VETERANS BENEFITS

VETERANS BENEFITS

THE COMPLETE GUIDE

Keith D. Snyder

Richard E. O'Dell

with Craig Kubey

HarperPerennial

A Division of HarperCollins*Publishers*

HarperCollins books may be purchased for educational, business, or sales promotional use. For information, please write to: Special Markets Department, HarperCollins Publishers, Inc., 10 East 53rd Street, New York, NY 10022.

FIRST EDITION

Test design by Marsha Cohen/Parallelogram

Library of Congress Cataloging-in-Publication Data

Snyder, Keith D.
  Veterans benefits : the complete guide / Keith D. Snyder,
    Richard E. O'Dell, Craig Kubey.
      p.   cm.
    ISBN 0-06-273146-7
  1. Veterans—Services for—United States—Handbooks,
  manuals, etc. I. Snyder, Keith D., 1950– . II. O'Dell,
  Richard E. III. Title.
  UB357.K83 1994
  362.86'0973—dc20   92-52540

94 95 96 97 98 RRD 10 9 8 7 6 5 4 3 2

CONTENTS

PART TWO

Special Programs, Opportunities, and Problems

211

PART THREE

Servicemembers and Their Families

243

DEDICATION

★★★★★★★★★★★★★★★★★★★★★★★★★★★★★★★★★★★★★★

We dedicate this book to American military veterans and servicemembers. For the blessings of American life that they have achieved and then protected, the people of this nation owe them our most solemn and heartfelt gratitude.

Keith D. Snyder dedicates this book to his parents, David and Leota Snyder, and to his father-in-law and mother-in-law, Meyer and Minnette Leichman.

Richard E. O'Dell dedicates this book to his wife, Dale, for her encouragement and love, and to departing Virginia Governor Lawrence Douglas Wilder, a decorated combat veteran of the Korean War, who has never forgotten to help his fellow veterans.

Craig Kubey dedicates this book to his parents, Sidney and Joan Kubey, and to the memory of his father-in-law and mother-in-law, Nathan and Symeta Kuper.

ACKNOWLEDGMENTS

Acknowledgments by Keith D. Snyder:

Special thanks are due to P. J. Budahn and Soraya S. Nelson, who wrote Chapters 21 and 24 on military medical care and programs available to dependents and survivors of active duty personnel. Budahn is the author of a weekly "Careers" column that appears in the *Army, Navy* and *Air Force Times:* he is also the author of the *Drawdown Survival Guide,* published by the Naval Institute Press in 1993. Nelson is the medical affairs reporter for *Army, Navy* and *Air Force Times* and has written extensively about the military and health care for several years.

It is difficult to express how much I have learned from my clients over the years. Their front-line view of the VA and their confirmation of recurring problems has shaped much of this book.

A number of long-time veterans advocates offered suggestions and comments at various stages of the writing of this book and unselfishly made themselves available to share valuable insights into the VA system; among them, Buzz Tiffany, Joe Nevin, Robin Temple, Brian Campbell, Bill Smith, Ken Carpenter. A debt is owed as well to former colleagues at the National Veterans Legal Services Project, including David Addlestone, Bart Stichman, Michael Wildhaber, and Roger Wedel, who have continued to procure and publicize essential information for veterans and their advocates.

Innumerable VA officials have shared copies of reports, steered me to sources of information, patiently offered official explanations, and, occasionally, offered candid observations on bureaucratic difficulties.

Last, but really first, I must acknowledge the support of my wife, Sherry, who tolerated an absurd working schedule, and my three children,

Max, Ruby and Russell, who were forced to learn an extra measure of patience during the course of this project.

Acknowledgments by Richard E. O'Dell:

I want to thank Ron Abrams, training director for the National Veterans Legal Services Project (NVLSP) and editor of the *Veterans Advocate*, for taking the time to comment on certain sections of this book. I also want to thank Ron, as well as David Addlestone and Bart Stichman, also of NVLSP, for all they have done as advocates to secure the rights of veterans and their families.

I also want to express my gratitude to Ruby G. Martin, Secretary of Administration of the Commonwealth of Virginia, who, although not a veteran, has provided me with encouragement and support in this project and in my role as an advocate for Virginia veterans and their families.

Acknowledgments by Craig Kubey:

This book would not exist were it not for the success of its predecessor, *The Viet Vet Survival Guide* (Ballantine, 1985). I therefore want to thank everyone connected with that book, in particular my co-authors (David Addlestone, Rick O'Dell, Keith Snyder, and Bart Stichman), the agent (Joe Spieler), the publisher (especially Bob Wyatt and the late great Richard McCoy), and Abigail Van Buren and her office (in particular Jeanne Phillips); Abby's mention of the *Viet Vet* dramatically increased the number of veterans who bought—and were benefitted by—the book. I also want to thank the agent for this book, Mitch Rose; its original and final editors, Nick Bakalar and Robert Wilson; and the production staff and others at HarperCollins who, like the editors, withstood the unusual demands of an unusual project.

INTRODUCTION

★★★

The War in the Persian Gulf and the intervention in Somalia have made the American military man and woman newly popular. American citizens have a new awareness of the dedication, courage, and sacrifice shown by current servicemembers and the 26 million living veterans (discharged former servicemembers), including the 20 million who fought in World War I, World War II, Korea, and Vietnam. American citizens have given these servicemembers parades, some citizens have given them jobs.

Nevertheless, servicemembers from the Persian Gulf and other areas, as well as veterans of earlier wars, often need more. They need the vast amount of financial, medical, psychotherapeutic, and educational help available from the army, the navy, the air force, and the Marine Corps. Veterans also need the similar kinds of assistance available from the U.S. Department of Veterans Affairs (formerly the Veterans Administration, this cabinet-level department is still called "the VA").

Each military era's group of servicemembers has its special problems. The earliest war with a large number of living veterans is World War II. More than eight million World War II veterans, known as the Class of '46 (the year most were discharged), are still alive. Their special problems are those of age. A soldier who was 25 when the war ended in 1945 turned 73 in 1993. Yet the hospital and nursing home facilities of the VA are seriously inadequate in number and resources to serve the increasing number of WWII vets who need geriatric care, hospitalization, and long-term nursing home care.

The more than four million veterans of the Korean War are not much younger. The soldier who was 25 when the cease-fire was declared in 1951 (sporadic fighting continued until 1953) became 67 in 1993. Many Korean vets, especially those who also served in World War II, are older. In addition, these vets have much in common with the Vietnam War vets, both having served in controversial wars. But even though Vietnam War vets have recently received some attention, Korean War vets remain unnoticed. They still hunger for the credit and honor they never received.

Vietnam War vets remain the ultimate U.S. veteran horror story. Numbering more than eight million, Vietnam War vets have made household words of "PTSD" (post-traumatic stress disorder) and "Agent Orange" (a herbicide containing dioxin). PTSD is a new name for an old tragedy known in previous wars as "shell shock." The incidence of PTSD is higher among Vietnam War vets, in part because, unlike their World War II counterparts who returned slowly (mostly on ships) and as heroes, the Vietnam War vets jetted directly from jungles to American living rooms, finding not yellow ribbons and parades, but humiliation and hatred. Lyndon Johnson and Richard Nixon continued an unpopular war, but the veterans received much of the blame.

Only recently did Congress force the VA to provide financial compensation for veterans suffering from diseases caused by exposure to Agent Orange, but even now only a handful of diseases are covered by the compensation package. Now, Vietnam War veterans must fight a new war: the war to keep the public and Congress attentive as new, younger vets are discharged after more popular duty, telling stories not from Da Nang and Saigon but from Kuwait City and Mogadishu.

Many of the more than two million current servicemembers have had their own hard times. Some have served routine tours in the United States or Europe. But those who saw duty in the Persian Gulf have, or soon may have, serious problems. Deaths and disabilities (on the U.S. side) were mercifully few, but 540,000 servicemembers were extensively exposed for many months to a harsh desert environment, to intense sunlight that can cause skin cancer and eye injuries, and to the many indigenous diseases of Saudi Arabia, some of which may remain latent for months or years.

Some veterans of the Gulf War still require extensive medical treatment for battlefield wounds. Others require long-term psychiatric treatment for conditions caused by exposure to horror and by fear. Still others will feel the full psychological effects of the war only in future years. Veterans of the U.S./U.N. action in Somalia will have similar problems.

Those in need of assistance from the military branches and from the Department of Veterans Affairs are not limited to those who have served. Also included are their *families*. The approximately 40 million immediate family members of U.S. servicemembers and veterans are entitled to benefits for everything from prenatal care for military women and servicemembers' wives to VA burial benefits for deceased veterans.

Consequently, it is clear that servicemembers, veterans, and family members have extensive needs. The military branches and the VA are there to serve them. Unfortunately, despite their efforts to provide adequate services, the military and the VA serve their constituencies in one way above all others. They serve them *inadequately*.

The military often provides no benefits to families who are entitled to them. More often, it provides too little, too late. All too commonly it unfairly releases its members with "less-than-honorable" discharges, leading to everything from disqualification from military-financed college education to lifetime disadvantages in gaining employment. Military hospitals, supposedly available to military families, are often closed to these dependants. In addition, care in military hospitals is on average far inferior to that available in private facilities.

The VA presents a bigger system and more problems. VA staff frequently give veterans' disabilities unfairly low ratings (ratings range from 0 percent to 100 percent), and as a result veterans often are awarded inadequate disability compensation. Veterans' pension payments are inadequate to provide a decent standard of living. The VA hospital system varies in quality; sometimes it is excellent, but more often it is not.

Worse, the VA medical system is so crowded that tens of thousands of veterans qualified for VA hospital care are turned away because not enough beds are available. Specialized programs either do not exist or are not sufficiently widespread to care for enough veterans with special problems, such as the psychiatric symptoms suffered by Vietnam War veterans with PTSD.

Veterans Benefits is best described in a single word: *realistic*. It makes clear that the military and VA systems are extensive, provide some wonderfully effective services, and have among their staff many professionals and others who are both highly competent and highly compassionate. It also explains where the systems fail to fairly and adequately meet the needs of the servicemember and veteran. The goal of this book is to help the reader know what to do when this happens.

The book will help the servicemember, veteran, and family member to find the benefits that are available: disability compensation, pensions, medical services, psychotherapeutic services, employment assistance, education and rehabilitation, housing (especially VA loans), and others. Often all the reader needs to know is what's available and how to apply: Often the system works.

But when it doesn't, *Veterans Benefits* is of critical value. It tells the servicemember and veteran how to appeal a wrongful denial of benefits (under a 1988 federal law, veterans can now appeal VA decisions to the new Court of Veterans Appeals, a federal court separate from the VA), how to obtain his or her records, how to have harmful entries corrected, and how to have a "bad discharge" upgraded. The book also deals with the special problems of veterans from each war era, of women and minority servicemembers and veterans, and of veterans in the criminal justice system.

As much as possible, chapters are written so that they can be read independently of the chapters that precede and follow them. This allows a veteran or servicemember with a specific problem to go directly to the chapter relating to a particular issue and need not read the entire book. Consequently, some chapters repeat information found earlier in the book.

Part One is for veterans, but is important for servicemembers because servicemembers eventually become veterans. Part Two, some of which is for veterans and some of which is for servicemembers, covers special programs, opportunities, and problems. Part Three is for servicemembers but may be of interest to some veterans. The book ends with four appendices. Please note that dollar figures and other numbers mentioned in the book are current as of this writing and are subject to change. Read on!

PART ONE

VETERANS AND THEIR FAMILIES

CHAPTER ONE

BASIC SURVIVAL SKILLS

★ ★

You are not alone. There are almost 27 million veterans in the United States. Veterans and their families make up almost one-third of the entire U.S. population. Still, sometimes you will feel all alone on a never-ending assembly line. Use this chapter first to locate a service representative or lawyer and then to prepare yourself to work with the VA, the U.S. Department of Veterans Affairs.

HOW TO FIND HELP

See Appendix C at the end of this book for a state-by-state list of state departments of Veterans Affairs. Appendix D lists veterans' organizations

---
★ IMPORTANT ★

We will say again and again starting right now: *get help*. Whether you need cash to make up for what you cannot earn because of a military injury, or whether you need medical treatment, too much is at stake to go it alone. Most times, help is available free of charge from service representatives associated with veterans' service organizations and located in each of the 58 VA regional offices. Examples of such organizations are the American Legion; American Veterans of World War II, Korea, and Vietnam (AMVETS); Disabled American Veterans (DAV); Vietnam Veterans of America (VVA); Veterans of Foreign Wars (VFW); and Paralyzed Veterans of America (PVA). In addition, sometimes you may want to pay a lawyer to represent you.

---

that offer services to veterans and their families. Call the telephone number listed in Appendix D for the national headquarters of an organization and ask for the telephone number of the nearest local service representative. Also check your local telephone directory for a local listing. Some states— for example, New York and Ohio—have county-funded veterans' service agency offices.

Veterans Service Organizations

You do not always need to belong to a particular veterans' organization to receive help from it, and you cannot be charged a fee for services provided by such an organization. Just like any business, the quality of service may vary from organization to organization. Just like any good consumer of any other service, you are free to comparison shop. There are no hard-and-fast rules on how to recognize a good advocate. Sit, talk, listen. As you do so, check the following:

- [ ] Does the service representative really listen to you?
- [ ] Can the service rep show you the VA's rule books?
- [ ] Do the books look well used?
- [ ] Does the service rep mention any decisions of the U.S. Court of Veterans Appeals?
- [ ] Does the service rep offer you pamphlets explaining VA programs?
- [ ] Does the service rep promise to send you copies of letters he or she might write on your behalf and promise to send you copies of VA rating decisions?
- [ ] Does the service rep promise to return your telephone calls?
- [ ] Does the service rep promise to prepare you well in advance of a hearing and then to go with you to present your case at a hearing?
- [ ] Does the service rep promise to prepare a written summary of the evidence that supports your claim and the reasons that, under the VA's rules, you should win?

There are limits on services available from some service organizations. Some service representatives may operate on a volunteer or a part-time basis and thus may not be able to offer all the help you need. Find out. Sometimes the best help a rep can give you is to tell you up front that you do not qualify for a benefit. Ask for an honest assessment of your chances. Some service reps may be under orders never to say that a person cannot win, and instead will let you waste your time going through the entire VA process. Ask the representative whether he or she has ever heard of any vets winning in a situation like yours. Be wary of guarantees of success.

After you find someone you trust, you will be asked to officially appoint the organization to represent you. Doing so gives certain employees of the organization access to your VA files. It also gives them authority to sign VA forms for you. Your representative has a duty to you to meet VA deadlines; however, you, not the representative, will be hurt if the deadline is missed.

Likewise, you have a duty to work with your rep. When your representative asks for documents, give them to him or her to review before filing them with the VA. Keep a copy of any records you turn over. When the VA writes you, it should send a copy of the letter to your representative. Call your representative to make sure that this actually happened. Double-check any deadlines that must be met and ask for advice from your service representative about the actual meaning of the VA letter. Then, be sure you are clear as to who will answer the VA letter and meet the deadline. Letters you send to a service rep are often simply turned over to the VA, so be polite in what you say.

If you are unhappy with the performance of your service rep, write to his or her boss (see Appendix D for the addresses of national headquarters). Some states have a fund to reimburse you if you lose money as a result of bad advice from a state department of veterans' affairs or a county employee, or because an employee missed a deadline. If you think the assistance you received was ineffective—for example, no one actually presented an argument on your behalf to the Board of Veterans' Appeals (BVA)—ask the BVA to ''vacate'' (nullify) its decision and give you another chance to present your appeal.

Attorneys

Hiring an attorney to represent you is more difficult. The old post–Civil War $10 limit on the fee you can pay an attorney was dropped in 1988. The new law says that you can pay an attorney a reasonable fee (but only at a certain time) in the processing of your VA claim. You can hire an attorney only after the BVA denies your appeal. Beginning on the date of denial, you have 1 year in which to hire an attorney. If you want to appeal to the U.S. Court of Veterans Appeals, also created in 1988, you must meet a shorter deadline: 120 days after the board's denial.

There are exceptions to the 1-year-after-board-denial deadline for hiring an attorney. For example, if the VA sues you to collect money it claims you owe it, you can hire an attorney. If the VA demands that you repay money (but is not suing you just yet) for an alleged debt due under a VA-guaranteed home loan, you can hire an attorney immediately. If someone else (not you) is willing to pay an attorney to help you, he or she can. That person should not be a member of your immediate family, and you cannot agree on the side to reimburse him or her.

The same rules apply for selecting an attorney as for selecting a veterans' service representative: Ask questions, get assurances, beware of guarantees. Call your nearest county, city, or state bar association's lawyer referral service for the name and telephone number of an attorney who accepts VA cases. A list of the attorneys who practice before the U.S. Court of Veterans Appeals and who actively represent veterans is available from the National Organization of Veterans Advocates (P.O. Box 42334; Washington, DC 20015). Some legal organizations provide free attorneys to help veterans. For some of these organizations—for example, a legal aid society or legal services offices—you must have limited income to qualify for services.

If you hire an attorney to represent you, be sure to get a written contract that describes what you will have to pay. Contracts can be for a flat fee, at an hourly rate, or on a contingency basis. A contingency basis means that if you do not win, you won't receive any money from the VA and your attorney will not receive any either (nevertheless, the attorney will ordinarily expect reimbursement for expenses). Even if he or she thinks you will win, an attorney may refuse your case if you will not win much in back benefits.

If you can find an attorney to accept your case on a contingency basis, the usual limit is 20 percent of any past-due benefits that are awarded. You can agree to pay more than 20 percent, but the VA will not be responsible for automatically paying your attorney from your award. (Ordinarily, the VA pays 80 percent of any award directly to the vet and withholds 20 percent for the attorney, which is not paid until the Board of Veterans' Appeals (BVA) reviews the contract between the veteran and the attorney.) A contract with an attorney will also require that—whether you win or lose—you pay court fees, copying expenses, postage, long-distance telephone calls, travel expenses, and other similar expenses.

You should ask the attorney to consider filing a claim under the Equal Access to Justice Act because that act may require the VA to pay the attorney an hourly rate for his or her services. The money the attorney receives from the VA under the Equal Access to Justice Act should reduce the amount that you must finally pay the attorney. Because this law is new (it became effective in 1992), it is not yet clear as to what extent it will help the vet. It applies only if you are finally successful and only if the VA's arguments are not ''substantially justified.''

The contract for representation at the Court of Veterans Appeals must be filed by the attorney with the court and should also be filed with the BVA and the VA regional office. If you don't like the contract, don't sign it. If you sign it and then think that the attorney will benefit too much, you can complain to the court (Court of Veterans Appeals; ATTN: Clerk of the Court; 625 Indiana Ave., NW, #900; Washington, DC 20004).

If your attorney does not meet the deadlines in your case or does not return your telephone calls, complain to the disciplinary office (which may be called a ''committee on discipline,'' ''disciplinary board,'' ''grievance commission,'' or something else) in the office of your state's bar association and to the clerk of the Court of Veterans Appeals.

If your contract called for representation at the VA, you can complain to the BVA (Board of Veterans' Appeals; ATTN: Counsel to the Chairman [01C]; 810 Vermont Ave., NW; Washington, DC 20420). When writing to the court, the board, or a state disciplinary body, send your complaint by certified mail, return receipt requested, and send a copy to your attorney.

After you locate a service rep and/or a lawyer, you are ready to deal with the VA.

WHAT EXACTLY IS THE VA?

The straight answer is that the VA is the Department of Veterans Affairs, a cabinet-level department of the federal government that is a revised version of the Veterans Administration. The less straight answer is that it is a factory that is supposed to produce three products: checks, well people, and burial plots. In reality, it often denies checks to deserving veterans, makes patients worse, and offers burial plots in few convenient locations.

The head of the VA is the Secretary of Veterans Affairs. The first secretary was Edward J. Derwinski, who resigned in October 1992 under pressure from veterans' service organizations and joined then-President Bush's reelection campaign. President Clinton appointed a new secretary, Jesse Brown, in 1993. In the chart of the VA organization, Brown is at the top. Under him are assistant secretaries; under the assistants are deputy assistants.

Of greater importance to you are four offices within the department: the Veterans Benefits Administration (headed by a Deputy Secretary), the

Veterans Health Administration (headed by a Deputy Secretary), the National Cemetery System, and the Board of Veterans' Appeals (headed by the chairman). All are located in Washington, DC.

Although your paperwork (and you) may eventually end up in Washington, your claim for benefits or your request for medical care begins in your state at either a local VA office, a so-called "regional office" of the VA, or a VA medical center. There are 58 regional offices and 172 VA medical centers. Some regional offices and medical centers share the same building.

Each regional office has a veterans' assistance division (it includes a telephone answering department), a loan guaranty division, and an adjudication division. The adjudication division is further divided into the authorization division and the rating board. The authorization personnel review your claim to determine what additional evidence must be obtained. They send letters (or computer-generated requests) to the National Personnel Records Center in St. Louis to confirm that you were in the military. They request an appointment for you at the nearest VA medical center for a "compensation and pension examination." After they collect enough information, they pass your case to the other side of the adjudication division—to the rating board.

A rating board consists of three persons, usually two full-time employees and one part-time physician. The board members consider the evidence and vote on your claim. Also within the adjudication division is a hearing officer. You have an opportunity to appear in front of the hearing officer both before and after the rating board makes a decision. The purpose of a hearing is to ensure that the VA understands what you are claiming and why and to provide you an opportunity to find out directly from the VA what evidence you must present in order to win.

BENEFITS AVAILABLE FROM THE VA

Cash, medical treatment, and burial are available from the VA. Cash may be in the form of a monthly payment from the programs for compensation, pension, or education, or a guaranty on a loan to buy a home. Medical treatment may be surgery in a VA medical center or an informal group session at a storefront readjustment counseling vet center.

The VA provided $16.3 billion in compensation and pension benefits in fiscal year 1992 to 2,673,820 veterans and 753,980 surviving family members. Another 432,932 veterans and family members drew $872 million in educational benefits. Home loan guaranties were extended to

226,021 others. VA medical centers cared for 1,053,238 veterans as inpatients; and a total of 22,788,431 visits were made for outpatient care. In addition, the VA maintains 114 national cemeteries in 38 states and Puerto Rico. Of these cemeteries, 53 are full. In fiscal year 1992, 64,602 veterans and survivors of veterans were buried. Another 315,888 applications for headstones or markers were received (virtually all were granted).

VA programs that offer monthly cash benefits include these:

★ compensation for veterans disabled due to their military service (see page 78)
★ compensation for survivors of veterans who died due to their military service (see page 188)
★ pension for wartime veterans who are totally disabled and have a limited income (see page 118)
★ pension payments for survivors of wartime veterans who have a limited income (see page 192)
★ educational assistance (money) to veterans to attend school (see page 133)
★ educational assistance or vocational rehabilitation assistance (money) to certain family members to attend school (see page 185)

Other cash assistance includes the following:

★ burial benefits (see page 149)
★ clothing allowance (see page 109)
★ allowance to buy a specially adapted van or to make modifications to your home (see page 109)

Noncash benefits include the following:

★ loan guaranties, which often give you the ability to purchase a home with little or no down payment (see page 141)

VA health care programs include these:

★ inpatient care at hospitals (see page 165)
★ outpatient care (see page 165)
★ nursing homes (see page 166)
★ domiciliary homes (see page 167)
★ specialized post-traumatic stress disorder treatment (see page 167)

★   vet center readjustment counseling (see page 167)
★   alcohol and drug abuse treatment (see page 167)
★   prescriptions (see page 168)

HOW TO FIND THE VA

See Appendix B for a state-by-state list of each VA regional office, medical center, outpatient clinic, vet center, alcohol and drug treatment facility, and cemetery.

PREPARING TO DEAL WITH THE VA

On the page provided at the back of the book, the Key Information Sheet, write down your social security number, your military service number, your dates of service, your VA claim number, your VA insurance number, and your VA home loan number. Perhaps you have memorized all these numbers, but write them down for your family's sake. Also write down the telephone number for the nearest VA regional office and medical center, as well as the name and number of your service rep.

You can deal with the VA in two ways: You can adopt a warm, trusting attitude, certain in the belief that all your needs will be met with one phone call and that you will be extended the benefit of the doubt. Or, you can take a somewhat less confident, more guarded attitude: Perhaps you will get what you need when you need it; perhaps you won't.

Rather than be so shocked by a bad experience with the VA that you simply stop pursuing what you need, be prepared for a bad experience, be prepared for the long haul. For example, if you are rated as 10 percent disabled, and you know that your condition has worsened, do not expect the VA to immediately increase your payments just because you tell it you are worse. Anticipate several months of delay before you get an answer. If the answer is no increase or only a small increase, anticipate many, many more months of appeal through the VA process. If you must appeal to the U.S. Court of Veterans Appeals, add another 2 years to the process. Prepare for the worst and be pleasantly surprised with a good outcome.

A complaint frequently heard about the VA is that it seems as if the VA is just waiting for you to die so that your claim can be closed. Officially, of course, there is no truth to such a concern. Unofficially, it can seem that way sometimes. Hang in there anyway. Millions before you have been rewarded for doing so.

┌─────────────────── ★ SUGGESTION ★ ───────────────────┐

Do not ignore other federal and state agencies that may be able to help you. If you are disabled and cannot work, go to the nearest district Social Security Administration office and apply for disability benefits. If the SSA agrees that you are disabled, you may get a higher payment from the VA. See Chapter 14.

└───┘

Tips on Managing Your Claim

You want your claim to be processed quickly and smoothly. You also want to get special attention when it is necessary. Remember that the VA, like a factory, processes your paperwork on an assembly line. You can help make some parts of the VA process work more quickly.

Start by assuming that every VA employee wants to do right by your claim. Next, assume that VA workers are evaluated primarily on a piece-rate basis (i.e., they get credits [and promotions] for how quickly and how much paperwork they handle). Finally, assume that every VA employee, from the first worker who opens the mail to the worker who votes on your case, has very, very large piles of papers on his or her desk (and the floor around the desk and behind the desk) from many, many veterans.

Anything you can do to make the VA employees' work go faster can also help you. Also, anything you can do to make your claim stand out from the pile may help. One way to help is to put your VA claim number on every piece of paper you mail to the VA. If you are answering a VA letter, start your letter by referring to the "VA letter dated ———." Include your current address. If your address changes, tell the VA (and the post office). If at all possible, type (with double-spacing) letters you send to the VA. If you cannot type, print neatly. Keep in mind that if the VA employee must take extra seconds, much less minutes, to read your letter, it may not get read as carefully as it should be.

Private Medical Records

If you have seen a private doctor or a therapist, and you want the VA to have a copy of the records from that person, you have three ways to get them to the VA: Ask the doctor to give them to you to relay to the VA, ask your service rep to get them, or wait for the VA to get them. As a general rule, you should see every piece of paper before it goes to the VA or is used by the VA to make a decision. The advantage to you and your representative in having these records before the VA gets them is that you and your rep can review them and ask the doctor to prepare an expert opinion that interprets the information and assesses the effects of your condition on your ability to work. Records of current treatment seldom provide an interpretation of past problems and their potential connection to illnesses or injuries during military service. Your doctor, who may have treated you for several years, may have a valuable perspective on the reason for your current problems that can make the difference between winning or losing your claim. Your treating doctor's opinion *should* carry extra weight in the VA system.

If you are sending the VA records that you think will help your claim, arrange the records in chronological order, number each page, and include a list that identifies each document. On top of your list, staple a letter identifying the benefit you are claiming and how these records help prove your claim. Do not simply say, "The enclosed records clearly prove my case." Keep in mind the limited time available to each VA worker to process your claim. In your letter, identify the statement that you believe is helpful, and provide the date and the name of the doctor associated with it. Refer to the page number of your enclosure where the full text of the doctor's statement is found. If you deliver these records to your service rep to give to the VA, make sure he or she reviews them first to make sure each page is relevant to your claim. You should not give the VA mounds of paper that are not relevant. Later in this book, we will discuss some of the evidence that may be especially relevant to your claim and how to get it.

Don't Complain About the Little Stuff

You do not help yourself by complaining loudly about the routinely irritating practices of the VA, such as its practices of never signing letters and of sending form letters that don't quite answer your last letter. Ask your service rep to explain the bureaucratic double-talk. If it appears that the VA doesn't understand what you have applied for or if the VA tells you to send the same information that you already sent, write back and politely reexplain the benefit you are seeking or explain that you already mailed the requested information on a previous date (be sure to send the information again in case the VA lost it).

Keep Copies of Everything

Keep a file of the letters you send to the VA. If a letter is especially important, if you are close to missing a deadline, or if you are writing to an office (such as the VA regional office in Manhattan and Washington, D.C.) that has a reputation for losing mail, be sure to use certified mail, return receipt requested. Keep a copy of your letters and the VA's letters in a folder, in chronological order so that you can keep track of the latest developments. Keep this folder in a safe place.

Get a Copy of Your VA File

Get a copy of your entire VA file. You are entitled to a copy free of charge. (See Chapter 11 for instructions on how to request your file.) While you are actively pursuing a claim, go look at the original file, which is located at the VA regional office. If you do go to the VA regional office, ask to review a copy of the *Adjudication Procedure Manual*, M21-1. It is a huge set of three-ring binders that provides details on the way your case should be handled and the evidence you need to supply the VA in order to win. You have a right to see and photocopy this manual. (See Chapter 11 for details on this and other resource materials.)

Qualifying as a Veteran

Not every former servicemember—even one with combat experience—is officially considered by the VA to be a veteran. Certainly, the majority of former servicemembers are officially veterans. Under the law, the term "veteran" means a person who served in the active military, naval, or air service, and who was discharged or released under conditions other than dishonorable.

The factors most significant to your status as "veteran" involve whether you were in active service and the character of your discharge. In 1980, another reason that you might not be considered to be a veteran was added. It involves minimum length of time served: In 1980, Congress defined veterans to be those persons who had completed a minimum period

---

★ CAUTION ★

When you have questions, you can call the VA for an answer. The VA offers a single toll-free telephone line, 1(800)827-1000, that automatically routes your call to the nearest VA regional office. The workers who answer the phones are called "veterans' benefits counselors." They are quite knowledgeable. However, they do not make decisions about your case, so they cannot guarantee anything. Nevertheless, ask for the counselor's name and make a note of what you asked, what you were told, and the date and time of your call.

─────────────── ★ EMERGENCIES ★ ───────────────

If an emergency arises, there are ways to cut through some of the red tape. Each regional office has a director; each director has a special assistant. In an emergency, the special assistant is the person to talk with. You probably will not get past the veterans' benefits counselor to speak directly with the special assistant. However several people and offices available to you can get in touch with the special assistant; they include an attorney, a service organization representative, the local office of your U.S. senator or representative, the office of the President of the United States, and a member of the local news media. Start with your service rep.

of active duty—either the whole period for which they enlisted or 2 years, whichever was less.

Character of Discharge

If your DD 214, Report of Separation, lists "honorable," or "under honorable conditions," or "general" discharge, you probably are officially a veteran. If your DD 214 says "under other than honorable conditions," "undesirable," or "bad conduct discharge from special court-martial," the VA is almost certain to deny you veteran status. If your DD 214 says "bad conduct discharge from general court-martial" or "dishonorable discharge," the VA will deny you veteran status, and it will probably be right.

If the VA says that your discharge was "under dishonorable conditions," you should consider three things:

1. Determine whether, for this claim, you can use another period of service that resulted in a better discharge.
2. Apply through a service discharge review board and board for correction of military records for a change in your discharge. (See Chapter 17.)
3. Appeal the VA's character of discharge determination.

If you have more than one period of service, for example, one that ended with an honorable discharge, but the last one ended with a dishonorable discharge, you may be able to use the honorable period of service to qualify officially as a veteran. For example, if you were ill during your first enlistment, which ended with an honorable discharge, and now you are reexperiencing health problems related to that illness, a dishonorable discharge following your last tour of duty should not prevent you from receiving VA compensation. On the other hand, if you were ill during the last tour, which ended with the dishonorable discharge, you have a problem. To fix that problem, you need either to change the discharge through a review board or a correction board or to appeal within the VA.

A discharge review board or a correction board is not part of the VA; it is part of the branch of service to which you belonged. Even if the VA agrees that your dishonorable discharge is not so bad, it cannot give you a new DD 214. Also, sometimes the VA does not have to follow what a discharge review board says, but the VA must follow what the *correction board* says. See Chapter 17 for more details about upgrading your discharge.

Another, separate process is available within the VA. The VA process is called a "character of discharge determination." You can pursue both the service discharge upgrading process and the VA character of discharge determination simultaneously. The VA process to appeal a denial is described in Chapter 3. Both processes are tough to win. You need expert help.

Active Service
To officially be a veteran, you must have served in the *active* military, naval, or air service. *Active* military service includes the following:

★ active duty
★ any period of *active duty for training* during which you become disabled (or die) from an injury incurred in the line of duty
★ any period of *inactive duty training* during which you become disabled (or die)
★ any service as a civilian that the Air Force certifies is active military service

The law defines "active duty," "active duty for training," and "inactive duty training." "Active duty" means full-time duty in the armed forces and includes certain officers of the Public Health Service and the National Oceanic and Atmospheric Administration, as well as cadets at the military academies. Active duty also includes travel time to or from active duty.

"Active duty for training" means full-time duty in the armed forces performed by reserves for training purposes, the duty of certain Reserve Public Health Service officers, and the duty performed by senior ROTC members when you are ordered to such duty for the purpose of training or a practice cruise for at least 4 weeks. Also qualifying is travel time to and from active duty for training. Full-time duty periods of Army or Air National Guard members are also included.

"Inactive duty training" means other than full-time duty ordered by the Secretary for Reserves and certain special additional duties authorized for reserves. Inactive duty training in the case of Army or Air National Guard members means other than full-time duty. Because there is no definition in VA law of the term "full-time duty," the VA has the flexibility to rule that a guard member ordered to duty for 14 days, not simply a weekend drill, has been ordered to active duty for training.

There are several categories of reserve duty:

★ initial active duty for training (IADT)
★ annual training (AT)
★ active duty training (ADT)
★ active duty for special work (ADSW)
★ active duty (AD)

The first three of these reserve categories (IADT, AT, and ADT) are considered service in the reserves for training purposes. When the ADSW and AD involve operational or support duties, not training, the service counts as active duty. A DD 214 may not indicate if your duties involved operational or support duties. If they did, ask the VA to investigate this further.

Although the National Guard and the Air National Guard operate similar full-time operational and support programs, such service performed by guard personnel in active duty for training status does not qualify as active duty for the purposes of VA benefits unless you have a service-connected disability that was incurred or aggravated during the period. National Guard service that is characterized as federal active duty is qualifying service for VA purposes if your order to active duty states that the service is under Title 10 of the United States Code. National Guard service under Title 32 is not qualifying service for VA purposes. Refer to your DD 214 for a reference to either "Title 10, USC," or "Title 32, USC." To convince the VA, you may need to produce a copy of the order to active duty.

Civilians as Veterans

Recently, several groups of civilian workers, including merchant marines, who provided services under hazardous conditions, have been granted veteran status. Some members of these groups presumably do not even know they qualify as veterans.

In 1977, a law granted a group of federal civilian employees attached to the U.S. Army Air Force during World War II, Women's Air Forces Service Pilots (WASPs), the status of having had active duty in the military. The law also gave the Department of the Air Force authority to certify that if the duties of other groups of civilians were similar to that of the WASPs, those groups' members qualify as having had active military service. Details on applying for certification of a group can be obtained from Department of the Air Force (SAF/AFPC; DoD Civilian/Military Service Review Board; The Pentagon; Washington, DC 20330). If you believe you are a member of one of the following groups (or if you believe your parent was), get an application form, a DD Form 2168 (Application for Discharge of Member or Survivor of Member of Group Certified to Have Performed Active Duty with the Armed Forces of the United States), from the nearest VA regional office. According to the Code of Federal Regulation, as of July 1993, the certified groups included these:

★ Women's Air Forces Service Pilots (WASPs)
★ Signal Corps Female Telephone Operators Unit of World War I
★ engineer field clerks
★ Women's Army Auxiliary Corps
★ Quartermaster Corps female clerical employees serving with the AEF (American Expeditionary Forces) in World War I
★ civilian employees of Pacific naval air bases who actively participated in the defense of Wake Island during World War II
★ reconstruction aides and dietitians in World War I
★ male civilian ferry pilots
★ Wake Island defenders from Guam
★ civilian personnel assigned to the secret intelligence element of the Office of Strategic Services (OSS)
★ Guam combat patrol
★ Quartermaster Corps Keswick crew on Corregidor (WWII)
★ U.S. civilian volunteers who actively participated in the defense of Bataan

★ U.S. merchant seamen who served on blockships in support of Operation Mulberry

★ American merchant marines in oceangoing service during the period of armed conflict from Dec. 7, 1941 to Aug. 15, 1945

★ Civilian Navy IFF (Identification Friend or Foe) technicians who served in the combat areas of the Pacific during World War II (Dec. 7, 1941 to Aug. 15, 1945)

★ U.S. civilians of the American Field Service (AFS) who served overseas operationally in World War I during the period Aug. 31, 1917 to Jan. 1, 1918

★ U.S. civilians of the American Field Service (AFS) who served overseas under U.S. armies and the U.S. army groups in World War II (Dec. 7, 1941 to Aug. 15, 1945)

★ U.S. civilian employees of American Airlines who served overseas as a result of American Airlines' contract with the Air Transport Command during the period Dec. 14, 1941 to Aug. 14, 1945

★ Civilian crewmen of U.S. Coast and Geodetic Survey vessels who performed their service in areas of immediate military hazard while conducting cooperative operations with and for the U.S. armed forces during the period of Dec. 7, 1941 to Aug. 15, 1945

★ Honorably discharged members of the American Volunteer Group (Flying Tigers) who served during the period Dec. 7, 1941 to July 18, 1942

Length of Service

Before 1980, it did not matter if you signed up for 4 years and served only 18 months. You were still a veteran (as long as you met the other requirements). New rules apply beginning with servicemembers who entered active duty after Sept. 7, 1980. Among such members, those discharged before completing either 24 months of continuous active duty or the full period for which they were called to active duty are not eligible for VA benefits based on the service connected with the discharge. Keep in mind, though, that if you had a prior "full" period of duty, you may be able to base your eligibility on that period of duty.

The minimum active-duty service requirement does not apply if you were discharged for hardship or because of a disability incurred or aggravated in the line of duty. Also, the minimum requirement does not apply if the VA decides that you have a service-connected disability or that you are seeking benefits in connection with a service-connected disability. The minimum service requirement also does not apply to insurance benefits. There are other exceptions to the minimum service requirement when you are seeking educational assistance under the Chapter 30 program (for servicemembers who went into active duty after June 30, 1985) and you were discharged because of a reduction in force or for certain medical conditions. See Chapter 6 for details on the education program.

Wartime Service

Getting most VA benefits is not tied to whether you served during a time of war or peace. Entitlement to the VA pension program does require service during a period of war. Also, the VA should not deny you benefits if your service was during wartime but the records that document your exact duties are missing.

For example, if you are claiming post-traumatic stress disorder (PTSD), you must document the details of a stressful combat or another experience. Often there are no official documents that provide the evidence you need. Therefore the VA should allow you to document your experience through "buddy statements" and other unofficial documents. When entitlement to a program does require wartime service, it does not require that you saw combat, only that you served during the period officially designated as wartime.

Congress has designated the following dates as periods of wartime. (We are not including periods prior to World War I). The Grenada and Panama Canal operations were not designated as wartime. Note, too, that, as of this writing, the Persian Gulf era did not have an ending date.

★ World War I: Apr. 6, 1917 through Nov. 11, 1918; if the service was in Russia, the ending date is Apr. 1, 1920; if the service was up to July 2, 1921, it still counts as WWI service as long as there was service after Apr. 5, 1917 and before Nov. 12, 1918
★ World War II: Dec. 7, 1941 to Dec. 31, 1946, extended to July 25, 1947, where continuous with active duty on or before Dec. 31, 1946
★ Korean "Conflict": June 27, 1950 to Jan. 31, 1955
★ Vietnam War: Aug. 5, 1964 to May 7, 1975
★ Persian Gulf: Aug. 2, 1990 to [undetermined]

CHAPTER TWO

FINANCIAL ISSUES

★ ★

Skip all of this chapter—except the first three paragraphs—if you have never received money from the VA, you have not applied for such money, and if you know what money is available to veterans from the VA but know that neither you nor your family is eligible for it.

Read this chapter, and the next, if the VA now says you owe it money or if once in the past, you owed money and repaid it. Also, read these chapters if you are curious about what you might get in cash benefits. (And, remember, VA benefit payments are tax exempt.)

Read this chapter, and the next, if you received an award letter telling you that you will soon get a check. Also read this chapter, and the next, if you are now receiving some VA money and you wonder whether you should be getting more.

AWARD LETTERS IN GENERAL

When the VA first determines that you are eligible for an award, it will send you an award letter. In general, the letter includes two columns of

─────────── ★ IMPORTANT ★ ───────────

Get help. If the VA is demanding that you pay money back, you know exactly how much you stand to lose. Depending on what measures the VA is taking to collect the money, you may be able to hire an attorney to represent you. You can, and should, hire an attorney if the VA has taken you to court to collect money. (See Chapter 1 for tips on locating a good attorney.)

information: the left-hand column lists a monthly amount and the right-hand column lists the beginning date for that amount. For example, if you applied in August 1991, the information columns of your award letter (dated in late 1992) might look something like this:

Your claim for disability compensation has been approved as follows:

Monthly Rate	Effective Date
$626.00	9-01-91
$601.00	3-25-94
$576.00	12-24-94

Included are additional benefits for the veteran's spouse and children. You must notify us immediately if there is any change in the number or status of dependents. Failure to promptly notify the VA of a dependency change will result in the creation of an overpayment in your account.

Soon after the award letter, you should receive a big "retro" check to pay you for the months since you first applied for the benefit. Within a month or two after this award letter, you will receive the first monthly check.

Compensation Award Letters

When you receive disability compensation awards, the letter you receive should include one or two lines listing the disability for which the VA agrees it will pay you, as well as the percentage of disability. This information may be a separate enclosure. On either the back of the award letter or enclosed with the award letter, but on a separate piece of paper, should be a notice of your right to appeal the amount of money the VA has awarded you. Read it.

On one of the enclosures, you will find very small print. The top of the page is headed "IMPORTANT INFORMATION." The bottom of the page says "CONDITIONS AFFECTING RIGHT TO PAYMENTS." Read all the words. If your primary language is not English, ask the VA to send you this notice in your primary language.

Pension Award Letters

If the payment you are to get is from the pension program, the letter will list the amount of money you can expect monthly and the effective date of the award. The letter will also list any other money you are receiving from other sources that affects the pension payment. An enclosure will explain your obligation to inform the VA if there are changes in your non-VA income or the number of dependents. Read all of it carefully. If you do not understand something (the letter is a classic example of bureaucratic language), ask your service rep to explain it.

THE FIRST CHECK

Your claim is effective on the date that the VA receives it. The VA may agree that you are entitled to receive monthly payments effective on June 2, but it will not pay you for June 2 through June 30. Under VA law and regulations, you begin to receive payments as of the first of the month *after* your claim is effective. Keep this in mind if you have the choice of hand delivering (or mailing by express mail) a claim on the 29th of the month or mailing it to arrive on the second of the next month.

If you are not happy with the amount of the monthly check and intend to appeal, you may accept the checks that the VA sends. Cashing those checks will not interfere with your ability to argue that you should receive more money.

THE RETRO CHECK

Back, or retro, awards continue to increase the longer the VA takes to process your claim. Although a large check is nice to receive, often the check cannot make up for the many months that you went without any payment. If you are not happy with the amount of the retro check and intend to appeal, you may cash the check. Doing so will not interfere with your ability to argue that you should receive more money.

DIRECT DEPOSIT

You can have the VA deposit the monthly checks into your bank account automatically. This may be more convenient for you (especially if you are disabled or if the bank is a long distance away). If so, ask your bank to arrange to have this done. Whatever you do, don't hold on to a VA check for more than 1 year. If you do, you will have to apply for a replacement check.

If you decide to cancel direct deposit, you'll need to file VA Form 572, Request for Change of Address/Cancellation of Direct Deposit. A copy of this form is provided in Appendix A.

LOST CHECKS

Normally, checks are mailed to arrive by the first or second of the month. If you do not receive yours by the fifth, call the regional office and let them know. You may be told that you have to write to the VA and request a replacement check. This process can take several weeks to complete. If you need the money to pay your rent or to eat (or for some other real emergency), go to the regional office, speak with the agent cashier, and ask for immediate payment. If your situation is urgent, the district office of your U.S. senator or representative may be willing to help you.

EFFECT OF VA PAYMENTS ON OTHER GOVERNMENT MONEY

If you receive general assistance payments from your state, or supplemental security income (SSI) through the Social Security Administration (SSA), or other payments to help ends meet, receiving a VA check will probably reduce the other payments. For example, perhaps you applied for VA and SSA benefits at the same time, but the SSA payments started first and began to pay SSI of $550 each month. Later the VA may decide that you will receive $592 for a 60 percent service-connected disability. If you continue to accept both checks, the SSA will demand repayment. To avoid the extra hassle of having to pay back the SSA, get in touch with the SSA as soon as you begin to receive VA checks. From the day you have the VA check, you are not entitled to the SSI check.

If the check from the SSA is a disability insurance benefit check, and the VA awards you service-connected compensation, you can keep both checks. If the SSA check is for disability insurance benefits, and the VA awards a pension, the VA must take into account what you receive from the SSA and must reduce (or cut off) the VA pension check. Immediately call and write to the VA when you begin to receive SSA checks, and tell the VA the exact date when you began to receive the checks.

★ IMPORTANT ★

If you receive a retro check from the VA because your claim was effective 1 year ago, you do not have to pay back SSI checks you have been receiving for the past year. The money you receive from the VA may cause a reduction or cutoff of *future* government assistance, but you should not have to repay past benefits.

Also, if you are a federal worker and claim Federal Employees Act Compensation for the same disability paid for by the VA, you will have to elect which payment to accept. You cannot receive payments from both programs for the same disability.

CALCULATING WHETHER THE MONEY IS RIGHT: EFFECTIVE DATE OF AWARD

The amount of money the VA will pay you is tied to several factors: the date of your claim, the date of your discharge, the nature of your disability, the date you became disabled, and the number of dependents you have. VA pension payments are also tied to your outside income. If you suspect that the payment you are receiving is not correct, call your service rep, and, if appropriate, appeal for more money. See Chapter 3.

New Compensation Claim

A general rule for new compensation claims is that a claim is effective as of the date the application arrives at the VA office. Whether you were discharged recently or not, do not worry about getting the proper application form before you file. Send a letter to the nearest VA regional office saying "I claim compensation benefits for my [*whatever*] condition." The VA will then send you the right form. If you return that form within 1 year and eventually win, you will be paid retroactive to the date on which the VA received your letter.

To calculate whether your monthly compensation payment is correct, you must know to what extent (percentage) the VA says you are disabled. Cross-check this percentage against the rate listed on page 98. If the amount you are receiving does not correspond to the rate chart, find out why it does

---

★ NOTE ★

There is a special rule for recently discharged veterans: If you were discharged within the past year, be sure to send a claim to the VA *before* the 1-year mark. If you do, and the VA agrees that you are entitled to disability compensation payments, the payments are effective *the day after you were discharged*. Sending a claim a year and 1 day after discharge is too late, and your claim will be effective as of the day it was filed. If, for instance, you are entitled to $600 a month, filing after the first year will cost you at least $7,200 (12 months at $600) of unpaid compensation.

not. If you receive a 2-year back-benefits award, the VA calculates the amount it will pay you from the rate charts that were in effect for the years involved.

Reopened Compensation Claim

If you applied for compensation in the past but were denied and now you have new evidence, your claim will be effective as of the date you refile (or reopen) it. Your claim will not become effective retroactive to the first time you filed. (However, see the discussion later in this chapter of the effect of "clear and unmistakable error" by the VA.)

Claim for Increase in Compensation

The VA says a claim for increase is effective only as of the date the VA receives the claim. In fact, the VA has a duty to calculate whether your disability had increased as long as 1 year before you asked for the increase—and to pay you retroactive to the date of the increase in disability. If the VA pegs the effective date of an increased payment to the date when you wrote to the VA or sent medical records to the VA, appeal for an earlier effective date. Watch out for an award that is effective when you filed a VA Form 21-8940, Veteran's Application for Increased Compensation Based on Unemployability (see Appendix A for a copy of this form): The VA almost always says any increased payment based on unemployability is payable only as of the day the form was filed. The VA is correct if the day you became unemployable was the day that you filed the VA form. If you became unemployable before you filed the form, tell the VA. Also, see the section later in this chapter (and in Chapter 3) about "clear and unmistakable error."

Claim for Increase in Compensation Based on Hospitalization

Compensation payments temporarily increase to the 100 percent rate if you are hospitalized for treatment of a service-connected disability for more than 21 days. You do not have to be hospitalized in a VA medical center. Tell the regional office that you were hospitalized and where you were. It will ask the hospital for a copy of a summary of your treatment. Even if you were admitted for some other condition, this special increase will apply to you if you needed more than 21 days of treatment for a service-connected disability. Even after discharge from the hospital, the 100 percent rate can be continued for as long as 3 more months of convalescence (example: if you underwent surgery and need at least 1 month of convalescence, or if surgery left you with severe postoperative problems such as unhealed surgical wounds, a body cast, the need to use crutches, or a wheelchair). Hospitalization is not necessary before you qualify for the 100 percent rate for convalescence. Surgery performed on an outpatient basis that produces the above-mentioned problems is sufficient. The need for a cast covering of a major joint, even without surgery, is sufficient for the convalescent rating increase.

Usually this temporary increase will revert to the prehospitalization or preconvalescent rating, but the need for hospitalization can mean your disability worsened and that your rating should be increased. In this case, apply for a higher rating. On the other hand, if you had surgery that corrected a previous medical problem, the VA may reduce your rating.

New Pension Claim

The general rule for pension claims is that they, like compensation claims, are effective on the date when the claim is received by the VA. There is an important exception to this rule, but you or a member of your family has to ask for it! Your pension claim can be made effective up to 1 year before you filed it if you also file a claim for a retroactive award. Your claim can be a letter that says, "This is a claim for a retroactive award of disability pension." To succeed, you must prove:

★ you were permanently and totally disabled,
★ the disability was not a result of your willful misconduct, and
★ the disability was so incapacitating that it prevented you from filing a pension claim for at least 30 days after the date when you became permanently and totally disabled.

If you were hospitalized for an extended time period—for example, after suffering a stroke or a heart attack—that period of hospitalization should convince the VA that you were incapacitated and that you could not file your claim.

As with compensation claims, to get an early date, write a letter claiming pension rather than waiting for the form to come in the mail or waiting to visit the VA. Our best suggestion, though, is that you talk to a service representative and get help filling out the form because it is long and detailed. You will have to supply details about dates of medical treatment and your finances as well as the finances of your spouse and your children.

CALCULATING WHETHER THE AMOUNT IS RIGHT: EFFECT OF EXTRA DISABILITIES

When your disabilities require that someone attend to your needs, or the disabilities result in your being housebound, or you have a particular combination of disabilities, the VA will pay extra in the compensation and pension programs (you can draw from only one program at a time). This extra allowance is called special monthly compensation (SMC), aid and attendance (A&A) or housebound (HB) allowance.

Special Monthly Compensation

If you have certain service-connected disabilities, the VA will pay an amount in addition to the usual rate. For example, as of this writing, if you lose the use of your foot, hand, an eye, a procreative organ; lose both buttocks; or are deaf in both ears, you will be paid $70 extra for each disability. These awards are referred to as K awards because they correspond to subsection (k) of the VA law (38 U.S.C. § 1114) on compensation rates.

Other awards (l, m, n, o, p, r, and s) are available, depending on the degree of blindness or deafness, the level of an amputation, and whether there is a need for aid and attendance or you are bedridden. For a detailed list of these conditions see VA regulations (38 U.S.C. § 3.350).

Pension A&A and HB Allowances

As of this writing, the maximum VA pension you can receive is $651 per month. With the A&A allowance, your maximum rate increases to $1042 per month. The increase for the HB allowance is not quite as large: $796 per month. See Chapter 4 for details.

CLEAR AND UNMISTAKABLE ERROR BY THE VA

The general rule is that a claim becomes effective on the date when the VA receives your claim. However, if you discover that the VA made a serious mistake in an earlier claim that it denied, you can successfully argue that the effective date should be retroactive to your original claim.

For example, assume that you were injured in World War II and shortly after discharge the VA agreed that you should be paid for injuries to certain groups of muscles. The VA made its decision after looking at the service's medical report, which identified the muscles through which shrapnel passed. Let's also assume that a sharp-eyed service representative in 1992 took the time to review the original service's medical report and discovered that the VA had missed one of the muscles that the shrapnel had not missed. Furthermore, let's assume that the service rep files a claim at the VA regional office on your behalf for an increased disability rating and says that the need for an increased rating is due to the "clear and unmistakable error" of the VA. If the claim is allowed, it is effective as of the date that it would have been if the original mistake had not been made. A large sum of money may be involved.

As a practical matter, such cases are unusual. If, however, you have a nagging feeling that the VA may be wrong, it may be worth your while to review the original service department records, the old VA decisions, and the old VA rules that were in effect at the time of the original claim. Also, make up a chart of each claim and list on your chart whether the VA properly responded to each claim. Review Chapter 3 for the correct process for responding to a claim, which states, among other things, that if the VA denies a claim it must do so in writing and send you a letter.

CALCULATING WHETHER THE AMOUNT IS RIGHT: EFFECT OF FAMILY

If you have a spouse or children, the VA will sometimes pay extra to support them. VA award letters may say, "Included are additional benefits for the veteran's spouse and children." But VA letters seldom specify exactly what amounts are for the family. Of course, you first must convince the VA that the people living with you are your family. As you can imagine, there are laws that explain who, officially, is a spouse or a child.

Qualifications of a Spouse

Under VA law, a spouse is a member of the opposite sex who is married to a veteran. A marriage does not have to be a formal wedding with a license. If the state where you were married recognizes common-law marriages, so will the VA.

The VA will demand proof of marriage. Proof can be in the form of a certified copy of your marriage license, an affidavit from the magistrate who married you, or an affidavit from eyewitnesses. You can get a certified copy of your marriage license for a nominal fee from (depending on the state) your state or county government (state departments, sometimes called departments of vital statistics, are usually located in state capitals). Proof of common-law marriage can be in the form of an affidavit setting out all the circumstances of the marriage; for example, when you began living with your spouse and where you were living. The VA also demands affidavits from two people who personally knew that you and your spouse were accepted in your community as husband and wife.

For purposes of the VA pension program, you do not have to live with your spouse to receive the additional amount; for example, you may be in a nursing home while she or he is still living at home. However, you may not be estranged from your spouse.

See Chapter 10 for an explanation of who is officially a surviving spouse of a veteran.

Qualifications of a Child

Children are children until they reach age 18. Children you adopt before age 18, stepchildren who are members of your household, and illegitimate children all meet the VA's definition of children. Sometimes, though, children are not children—for example, if they are married before age 18. Sometimes, too, children remain children beyond age 18. For example:

★ If before reaching age 18 the child becomes permanently incapable of self-support, he or she is considered a child for the duration of his or her life.

★ If the child is attending school (at a VA-approved educational institution), the child is considered a child until his or her twenty-third birthday.

The VA will demand proof of your relationship to the children. This proof can include a certified copy of a birth certificate, an affidavit from the doctor who delivered the child, two affidavits from persons who have personal knowledge that the children are yours, or school records.

Benefits for Having a Spouse and Children

The effect of family varies depending on the VA benefit program involved. For neither the compensation program nor the pension program does the extra amount even approach the expenses related to supporting a family.

Compensation

The dependent's allowance does not begin until your disability rating reaches at least 30 percent. In 1994, Congress set the payment at $105 extra per month if you are rated 100 percent disabled and you are married. If you are rated at 30 percent, you will receive the prorated minimum amount: $31. If you have a spouse and one child and are rated at 100 percent, you will receive $178 per month (and 30 percent of $178 if you are rated 30 percent disabled). For each additional child, the VA pays a maximum of $55.

If your spouse is disabled, you can receive an additional amount, which is also prorated depending on your percentage of disability. The VA will accept that your spouse is disabled if she or he is in a nursing home, is blind, is almost blind, is helpless, is almost helpless, or is in need of the aid and attendance of another person.

Pension

The extra pension for a spouse is approximately twice the $105 amount that the compensation program provides for the 100 percent disabled veteran. At this writing, for a veteran with one dependent, the maximum additional payment is $201 per month (or $2,422 per year). For each additional dependent, the VA pays $110 per month.

WAYS TO LOSE MONEY (OR LOSE CONTROL OF IT)

Your children might grow up, your spouse might become an ex-spouse and get custody of the children who have not yet grown up, you might be judged incompetent, you might be drawing A&A along with compensation and go into a VA medical center or a VA nursing home, you might actually get better, or the VA might think you are better: In all these cases, your compensation might be reduced or even eliminated.

Changes in Dependents

If, while you are drawing extra money for a spouse you get a divorce, you aren't allowed to keep the extra money—even if you are paying alimony. If your former spouse takes the children, you can continue to draw the extra amount for them. But you must turn it over to them for their use. If not, they might read about "apportionment" in Chapter 10 and ask the VA to pay them directly. After you are divorced, send the decree to the VA. If they continue to send the wrong amount, send another copy of the decree by certified mail, return receipt requested. Be sure to set aside the extra money either to repay the VA or to use after the VA makes a double reduction in your check. (It's a double reduction because first the VA makes the reduction to the proper payment, then it further reduces payments in order to recover the overpayments it made.)

Changes in Your Competency

The VA may decide that you are not altogether "with it"—at least not together enough to handle your finances. If so, the VA will stop sending money directly to you.

Incompetency

If you are incompetent, you lose control of your VA money: The VA does not generally send benefits to individuals found to be incompetent to handle the funds. Before the VA can determine that you are incompetent, it must tell you that it plans to consider making that determination. The VA should have medical evidence that you lack the mental capacity to manage your affairs. Unless a court has already declared you incompetent, the VA must also tell you that you have the right to a hearing. You can appeal the VA's decision that you are incompetent. See Chapter 3 for further information about appealing an incompetency ruling.

After the VA decides that you are incompetent, it will send your money each month to a fiduciary (a person legally required to act in your interest). Often, a fiduciary is a vet's spouse or a parent. Sometimes it is a bank or someone who handles a number of other veterans' accounts. The fiduciary is supposed to spend your money to help you. If the fiduciary is not a member of your family, he or she keeps 4 percent of your payments as a commission.

If you are not happy with the way the fiduciary is using your money, complain to the VA employee called the Veterans Service Officer (VSO) at the regional office. Ask the VSO to require the fiduciary to produce accounting records showing exactly where your money has been going. If the VSO refuses to do this or to change the fiduciary, call the VA Inspector General at 1(800)488-8244 and ask for an investigation. Also call a lawyer or, if you cannot afford one, the nearest legal aid society office.

Incompetent, in a Private Facility, Getting Compensation

Until September 1992, if the VA determined you were incompetent and you had no immediate family and had a net worth of more than $25,000, it would cut off your compensation payments until your net worth was $10,000. The VA considered your immediate family to include only a spouse, a child, or a dependent parent. The $25,000 limit on your net worth included cash in the bank, stocks, CDs, and other assets. If there was a chance that you would return to your house, the value of the house would not have been used in calculating the value of your estate.

The program to cut off benefits for incompetent veterans began in 1990 and expired in September 1992. Before that, it was challenged in federal court in a lawsuit brought by the Disabled American Veterans (DAV). DAV and the VA agreed to a settlement that restored some of the money that had been withheld. If you did not receive a refund, contact DAV.

Incompetent, in a Public Facility, Getting Compensation or Pension

If the VA has officially determined that you are incompetent, and you have no immediate family and are hospitalized at government expense, your compensation or pension payments may be cut off. "At government expense" includes state, county, or municipal institutions. The cutoff occurs when your estate is worth $1,500 or more but resumes when your estate is reduced to $500. You can ask for a waiver of this cutoff if the discontinuance would cause a financial hardship.

Changes in Your Health

Medical problems sometimes improve. Such changes may permit you to move from part-time to full-time employment or to qualify for a more skilled job than the one you've had. (On the other hand, the theory that you should be able to work full time may not be close to the reality of today's depressed job market.) Because the purpose of VA compensation payments is to make up for the service-connected impairments in your ability to earn a living, you can expect the VA to cut its payments as your ability to work improves.

You can expect the VA to periodically reexamine you to monitor your condition. After an exam, the VA may decide to cut your benefits. The VA must follow strict procedures before your benefits are cut. These procedures are discussed in Chapter 3.

Sometimes it is not a change in your health that causes the VA to say you have improved. Instead, the VA may change the test (for instance, a test to measure hearing loss) that it uses to measure your condition. The change in the test may falsely show that your condition has improved. Also, the VA may change the rules governing the percentage of disability that corresponds to your condition so that your condition may now be worth a lower percentage of disability.

Major changes are in the works to update the VA's almost 50-year-old

---

★ WARNING ★

If you get a notice from the VA that your percentage of disability is going to be reduced, you must act quickly and carefully. Visit your service representative or legal services attorney for help or hire an attorney through a third party. To avoid an immediate reduction in your checks, you usually have to write to the VA and say that you want a hearing on the matter. Usually, the VA must receive your request within 30 days from the date on the notification letter (not from the date you receive the letter). Do not waste time calling the VA to tell them you want a hearing. You must put your request in writing. Send it certified mail, return receipt requested.

---

schedule for rating disabilities. Still, a new law directs the VA not to reduce your rating just because the schedule changes. A reduction must be based on a real improvement in your condition.

WAYS TO PROTECT YOUR MONEY

By law, certain compensation ratings are protected from reduction. If you are receiving a pension, you might need to give it up temporarily to protect it.

Protection for Compensation Ratings

If you have been receiving compensation (for example, for a 20 percent disability) for at least 20 years, the VA cannot reduce the rating unless you committed fraud in getting it in the first place. Your rating is protected.

If you are under the 20-year mark, you may be afraid that by asking for an increase in rating you'll risk losing what you have. You may think you can protect what you have by not asking for more. We cannot assure you that your fear is unrealistic. The VA may not agree that you are worse just because you say you are. Also, just before the 20-year protection begins, the VA may call you in for an examination. Everything considered, if you need more money because your disability is worse or you can't work at all because of it, don't hesitate to ask for an increase.

First, sit down with your service representative and your doctor. Review the VA rules involved. Find out from your service representative what he or she has seen happening with the VA's rating boards. Ask the rep whether there is pressure at the regional office to review and reduce ratings for your particular disability. In the early 1980s, the VA instituted a review of unemployability ratings for veterans younger than age 50. The VA "discovered" that thousands of the 100 percent unemployability ratings were granted "in error" and cut them off. Many of those veterans who had not been employable for years and still are not employable are only now having their cases heard in the U.S. Court of Veterans Appeals.

★ SPECIAL OPPORTUNITY ★

If you were receiving compensation benefits at the 100 percent rating because of unemployability and the VA cut the benefits off, you may be able to argue that the VA committed "clear error" in its decision. This could force the VA to restore your 100 percent rating retroactive to the cutoff date. Talk to your service representative; talk to an attorney. Find out about the latest decisions from the Court of Veterans Appeals on this topic.

Giving Up Pension to Get More

You have the right to give up (renounce) any VA benefit you are getting. There is at least one time when this right may protect you from a longer reduction in pension benefits than you otherwise might incur. Assume, for example, that you are receiving $7,000 in VA pension benefits and those benefits are your only source of income. Assume that your father dies and names you as the beneficiary of his $7,000 life insurance policy. Under normal circumstances, after you report receiving this money, the VA will cut off your pension payments for the next 13 months.

You may be able to protect your pension if you formally renounce the pension 1 month *before* you get the $7,000 life insurance proceeds. The strategy is to make sure you receive the $7,000 insurance proceeds during a month when you are not entitled to receive a pension.

After receiving the proceeds, reapply for a VA pension. When reapplying for a pension, you may have to report to the VA that you have $7,000 in your bank account as a resource, but the VA cannot count this money as income that requires it to cut off your pension for 13 months. You may lose as much as 2 months of pension payments.

```
┌──────────────────── ★ WARNING ★ ────────────────────┐
│ Renouncing pension is a dangerous tactic. You must work with an      │
│ experienced service representative to be successful. You may not     │
│ know when you will get the extra payment. Because timing is          │
│ critical and you may not be able to control the timing, this may not │
│ be realistic for you. You also face the possibility that you will not│
│ qualify for a pension when you reapply. Since 1991, qualifying       │
│ for a pension has been much more difficult than it was 5 years ago.  │
│ Make certain you would re-qualify under today's rules before you     │
│ renounce your current pension.                                       │
└──────────────────────────────────────────────────────┘
```

WAYS TO FIGHT BACK IF THE VA SAYS IT WANTS MONEY FROM YOU

DEADLINES: If the VA is demanding that you repay money and you want to dispute its claim, you will have to meet strict deadlines:

★ Waiver: 180 days from the date on the first VA letter telling you about the debt
★ Waiver of home loan debt: 1 year from the VA letter telling you about the debt
★ To postpone reduction of monthly check: 30 days to ask for a waiver and a hearing
★ Dispute: No deadline

The VA gives you money, and it can take it away and tell you that you can ask for forgiveness. It has a biblical ring to it.

There are several reasons the VA may have overpaid you or think it did:

★ The VA learned from the Social Security Administration that you were getting more SSA benefits than you reported.
★ You reported that you received less SSA benefits last year than you actually received.
★ The VA matched its computer records against those of your state and found out that you or your spouse was working even though you told the VA you were not.
★ You cut back your school course load from full-time to half-time.
★ Your spouse died or divorced you.

★ The person to whom you sold your VA-guaranteed house stopped making payments and the house was sold at a foreclosure sale.

★ The VA hospital you've been in for the past 2 years finally told the regional office you were there and that it should stop paying you extra A&A.

★ The VA failed to collect the $2.00 prescription copayment.

Whatever the official reason or real reason, the VA has enormous power not only to stop future VA payments to you, but also to ruin your credit rating, to have bill collectors call you at home, to have the IRS seize your tax refund, to garnishee your salary, and to take you to court. The VA's debt-collection machinery is frustrating to work with. You will have to juggle phone calls from debt collectors in Atlanta or Houston; letters from the VA Debt Management Center in St. Paul, Minnesota; and letters from the nearest VA regional office.

Fight Your Initial Reaction

Although your initial reaction to a form letter from the VA demanding repayment of $10,000 within 30 days may be to pound a tabletop, get a grip on yourself and reread the letter and any enclosures three times. Then get help.

Also, try to maintain an appropriate perspective on the situation. Keep in mind that the VA's official position on its debt-collection efforts is that its actions to force you to repay money are not adversarial but simply part of its informal, nonadversarial system designed to benefit you. Having said this, our best advice to you is to get very, very good help.

Get Good Help

The best help will be from someone who understands (or will learn) the details of the VA program (pension, compensation, educational assistance, or home loan program) that overpaid you so that you can be certain that the VA determined correctly the amount of the debt.

★ WARNING ★

Do not immediately call the toll-free number listed by the VA in its letter. The VA employees answering the telephones will be happy to hear from you. Some of them may sound and be sympathetic. However, calling the VA before consulting expert help may hurt you more than it can help you.

Service Representatives

Your service representative is the most likely person to know the details of the VA program that overpaid you. If your service rep gives you the clear impression that he or she is not confident that you can avoid repayment, find out whether this is because he or she thinks you were wrong or because he or she knows that the VA employees who consider these cases are not likely to give you a break. If your service rep convinces you that you were wrong and can show you the rules that prove it, get a second opinion. If the second opinion is the same, your options may be limited to asking for forgiveness from repayment or working out a repayment plan.

Attorneys

If the debt that the VA wants you to repay is from the VA home loan program, you are probably facing a debt of $15,000 to $30,000. Get an attorney who can review your loan guaranty file and confirm that the debt was calculated properly. Retain either a real estate attorney or an attorney specializing in consumer matters.

Since October 1992, veterans facing home loan program debt collection have had the right to hire an attorney without any restrictions. Nevertheless, restrictions still exist for veterans encountering debt collection because of overpayments of compensation, pension, or educational assistance.

If your debt is not from the home loan program, you cannot pay an attorney to request a waiver, but you can pay an attorney to dispute the debt; to argue with the IRS, credit bureaus, bill collectors, or your employer.

An attorney whom you pay to do all of the above might also agree to prepare a waiver request free of charge if that is your best option. Only after you appeal a waiver denial to the Board of Veterans' Appeals (and lose) can you pay an attorney to go forward to the Court of Veterans Appeals on the waiver. Of course, a third party can pay an attorney to represent you and then there are no restrictions on the work the attorney can do for you. Also, if you qualify for free legal assistance from a legal aid office because you have limited income, there are no limits on what that attorney can do for you. If the VA has taken you to court over the debt, none of the above restrictions apply and you can hire an attorney to defend you.

How the VA Tries to Collect Debts

Initially, the VA will try to scare you enough to make you repay the debt. It will tell you that unless you pay in full within 30 days, interest and administrative charges will begin to accrue. The rate of interest floats, but after it begins to accrue, it is not adjusted. Some education debts are increasing at the rate of 15 percent each year. Home loan debts accrue interest at the rate of 4 percent. The VA has not been charging interest on compensation or pension debts but may begin to do so soon.

If the first letter doesn't work, it begins a series of actions to convince you that it is more cost effective to repay than to ignore the debt. The VA never tries to convince you that it is right by offering you records to show exactly how it calculated the debt. After the VA decides that you owe it money, it uses different form letters with different explanations for you, depending on whether you are currently receiving VA benefits and whether you are a federal employee.

If You Are Currently Receiving VA Benefits

If you are currently in receipt of a running award, the VA will first warn you that it plans to adjust your award to the correct amount. You can (and almost always should) contest this, but benefit reduction is not, strictly speaking, part of the debt collection process. See Chapter 3 for how to contest proposed reductions or terminations of awards.

Second, after deciding that the adjustment must be made, the VA notifies you that the adjustment resulted in an overpayment of $X,XXX. The form letter will also explain that you can dispute the debt or request a waiver of the debt and that you can ask for a hearing.

★ DEADLINE ★

The VA letter will probably tell you that you have 30 days in which to request a hearing and that if you do not request a hearing it will begin to collect the debt by reducing your checks. If you have any hope of forcing the VA to postpone the reduction, you must meet this 30-day deadline. The deadline runs from the *date on the letter*, not when you receive the letter. Send your letter by certified, return receipt mail. State in your letter: "I dispute this debt and request a waiver and a hearing on these matters. Send me an accounting of how you calculated this debt. Defer debt collection until after the hearing."

If You Are Not Currently Receiving VA Benefits

If you are not currently receiving monthly VA benefits, the VA will send a series of demand letters. The first letter will notify you that your participation in the compensation, pension, education, or home loan program resulted in an overpayment of $X,XXX. The form letter must also explain that you can dispute the debt or request a waiver of the debt and that you can ask for a hearing.

If you ignore the first letter, the VA will send a second letter, reminding you that you failed to respond to the first letter. The second letter will not repeat your right to dispute the debt or request a waiver, but it will warn you that the VA plans to send the bad debt information to consumer reporting agencies around the country unless you make arrangements to pay back the money.

The next letter will tell you that the VA has sent the information to consumer reporting agencies. Later letters will tell you to pay the money or the VA will send your name to a private debt collection agency. The next letter will tell you that the VA has sent your name to a particular agency. Then you can expect to get obnoxious telephone calls at home. Later, the VA will tell you to pay or it will send your name to the IRS to seize any tax refund to which you might be entitled.

If you persist in doing nothing, the VA might ask its attorneys, attorneys in the U.S. attorney's office, or private attorneys to sue you. If the VA sues you, it must file suit within 6 years after it discovers your debtor status. After 6 years it might still sue you, hoping that you do not know about the 6-year statute of limitations.

If You Are a Federal Employee

If you are a federal employee and owe a debt to the VA, you face the prospect of having as much as 15 percent of your salary garnisheed to repay the VA. By law, this can happen only after you ignore the initial demands for repayment and only after you are warned that salary offset is being considered. You also have the right to have a hearing on whether a 15 percent reduction would impose a hardship.

Your Rights

The first VA letter explains some of your rights but not all of them or even the most important ones. The letter is written in classic bureaucratic gobbledygook and in small print.

Right to a Personal Hearing

If you are currently receiving VA benefits and the VA is threatening to reduce or cut off your benefits to collect an overpayment, asking for a hearing is especially important. If you request a hearing in writing within 30 days of receiving the VA letter giving you this option, the VA is obligated to postpone or defer the reduction until after the hearing. A hearing at the VA regional office will be before a Committee on Waivers and Compromises.

Take advantage of the opportunity. Show the VA employee that you are a human being. If the debt occurred because you did not understand what you were to do, go to the hearing and explain this. Explain that you had no way of knowing otherwise. In a home loan case, go to the hearing and explain the problems you and your family were having and the efforts you made to sell the house to avoid foreclosure. Hearings are also a good opportunity to answer the VA's questions. The VA will also want to know about your financial ability to repay a debt today and will want to discuss your Financial Status Report form (VA Form 20-5655). Make sure a representative goes with you to this hearing.

Right to Your Records to Confirm the Debt

Although the VA does not volunteer this, you have a right to a free copy of your VA records to confirm that the way the VA calculated the debt is correct. Even if you believe that the VA is correct in stating that you were overpaid, it is a good idea to confirm that the VA added the numbers correctly. Prior to sending the first letter of indebtedness, someone at the VA will have scribbled down three columns of numbers on a piece of paper. The headings for these columns should say:

Date Paid	Amount Paid	Amount Due

This is the accounting or the "paid and due" statement. Get it and add the columns yourself. If the figures do not add up to what the VA is demanding, you have good grounds to dispute the debt. If you learn that the VA Inspector General investigated your case and this is how the debt was discovered, ask for a copy of the IG's report of the investigation. Before you go into a face-to-face hearing, get all these records. If your debt arose from the home loan program, ask for both your VA claims file and your VA loan guaranty file.

Right to Dispute the Debt

Although the VA does not volunteer this, it is much better to successfully dispute the debt than to get a waiver. The VA also does not volunteer that there is no deadline for you to file a dispute. In fact, even if you already paid a debt, you can still dispute it and, if successful, get a refund.

If you dispute the debt, you may succeed in showing that the debt actually is less than the VA claims, or you may succeed in showing that there was no debt at all. Until September 1992, if you got a waiver, the VA reported the waived money to the IRS, which expected you to pay taxes on it.

In addition to checking the VA's arithmetic, there are three strategies to pursue to dispute an alleged debt: (1) demonstrate that the VA was solely at fault, (2) present mitigating circumstances surrounding an educational debt, or (3) ask for a retroactive release of liability of a home loan debt.

Right to Dispute Debt: VA Administrative Error

What if your debt occurred because the VA didn't do what it was supposed to and you didn't know better? For example, if you are receiving compensation and the higher level A&A and you go into a VA hospital, the A&A allowance should be cut off. The hospital is required to inform the regional office of your admission. In the past, hospitals seldom did this.

If the VA did not warn you that you would lose the A&A allowance (i.e., you were never sent anything by the VA that explained this) and you did not know you were supposed to lose the A&A allowance, the alleged debt is not a debt at all. It was created solely due to administrative error. Administrative error includes the VA's clerical mistakes, overlooking facts of record, and failing to properly follow VA regulations or instructions. The VA may tell you that you "should have known" the payments were wrong and that you were at fault for accepting the wrong payments. Unless the VA can point to some particular fact that clearly shows that you really should have known better, you should get the benefit of the doubt.

Right to Dispute Debt: Education Cases

What if your education debt occurred because you reduced your course load from full time to three-fourths time or you dropped out of school for one of the following reasons?

★   You were sick.
★   There was an illness or a death in your family.
★   You were unavoidably transferred as part of your employment.
★   There was an unavoidable change in the conditions of your employment.

★ Immediate family or financial obligations beyond your control required suspending attendance at school to obtain employment.
★ The course you were taking was discontinued by the school.
★ You had to report for unanticipated active duty service, including active duty for training.
★ You had unexpected difficulties arranging for child care.

These are examples of what the VA calls "mitigating circumstances," which can mean there is no debt at all. Since June 1989, the VA should automatically consider that mitigating circumstances exist for the first 6 semester hours of courses from which you withdrew. Also, withdrawing from a course during a drop-add period is automatically a mitigating circumstance. You must notify the VA of such circumstances within 1 year from the date of receiving the VA letter telling you of your opportunity to notify it. If you do not recall getting such a letter, review your claims file for a copy of it. If there is none, argue that you never received the letter and you now want the opportunity to submit your explanation.

Right to Dispute Debt: Home Loan Cases

Because the interest rate on VA loan guaranties is usually lower than what is available through conventional financing, veterans or active duty servicemembers frequently sell their homes by letting someone else assume their mortgage. Failing to get all the paperwork (i.e., a release of liability) done and approved by the VA in advance of such a transfer can mean that the VA will come after the veteran many, many years later. Although neither the VA nor the private debt collectors calling you at home will tell you this, you can apply today for a retroactive release of liability if you bought the home before March 1988. If you are successful, you have no further financial obligation to the VA. The VA still believes, however, that you have no right to future loan guaranties from the VA until someone pays off the alleged debt. A retroactive release of liability is appropriate if all three of the following conditions are met:

1. At the time of the transfer you were up-to-date on your mortgage payments.
2. There is a valid contract for the sale of the house that states that the purchaser assumes full liability for repayment of the loan and all your obligations.
3. The purchaser was qualified from a credit standpoint on the day of the transfer.

After you get a copy of your loan guaranty file, you may discover that the VA regional office's loan guaranty service already considered you for a release of liability and denied it. The reference might be only a stamp that says, "Release denied under 1813." That, of course, may be news to you because the VA failed to inform you of this secret determination.

In 1991, the U.S. Court of Veterans Appeals ruled in a case called *Travelstead v. Derwinski* (No. 89-5) that, before considering the veteran's waiver request, the VA was obligated to inform veterans of such determinations and to consider whether a release of liability was appropriate on the day of the sale.

In addition to disputing the debt by requesting a release of liability, you should confirm whether the VA already collected money from your lender because of questionable practices in your case. Over the past five years, the VA Inspector General has conducted investigations into the lending practices of several lenders. The IG has found many serious deficiencies and several lenders have repaid the VA for losses the VA sustained when it repaid the lender under the loan guaranty. The VA has not credited the accounts of individual veterans for the money it has recovered from the lenders. If the VA recovered money from your former lender, you have a good argument to dispute the very existence of a VA debt. To find out if your lender was investigated, contact the VA Inspector General (Assistant IG for Policy); Planning & Resources (53B); U.S. Department of Veterans Affairs, 810 Vermont Ave., N.W., Washington, DC 20420).

Right to Request Termination or Suspension of Debt Collection

If you cannot dispute the correctness of the debt and you have no ability to repay any significant amount of it, ask the VA to stop collection actions. The VA will terminate debt collection if it is convinced that you have no ability to repay any significant amount of the debt. In deciding on your ability to pay, the VA considers your age and state of health, your present and potential income, whether you will inherit money soon that could be used to repay the VA, and whether you have hidden or transferred assets that could be used to repay the VA.

On the other hand, if you want to repay it in the future but simply cannot now, the VA may be willing to suspend collection action. The VA will look at your future prospects to evaluate whether you will be in a position to repay later. The VA will also consider whether you have substantial equity in your home. Before suspending collection, the VA will ask you to agree to pay interest on the amount of the debt that is suspended. You should also routinely ask for suspension of collection actions pending review of a waiver request.

Right to Request a Waiver

If the VA is not successful in persuading you to repay the debt, it focuses almost exclusively on a waiver as your only other option. It's not. Only after you have tried to dispute the debt should you consider a waiver. Because of the short deadline involved, however, you will have to ask for a waiver before your dispute is resolved. Ask for both at the same time, but insist that your dispute be handled first. Asking for a waiver means giving the VA an opportunity to wave good-bye to you. Technically, requesting a waiver is acknowledging the debt but asking the VA to forgo collecting it; to forgive the debt.

★ DEADLINE ★

There are different deadlines for requesting a waiver, depending on whether your debt is from the home loan program or another VA program. If your debt is *not* from the home loan program, you must request a waiver in writing within 180 days from the date on the VA letter.

REASONS THE VA WILL GRANT A WAIVER REQUEST

The law says that the VA must grant a waiver (i.e., not collect an overpayment) if collecting it would be "against equity and good conscience." At the same time, the law also says that the VA may not grant a waiver if you committed fraud, misrepresented matters, or showed bad faith. Fraud, misrepresentation, and bad faith are big-time offenses. For example: You purposely supplied wrong information to get the VA benefit or you walked away from your VA-guaranteed house because the color of the walls in the dining room was not to your liking. Anything short of actions such as these should not prevent you from getting a waiver.

In deciding whether to grant a waiver, the VA focuses almost exclusively on what it believes is your present or future financial ability to repay the money. In fact, financial hardship is only one of at least six factors that the VA must consider. In presenting your request for a waiver, argue every other factor first and only as the last item talk about whether debt collection would impose a financial hardship. Also argue that the VA is required to give you "the benefit of the doubt." The factors that the VA must consider (and the official VA descriptions of these factors) include the following:

★ NOTE ★

If you ask the VA, it will tell you that it never makes a mistake: It always sends you the correct letter, to the correct address, and if it did not, the letter would have been returned by the postal service and its return would have been recorded. Regardless of VA assurances, the law states that if there was a delay in your receiving the notice, either because of VA error or postal service error, or because of other circumstances beyond your control, the 180 days extends from the date when you actually receive the notice. Circumstances beyond your control might include that you were hospitalized when the notice was sent or you had a disability that made it impossible to appreciate the significance of the notice.

Under a law passed in June 1991, if your debt originated from the home loan program, you have 1 year from the date when you receive a VA letter that was sent by certified mail. If the VA has not yet sent you a notice about your home loan debt, it must now do so by certified mail.

---

1. *Fault of debtor*: actions of the debtor contribute to creation of the debt
2. *Balancing of faults*: weighing your fault against VA fault
3. *Undue hardship*: whether collection would deprive you or your family of basic necessities
4. *Defeat the purpose*: whether withholding benefits would nullify the objective for which benefits were intended
5. *Unjust enrichment*: whether failure to make restitution would result in unfair gain to you
6. *Changing position to one's detriment*: whether reliance on VA benefits resulted in your giving up a valuable right or meant you incurred a legal obligation

If your actions did not contribute to the creation of the debt, be sure to consider disputing the debt as one that was solely due to administrative error by the VA. If the debt is in the home loan program, explain in detail how you got into trouble and could not maintain mortgage payments, and how the lender refused to accept your partial payments, and how you tried to sell your home.

If you were at fault but the VA's mistake was more serious, say so and explain why. If you are getting VA pension benefits that are available only because you have extremely limited income, argue that taking away your pension would put you below the poverty level and would defeat the purpose of the program, which is to ensure that you stay above the poverty level.

Whether the enrichment is "unjust" is a highly subjective matter that varies depending on which VA employee is making the decision. An example of changing your position to your detriment is letting someone else assume your VA mortgage, and, under the mistaken impression that you were free of your VA obligations, buying another house (i.e., taking on a major legal obligation).

As we just noted, the factor that the VA almost exclusively focuses on is whether demanding repayment would be a financial hardship. The VA will ask you to submit a VA Form 20-5655, Financial Status Report, which itemizes income, expenses, and assets. The form also asks you how much of the difference (assuming you have anything left over) between your income and your expenses you can apply to your debt to the VA on a monthly basis.

Although the VA form does not ask, take the time to explain whether you expect any major medical expenses or new educational or child care expenses during the next year. Also explain whether you will be laid off or retiring soon, thus taking a sharp cut in income.

The VA often takes a hard line regardless of your financial situation. For example, even if you show only a $10 balance each month, but you are making monthly payments on one credit card, the VA will say that you should give the same regard to the VA debt as you do your credit card bill. Also, even if you are now unemployed, the VA may say that because you are "relatively young" and have some prospect for employment in the future, it is not presenting a financial hardship by refusing to grant a waiver now. Anticipate these VA responses and address them in person at a hearing so that the VA Committee on Waivers and Compromises can see and hear you and personally judge whether you are telling the truth. It is usually more difficult for a VA employee to refuse to help you when he or she has met you and heard your story.

The committee can waive all the debt or part of it. The decision is recorded on a VA form called a "rating decision." If it does not waive all the debt, the committee is obligated to explain its decision and to summarize the evidence it considered.

If the VA Denied Your Waiver Request

Carefully review the letter that you receive from the committee. It may be clear that the committee rejected your request for a waiver, but it may not be clear why. To get a better understanding and to help decide whether to appeal further, ask the committee to send you a copy of its rating decision. You are entitled to a copy free of charge. If the rating decision reveals that the committee made mistakes in evaluating the facts surrounding your case, request correction of those mistakes and reconsideration by the committee.

You have 1 year from the date on the committee's denial to start your appeal by filing a Notice of Disagreement. See Chapter 3 for information on the appeal process. After the committee denies your request, any debt collection actions that were postponed will now go forward. If this means the VA begins to reduce your monthly check to less than your subsistence level, ask for an adjustment in the amount withheld each month.

Compromise and Repayment Plan

When you believe you should repay the debt but cannot handle repayment in one lump sum, offer to repay on a monthly basis. The VA generally likes you to repay enough each month so that the debt is repaid in full with the thirty-sixth payment. If this is not possible, say so and offer to repay an amount you can manage.

When you believe you should repay some of the debt but not all of it, offer to repay half. The VA will insist on having a current financial status report from you when it considers your offer. If your mortgages on your primary residence and a summer home are paid off, and you have $20,000 in CDs, the VA is likely to laugh at an offer to repay $5,000 of a $10,000 debt. If your financial situation is not so secure, the VA is likely to give serious attention to your offer. The VA says that you cannot appeal its rejection of your offer. You *can* make a second, third, fourth, or more offers.

Bankruptcy

If the VA is really knocking down your door and you are desperate, get professional financial counseling. Credit counseling services sometimes offer services free of charge. The focus of these services is to ensure that you avoid bankruptcy and continue to pay your credit card debts. If it is unrealistic to contemplate continuing to pay the credit card debt, much less pay off the VA, consider bankruptcy.

Filing bankruptcy will halt VA debt collection actions. If your petition for bankruptcy is granted, your debt to the VA is eliminated. If you're facing foreclosure on your VA-guaranteed home, filing bankruptcy will delay the final foreclosure proceedings. Unless you are very careful to name the VA as a creditor (in addition to the lender to whom you were making your monthly payments), you will not discharge the VA as a creditor. And the VA will still come after you.

★ **WARNING** ★

Bankruptcy is a major move. Your credit reports will carry the fact of bankruptcy for 10 years and effectively bar your getting credit for a car or home appliances or getting a mortgage.

Possibility of Refund

If you applied for a waiver in 1990 or more recently, skip this section. Requests for waivers that were considered in 1989 or earlier were considered by the VA under a harsher law. The current law is more liberal. If you began repaying a debt before 1990 or the VA before 1990 began reducing your monthly benefit checks to recover a debt and you are still paying it off, you may be able to obtain a waiver now. If you do, all the money you paid should be refunded. Talk to your service representative about this possibility. You can also call the VA Debt Management Center in St. Paul, Minnesota, for details; ask about reconsideration under Public Law (PL) 101-237. Call 1(800) 827-0648.

When the Bill Collector Calls or Your Credit Report Is Affected

When the VA refers information about your debt either to a private bill collector or to consumer reporting agencies, you have additional rights. For example, under the Fair Debt Collection Practices Act, you have the right to have the debt "verified." You have the right not to get telephone calls from the collector. If an attorney is representing you, send the bill collector a note, telling him or her your attorney's name and not to call you again. The bill collector cannot call you late at night or call you again and again to harass you. The bill collector cannot threaten to take you to court because he or she has no authority to do so. The line between illegal threats and obnoxious behavior is sometimes difficult to determine. Keep notes of what is said and when the call came in. Consult an attorney who specializes in consumer law. Depending on the tactics used by the bill collector, it may be possible to sue the collection company and get more out of it than it was trying to get from you.

You should understand that the VA will not pay the bill collector unless he or she is successful in getting you to send money to a special address (of his company). If you do decide to repay a VA debt, make arrangements with the VA directly. If the private collector is not successful after a certain number of letters or phone calls, your account is sent back to the VA.

If the phone call from the bill collector is the first indication that you owe the VA anything, tell the bill collector that you are disputing the debt within the VA and will not discuss repayment until after the VA resolves the matter. The private bill collector calling you does not know anything about your rights under VA law. It is useless to attempt to discuss with the bill collector the options you have at the VA.

Under the Fair Credit Reporting Act, if you are denied credit because of adverse information in your credit report, you are entitled to a free copy of your report. You also have a right to notify the credit bureau that you dispute the debt and a right to ask the company to verify the accuracy of the debt. If you write to the VA and request a waiver of the debt or dispute it before the VA has time to refer the account to the credit bureaus, the VA is not supposed to send the information to them.

The VA is required to notify you that it intends to report the information. If you do not respond, it will ship magnetic tapes that include your account information to several major consumer reporting agencies, which in turn sell the information to local credit bureaus. The VA also must tell you that it has shipped the information to the agencies, but it does not routinely give you the names and addresses of the agencies. You are entitled to their names.

After you work out a repayment plan or a waiver is granted, the VA should cancel the bad debt information it previously sent out. You may have to write many times to the VA's Debt Management Center in St. Paul to clear your records. And, if the information has been distributed to a local credit bureau, you will have to contact it, too.

CHAPTER THREE

★

WHEN THE VA SAYS NO

★ ★

Because the VA often says no, we'll explain now what you can do when you hear that word—even before we explain the details of VA programs. Our purpose in doing this is to prepare you for the worst and to give you an overview of the entire process that you may have to undergo. We think that if you have an idea about how the assembly-line process works you will prepare a better application in the first place and perhaps avoid a "no" and the lengthy appeals that might follow. This chapter also addresses your options if you are currently receiving benefits and the VA proposes reducing its payments or cutting them off altogether.

We have divided this chapter into alternating sections: (1) actions you are responsible for taking and (2) VA responses. We will describe a worst-case scenario: one that takes you through the entire VA appeals process. In fact, very few persons who apply for VA benefits go through the entire process.

The scenario described here is also relatively simple: It involves processing only one disability. Your situation may be that you have two disabilities for which you applied for benefits at two different times and for which you are in two different stages of appeal.

Finally, the scenario is only one example of how a claim might be processed. You may never have a hearing or you may have a hearing at a different stage of the process than described next. You may ask for a hearing when you file your claim even before anyone at the VA has considered your case. There are lots of options and variations.

★ IMPORTANT ★

Get help. No book can substitute for the assistance of a service representative who has daily, hands-on experience with the VA process and the VA decision makers. Remember, unless your claim was denied by the Board of Veterans' Appeals (BVA) within the last 12 months, you cannot hire a private attorney. Although you may not be able to hire and directly pay an attorney, a third party could do both for you at any time. See Chapter 1 for details on locating a service representative or an attorney.

ONE BIG PICTURE OF THE VA PROCESS

Your Action: File a claim for benefits at the nearest VA regional office or through a service representative; send evidence to support your claim.

VA Response: It requests certain military records from the National Personnel Records Center and schedules you for an examination.

Your Action: Keep the appointment for the examination.

VA Response: It reviews the examination results but does not agree that your condition is related to your military service. The VA sends a form letter saying that your claim for service connection for XYZ disability is denied.

Your Action: Send a Notice of Disagreement to the VA.

VA Response: It sends you a letter with two enclosures: a Statement of the Case and a VA Form 9, Appeal to the Board of Veterans' Appeals.

Your Action: Ask for a hearing at the regional office and collect additional information.

VA Response: A hearing officer convenes a hearing and issues a decision denying the claim.

Your Action: Send VA Form 9 back to the regional office in time to meet the deadline.

VA Response: The VA regional office sends the case to the Board of Veterans' Appeals in Washington, DC.

Your Action: You should prepare for a BVA hearing.

VA Response: The Board of Veterans' Appeals in Washington, DC, sends you a letter with an enclosure: its decision denying your appeal. With the board's denial is information about the U.S. Court of Veterans Appeals in Washington.

Your Action: See the next section on the Court of Veterans Appeals.

Claiming VA Benefits

Your Action: You must file the claim and supporting evidence. You are responsible for getting a claim to the nearest VA regional office. If you work with a service representative, he or she may deliver the claim to the regional office. Generally, if you need health care, call the nearest VA medical center for an appointment. Fill out the application there.

You do not need a VA form before you apply for VA benefits. You can apply by sending a letter to the nearest VA regional office and telling the VA that you are disabled because, for instance, you fell off the back of a truck and hurt your back while in the army on XYZ date. This is an informal claim. You do not have to know the exact medical diagnosis for your condition before you apply. The more details you can supply, the better because this will permit the VA to know what it should do next.

Although you do not have to start with the correct VA form, you almost always have to fill one out. Be sure you do so within 1 year of sending in your informal claim.

Making Your Claim Stronger

You can rely on the VA to get the records to prove your claim, or you can get them yourself. The VA may end up getting duplicate records from the hospitals, but duplicates are better than nothing at all.

Some general instructions apply to almost all disability claims. For example, if at all possible when you file your claim, include discharge

---

★ DEADLINE ★

There is no deadline to file a claim. The sooner the better, though. See Chapter 1 regarding effective dates. The VA has no deadline by which to process your claim. But once the VA says no, you have a deadline of 1 year from the date on the VA denial letter. A new law was proposed in 1993 that would reduce this amount of time. Check with your service rep to see if the proposal became law. It is wise to respond as soon as possible.

summaries from hospitals that treated you. Include a list of the medicines you must take for your condition. The most important supporting evidence you can get are statements from the doctors treating you.

Before getting such statements, work with your service representative to make sure that you can explain to your doctor what you have to prove to the VA to make a connection between your current condition and your military service and what you have to show to obtain the highest possible percentage of disability. Work with your service representative to get an excerpt from the VA Schedule for Rating Disabilities that lists your condition and an excerpt from the *VA Physician's Guide to Disability Evaluation Examinations* that explains what tests the VA doctors use when they examine veterans with conditions such as yours.

It is useful to obtain doctors' statements that identify the treatment they have provided you and the dates of treatment, and that explain why your current condition is related to your in-service injury or disease. If you are trying to show that you are totally disabled and cannot work because of your condition, make sure that the doctors who have been treating you discuss this in their reports. For example, if you are taking medicines that affect your ability to drive, make sure your doctor explains this.

If the Social Security Administration has already evaluated you and agreed that you are totally disabled, attach a copy of the SSA award letter to your VA claim. If you had a hearing before an administrative law judge, give the VA a copy of that decision, too. The VA may not agree with what the SSA said, but the VA must consider it carefully.

VA Response to Your Claim: The regional office authorization staff will review the papers you submitted. They will request verification of your military service. If you identified an episode of in-service medical treatment, they will ask the National Personnel Records Center in St. Louis to forward copies of those treatment records.

This work is called "developing your claim." If you did not supply private medical records and instead simply listed the dates of treatment and the names and addresses of the doctors who treated you, the VA will develop your claim by requesting records from those doctors. The VA will ask you to sign VA Form 21-4142, Authorization for Release of Information, giving it permission to obtain the records. To speed the process, we have included a copy of this form in Appendix A. Make a photocopy of the form for each physician or hospital that treated you and submit the form with your claim.

After the records are collected, and if the VA thinks you have a reasonable possibility of a valid claim, the VA regional office will contact the nearest VA medical center and schedule an appointment for you to undergo a physical or psychiatric examination. This examination is referred to as a "C&P exam"; this stands for compensation and pension exam.

Your Action: Keep your appointment. If the letter scheduling your appointment tells you to go to the general medicine clinic and you have a problem with your shoulder, call the telephone number on the letter to find out whether you will be seen by an orthopedist. If not, ask to see one. Similarly, if you have a psychiatric problem, you will likely benefit by seeing a psychiatrist rather than a physician with a more general practice.

Although your VA claims file should be in the office with the doctor during your examination, it may not be. If you have letters from your doctors describing your condition, take those letters. Sharing these letters with the VA doctor will help him or her to understand your condition. Offer to leave the letters with the doctor.

The examination may be short. Record exactly how long it lasts. Listen very closely to whatever the doctor asks. If you don't understand, say so. If the doctor asks why you are there, explain your problem and explain how the problem interferes with your ability to work. If this is your first examination since discharge from the service and you are claiming that you hurt your right shoulder in the service, explain exactly how you got hurt. If the arm has bothered you ever since, say so and explain how often it bothers you, whether it bothers you more at a certain time of day, what you are doing when it bothers you, and what you can't do now that you used to be able to do.

If the doctor asks you to lift your right arm and you can do so only by gritting your teeth to fight back the pain, do what you have to do but also explain at exactly what level your arm or shoulder begins to hurt. If you can bear the pain or can lift your arm only because you took pain medication an hour ago, tell the doctor this. Bear in mind that the doctor will be secretly observing you as you climb on and off the examining table and as you dress and undress.

When you go home, ask the regional office for a copy of the doctor's notes and the typewritten report of the exam and of any laboratory reports. You are entitled to a free copy of these. If the exam does not include a description of the pain you mentioned you were having or a description of the difficulties you explained to the doctor, write a letter to the VA regional office and include those descriptions.

VA Response: The VA will review the C&P exam and make a decision. The C&P examination results may be scribbled on a report or typed. The results must follow a particular format as outlined by the *VA Physician's Guide to Disability Evaluation Examinations*. The guide requires that certain tests be conducted to confirm a particular diagnosis or condition. If these were not done or the doctor's report did not include an assessment of the pain you experienced, the exam should be rejected as not adequate for rating purposes and should be done again.

A rating is the decision by the rating board. The rating board consists of three members (sometimes two). One member is a doctor. For a compensation claim, the rating board is required first to determine whether your present disability is related to the injury you said you incurred during military service (i.e., whether it is service connected). Only if you are successful on that point does the board proceed to determine where you fit in the VA's Schedule for Rating Disabilities and what percentage of disability you have. See Chapter 4 for a discussion of the VA Schedule for Rating Disabilities.

The rating board's decision is typed on a VA form headed "Rating Decision." The VA does not send the form to you. If your service representative works in the VA regional office, he or she has an opportunity to review the rating decision before you are told the results. Your rep may be able to return it to the rating board if he or she finds a mistake.

If the rating board decision is to deny you service connection, you will be sent a form letter. The VA is obligated to explain its decision and to summarize the evidence it considered. It does not explain what regulations or policies warrant the denial.

★ IMPORTANT ★

VA law requires that VA decision-makers give you the "benefit of the doubt" (38 U.S.C. 5107). Generally speaking, if the evidence in your favor and the evidence against you are roughly even, the VA should side with you. This policy sounds nice, but don't rely on it. Although asking to be given the "benefit of the doubt" is the most common request by veterans and service representatives, it is seldom granted and almost impossible to enforce. Do not sit back and neglect to get one more favorable medical opinion because you think the VA will give you the benefit of the doubt.

Appealing VA Denial

Your Action: You should send a Notice of Disagreement to the VA. A Notice of Disagreement (NOD) is your statement to the regional office that you disagree with its decision. You do not need to write a detailed explanation of your reasons for disagreement. In fact, you may not know in enough detail why the VA denied your claim to understand exactly how to counter the VA's decision. You can simply state that you disagree with the decision of XYZ date that denied service connection for your disability. Be sure to include your VA claim number. Also ask for a hearing before the regional office's hearing officer.

Consider as an alternative asking for a hearing before the regional office's hearing officer and *delaying* your NOD until after you have seen the rating decision and the C&P exam report and have received the hearing officer's decision. Review and discuss these documents with your service representative.

VA Response: The VA will issue a Statement of the Case. A few weeks (and sometimes months) after you file your NOD, the VA will send you a letter with two enclosures: a Statement of the Case (SOC) and a blank VA Form 9, Appeal to the Board of Veterans' Appeals.

The cover letter acknowledges that you filed an NOD and explains that the VA is not enclosing another decision but rather a document required by law, a Statement of the Case. The cover letter also routinely says, "If we do not hear from you in 60 days, we will assume you do not intend to complete your appeal and we will close our record." If this sounds as if you have 60 days in which to file your appeal, this may or may not be true. See the explanation of the deadline for VA Form 9 later in this chapter.

On page one of the Statement of the Case, the VA states the issue as it understands it (for example, whether a specific condition is service connected or whether an increased disability rating should be granted). Page two provides a cursory listing of the evidence the VA considered,

---

★ DEADLINE ★

You have 1 year from the date on the VA denial letter to mail your NOD to the regional office. Give yourself extra time to be sure you meet the deadline. Act as though the deadline is a day or two earlier than it really is. (Note that if the deadline would fall on a weekend or holiday, the deadline is the next business day.) Make a note of this deadline and put it on your refrigerator or calendar. An extension of this deadline may be possible if you have "good cause" for asking. If you were sick or on medication that impaired your ability to function, file the NOD even if it will be late. Include an explanation. If the regional office refuses to accept the NOD, you can appeal that to the BVA.

along with the date of filing the claim, the date of the rating decision, and the date of receipt of the NOD. Another section lists the "pertinent laws, regulations and rating schedule provisions." A very short decision is recited (for example, "Service connection is denied for residuals of shoulder injury"). At the end of the SOC is a short reason for the decision. A typical reason might be, "Complaints of shoulder pain in service were attributed to muscle strain. Degenerative joint disease was not shown until some time after service."

Your Action: Collect more evidence and present it at a hearing before the regional office's hearing officer. The regional office sent you a blank VA Form 9 with the Statement of the Case and also strongly suggested that you have only 60 days in which to return the form.

Instead of rushing to file the VA Form 9, talk to your service representative. Talk to him or her about collecting more evidence to submit to the regional office and asking for a hearing before the hearing officer. After you file the VA Form 9, you undercut the discretion the hearing officer has to allow your claim. At the *same time*, you must keep the deadline in mind (and in sight) while you consider the following options. These options do *not* change your deadline for filing the VA Form 9.

Collect More Evidence

Because the VA Statement of the Case is not likely to explain much, get a copy of the VA rating decision. If you did not get a copy of the C&P exam, do so. If the C&P examiner recommended follow-up tests or evaluations by a specialist, promptly ask the regional office to schedule them.

★ DEADLINE ★

The deadline for filing a VA Form 9 is 60 days from the date on the VA cover letter transmitting the SOC or, if it is longer, the 1-year anniversary of the date on the original VA letter that said your claim was denied. Write both dates on the VA letter. Then stick a large note on your refrigerator or mark your calendar with the later deadline. To meet this deadline, the VA Form 9 must be in an envelope and postmarked by that date. An extension of this deadline may be possible if you have "good cause" for asking. If you were sick or on medication that impaired your ability to function, file the appeal form even though it will be late. Include an explanation. If the regional office refuses to accept the appeal, you can appeal to the Board of Veterans' Appeals.

The rating decision should point out why the rating board was not convinced that your condition should be called service connected. Take a hint. Go back to your doctor and ask for a stronger statement (for example, a statement that the physician believes there is "definitely a relationship between the current problem and the injury the veteran sustained on active duty").

If the rating board said there were no records of treatment between the date of your discharge from the service and the next 10 years, go back to any doctors or clinics that treated you and get such evidence. If you received no formal treatment but people with whom you were working (or members of your family) remember your continuing problems, ask them to write and sign a statement to that effect. Have the statements notarized and then submit them to the VA at a hearing before the regional office's hearing officer.

Present Evidence to the Hearing Officer

The hearing officer (HO) is an experienced, former rating board member. The HO might be an attorney but is not required to be. The HO can overturn the rating board's decision, and does so in about 25 percent of cases. The HO can also order further development for pertinent records or order additional laboratory tests or an examination by a specialist.

Before choosing a hearing before the hearing officer, consult with your service representative. Confirm whether he or she has made presentations to the HO and whether the rep believes this step is worthwhile. You almost always want to maximize your chances for winning at the regional office level by taking the time to attend a hearing. Work with your service representative to review well in advance of the hearing date exactly what you should say, and write your statement. Also write down answers to the questions you expect to get from the HO.

Ask your service representative to tell you what is irrelevant so that you will keep the hearing focused only on what is necessary. Finally, ask your service representative to prepare a written argument, a written summary of your evidence, and an explanation of how your evidence satisfies each requirement in the regulations (together, these elements make up your "brief").

If possible, deliver the brief a few days prior to the hearing and be sure to take an extra copy to the hearing in case the hearing officer didn't receive your original. Keep a copy of this and all other documents for yourself. Your brief is not something you read at the hearing, nor do you read the statement you wrote, but you can use both to make sure you cover all the important points at the hearing as you testify.

Also discuss with your service representative whether you want the hearing officer to have a VA doctor present at the hearing or whether you should have your own private doctor present.

There is no formal procedure to follow in presenting your case to the hearing officer. A typical presentation consists of an opening statement that confirms exactly what benefit you are seeking and that briefly outlines your case. Your service representative may then ask you a series of questions designed to expand on the evidence in the record but mostly designed to fill in facts that only you can supply because they are missing from the official record.

Your representative may then highlight the regulations that apply to your case and emphasize how your evidence satisfies those regulations. At the end of the presentation, or perhaps during your testimony, the hearing officer may ask you questions. You should assume that the questions are significant even if you don't believe they are. Try to answer completely, but don't volunteer more than what you're asked. If your service representative knows that you should say more, the rep will follow up and prompt you to say more.

The hearing will be audiotaped, but take your own tape recorder, too.

★ **IMPORTANT** ★

In the past, the VA generally ignored the veteran's testimony at hearings. The Court of Veterans Appeals now requires the VA to consider that testimony carefully. If the VA official thinks you are lying, you will lose. Make sure that the official does not mistakenly discredit your testimony or mistakenly conclude there are certain "inconsistencies" in your testimony or past statements noted in your VA claims file. At the beginning and at the end of a hearing, invite the VA hearing official to question you about any aspect of your testimony. Remind the official that you are testifying under oath and that if he or she has any suspicions or reasons to doubt the truthfulness of your statements you want to know that now. You also want the official to state during the taped portion of the hearing whether he or she finds your testimony "credible." Also state that if the official discovers any inconsistencies in the records after the hearing, you want an opportunity to clarify or explain that before a decision is made.

At the end of the hearing, if you have thought of additional records that could be helpful, ask the HO to keep the record open for 30 days so that you can supply the information. Also, ask the HO to prepare a written decision and a transcript and to send them both to you and your representative.

VA Response: The hearing officer will issue a decision. Before he or she issues a decision, the hearing officer may order you to undergo an additional examination. He or she may also order that more records be collected. Upon receipt of that evidence, the HO may issue the decision. There are two possible decisions: to affirm the rating board's denial or to overturn it.

Your Action: If the HO affirms the denial, send VA Form 9 to your regional office. Form 9 presents some important choices to you: Do you want a hearing; if so, where? Hearings are important. The BVA reviews about 27,000 cases a year. Only about 3,000 hearings are held each year. A hearing will give you the chance to make your case stand out from the field. Consult with your service representative. Find out whether he or she will go with you to Washington or is available only for a hearing at the regional office or believes a hearing is not useful.

Your choices for a hearing include (1) travel to Washington, DC, or (2) wait for a traveling panel of the BVA to come to your regional office.

Traveling to Washington, DC, is expensive. It may be too expensive. Waiting for a traveling panel of the BVA to come to your regional office may take several months. Nevertheless, statistics indicate that a live appearance before a panel produces the highest allowance rate.

In addition to indicating on VA Form 9 that you want a hearing, you must also state the issues that you are appealing. Be very careful in doing so. The Statement of the Case may have listed the "official" version of the issue or issues involved.

Make sure you list on VA Form 9 what you believe the issues are. For example, if the VA has ignored your statements that your disability prevents you from working, and the official issue is that you want an increased rating, make clear again on Form 9 that an increased rating is one issue but

---

★ NOTE ★

Major changes in how the BVA reviews appeals went into effect in March 1992. Ask your service representative how these changes may affect your case. Also ask about decisions of the Court of Veterans Appeals that may have made more changes in how the BVA must consider cases.

★ DEADLINE ★

VA Form 9, Appeal to the BVA, must be in the mail to the regional office by the 1-year anniversary of the date on the initial denial letter or within 60 days of the date on the Statement of the Case. You do not get extra time to file the Form 9 just because you requested a hearing by the HO. If you have a good reason for filing the form late, file it along with your explanation. If the regional office refuses to process the form because it is late, file a Notice of Disagreement over that.

---

a total rating due to unemployability is another. It may help if you number the issues. If you were not examined by a medical specialist and you think an exam is necessary, make that an issue, too. If the VA has consistently ignored a particular document that you think is relevant, say so and give the name of the document and its date.

VA Form 9 also asks you to state in block 8 "in specific detail" your reasons for "believing that the action appealed is erroneous." Unless you go to a hearing before the BVA, what you put in block 8 will be your last opportunity to say anything to persuade the BVA to grant your appeal. Your service representative at the regional office has an opportunity to make some additional remarks before the case goes to the BVA. Work closely with him or her to coordinate your statements. In Washington, DC, the major service organizations and some state departments of veterans' affairs provide representation before the BVA.

If, however, you do not go to a hearing, in most cases the Washington, DC, representatives simply dictate a short statement into a microphone. That statement is transcribed by VA secretaries onto a piece of paper called an "informal hearing presentation." Therefore, unless you go to a hearing, no one is likely to appear on your behalf to personally present your case to a Board member.

If you are not going to a hearing, and if your service representative cannot promise to discuss with you and send you a copy of the brief he or she plans to present to the BVA, you must be careful about what you say in block 8. There is not enough room on the VA form to say what needs to be said, but you do not have to say everything before you send the form to the regional office. You can simply state on the form, in block 8, "Brief will be supplied within 90 days; make no decision prior to receipt of my brief."

VA Response: The VA will send the file to the BVA. The regional office prepares a "certification of appeal" and sends you a letter stating that your case has been certified to the BVA. From this date on, send any letters about your appeal directly to the BVA in Washington, DC, not to the regional office. Be sure to include your claim number. The regional office's letter also says you *may* have at least 90 days from the date on the letter to submit additional evidence, to find a representative, or to find a new representative. The 90-day period may be shorter: The letter says you have either 90 days or whenever the BVA makes a decision, whichever comes first. As a practical matter, the BVA does nothing quickly. If you need more than 90 days, however, write a letter to the board in Washington, DC, asking for more time. The BVA will also send you a letter acknowledging that it received your file and giving you phone numbers to call if you have questions about your case: (202) 233-3336 or 233-3346.

Your Action: Prepare for and attend the BVA hearing. The same advice we offered for preparing for a hearing before the regional office's hearing officer also applies to this hearing. If a hearing is unrealistic for you or you have nothing to say, your brief to the BVA has added importance. The advice we offered about preparing a written argument for the hearing officer applies here, too. You now have the advantage of knowing why the hearing officer denied your claim. He or she has identified weaknesses in your case that you must take seriously.

If you need additional expert medical opinions about the connection between your current problems and in-service problems, get them. If the hearing officer insisted that even though you are not working you *could* work, find a rehabilitation center and ask for testing and an evaluation to

---

★ IMPORTANT ★

The BVA can speed up the processing of your appeal if it thinks speed is important. If your health is deteriorating and your doctor can give you a statement that your condition is grave or terminal, that might work. Ask your members of Congress to help on this. Money-wise it is very important to you and your family to stay alive until after a BVA decision. If you win a 5-year-old case, you may receive a large award; if you die before the case is decided, your surviving family will not get 5 years of back benefits. Unlike the Social Security Administration, the VA has a very harsh law (38 U.S.C. 5121) that says if you die, your claim turns into a claim for accrued benefits and your family can get only 1 year of past benefits.

determine what jobs you realistically can perform, given your disability, your education, and your training background.

VA Response: The BVA convenes a hearing and considers your case. The BVA hearing used to include a panel of three BVA members. In 1992, the BVA began to have only one member hear a case. Even if your service representative presented your brief in advance of the hearing, do not assume that the BVA member has looked at it or your claims folder.

The BVA panel will not shout at you or be sarcastic. The members will appear concerned about your situation and will assure you that they will give your case a very careful, thorough review. They may shake your hand and thank you for coming. They may or may not ask you very pointed questions. They will not give you a decision at the end of the hearing. It may be 3 to 6 months before you get a decision.

In 1991, the BVA considered 46,000 cases. It decided in favor of veterans in only about 14 of every 100 cases, about 55 of 100 cases were denied, and the remainder were remanded (i.e., returned) to the regional office for additional processing. In 1993, the BVA considered only about 27,000 cases, decided for veterans in about 16 out of every 100, returned about 48 of 100 to the regional office, and denied the remainder of appeals.

After the Board of Veterans' Appeals Hearing

Before you get a decision from the BVA, your health may worsen or you may discover that you have another disability unrelated to the one on appeal but related to your military service. Don't wait for your file to be returned from Washington, DC. File the new issue at the regional office as soon as possible. If this new claim is allowed, you will probably get paid retroactive only to the date when you filed it.

If your new evidence relates to the claim pending at the BVA, send it to the BVA. For example, perhaps the Social Security Administration will come through while you are waiting for the BVA. The BVA may refuse to consider this evidence, but you should send it anyway.

After the Board of Veterans' Appeals Decision

The BVA may remand, allow, or deny your claim. If you were raising two or three issues, the BVA may remand on one issue, allow one, and deny another. It may also refuse to deal with certain matters and "refer" them back to the regional office. Discuss with your service representative whether this referral was proper, what action the regional office is taking on the issue referred to it, and what action you should take to make sure the regional office acts on that issue.

Remand from the BVA

The BVA decision may be no decision at all but rather a remand to the regional office ordering it to perform another medical examination or to get some additional evidence. Take a hint. The regional office will do what the BVA said, but you should too. If the BVA instructed you to be examined by a certain kind of specialist and asked that specialist specific questions, you can do the same with your doctor or a specialist you select.

After you complete the "official" VA exam, be sure to get a copy of the report. If the official report does not look favorable to you, give it to your specialist physician and ask him or her to review it. If your specialist can point to problems with the VA's official report, have him or her put those problems in writing and present the statement to the regional office.

The regional office's rating board will prepare a rating, and, if it still says no, it will send you a Supplemental Statement of the Case. You can reply to the Supplemental Statement of the Case, and your case will automatically be returned to the BVA to further review the evidence that was collected. You can ask for another hearing either at the regional office or at the BVA.

Allowance by the BVA

If the BVA gave you everything you wanted and you are completely satisfied, congratulations are in order. If you were trying to establish that your current problem is service connected and the BVA agreed, you still get no money until the regional office reviews your case again and decides at what percentage you are disabled as a result of this particular disability. You should expect to be scheduled for an examination to assess this. If you are not completely happy with the percentage that is assigned, you can go through the entire appeals process again on that issue.

If you get a 100 percent rating retroactive to the day after you were discharged from the service, there may be nothing else to ask for. But what if the BVA agrees that your 30 percent rating should be increased to 50 percent and you think it should be 70 percent? Or what if the BVA says that the effective date should be the day you filed an application and you think it should be the day you became disabled? If this is your situation, consider your claim denied and read on.

Denial by the BVA

Your Action: You may be able to appeal to the U.S. Court of Veterans Appeals, but don't do so without first considering three alternatives: (1) getting new evidence to address the reason the BVA denied your claim and presenting that evidence as a reopened claim to the regional office, (2) asking the BVA to reconsider its denial, and (3) dropping the matter. If you want to pursue the matter, you may be able to simultaneously reopen, appeal to the court, and ask for reconsideration.

Reconsideration by the BVA

Only a few cases are reconsidered by the BVA. In fiscal year 1992, the BVA denied 498 requests for reconsideration. It agreed to reconsider 221 other cases but decided for the veteran in only 71 of them. You have to identify a specific mistake made by the BVA. For example, if one of the issues in your case was an increased rating based on unemployability and the BVA decision did not recite the VA regulation on unemployability and how it was applied, this may be an error sufficient to require reconsideration. If the BVA completely ignored one of the statements from your doctor about your condition, this may be an error sufficient to require reconsideration. If the BVA failed to obtain pertinent military service records, this error requires reconsideration. Reconsideration may be especially important to you if you have missed the 120-day deadline to appeal to the Court of Veterans Appeals. The advantage of reconsideration is that if you are successful, you should be paid retroactive to the date that would have been set if the error had not been made.

Another kind of problem may also convince the BVA that it should "vacate" (nullify) its decision and reconsider your case. For example, if you asked for a hearing and instead of getting a notice scheduling you for the hearing you got a decision denying your case, the BVA should "vacate" its decision. Send your request for reconsideration or "vacation" directly to the BVA, not to the regional office. If the BVA agrees that your case should be reconsidered, it will "vacate" or withdraw the earlier decision.

Reconsideration by the board effects an appeal to the Court of Veterans Appeals. If you file a motion for reconsideration to the BVA within 120 days of its decision, the deadline for filing your appeal to the court is postponed. Not until the BVA rejects your motion for reconsideration—or, if it agrees to hear your case again, then denies it again—will the 120-day deadline to file in court begin to run again. Certain requests for reconsideration that are denied by the BVA chairperson can be appealed to the Court of Veterans Appeals. For example, if you presented the BVA with newly discovered military records or other new evidence and the BVA still refused to reconsider its decision, the court might act on the appeal and force the BVA to reconsider your request. If you give the BVA nothing new to consider, the court probably will not accept an appeal of the denial of reconsideration.

Reopening the Claim

Trying again at the regional office or reopening your claim may be a possibility. Do not simply say to the regional office, "I reopen my claim for XYZ disability." Unless you give the regional office quality evidence, the regional office is likely to refuse to reopen your claim. Then you will be in the position of having to appeal through the entire process on whether your evidence really warrants reopening. If you are successful on that narrow, technical issue, you may succeed in forcing the regional office to consider the evidence—but not necessarily to allow your claim.

To reopen your claim, you must present "new and material evidence." "New" is something the VA has not seen before. It is not the same letter from the same doctor but with a different date. "Material" means more than just relevant; "material" evidence really matters: It might make a real difference if it is considered. The new and material evidence by itself does not have to convince the VA to allow your claim. If the VA reopens your claim because it is persuaded that your evidence is new and material, it must then review the new material along with the earlier evidence to make a decision.

The advantage of reopening your claim is that you can have your claim reviewed again and present evidence to support it. If you go forward to the Court of Veterans Appeals instead of reopening the claim, you are locked out of presenting new evidence to the court. The Court of Veterans Appeals does not give you a "day in court" to tell your story in person. The court looks only at what the BVA saw before.

The disadvantage of reopening a claim is that if you eventually succeed, the VA will pay you retroactive only to the date when you reopened the claim, not to the date when you began the appeal that was denied by the BVA. The best advice is to both reopen your claim at the regional office and appeal to the Court of Veterans Appeals.

★ **IMPORTANT** ★

In March 1992, the BVA proposed imposing a 45-day deadline to request reconsideration. Confirm with your service representative or attorney whether this proposal was ever put into effect. Until this proposed change goes into effect, there is no deadline to request reconsideration.

★ IMPORTANT ★

Recent cases at the court suggest a problem with trying both to reopen and to appeal. The court might say it cannot consider the exact same issue that is pending at the regional office and might dismiss your appeal. To try to avoid this potential problem, make your reopened claim slightly different. Perhaps you can say that instead of just an increased rating, you want a total rating due to unemployability. Consult an attorney experienced with the court's cases.

Fighting a Proposed Reduction in Rating

There is extra processing the VA must offer you in connection with a reduction in your benefits. Sometimes the VA will send you a notice of a reduction before the reduction goes into effect. This notice is a pretermination or prereduction notice. Sometimes, as part of such a notice, the VA will offer an opportunity for a special hearing *before* it reduces or terminates your benefits. This hearing is a predetermination hearing. Although you have a right to request a hearing at any time in the VA processing of your claim, what is special about a predetermination hearing is that the VA cannot act to terminate or reduce your benefits until it has held the hearing.

The notices and hearings are additional due process rights. The extra process is intended to make sure that before the VA takes such drastic action it will be sure it's right. To make sure it's right, the VA gives you a chance to explain in writing or in person at a hearing that it might be wrong if it reduces your benefits.

Sometimes the VA tells you nothing in advance. For example, if the VA hears from a reliable source you are dead, it will simply stop making payments. Sometimes the VA will tell you that it is making an adjustment in your payments at the same time it makes the adjustment. For example, if you wrote to the VA and told it you are no longer married, the VA makes the adjustment and tells you it did it. The VA presumes since you sent the letter and you signed it that the information was correct and there is no possibility of a mistake. Also, if you return the pension Eligibility Verification Report and indicate you won $5,000 playing the lottery, and you sign the report, the VA will presume the information is correct and will further presume you know that the VA is required to reduce your pension payments for the next 13 months to offset your winnings.

Other times, the VA will tell you in advance that it is going to adjust your benefits and give you 60 days to respond in writing. If you convince the VA not to reduce your payments by what you send in writing, the reduction should not happen.

Other times, the VA must offer you a hearing before the reduction and hold the hearing before the reduction kicks in. For example, a predetermination hearing is required if the VA is proposing a reduction or termination for any of the following reasons:

★   Service connection is to be severed
★   Percentage of disability is to be reduced
★   Total rating based on unemployability is to be terminated
★   Pension payments are to be reduced based on report of improved health or employability

The timing of your response to a pretermination or prereduction notice giving you an opportunity to a predetermination hearing is critical and very tricky. The pretermination or prereduction letter will tell you that you have 60 days to respond in writing but only 30 days to request a hearing.

Deadline: To postpone a proposed reduction when you have been offered a predetermination hearing, you must make a written request for a hearing within 30 days of the date on the VA letter.

If you meet the 30-day deadline, the VA is required to continue your payments until it has held the hearing. The hearing will be held before the regional office hearing officer. If you miss the 30-day deadline for requesting a hearing, you can still have a hearing but the VA will not be obligated to postpone the reduction until after that hearing. You also have until the 60th day to submit evidence that your current level of payment is correct and should continue.

Preparing for Predetermination Hearing

The "predetermination" hearing is somewhat misnamed since the regional office has already prepared a rating decision explaining why it thinks the termination or reduction is necessary. Get a copy of that rating decision. The VA is required to give you a reason for the proposed reduction but that reason may not be very complete. The rating decision will give you a better explanation. You must see it before you go for the hearing so you will know exactly what to prepare for.

If the reduction is based on the results of a periodic C&P examination, ask the doctor who is treating you to prepare a report refuting the C&P

exam's findings. If the VA refuses to supply a copy of the rating decision in advance of the hearing, or you get sick or someone in your family dies and you cannot attend the hearing on the date it is scheduled, call and tell the hearing officer you need to reschedule. Also repeat that request and your explanation in writing. You should be given at least 10 days' notice of the date of the hearing.

Predetermination Hearing

Review the suggestions noted above for preparing for a hearing before the hearing officer. Work closely with your service representative. If the reason for the reduction is a C&P reexamination, make sure that the report from that exam is consistent with the requirements in the *VA Physician's Guide to Disability Evaluation Examinations.*

If the report is not adequate, it cannot fairly be used to reduce your rating. Look in particular for the absence of references in the report to pain (if your condition actually is painful); look for the absence of any consideration of the past history of your disability. These are defects in the exam and factors that you will want to emphasize to the hearing officer.

IMPACT ON PAYMENTS

If you lose after a predetermination hearing, the effective date of the reduction is in the future, not back to the date of the first notice. No overpayment of benefits should occur. In fact, you will continue to get at least two more months of the same payment if the reduction was due to severance of service connection or reduction of a service-connected disability rating. If the reduction of pension was based on improved health or employability, the reduction will go into effect at the end of the month in which final action is approved.

APPEAL AFTER THE PREDETERMINATION HEARING

You will be given notice of the results of the hearing or of the VA's consideration of any evidence you submit up to the 60th day. That notice, if unfavorable, is a notice of denial that triggers your opportunity to submit a Notice of Disagreement. You then can go through the entire normal appeals process outlined above.

You should understand that if you ask for a hearing at the regional office again, it should be held before a different hearing officer, not the same one you previously saw. Having an impartial hearing officer is important. Someone who has already heard your case and turned you down is not impartial. If necessary, ask the regional office adjudication officer to assign a different hearing officer.

Appealing to the U.S. Court of Veterans Appeals

```
──────────────────── ★ IMPORTANT ★ ────────────────────

Deadline: You have 120 days from the date on the front of the
BVA's decision to get a Notice of Appeal in the hands of the clerk
of the court. Do not put your appeal in the mailbox on the 120th
day: it must arrive at the courthouse before the end of the 120th
day. You can send it via facsimile to (202) 501-5848. If you need
information, note that the court has a new, toll-free phone number,
(800) 869-8654. A blank Notice of Appeal is included in Appen-
dix A. Fax or mail your Notice of Appeal to:

Clerk of the Court
U.S. Court of Veterans Appeals
625 Indiana Avenue, N.W., Suite 900
Washington, DC 20004
```

```
──────────────────── ★ WARNING: ★ ────────────────────

Get help. Consider the following: The attorney representing the
VA is out to make you lose. Because this is a court proceeding,
the decision can establish a precedent. If you lose, and establish a
bad precedent, the decision will affect you first but the decision
may well affect many, many other veterans who were hoping to
win their cases. Taking your case to the court just because you are
stubborn and won't let go is not a smart move. Sit down with
someone who has copies of all the court's decisions and who will
give you an honest assessment of your chances.
```

The Clerk of the Court wants you to have a representative. If you file an appeal and do not have a representative, he or she will send you a list of attorneys and non-attorney practitioners authorized to practice at the Court. If your case has merit, you should be able to find a representative.

Fees charged by private attorneys vary widely. Many attorneys accept cases on a contingency basis, which means your attorney gets a fee only if you win. In these cases, you can expect to be asked to give up 20 percent of any back benefits you win. Sometimes you may be asked to agree to turn over more than 20 percent. You may also be asked to pay some money up front or to pay an hourly rate whether you win or lose. Contracts with attorneys are negotiable. The fees you pay cannot be "excessive or unreasonable." Also, the contract must be filed with the court and if the attorney wants the VA to automatically withhold his or her 20%, it must also be filed with the BVA and regional office. If you think the fee is excessive or unreasonable, tell your attorney first. If you get no satisfaction, tell the court and the BVA.

A list of attorneys admitted to practice before the Court of Veterans Appeals and who are actively representing veterans and survivors is available from the National Organization of Veterans' Advocates; P.O. Box 42334; Washington, DC 20015. You may not find an attorney in your state who is available but you do not have to use an attorney from your state.

Limit on Appeals
You have to have been denied by the BVA to appeal to the court. You also have to have filed a Notice of Disagreement on or after Nov. 18, 1988. (Congress is considering changing the requirement for a Notice of Disagreement).

What is the Court of Veterans Appeals?
The court was created by Congress in 1988 to hear cases that had been denied by the Board of Veterans' Appeals. It is not part of the VA. There are seven judges. As of this writing, they are:

★ Frank Q. Nebeker (formerly a judge of the District of Columbia Court of Appeals)
★ Kenneth B. Kramer (formerly Assistant Secretary of the Army for Financial Management and U.S. Representative from Colorado)
★ John J. Farley III (formerly Director, Torts Branch, Civil Division, U.S. Department of Justice)
★ Hart T. Mankin (formerly vice president of the Columbia Gas System)
★ Ronald M. Holdaway (formerly Chief Judge, U.S. Army Court of Military Review)
★ Donald L. Ivers (formerly General Counsel, U.S. Department of Veterans Affairs)
★ Jonathan R. Steinberg (formerly Chief Counsel, U.S. Senate Committee on Veterans Affairs).

Nebeker is the Chief Judge. Each of the others is referred to as an associate judge. Farley (who received Purple Hearts and Bronze Stars from service in Vietnam), Holdaway, Mankin, and Ivers are veterans. The law creating the court permitted the President (at the time, President Bush) to nominate four members of his political party to the court. He did just that.

The Court's Appellate Process

The following portion of this chapter is broken into three alternating sections: (1) actions you are responsible for taking, (2) actions the court takes, and (3) response the VA makes. The scenario described here is a fast-track scenario, i.e., the way a case would proceed if no one asks for additional time to prepare papers. If you need more time to meet a deadline, you must ask the court before the deadline has passed. So long as you are asking for only a 30-day extension, the clerk of the court is very likely to grant your request. When you write to the Clerk, be sure to use your court docket number and your VA claim number on your letter.

ONE BIG PICTURE OF THE COURT PROCESS

Your action: Within 120 days of the BVA decision, your notice of appeal reaches the court and you send the $50 filing fee or ask permission to not have to pay the fee.

Court action: Clerk acknowledges receipt of your appeal, assigns a docket number, and directs you to file a Statement of Issues within 30 days.

Your action: You file a very short statement (your Statement of Issues) explaining what part of the BVA's decision you are appealing. For example, "I appeal the denial of service connection for asbestosis."

VA response: The VA attorney prepares a list of the pages in your VA claims file that he or she believes are relevant for the court to review (this list is called the Designation of Record) and mails that to you within 30 days.

Court action: Clerk will direct you to file your list of any other records in your VA claims file you believe are relevant for the court to review (your Counter Designation of Record) within 30 days.

★ **IMPORTANT** ★

The rules and deadlines used by the court are likely to change in 1994. Ask the clerk for a copy of the latest edition of the rules. The National Organization of Veterans' Advocates offers appellants a self-help pamphlet on the court's procedures free of charge. Send a self-addressed stamped envelope to: NOVA, P.O. Box 42334, Washington, DC 20015.

Your action: File your Counter Designation after reviewing a photocopy of the claims file against the pages designated by the VA attorney to see what else should be added. If you do not have a copy of your entire file, ask the VA attorney to send you one free of charge.

Court action: Clerk will direct the VA to transmit the Record on Appeal within 30 days.

VA response: The VA attorney will compile the pages of your claims file he or she selected and you selected and assemble them in chronological order, number each page, and file it with the clerk.

Court action: The clerk will direct you to file within 30 days your reasons (your brief) explaining why the BVA's decision was wrong.

VA response: The VA will prepare its brief explaining why the BVA decision should be affirmed and you should lose.

Your action: You get 2 weeks to reply to the VA's brief.

Court action: Judges review the briefs and issue a decision.

There is no deadline for the judges to reach a decision. It can be as little as a few weeks to more than a year. Most cases are decided in 6 to 9 months. From the time you file a Notice of Appeal until your case is in the hands of the judges is about 6 months if everything goes according to the rules. The reality is that in virtually every case you will need extra time and the VA attorney will need extra time and you really face no less than a year to get a final decision.

The reality also is that the VA attorney will probably not file a brief at all but instead will file a short memo (a "motion") asking the court to uphold (or "affirm") the BVA's decision. The VA attorney will argue that your case is easy to decide and should be quickly disposed of. You will have 2 weeks to respond. If you think your case is complicated and requires the VA attorney to write a brief explaining his or her reasons for wanting the court to deny your case, tell the court that. It is very important to point out exactly how the VA attorney is wrong in his or her description of your case.

Finally, you might not want to file a brief yourself at all. If the BVA did not discuss important evidence you presented to it, or if the BVA did not get SSA records or VA medical records you told it were available, ask the court to remand your case to the VA to get that information and to redo your case. If you point out this kind of problem to the VA attorney, the VA attorney may be willing to work with you to file a "joint motion for remand."

What the Court Can Do

The court has authority to overturn or reverse the denial by the BVA. It also can uphold the denial, i.e., affirm the BVA's decision. The court also

> ─────── ★ **WARNING ABOUT YOUR PRIVACY:** ★ ───────
>
> Parts of your VA file may contain extremely sensitive information (only you know for sure): perhaps intimate details about your mental health, your inability to have sex, the fact that you had a venereal disease, or that you are incontinent. The VA has been required to maintain your privacy. As outlined above, however, portions of your VA claims file will be turned over to the clerk of the court.
>
> Any member of the public can walk in off the street and review and make copies of the files at the clerk's office. If you have a good reason for wanting to keep your records confidential, ask the clerk to keep your records out of reach. You must explain in detail why the records should be kept confidential; do not just say it would be embarrassing if your records were released.

has authority to remand the case back to the BVA. Under the law creating the court, determinations of the BVA on factual matters cannot be overturned unless they are clearly erroneous. The court has interpreted this to mean that if there is a plausible basis in the record for the BVA's decision, the court will not overturn it. Basically, the court defers to the BVA on factual matters.

On the other hand, if the issue is a matter of law, the court is not so deferential. Also, if the BVA's decision or conclusions were arbitrary, capricious, an abuse of discretion or otherwise not in accordance with proper procedures, the court can overturn the BVA decision. The court can force the VA to act if it has unreasonably delayed acting or has refused to act.

There is one other power this court has. Like other federal courts, it has the power to order the VA to act if the VA's failure to act "frustrates its jurisdiction"; that is, if the VA takes so long (perhaps years) that it in effect keeps the court from being able to do what it is supposed to do. This power is exercised under the All Writs Act. See Court Rule 21 in the rule book the clerk of the court sends you when you file your appeal. The court almost never actually uses this power but sometimes just asking for relief can persuade the VA to move.

What the Court Has Been Doing
During the period 1989 and 1991, Congress gave the court $17 million. With that money, the court built a courtroom and several offices. It

also hired 85 employees to process the enormous number of documents filed with it.

Originally, it was thought that some 5,000 veterans and survivors each year would appeal. In fact, from January 1990 through December 1991, the first 2 years of the court's operation, only 4,046 veterans or survivors filed notices of appeal. In 1993, fewer than 1,300 appeals were filed. Many cases are dismissed because the court has no jurisdiction to consider them; for example, there was no final BVA decision, or the Notice of Disagreement was before Nov. 18, 1988.

The bulk of the court's actions have been to summarily affirm (or uphold) the BVA's denial without issuing a published decision. Through 1993, it had permitted representatives for about 100 veterans to appear and present oral argument. Of these, almost half were presentations by one organization: the Disabled American Veterans. Many of DAV's arguments were presented by its non-attorney practitioners.

The court issued 150 published opinions during its first two years of operation. In most of these opinions it remanded the case back to the BVA for further consideration. The most common reason for doing that was that the BVA had not fully explained why it had denied the appeal. In 33 cases of the published decisions, the court affirmed the BVA's decision. In three of the published cases, the court reversed the denial by the BVA and ordered that service connection be granted; in four cases it ordered the BVA to restore a rating that had been reduced.

There have also been important cases that have begun to change how the BVA writes its decisions and considers veterans' cases. One case in 1990 required the BVA to better explain why it took the action it did. Unfortunately for that veteran, once the BVA did that, the court was satisfied the BVA had made the right decision in the first place. These cases have had a significant impact on the BVA and are beginning to have an impact on operations at the regional offices.

The court does not keep statistics on what happens to those cases remanded to the BVA for further processing. It appears that in most of these cases, the BVA remands the case to the regional office for the collection of more evidence.

After the Court Has Denied Your Appeal
You can appeal to the U.S. Court of Appeals for the Federal Circuit. The court has no authority to overturn a decision by the Court of Veterans Appeals if the decision involved only findings of fact. Only if the Court of Veterans Appeals ruled on an issue of law does the circuit court have

authority to review the decision. The VA can also appeal if the Court of Veterans Appeals said you should win. Get help.

Of course, even if the Court of Veterans Appeals says the BVA was right to deny your appeal based on the evidence in your file at that time, you are still free to collect new evidence and try to reopen your case at the VA regional office or seek reconsideration.

★ IMPORTANT ★

If your disability gets worse or another disability develops, ask the regional office to get your file back from the Office of the General Counsel in Washington. The Court of Veterans Appeals never gets your original claims file and the VA attorney does not use it after the first few weeks of your court appeal. Do not let the regional office postpone processing a new claim because it mistakenly thinks your file is unavailable until after the court is done.

CHAPTER FOUR

COMPENSATION

★ ★

This chapter describes monthly cash benefits available if you have health problems related to the time in your life when you were on active duty. These benefits are also available if you were injured while in a VA hospital. If the VA agrees that your condition is service connected, it will then consider whether you are disabled by the condition, and if so, to what percentage you are disabled. The percentage of disability dictates how much money you will receive each month. You might find it necessary to go through the entire appeals process described in Chapter 3 on the issue of service connection before you get a chance to argue exactly how disabled you are.

As of December 31, 1993, the amount of money paid by the VA for service-connected disabilities ranged from $87 per month for a 10 percent rating to $1,774 for a 100 percent rating. Another $3,300 (approximately) per month, in addition to the amount paid for the 100 percent rating, may be paid for particularly severe disabilities. Only 6 percent of veterans currently receiving compensation get the 100 percent rate; 40 percent receive only the 10 percent rate.

We have divided this chapter into two sections: (1) how to establish service connection and (2) how to get the most money. Compensation for survivors is discussed in Chapter 10. If your disability is already service connected and you want to pursue an increased rating, skip to the section in this chapter entitled ''How to Get the Most Money.'' If you are applying for the first time, read the entire chapter and prepare your case for both service connection and the highest possible payment.

The formal application for compensation for veterans is VA Form

---

★ **IMPORTANT** ★

Get help. No book can substitute for the experiences of a service representative who has daily, hands-on experience with the VA process and the VA decision-makers. Remember, unless your claim was denied by the Board of Veterans' Appeals (BVA) within the last 12 months, you cannot hire a private attorney. Although you may not be able to hire and directly pay an attorney, a third party could do both for you at any time. See Chapter 1 for details on locating a service representative or an attorney.

★ **EXTREMELY IMPORTANT** ★

It is essential that you make the strongest case the first time. You do not want to waste your time on a half-hearted effort. If you lose, you have to overcome difficult legal requirements just to reopen your claim, much less win it. Take the time to talk to a service representative. Ask the rep what kind of evidence is essential. Get that evidence. Get it right the first time.

21-526, Veteran's Application for Compensation or Pension. A copy of this form can be obtained by calling the nearest VA regional office. Before you sit down with your service representative to complete a full-size form, compile the dates of past medical treatment and the names of the facilities that provided the treatment.

SERVICE CONNECTION

A disability that is service connected is one that you have proven resulted from an injury or an illness you had in the military. Such a disability can also be a condition that you had before you went into the military and that worsened as a result of your service. Your injury does not have to have occurred on the base, at the fort, on a ship, or while in uniform; your injury does not have to have occurred in combat. VA law is not like workers' compensation programs, where you have to prove that your injury was related to specific work-related chores. If you are in the military, you are considered to be at work almost regardless of what you are doing. See Chapter 1 for an explanation of what constitutes service (regular, reserve, National Guard, etc.).

There are five general ways in which you can show that your condi-

> ─────── ★ IMPORTANT ★ ───────
> Don't procrastinate about working on your case. Establishing service connection for certain diseases, even if you cannot get much by way of a disability rating now, may be very important later in your life. But don't wait until later to work on your case.

tion is service connected: (1) directly, (2) by using a presumption, (3) by showing that a new condition is secondary to another that is already service connected, (4) by showing that a preservice condition was aggravated by your military service, or (5) by showing that you were injured in a VA hospital or while pursuing a VA vocational rehabilitation program.

Although there are five ways in which you can argue that your condition is service connected, usually only one of them applies to your specific situation. Unfortunately, the VA has numerous ways to deny your claim. For example, if you were injured in an auto accident while on active duty and convicted of drunk driving, the military may have found that your injuries were not in the line of duty. The VA can agree and deny service connection. The VA will not pay compensation if your disability is a result of your own willful misconduct. Since 1990, the VA will not pay compensation if your disability is a result—directly or indirectly—of alcohol or drug abuse. For example, if you became HIV positive in the service due to IV drug abuse, the VA will deny service connection. On the other hand, the VA will grant service connection for HIV-positive status arising from sexual behavior.

Whether you were injured or ill in the military can be documented in a number of ways and sometimes does not require an actual diagnosis of your condition in official military records. In fact, for many disabilities, the law orders the VA to presume that conditions were service connected even when there were no signs of the condition while you were in the service.

Begin with a Disability

Unless there is a name for what ails you, you will not get far in the VA compensation program. You can begin the process without knowing the exact medical term for your problem, but a doctor, psychologist, or psychiatrist must eventually put a specific name to your condition. Only with that can the VA rating board decide your claim. You and the VA must make an early decision as to which records are important to your case.

Depending on the diagnosis, records of medical treatment in the service may not be necessary at all. For other diagnoses, in-service records are essential.

After you have a diagnosis, VA law may dictate that the condition is service connected. Service connection for these conditions is presumed. After the following discussion on presumptions, we will address establishing service connection for injuries and many other illnesses that the VA will not presume are service connected.

Conditions Presumed to Be Service Connected

VA laws and regulations list many conditions that must be presumed to be service connected—if they appeared at the right time after you were discharged. A presumption is supposed to make your life easier; if a presumption applies, you do not have to work as hard to prove your case. Six different lists of diagnoses follow. For each of these conditions, a presumption of service connection may be available.

Be sure to review the first list, chronic diseases. The headings for the other five lists will indicate whether you need to bother reviewing them: tropical diseases, diseases specific to former POWs, radiation-related diseases, diseases related to service in Vietnam, and diseases related to mustard gas exposure.

In the following lists, circle the diagnosis (or diagnoses) that you have. The time noted in brackets after the diagnosis (e.g., [1 year]) indicates how quickly the disease must become "manifest" (apparent) following discharge. VA rules on calculating the date when a deadline begins to run, whether the disease is sufficiently manifest, whether you were exposed to radiation or Agent Orange, or at what point you are officially considered to be a POW are discussed later in the chapter.

★ NOTE ★

The use of a presumption does not appear to apply if your service was not officially active duty and you are trying to say (through use of a presumption) that because you were disabled your service should be considered active duty. Chapter 1 discusses the definitions of active duty, active duty for training, and inactive duty training. However, for radiation-related conditions, the presumption applies to you if you were in the reserves.

Chronic Diseases

Anemia, primary [1 year]
Arteriosclerosis [1 year]
Arthritis [1 year]
Atrophy, progressive muscular [1 year]
Brain hemorrhage [1 year]
Brain thrombosis [1 year]
Bronchiectasis [1 year]
Calculi of the kidney, bladder, or gallbladder [1 year]
Cardiovascular-renal disease, including hypertension [1 year]
Cirrhosis of the liver [1 year]
Coccidioidomycosis [1 year]
Diabetes mellitus [1 year]
Encephalitis lethargica residuals [1 year]
Endocarditis (this term covers all forms of valvular heart disease)
    [1 year]
Endocrinopathies [1 year]
Epilepsies [1 year]
Hansen's disease (leprosy) [3 years]
Hodgkin's disease [1 year]
Leukemia [1 year]
Myasthenia gravis [1 year]
Myelitis [1 year]
Myocarditis [1 year]
Nephritis [1 year]
Osteitis deformans (Paget's disease) [1 year]
Osteomalacia [1 year]
Other organic diseases of the nervous system [1 year]
Palsy, bulbar [1 year]
Paralysis agitans [1 year]
Psychoses [1 year]
Purpura idiopathic, hemorrhagic [1 year]
Raynaud's disease [1 year]
Sarcoidosis [1 year]
Scleroderma [1 year]
Sclerosis, amyotrophic lateral [1 year]
Sclerosis, multiple [7 years]
Syringomyelia [1 year]
Thromboangiitis obliterans (Buerger's disease) [1 year]

Tuberculosis, active [1 year]
Tumors, malignant, or of the brain or spinal cord or peripheral nerves
 [1 year]
Ulcers, peptic (gastric or duodenal) [1 year]

Tropical Diseases

Amebiasis [1 year]
Blackwater fever [1 year]
Cholera [1 year]
Dracontiasis [1 year]
Dysentery [1 year]
Filiariasis [1 year]
Leishmaniasis, including kala-azar [1 year]
Loiasis [1 year]
Malaria [1 year]
Onchocerciasis [1 year]
Oroya fever [1 year]
Pinta [1 year]
Plague [1 year]
Schistosomiasis [1 year]
Yaws [1 year]
Yellow fever [1 year]
Resultant disorders or diseases originating because of therapy admin-
    istered in connection with such diseases or as a preventative
    thereof [1 year]

Diseases Specific to Former POWs

Avitaminosis [no time limit]
Beriberi (including beriberi heart disease) [no time limit]
"Wet" beriberi (accompanied by coronary artery disease) [no time
    limit]
Chronic dysentery [no time limit]
Helminthiasis [no time limit]
Malnutrition (including optic atrophy associated with malnutrition)
    [no time limit]
Pellagra [no time limit]
Any other nutritional deficiency [no time limit]
Psychosis [no time limit]

Any of the anxiety states [no time limit]
Dysthymic disorder (or depressive neurosis) [no time limit]
Irritable bowel syndrome [no time limit]
Organic residuals of frostbite [no time limit]
Peptic ulcer disease [no time limit]
Peripheral neuropathy except where directly related to infectious
    causes [no time limit]
Post-traumatic osteoarthritis [no time limit]

Radiation-Related Diseases

LIST 1, RADIOGENIC DISEASES (PUBLIC LAW 98-542)

Bone cancer [within 30 years of exposure to radiation]
Breast cancer [5 years or more]
Colon cancer [5 years or more]
Esophageal cancer [5 years or more]
Kidney cancer [5 years or more]
Leukemia, all forms except chronic lymphatic (lymphocytic) leuke-
    mia [any time after exposure]
Liver cancer [5 years or more]
Lung cancer [5 years or more]
Multiple myeloma [5 years or more]
Nonmalignant thyroid nodular disease [5 years or more]
Pancreatic cancer [5 years or more]
Posterior subcapsular cataracts [6 months or more]
Salivary gland cancer [5 years or more]
Skin cancer [5 years or more]
Stomach cancer [5 years or more]
Thyroid cancer [5 years or more]
Urinary bladder cancer [5 years or more]

LIST 2, DISEASES SPECIFIC TO RADIATION-EXPOSED VETERANS (PUBLIC LAW 100-321 AND 1992 AMENDMENTS)

Cancer of the bile ducts
Cancer of the breast
Cancer of the esophagus
Cancer of the gallbladder
Cancer of the pancreas

Cancer of the pharynx
Cancer of the salivary gland
Cancer of the small intestine
Cancer of the stomach
Cancer of the thyroid
Cancer of the urinary tract
Leukemia (other than chronic lymphocytic leukemia)
Lymphomas (except Hodgkin's disease)
Multiple myeloma
Primary liver cancer (except if cirrhosis or hepatitis B is indicated)

Vietnam Service/Agent Orange Exposure

Chloracne [1 year]
Non-Hodgkin's lymphoma [at any time after service in Vietnam]
Peripheral neuropathy [pending at the time of writing this]
Soft-tissue sarcoma [at any time after service in Vietnam]
Hodgkin's disease
Porphyria cutanea tarda
Respiratory cancers (lung, larynx, and trachea)
Multiple myeloma

Diseases in Naval Personnel Exposed to Mustard Gas

Asthma
Bronchitis
Conjunctivitis
Corneal opacities
Emphysema
Keratitis
Laryngitis

Did the Disease Become Manifest in Time to Meet the Deadline?

For any of the previously listed conditions to be presumed service connected, it "must have become manifest to a degree of 10 percent or more" within the time period noted (the presumptive period). To become manifest does not mean that the condition was formally or officially diagnosed by medical personnel within the presumptive period. You do not have to produce medical records with diagnoses that are dated within the period.

Nevertheless, you will need to produce either medical evidence or lay evidence that you had the symptoms characteristic of the disease (to a degree of at least a 10 percent disability) during the presumptive period and had a formal diagnosis shortly afterward. For example, testimony from your mother that you were exhibiting unusual behavior soon after you were out of service may be good lay evidence of schizophrenia, a psychosis. A formal diagnosis 3 or 4 months later—even though beyond the 1-year deadline—should be sufficient.

If the doctor who makes the first formal diagnosis can state with confidence that the behavior described by the mother constituted the "classical symptoms of a psychotic disorder from a layperson's viewpoint," the VA should not take issue with the matter. If the report of the doctor who makes the first formal diagnosis does not include this kind of assessment of the lay testimony, ask a specialist to review the statements to see if you can get such a report now.

The same pattern of lay testimony within the presumptive period followed by formal diagnosis outside the presumptive period should suffice for physical conditions, too. The purpose of the presumption is to make establishing service connection easier.

The VA may try to argue that some other injury or disease that occurred after you were discharged is the real reason for your condition. Of course, if you have a tropical disease but never served outside Alaska, it may be reasonable for the VA to deny service connection.

Definition of a POW
For the VA rules on presumptions to apply, a POW must have been detained for at least 30 days. There are no exceptions, even for unusually severe treatment.

Exposure to Radiation
There are three partially overlapping lists of radiation-related diseases. If your diagnosis is on List 1 or List 2 and you can show that you were exposed to radiation, the VA should agree that your disease is service connected. There are two lists because Congress initially gave the VA permission to develop one list—List 1 (under Public Law 98-542)—and then a few years later (May 1, 1988), Congress imposed its own list, List 2 (under Public Law 100-321 and modified in 1992), when it became convinced that the VA was not allowing enough claims. The VA also developed rules for deciding whether a veteran was exposed to radiation and later contracted the diseases on List 1. Although the VA-developed

List 1 of diseases is longer and sounds better, its rules regarding exposure are extremely difficult to satisfy. You can use whichever list is better for you. The starting point for a deadline, for example, a deadline of 5 years, means the stopwatch began to run on the last day of your exposure to radiation.

LIST 1 (PUBLIC LAW 98-542)

The VA list (List 1) applies not only to participants at nuclear weapons test sites and servicemembers in the occupation forces at Hiroshima or Nagasaki, but also to others who may have been exposed to radiation during their handling of nuclear weapons or during work aboard nuclear-powered submarines. Before the VA will consider a claim for service connection for one of these diseases, you must prove that you were exposed to some unspecified amount of radiation. The VA asks the Defense Nuclear Agency (DNA) to provide an official assessment of the dosage of radiation to which you were exposed. The DNA routinely says that there was only minimal or no exposure. Unless you counter that assessment, you lose.

You can submit your own assessment of the level of exposure, but these private dose assessments are expensive. The private assessments must be performed by a certified professional health physicist or nuclear medicine or radiology professional. If the private assessment of exposure is at least double the official DNA assessment, you have not won your claim; you are allowed only another level of review. If the private assessment is not, you don't even get that chance.

The additional level of review is conducted by an independent expert selected by the National Institutes of Health and paid for by the VA. The expert must review both the official and the private assessments and prepare a third dose estimate, which is the level of radiation exposure on which the VA then relies.

If you succeed in proving that you were exposed to radiation, your claim is sent to the VA Central Office in Washington, DC, for special treatment. Central Office personnel then decide whether "sound scientific and medical evidence supports the conclusion it is at least as likely as not the veteran's disease resulted from exposure to radiation." Although not part of VA regulations, the VA appears to consider any exposure of less

---

★ NOTE ★

The VA General Counsel has ruled that the cancers on either List 1 or List 2 must be primary cancers, not cancers that started in another part of your body and then spread (or metastasized).

than 5 rem to be of no consequence. Exposure to more than 5 rem might result in service connection for the disease.

LIST 2 (PUBLIC LAW 100-321)

The list dictated by Congress in 1988 (List 2) is not as long as that developed by the VA. However, Congress eliminated the lengthy and expensive dose estimate process and said that for its list you do not have to prove a particular level of exposure to radiation. You do have to prove you were present at a test site during the operation, that you participated in support activities related to the test, that you were a member of the Hiroshima or Nagasaki occupation forces, or that you were interned as a POW in Japan.

If you were not at a test site during the operation, it is sufficient that you were there within 6 months afterwards to help in decontamination work or that you worked at the Naval Shipyards decontaminating ships from Operation Crossroads. Finally, if you were a member of the garrison or maintenance forces on Eniwetok while nuclear weapons were being handled, this is sufficient evidence.

The names and dates of the various nuclear test operations follow:

★ Operation TRINITY (July 16, 1945–Aug. 6, 1945)
★ Operation CROSSROADS (July 1, 1946–Aug. 31, 1946)
★ Operation SANDSTONE (Apr. 15, 1948–May 20, 1948)
★ Operation RANGER (Jan. 27, 1951–Feb. 6, 1951)
★ Operation GREENHOUSE (Apr. 8, 1951–June 20, 1951)
★ Operation BUSTER-JANGLE (Oct. 22, 1951–Dec. 20, 1951)
★ Operation TUMBLER-SNAPPER (Apr. 1, 1952–June 20, 1952)
★ Operation IVY (Nov. 1, 1952–Dec. 31, 1952)
★ Operation UPSHOT-KNOTHOLE (Mar. 17, 1953–June 20, 1953)
★ Operation CASTLE (Mar. 1, 1954–May 31, 1954)
★ Operation TEAPOT (Feb. 18, 1955–June 10, 1955)
★ Operation WIGWAM (May 14, 1955–May 15, 1955)
★ Operation REDWING (May 5, 1956–Aug. 6, 1956)
★ Operation PLUMBBOB (May 28, 1957–Oct. 22, 1957)
★ Operation HARDTACK I (Apr. 28, 1958–Oct. 31, 1958)
★ Operation ARGUS (Aug. 27, 1958–Sept. 10, 1958)
★ Operation HARDTACK II (Sept. 19, 1958–Oct. 31, 1958)
★ Operation DOMINIC I (Apr. 25, 1962–Dec. 31, 1962)
★ Operation DOMINIC II/PLOWSHARE (July 6, 1962–Aug. 15, 1962)

A special opportunity for atomic vets or survivors exists. A new law in 1990 may give you the chance to obtain as much as $75,000 in a lump sum. Under the Radiation Exposure Compensation Act, the U.S. Department of Justice, not the VA, handles payments to veterans (or their survivors) who "participated on-site in a test involving the atmospheric detonation of a nuclear device." Most of the cancers on List 2 may qualify you for the payment. The two cancers added in 1992 (urinary tract and salivary gland) are not currently accepted by the Justice Department program. For details on this program, see the rules at 28 C.F.R. (Code of Federal Regulations), Part 79 (available in any law library), or contact Assistant Director; Radiation Exposure Compensation Program; U.S. Department of Justice; P.O. Box 146; Washington, DC 20044-0146. Or you can call (800) 729-7327.

Service in Vietnam and Exposure to Agent Orange

After you show that you have one of the diseases noted in the Vietnam Service list, you must still show that you were in the Republic of Vietnam. Service in Vietnam also includes service in the waters offshore. If your duty required visits to Vietnam, but you were not stationed there, this is still sufficient. If you can show that you had service in the Republic of Vietnam, the VA then presumes that you were exposed to a herbicide containing dioxin, for example, Agent Orange. The starting point for the deadline, if any, means that the stopwatch began to run on the last day you were in Vietnam.

Exposure to Mustard Gas

Mustard gas was a poison used in World War I. During the Persian Gulf War, it was feared that Iraq would use mustard gas. This probably did not happen. Apparently it was used, however, in secret tests on naval

---

★ IMPORTANT ★

The $75,000 payment may be reduced by certain VA payments or payments from the Social Security Administration that you have already received based on the condition; also, by accepting the Justice Department payment, you will give up the right to certain future VA benefits and SSA benefits for yourself and possibly for your survivors. Take the time to carefully calculate exactly what you will gain or lose. It is advisable to complete the application and let the Justice Department officially tell you the amount it will pay, as well as the consequences of accepting its payment. Then you can make an informed choice to accept or reject the payment.

personnel at the Naval Research Laboratory in Washington, DC, between 1943 and 1945. It may also have been used in testing at other locations during World War II. The tests were intended to develop protective clothing and equipment.

Participants in these classified tests were sworn to secrecy and medical records associated with the tests are not generally available. It is not clear whether a list of participants is available. It is clear that through the end of 1991, such veterans were at a "disadvantage when attempting to establish entitlement to compensation." In 1992, the VA recognized this difficulty and issued a new regulation to make it easier to get compensation. If you think this rule (38 C.F.R. 3.316) applies to you, write the nearest VA regional office.

Conditions Directly Connected to Service

You should not have much difficulty in establishing service connection if your current disability was originally diagnosed in the service and required a period of hospitalization and then a period of light duty after that. If the original in-service diagnosis said the condition was "chronic," your case is even stronger, but not airtight. If you are trying to show that you are disabled because of an in-service illness or injury, you are trying to establish service connection directly. In these cases, obtaining your service records is very important. You are entitled to these records. See Chapter 25 for details on requesting your records.

Unfortunately, millions of veterans' service records were burned in a fire at the National Personnel Records Center in St. Louis in 1973. Some official records may be located through alternate sources, but this is a tedious process. You may already know, however, that there is no record of hospitalization for the injury you sustained when you fell off the back of the jeep (or humvee) while under fire.

Sometimes unofficial records (for example, newspaper articles, photographs, letters you wrote to your parents or girlfriend, or statements from veterans who served with you) may provide the corroborating evidence you need. If official records are missing, it is very important that you take advantage of any opportunity to present your sworn testimony at a hearing. See Chapter 3 for details on obtaining a hearing.

The VA must presume that you were in good health when you walked in the door and began your military service—unless "defects, infirmities, or disorders" were noted on your entrance examination. If the VA believes your condition "existed prior to service" (EPTS), it is unlikely to grant service connection directly. But see the discussion later in this chapter on EPTS conditions that were aggravated by your service. Before the VA denies service connection because it believes a condition EPTS, it must conduct a "thorough analysis" and "careful correlation of all material facts." Look for that analysis on a rating decision. If you do not find such an analysis, work with your doctor—especially the family doctor whom you had before service—to get an independent review of the facts.

Chronic Disease

Service medical records that contain a diagnosis of a condition and a description of that condition as "chronic" should convince the VA that the same condition you have today is service connected. But it might not. The VA may deny your claim by saying that an illness labeled "chronic" was really not chronic if there was only one bout of it. The VA will deny your claim by saying that the episode was "acute and transitory and had resolved satisfactorily with treatment."

As part of your claim, be sure to list every instance of follow-up treatment you had before you were discharged from service, the number of days you were taking medication, and so forth. The longer your list, the stronger your case, and the less likely the VA can fairly deny it. Do not leave it up to the VA to review each page of your service medical records to identify every sick call visit. Also, ask the doctor treating you now to prepare an opinion letter stating that the episode you had in service was the first of several episodes of what is clearly a chronic condition.

If your in-service health problems led to a diagnosis of one of the chronic diseases listed previously, you should not have any trouble with the VA. A "chronic" condition is not limited to one of those on the VA's list of chronic diseases.

Not Chronic in Service, But Constant Problem Ever Since

You will have a harder time if you went to sick call several times but no one ever officially recognized your complaints as a specific disease. You will also have a harder time if you went to sick call several times and complained about hurting your back but your discharge physical exam showed no complaints about your back.

You can try to establish service connection for such complaints that eventually (after discharge and after any presumptive period) were diagnosed as a disease. To be successful, you will need to show that you continued to have the problem. It is not necessary to produce civilian doctor's bills for every month or two after discharge. Maybe you saw doctors shortly after discharge. Maybe you didn't, or you didn't think that 10 years later you would need the canceled check to prove it.

If you did not seek professional medical care or can't produce the bills or the doctor's records, but your family can testify to your constant self-medication or complaints, present your testimony at a hearing and ask your family to provide sworn testimony, too.

You can anticipate that the VA regional office will deny your claim by saying that your condition was diagnosed at a time "too far removed from your military service to be considered service connected." Because such a response is likely, ask the doctor who finally diagnosed your condition to review your military sick call records and give you an expert medical opinion that the complaints you had then were consistent with your disease and indicated that your condition was incurred in service.

Not Chronic, Not Constant, Just Appeared

Some conditions don't appear for many years. You may never have thought you'd have a problem 10, 20, or more years after discharge. These can be mental or physical conditions. Consider two examples: post-traumatic stress disorder (PTSD) and asbestosis. Despite a long dormant period, each can be directly service connected.

POST-TRAUMATIC STRESS DISORDER

PTSD is often associated with combat experiences in Vietnam. Between 600,000 and 800,000 Vietnam veterans are thought to have some symptoms of PTSD. The VA is paying compensation to about 10 percent of them. PTSD is a condition that also appears in civilians (for instance, concentration camp survivors) and veterans with no combat experience or combat in World War II, Korea, Grenada, or other theaters. It also appears in rape survivors.

According to the American Psychiatric Association's *Diagnostic and Statistical Manual of Mental Disorders,* the common feature among persons diagnosed with PTSD is that they experienced an "event that is outside the range of usual human experience and that would be markedly distressing to almost anyone." The VA refers to this event as a "stressor."

The VA accepts that combat is such an experience. If your service records reflect that you were awarded a Combat Infantry Badge or you received an award for valor or a Purple Heart, you should not have to convince the VA that you experienced a stressor. If your records instead indicate that your occupational specialty meant (in the VA's opinion) that it was unlikely that you saw combat, it becomes more difficult to prove that you experienced a stressor. The more difficult it is to prove, the more stridently the VA demands that you prove it. Even though you may have described the stressful event in enough detail to satisfy 5 psychiatrists that you have PTSD, the VA demands official documentation.

Official documentation of the nature of your combat experience may or may not be available. The Vietnam War generated, among other things, an enormous number of records describing various units' activities. If you describe a specific incident in which you were one of the few survivors of an operation, records of the deaths of your buddies will be available. See Chapter 11 for information on how to tap into the records of the Vietnam War collection and records of other wars.

If you survived the sinking of your ship in World War II, historical records of the event are available through the National Archives in Washington, DC. See Chapter 11 for how to gain access to these records. The VA should write to you after you file a claim for PTSD and ask for detailed information about the stressful event. The VA should then write to various sources of government records for documentation of your experience. You can wait for the VA to do this work and review whatever the VA finds when it gets filed in your claims folder, or you can contact the same sources.

In the absence of official documentation that will corroborate your description of the event, you must get statements from other members of the unit that will substantiate the experience. If you engaged in combat with the enemy during a period of war, VA law (38 C.F.R. 3.102) directs the VA to accept "satisfactory lay or other evidence" that is consistent with the circumstances, conditions, or hardships of such service and to "resolve every reasonable doubt" in your favor. Don't expect this to happen.

For stressful events not associated with combat, the VA is extremely insistent that you provide documentation. PTSD can develop as a result of a threat of harm to you or your family, or as the result of the destruction of your home, or from seeing another person who was seriously injured in an accident.

Documentation of a fire that burned down your house or of an auto accident may be obtainable. But if you were raped and did not report the rape to the authorities, or out of fear or embarrassment you did not seek immediate medical treatment, there may be no official documentation. These are very difficult cases. It is important to present believable testimony at a hearing in these cases. If you confided in a friend shortly after the attack, try to have that friend testify, too. If you have been undergoing psychotherapy, ask your therapist to testify why your description of the event is believable and not a fabrication. VA hearing officials, most of whom are men, have received no special sensitivity training about rape cases.

Documenting the stressful event is only one portion of PTSD claims; you still have to obtain a formal diagnosis of the condition. The *Diagnostic and Statistical Manual of Mental Disorders* (DSM) published by the American Psychiatric Association lists specific diagnostic criteria that the psychiatrist or psychologist must find in order to make the diagnosis.

Even if a mental health professional concludes that you have PTSD, his or her examination must itemize the particular criteria or enough of them to match what is in the DSM for the nonmedical VA rating boards or Board of Veterans' Appeals to find the diagnosis adequately supported; otherwise, the BVA will rule that it is not service connected.

For example, if you report nightmares about the stressful event, but the psychiatrist simply reports "nightmares," you may lose. This is one reason that you and your service representative or your private psychiatrist needs to obtain and review the VA's official examination. Make sure it accurately reflects what you said. If it does not, ask for another exam.

ASBESTOSIS

Exposure to asbestos can lead to asbestosis, mesothelioma, lung cancer, cancers of the gastrointestinal tract, and cancers of the larynx and pharynx as well as the genitourinary tract. The damage is not obvious very quickly. The VA officially recognizes that it may take 10 to 45 years after

---

★ IMPORTANT ★

PTSD is a condition that may be very difficult for a VA psychiatrist who has never seen you before to diagnose in one 15-minute interview. Given the often difficult-to-talk-about nature of the stressors, you may not feel comfortable quickly enough to give the VA examiner the information necessary to make a diagnosis.

If you have a civilian psychiatrist whom you have been seeing or some other mental health professional who knows the details of your experience and current condition, ask that person to prepare a thorough evaluation report on your condition. The VA should give greater weight to the report of a doctor treating you than to a report by a doctor who examines you once for a few minutes.

exposure before a disease develops. The VA also recognizes that exposure for as little as a month or two may result in the development of diseases.

If you allege exposure to asbestos while in the service, the VA should try to confirm exactly what your duties were at the particular location. The VA has a notion that there were certain "traditional occupations" that meant it was more likely that you might have been exposed (for example, in the navy, working on boilers or pipes, or working as a machinist).

The VA will also ask about exposure prior to service and after service in order to say that it was exposure during these other, nonservice periods that led to your problems. You should anticipate the VA's efforts to find information to deny your claim. To counter such efforts, ask your doctor to explain whether it is medically or scientifically feasible to say that one period of exposure was more likely to have caused your problem than another. If it is not reasonable to isolate your in-service exposure from your pre- or postservice exposure, you should win.

A Condition Secondary to a Service-Connected Condition

Consider the following discussion as one of the five ways to establish service connection but also as a method of getting the most money. If you already have one service-connected disease or injury, it may affect other parts of your body. If it does, the affected part is also considered service connected.

For example, an injury to your right leg may have resulted in its being shorter than your left leg. You may not walk with an even gait, and you may not be able to stand straight anymore. This may lead to problems with your lower back. The back condition is the result of your service-connected leg disability, and you now have another condition for which you may receive compensation.

If you are service connected because of an amputation of one leg at or above the knee or amputation of both feet at or above the ankle, the VA must agree that any ischemic heart disease or other cardiovascular disease is service-connected (38 C.F.R. 3.310).

A Preservice Condition Aggravated by Service

You may have been accepted for service despite reporting one or more medical conditions on your entrance examination. If you were discharged in the same shape as when you went in, you'll get nothing from the VA. However, if your condition worsened while you were in service, you may be compensated. The VA may agree that your condition should be service connected because your military service aggravated the preexisting condition.

Even if your condition clearly worsened during service, the VA may still deny your claim if the worsening was "due to the natural progress of the condition." Anticipate this response and ask your doctor to prepare a detailed report about your condition as it existed prior to service, how he or she thinks your condition would normally have progressed, and why, in his or her expert opinion, your military duties made the condition worse than it otherwise might have been.

The VA will not agree that certain conditions could have been aggravated by service (for example, personality disorders, mental deficiency, congenital or developmental defects, and refractive error of the eye). Before giving up on a claim for one of these disabilities, get an independent evaluation to confirm the diagnosis, especially if a personality disorder is involved.

There are also some loopholes regarding congenital or developmental defects. A congenital defect is not the same as a congenital disease. A defect is a structural abnormality. Just because a disease is of congenital, developmental, or familial (i.e., inherited) origin does not mean that you cannot get service-connected compensation for it. If the condition first became manifest or was diagnosed while you were in the service or was aggravated in the service, it can be considered service-connected. Retinitis pigmentosa and polycystic renal disease are two such conditions. Pes cavus, sickle-cell anemia, and Huntington's chorea are other examples.

Injuries or Death During VA Hospitalization

One additional way to show that a condition is service connected is to show that the person suffered an injury or aggravation of an injury (or died), as a result of VA hospitalization, medical, or surgical treatment. An injury (or death) sustained during an examination or while pursuing vocational rehabilitation is also considered service connected. If that injury resulted in additional disability, the VA should find that the additional disability is service connected. These claims are informal medical malpractice claims.

The VA does not have a specific application form to use in this situation. Before 1991, these cases were referred to as Section 351 cases, the section number of the VA law. VA laws were renumbered in 1991, and now these cases are referred to as Section 1151 cases. Make a claim by stating in a letter, "I claim Section 1151 benefits for disability suffered while hospitalized on [XYZ date] at [name of hospital]." Send your letter to the nearest VA regional office.

If the VA agrees that its staff made a mistake and it grants service connection for the additional disability, the amount of money it will pay is calculated the same as for any other disability. See the discussion later in this chapter on percentage of impairment.

Prior to 1991, the VA misapplied the law governing these claims. The VA incorrectly required you to prove that your injury was a result of the negligence or fault of VA personnel. Proving this was difficult to do. In November 1991, the U.S. Court of Veterans Appeals found the VA rules to be faulty (*Gardner v. Derwinski* [No. 90-120]).

The VA immediately announced a freeze on denying the cases while it decides what to do. The VA then appealed to the next higher court but lost again in September 1993. It should now issue new rules to handle these claims. It may also ask Congress to change the law to avoid paying claims.

★ SPECIAL OPPORTUNITY ★

If you were denied service connection in the past under the old Section 351, write to the VA and say, "I claim Sec. 1151 benefits on the basis of clear and unmistakable error of law."

HOW TO GET THE MOST MONEY

One of the great mysteries of the VA disability system is exactly how the VA decides that a particular diagnosis warrants a particular percentage of disability. You know that you had to fill out an application form and be examined by a VA doctor. Months later you got a letter awarding you a 10 percent rating and you began to get a check in the mail each month. Maybe later you wondered why your rating was 10 percent and not 20 percent or 30 percent. Maybe you wondered why your friend, with the same complaint, got a 50 percent rating. Maybe you decided to leave well enough alone. Think again.

After reading the following you might conclude the VA was right to

---

★ IMPORTANT ★

If you are injured in a VA hospital, you may recover more money through another process, called the Federal Tort Claims Act (FTCA). If you wait for the VA informal claim to be decided before exploring this option, it may be too late. As soon as you suspect you are worse after being in a VA hospital, contact an attorney who specializes in medical malpractice.

The deadline to file a Standard Form 95, Claim for Damage, Injury or Death (included in Appendix A), with the nearest VA regional office is 2 years after the injury arose. Exactly when the injury arose can be a complicated matter; it may be when the surgery was performed (for example, when you discovered that a clamp had been left inside your body). If you receive money from the FTCA claim, and the VA agrees to pay you under Sec. 1151, the VA will suspend (or offset) its payments until it recovers most of what you obtained under the FTCA.

---

set your condition at a 10 percent rating. On the other hand, you might decide that the VA was wrong. Using the VA's rules yourself will give you a chance to get an independent evaluation of your condition by a doctor of your choosing or by the doctor who has been treating you for several years.

★ CAUTION ★

Some doctors who have been treating you and who are wonderful providers of care may not want to help you apply for VA benefits. For example, if your disability is a mental disorder, the doctor may want you to focus only on getting better and not focus on how to prove to the VA that you have a serious condition.

The doctor may know how difficult the VA disability process is and know that you may become irritated by all the red tape. The doctor may therefore want to discourage you from pursuing the claims process because it might intensify your symptoms. You may need to explain your personal finances to your doctor and explain that until you can get a reasonable payment from the VA you will have to spend so much time and energy on day-to-day survival that you will be unable to focus as much on your treatment program as you would like to.

Definition of a Disability Rating

A disability rating is the percentage of disability that the VA officially says represents as far as can practicably be determined the average impairment in earning capacity resulting from diseases and injuries and their residual conditions in civilian occupations.

Amount of Money for the Percentage Rating

Congress sets the amount of money that you are to be paid for a particular disability rating. The amount generally increases each December by the same amount that the cost of living allowance increases. For example, in 1992 the increase was 3 percent. The benefit rates for compensation in 1994 follow:

%	Monthly Amt.	Annual Amt.
10	$ 83	$ 996
20	157	1,884
30	240	2,880
40	342	4,104
50	487	5,844
60	614	7,368
70	776	9,312
80	897	10,764
90	1,010	12,120
100	1,680	20,160

As discussed in Chapter 2, larger payments are made for certain disabilities that may require someone to care for you or for combination of disabilities.

How a Rating Is Assigned

A rating specialist looks at what the Compensation and Pension examiner (the C&P doctor) wrote and tries to fit those words into a detailed chart. That chart lists the medical diagnosis, symptoms ranging from mild to incapacitating, and corresponding percentages of disability. If the doctor provided enough clues and the rating specialist read the clues properly, the rating on the award letter may be right.

The chart that the VA uses, and that we strongly believe you should review, is called the 1945 VA Schedule for Rating Disabilities. It is part of the VA's rules (38 C.F.R. Part 4). Because most of this schedule is almost 50 years out of date, its use presents some problems for the VA and for you.

The VA was embarrassed recently by a highly critical evaluation of the schedule and has begun to propose changes to it. During the next 2 to 3 years, the entire schedule will be revised. Chapter 11 describes how to obtain the latest version. Although the VA will not volunteer the fact, you are entitled to examine the schedule at the nearest VA regional office. Service representatives will also have copies of the schedule.

The VA schedule is a series of 14 charts. There is one chart for each body system. For example, one chart deals with each of the following:

1. musculoskeletal system
2. organs of special sense (eyes, ears)
3. system conditions (e.g., TB, malaria, AIDS)
4. respiratory system
5. cardiovascular system
6. digestive system
7. genitourinary system
8. gynecological conditions
9. hemic and lymphatic systems
10. skin
11. endocrine system
12. neurological conditions and convulsive disorders
13. mental disorders
14. dental and oral conditions

Your disability is assigned a Diagnostic Code. For example, if you have severe back pain that shoots into your legs because of a disc problem, the relevant Diagnostic Code is DC 5293. After you have a Diagnostic Code, look it up on the chart to find out the appropriate percentage of disability. The VA schedule for this condition in effect in 1993 read as follows:

5293 Intervertebral disc syndrome:
    Pronounced; with persistent symptoms compatible with sciatic neuropathy with characteristic pain and demonstrable muscle spasm, absent ankle jerk, or other neurological findings appropriate to site of diseased disc, little intermittent relief . . . 60

Severe; recurring attacks with intermittent relief . . . 40
Moderate; recurring attacks . . . 20
Mild . . . 10
Postoperative, cured . . . 0

As you can see from the above example, the VA schedule consists of three parts: (1) the diagnostic code (5293) and its corresponding description (intervertebral disc syndrome), (2) various symptoms, and (3) a percentage. It looks simple. But the reality is much different.

Problems with the Schedule

Although the schedule looks simple, it is not easy to use for several reasons. The most significant one is that given the age of the schedule, there are numerous conditions that exist today that did not in 1945 and are not on the schedule. You may well not find your diagnosis on the schedule. In the absence of a specific diagnostic code directly corresponding to your condition, the VA rating specialist may have to guess at what other diagnosis on the schedule is most similar to yours. If the VA guessed wrong, the maximum percentage of rating might be lower with the wrong code than with a more accurate diagnostic code.

Another significant problem is that many doctors don't use the (outdated) terminology found in the VA schedule. Also, using the example of DC 5293, intervertebral disc syndrome, one doctor might describe the back pain as "moderately severe." Based on that report, a sympathetic VA rating board may set your rating at 40 percent (the rating corresponding to severe); a less kind rating board may set your rating at 20 percent (the rating corresponding to moderate). In 1994, the difference between these two ratings amounted to $2,340 each year.

The VA is beginning to move slowly to address the rating system problems. It appears to be planning to require more specific and exacting laboratory tests to produce more detailed findings, which it will then fix to a particular rating. Although at this writing only one system of the schedule appeared to be in nearly final form, the change in it (the genitourinary tract) also points to a VA plan to reduce the rating that will be assigned for the same diagnosis.

This reduction may reflect the shorter periods of recovery needed following surgical procedures or other advances in medicine that may lead to fewer long-term problems. If so, a lower rating may accurately reflect a lesser impairment on your earning capacity. As a concession to veterans who are currently rated under the 1945 schedule, Congress enacted a law in late 1991 that said that the new changes should not be used to lower existing ratings.

Using the Rating Schedule

There are three critical ways in which you should use the schedule: (1) if you do not have a rating, examine the criteria corresponding to your diagnosis and work with your doctor to determine which criteria you meet; (2) if you have a rating, confirm that it was correctly determined; and (3) if you want an increased rating, examine the criteria for a higher rating and work with your doctor to see if you meet those criteria.

Working with Your Private Doctor to Prepare a Report for the First-Time Rating

First, if you are applying for compensation for the first time and you know your diagnosis, scan the alphabetical listing of diagnoses found in 38 C.F.R. Part 4. You may have to guess at what other diagnosis on the schedule is most similar to yours. Find the diagnostic code on the schedule. Take a copy of the symptoms to your doctor and ask him or her to prepare an expert opinion letter that reviews your condition and, if the doctor can do so fairly, uses the terminology in the schedule.

If you already had your C&P exam, review it to see if it uses the criteria that you think fit your situation. If not, and you think other criteria that correspond to a higher rating are more accurate, ask your private doctor to review the C&P exam and the schedule and describe why, based

---

★ CAUTION ★

As you review the criteria in the rating schedule, keep in mind that if a list of symptoms or criteria correspond to a particular rating, the VA does *not* expect you to have each of the symptoms. For example, under DC 5293, intervertebral disc syndrome, the symptoms corresponding to a 60 percent rating include (1) pronounced [pain], (2) with persistent symptoms compatible with sciatic neuropathy with characteristic pain, (3) demonstrable muscle spasm, (4) absent ankle jerk, (5) other neurological findings appropriate to site of diseased disc, and (6) little intermittent relief. You *do need* "findings sufficiently characteristic to identify the disease and the disability."

---

on his or her long-term familiarity with your condition, the higher rating is more accurate.

Confirming That the Current Rating Is Correct

If you have a rating, confirm that it was determined correctly. Find the diagnostic code that was used on your rating decision. Find that code on the schedule, and then identify the criteria corresponding to the rating assigned to you. Do these criteria match the language used by the C&P examiner or the other medical reports? If the C&P examiner reported that you had "severe pain with intermittent relief" as part of your intervertebral disc syndrome, a 20 percent rating is wrong. The language "severe pain with intermittent relief" corresponds to the 40 percent rating. If the VA rating decision was wrong, tell the regional office that it made a "clear and unmistakable error."

Working with Your Private Doctor to Support an Increased Rating

If you want an increased rating, examine the criteria for the higher rating and work with your doctor to see if you meet that criteria. Use the same strategy discussed above to work with your doctor to prepare a strong opinion letter. If there have been changes in your symptoms over the years, if may be time for the VA to assign a new diagnostic code. A new code could raise the ceiling on the rating you could get.

For example, if your lower back pain is now shooting down to your right foot, DC 5295—lumbosacral strain—and its criteria may no longer accurately reflect your condition. Nothing in DC 5295 covers pain that shoots (or radiates, i.e., sciatic pain) down your foot. DC 5293 covers shooting pain and raises the ceiling from the 40 percent in DC 5295 to 60 percent in DC 5293.

Miscellaneous Rules About the Schedule

The VA does not assign a 43 percent rating or a 55 percent rating. Ratings such as those are rounded off to the nearest 10 (43 is rounded to 40, 55 is rounded to 60). In the VA system, 10 + 10 does not really "equal" 20; they "equal" 19, but 19 is rounded to 20. Twenty plus thirty, on the other hand, "equals" 44, which is rounded to 40. Multiple ratings are not added. They are combined by using a "combined rating table" found in VA regulations at 38 C.F.R. 4.25.

★ CAUTION ★

Having told you to work with your private doctor to get a report about your condition, we should warn you that the VA rating boards are not bound to follow those private reports. Obtaining a private doctor's report that parrots the "magic" language from the schedule is not the last word. A one-line report that says, "In my opinion, Mr. So and So is severely disabled" is of little value.

Even less helpful is a report that simply says: "Mr. So and So is 60 percent disabled." A private opinion letter should begin by explaining how long the doctor has worked with you and should follow the protocol used by the C&P examiners for examining veterans. This protocol is contained in the 1985 *VA Physician's Guide to Disability Evaluation Examinations* and can be reviewed at any VA regional office or VA medical center. This guide is being replaced by a series of computerized forms but those, too, are available.

The VA has traditionally favored its own C&P examiners and ignored everyone else. The U.S. Court of Veterans Appeals has directed the VA to give careful attention to private doctors' reports. A carefully written report by your doctor may also persuade the C&P examiner that your condition is as serious as you say it is.

What if you have so many aches and pains and problems with your left foot that you sometimes think that you might as well chop it off? Under the schedule, you may in fact have multiple problems that, when combined, warrant a high rating. However, under what the VA calls its "amputation" rule, the VA will not pay you more than it would if your foot were amputated.

What if you have a rating for your left hand and your right elbow? The VA will pay extra when both upper extremities or both lower extremities are involved. The so-called "bilateral factor" means that after combining the rates, the VA adds 10 percent of that. This is a "real" 10 percent added the way you learned arithmetic, not combined using the VA table.

Finally, the VA will not give you a special break and assign a higher rating on a compensation claim because of age.

What to Do If Your Disability Means You Really Cannot Work

If you cannot work because of your disability, the official VA policy in its rule book (38 C.F.R. 4.16) is that you should be rated totally (100 percent) disabled. Sounds fair. And, prior to 1980, the official policy appeared to result in many veterans being assigned a 100 percent rating based on "individual unemployability." In 1980, however, the VA began a series of "special" reviews of veterans who were rated at 100 percent and decided that it had committed "clear and unmistakable error" in awarding the total rating. The VA also announced that prior to granting new awards based on unemployability, the claims file had to be sent to the VA Central Office in Washington. Not coincidentally, the Social Security Administration also began a series of massive rereviews of its beneficiaries.

As a result of the VA's special attention, ratings for several thousand veterans were drastically reduced. Many vets are still fighting to restore their ratings. Recent decisions by the U.S. Court of Veterans Appeals offer some encouragement. The more long-lasting effect of the special reviews was the "unofficial" message sent to the regional offices: Stop granting awards based on unemployability. The message was received, and the number of total ratings granted since 1980 has dropped to only a few dozen each year.

Nevertheless, the official policy remains the same: The VA will grant a total rating if the veteran is unable to secure or to follow a substantially gainful occupation as a result of service-connected disabilities. As noted in the next section of this chapter, exactly what the official policy means is not clear. However, the U.S. Court of Veterans Appeals has issued a series of decisions that should make the VA follow its official policy.

It is up to you to present your case and get over the artificial hurdles that the VA uses to try to avoid awarding benefits. The value of this benefit to you is quite large: If you are currently drawing compensation for a disability rating of 60 percent, the monthly payment almost triples with the unemployability factor and you get a 100 percent rating. Even if you are just applying for the first time for service connection for a disability, but you cannot work because of your condition, argue that you are entitled to a 100 percent rating. Consider repeating some of the following explanation about unemployability in your letter to the VA regional office or Board of Veterans' Appeals (BVA).

First Hurdle: What Is Unemployability?

In the past, when veterans have appealed the reduction of an unemployability rating or appealed the denial of the rating, the Board of Veterans' Appeals has often said "Being unemployed is not the same as being unemployable." Neither the regional office nor the BVA says much more. They may recite that they have "carefully" considered your education and training. They conclude, however, that you have not proven that you cannot work.

The VA does not routinely conduct an evaluation of the skills you have and whether there are jobs that you qualify for or whether those jobs are available. You should get such an evaluation.

Private vocational rehabilitation experts regularly prepare reports to support social security disability claimants. Have one done for yourself. You can probably locate such experts through the nearest hospital's physical therapy unit or by contacting an attorney who handles social security or workers' compensation claims.

Unfortunately, there is no single, comprehensive VA rule on what "unemployability" is.

In March and April 1991, the U.S. Court of Veterans Appeals complained about the failure of the BVA to apply or explain the various rules involving unemployability (*Hatlestad v. Derwinski*, No. 90-103 [March 1991] and *Hyder v. Derwinski*, No. 90-254 [April 1991]). The court did not attempt to reconcile the differences itself. In July 1991, however, the court pushed the VA further and said that it should consider adopting a rule similar to that adopted in 1975 in another court that considered a social security disability claim (*Moore v. Derwinski*, No. 90-133).

According to the 1975 case, "It is clear that the claimant need not be a total 'basket case' before the courts find that there is an inability to engage in substantial gainful activity. The question must be looked at in a practical manner, and mere theoretical ability to engage in substantial gainful employment is not a sufficient basis to deny benefits. The test is whether a particular job is *realistically* within the physical and mental capabilities of the claimant."

Perhaps the VA will take the hint eventually. But you should now. Focus your explanation of why you cannot do the kind of work you have done in the past and how your disability prevents you from doing that work successfully now.

Second Hurdle: Forcing the VA to Accept Your Claim

Regional offices used to try to read your letters and look for a reference to the fact that your disability prevented you from working. If they saw such a statement, they would "infer" that you were claiming an increased rating based on unemployability, and process your claim accordingly. In the mid-1980s, the VA Central Office decided not to continue this practice and instead to require you to submit a specific application form, VA Form 21-8940, Veteran's Application for Increased Compensation Based on Unemployability. A copy of this form is included in Appendix A at the end of the book.

The VA Central Office managers also decided that if you had a mental disability, you could not use the form. Your claim would be evaluated using the normal criteria in the schedule for mental disorders. Until recently, that has meant few veterans with mental disorders received a 100 percent rating.

Whether you have a physical or a mental disability, if you cannot work because of your disability, write to the VA and say, "I want my rating increased to 100 percent because I am unemployable due to my service-connected disability."

Third Hurdle: Forcing the VA to Read Its Own Rules

Anticipate that a regional office's rating specialist must first look at the ratings you currently have when he or she reviews a request for an increase based on unemployability. The VA employee has memorized certain percentages that he or she has been told you must have before he or she will seriously consider your application. The percentages that the rating specialist has memorized come from the first part of a three-part VA rule: 38 C.F.R. 4.16(a).

Under the first part of this rule, to obtain a total (100 percent) rating for unemployability, you must already have one disability that is rated at least at 60 percent. If you have two or more disabilities, one has to be at least a 40 percent rating and your combined rating has to be at least 70 percent. This is only the first part of the rule. If you do not already have those ratings, you must make sure that the VA applies the next part of the rule.

Under the second part of the rule—38 C.F.R. 4.16(b)—even without the specific percentages itemized in the first part of the rule, "It is the established policy of the VA that all veterans who are unable to secure and follow a substantially gainful occupation by reason of service-connected disabilities shall be rated totally disabled."

In January 1992, the U.S. Court of Veterans Appeals ordered the VA to reconsider a veteran's claim that her disability rated at 20 percent warranted a total rating due to unemployability (*Mingo v. Derwinski*, No. 90-992). It is very clear that the VA can no longer simply ignore your claim just because you don't already have a certain rating or combined rating.

Under the third part of the rule—38 C.F.R. 4.16[c]—if you have a mental disorder rated at 70 percent and you cannot work, you should "almost" automatically qualify for a 100 percent rating. If your mental disorder rating is not 70 percent, but you cannot work because of the disability, argue that the second part of the rule—38 C.F.R. 4.16[b]—requires the VA to set your rating at 100 percent.

Part of the difficulty in getting the VA to read its own regulations is that there is no single, comprehensive definition of what the VA means when it says "unable to secure and follow a substantially gainful occupation by reason of disabilities." Several VA rules, besides the ones just discussed, apply to these decisions.

Fourth Hurdle: Some Work Does Not Preclude a Total Rating

You can anticipate that the VA may deny your claim if you have not had a steady job for the past several years but you have done some volunteer work or you have worked a few hours a week and earned some money. The VA will say that such work proves that you are employable. The VA is incorrect.

If in a year's time (or on the average during the past few years) you make less than the amount set as the poverty threshold, your employment is "marginal." Marginal employment is not "substantially gainful employment" and should not be used to deny a total disability rating. In 1993, the poverty threshold for an individual was $7,143.

Fifth Hurdle: What Is Unemployability Due to Your Service-Connected Disability If You Also Have Other, Nonservice-Connected Disabilities?

You should anticipate that the VA will deny your claim if you have one nonservice-connected disability—even if you have a combined rating of 90 percent for service-connected disabilities and because of those service-connected disabilities you have not been able to work for the past 10 years. The VA practice is to decide that if you have even one nonservice-connected disability, you must not be unemployable solely because of your service-connected disability. If the VA sees a nonservice-connected condition it simply stops further consideration and denies the claim.

Counter the VA's practice with an opinion letter from your treating doctor. The letter should say that he or she has reviewed your overall condition and each of your disabilities—both those said to be service connected and those said to be nonservice connected—and in his or her opinion the service-connected disabilities prevent you from obtaining employment or keeping gainful employment.

Because several disabilities seldom appear at once, review the dates that the VA said you were service connected for one condition and non-service connected for another. If you had to stop working before the nonservice-connected condition appeared, use that fact to counter the VA's argument.

Sixth Hurdle: Getting the VA to Take into Account an SSA Disability Finding

Unlike what you must do in the VA disability system, which assigns ratings between 10 percent and 100 percent, to obtain disability benefits from the Social Security Administration, you must prove that you are totally disabled (i.e., you cannot engage in substantial gainful activity). Otherwise you get nothing.

If you have convinced the SSA that you are totally disabled, it makes sense that the VA would read the SSA's decision to see if it should make the same determination. Until recently, however, the VA routinely and completely ignored SSA decisions.

In August 1991, the U.S. Court of Veterans Appeals ruled that the VA must consider the SSA's decision (*Collier v. Derwinski*, No. 90-839). The court has not ordered the VA to always accept the SSA's determination, but it is clear that the VA must obtain the records relied on by SSA to make its decision and the VA must fairly consider those records.

One Way to Lose Your Rating

If the VA schedules you for a reexamination, go. If it schedules you for two examinations in the same month, go. If it schedules you for three examinations in the same month, go, but complain about it. One of the easiest ways for you to lose the disability rating you have is to ignore a VA letter scheduling you for a reexamination. You can be as suspicious as you want to be about the VA's motivation for scheduling the exam, but keep the appointment anyway. If you fail to show up and do not give the VA a good explanation as to why you missed the appointment, you will lose your money.

If you can't go and you know in advance that you can't, call and write the VA Medical Center that sent you the scheduling notice and explain this. Be sure to say that you are willing to appear for the exam, but that you can't keep the appointment for whatever good reason you have. Good reasons to miss an appointment include being sick or having to take care of someone in your family who is sick.

VA rules state that after the VA conducts its initial examination, it should not recall you within the first 2 years. It also should not wait more than 5 years if a reexamination is thought to be necessary. In some circumstances "no periodic reexamination will be scheduled." Nevertheless, whether the VA "should" or "should not" schedule an exam is not a good reason for not going (38 C.F.R. 3.327). The VA should not use one isolated examination as the reason to cut your disability rating, especially if you have a 100 percent rating (38 C.F.R. 3.343). If this happens, be sure to appeal the decision.

Other Benefits or Breaks Related to Service-Connected Disability

Depending on the severity of your disabilities or given a particular combination of disabilities, you may qualify for certain cash allowances in addition to monthly compensation payments. These benefits include cash to purchase a car or a van with special adaptive equipment; cash to modify your house to make it wheelchair accessible, including installing an invalid lift; and an annual clothing allowance if you wear a prosthetic appliance that causes extra wear and tear on your clothes. If you are blind, the VA may pay for a guide dog. Mechanical or electronic devices to help you overcome the handicap of blindness or deafness may be available, too.

The VA may also purchase artificial limbs, braces, orthopedic shoes, wheelchairs, medical accessories, or similar appliances. If one of these items is damaged or destroyed by a fall or other accident caused by a service-connected disability, the VA might repair it. You can expect to wait awhile to get repairs completed.

CHAPTER FIVE

★

PENSION

This chapter tells you about the VA's current pension plan. This plan may provide modest monthly cash payments to you to keep you above the official poverty line. The three requirements to receive a VA pension include (1) service during wartime, (2) health problems that might not be related to military service but are serious enough to render you totally disabled, *and* (3) little or no income from any other source. These payments are also available to survivors of wartime veterans. Survivors' benefits are discussed in Chapter 10.

The VA's current pension plan, the "Improved Pension," paid benefits to 492,884 veterans in 1992. Of the veterans receiving pension payments, 69 percent were older than age 65. Veterans between ages 55 and 64 accounted for 25 percent of those receiving pension payments. Only a few veterans who are younger than age 55 (6 percent) receive pension benefits. Although the maximum payment possible was much higher, the average payment in 1990 amounted to $4,500.

Before the Improved Pension began in 1979, the VA offered a program that is now referred to as the "Section 306 pension." About 18 percent of veterans drawing VA pensions are getting the Section 306 benefits. Still, because only 7 percent of the VA pension payments go to veterans under the earlier pension plan, and because only the Improved Pension plan is now open to applicants, we will discuss the current plan.

In 1994, the maximum payment to a single veteran who had no other income was $7,818. Under the VA pension program, the VA reduces its payment dollar-for-dollar for certain other income that you or your family may receive.

The application form for a VA pension is the same form used for the VA compensation program, VA Form 21-526, Veteran's Application for Compensation or Pension. Before you sit down with your service representative to complete a full-size form, compile the dates of medical treatment and the names of the facilities that provided treatment. Also, make a list of medical expenses and collect copies of pay stubs from family members and tax returns or other information that will help you explain your financial situation for the past year and what it is likely to be for the next year. A copy of VA Form 21-526 can be obtained by calling the nearest VA regional office.

We have divided this chapter into three sections: (1) how to establish wartime service, (2) how to prove that you are totally disabled, and (3) how to show that you have a limited income. You must meet all three criteria to get a VA pension.

WARTIME SERVICE

Entitlement to the VA pension program requires service during a period of war. It also requires a minimum period of service. You did not have to see combat, you only had to serve during the period officially designated as wartime. Officially designated periods of war include World War I, World War II, the Korean War, the Vietnam War, and the Persian Gulf Era (see dates in Chapter 1). Service in Grenada and Panama is not designated as wartime.

In addition to serving during a particular time period, you also must have served a particular length of time that began, ended, or occurred during wartime. *One* of the following must apply: Your active military service was during wartime for 90 days or more, you were discharged for

---

★ **QUICK CHECK** ★

Read this chapter especially if you can answer yes to all the following questions:

Have you served during wartime?   yes/no

Are you too sick or disabled to work?   yes/no

Do you have an income of less than approximately $600 per month (or more, but you have lots of medical expenses)?   yes/no

Especially read on if you have income of more than $600 per month, and you also have a family.

★ **IMPORTANT** ★

Get help. Eligibility for a pension can depend on complicated questions about what counts as income in the VA program and on complicated calculations. If you make a mistake, not only can you lose future pension payments, but you can also provide the VA with a reason to collect money from you. You are also under a daily obligation to tell the VA about any changes in your family or disability or income (yours or your family's) that might affect eligibility for the program.

---

a service-connected disability, your service was for at least 90 days that either began or ended during a period of wartime, or, finally, your service during two or more periods of wartime totaled 90 days.

There is yet another requirement if you entered service after Sept. 7, 1980: 24 months of continuous active duty. Exceptions to this last requirement are discussed in Chapter 1.

TOTAL DISABILITY

Actually, total disability is not enough. You also have to show that the total disability is likely to be "permanent." A total disability rating means a 100 percent rating. You get a 100 percent rating in two primary ways: (1) by using the VA Schedule for Rating Disabilities or (2) by showing that your disability means that you are unemployable. You must apply and qualify for a disability rating under the pension program in about the same way as you would seek and obtain a disability rating under the compensation program.

Total Rating on the Schedule

Unlike the service-connected compensation program, where you have to prove that your disability is related to your military service, there is no such requirement with the pension program. Like the compensation program, though, you do have to use the VA's rules to show the extent (expressed in percentage) to which your disability impairs your ability to work. Those rules are contained in the VA Schedule for Rating Disabilities (38 C.F.R. Part 4).

A disability rating is the percentage of disability that the VA officially says represents, as far as can practically be determined, the average impairment in earning capacity in civil occupations resulting from particular diseases and injuries, and their residual conditions.

Unlike the compensation program, which will pay you if you have even a 10 percent rating, you will not receive a pension unless your single disability is rated at 100 percent or your ratings for multiple disabilities total 100 percent. Also, unlike the compensation program, which will not pay for congenital or developmental disabilities (for example, a personality disorder), the pension program will pay for those disabilities. Just like with the compensation program, however, if your disability is considered to be due to your "willful misconduct" or drug or alcohol abuse, you will not be paid a pension.

If you have a service-connected disability, but you do not get paid much for it and you have a severe nonservice-connected disability, the VA will combine the ratings for the two disabilities to see if you reach a 100 percent rating. You cannot draw payments from both programs and will be given the choice of electing the payment you want. Also, do not be confused by a rating of permanent and total disability for VA insurance purposes. Such a finding in connection with VA insurance technically does not affect compensation or pension ratings, but you still should point to this finding as evidence of your disability.

How a Rating Is Assigned

The VA usually will schedule you for an examination by one of its doctors, who are called Compensation and Pension examiners (C&P doctors). Sometimes the VA will accept medical records or a report from your personal doctor and will not schedule you for further exams. In setting a rating, a VA rating specialist looks for the diagnosis and the description of the severity of the condition that the C&P doctor wrote or that your private medical records show.

The VA employee tries to fit those words into the 1945 VA Schedule for Rating Disabilities. Because most of this schedule is almost 50 years out of date, using the schedule presents some problems for the VA and for you. You should know, too, that during the next few years, the entire schedule will be revised. Chapter 11 describes how to obtain the latest version. Although the VA will not volunteer the fact, you are entitled to examine the schedule at the nearest VA regional office. Service representatives will also have copies of the schedule.

The VA schedule is a series of 14 charts, one for each body system. For example, one chart deals with your muscles, another with your ears, another with your nerves, and so forth. Your disability is assigned a Diagnostic Code. For example, if you have severe back pain that shoots into your legs due to a disc problem, the relevant Diagnostic Code is DC 5293. After you have a Diagnostic Code, you look it up on the chart to find out the appropriate percentage of disability.

The VA schedule consists of three parts: (1) a four-digit diagnostic code and its corresponding description, (2) various symptoms, and (3) a percentage. It looks simple. But the reality is much different. Several of the problems with the schedule are described in Chapter 4.

Using the Rating Schedule

There are three critical ways in which you should use the schedule: (1) if you do not have a rating, examine the criteria corresponding to your diagnosis and work with your doctor to determine which criteria you meet and to prepare a report that explains why you meet those criteria; (2) if the VA has denied that your disability is 100 percent, confirm that it was correctly determined; and (3) if you want an increased rating, examine the criteria for a higher rating and work with your doctor to see if you meet those criteria. A detailed discussion of the three ways you and your doctor can use the VA schedule is included in Chapter 4.

Total Disability If You Count Unemployability

Perhaps, after reviewing your disability and where it falls on the VA schedule, you will discover that your condition is going to be rated at only 40 percent or 50 percent. At the same time, you know that because of your disability you cannot work. Don't give up. There are special rules that the VA applies to boost your rating to the 100 percent mark.

The official VA policy, according to its rule book, is that you should be rated totally (100 percent) disabled if you cannot work because of your disability. The technical language is, "All veterans who are unable to secure and follow a substantially gainful occupation by reason of disabilities which are likely to be permanent shall be rated as permanently and totally disabled" (38 C.F.R. 4.17).

Despite the kind sound of this policy, it is up to you to present your case and get over several hurdles that the VA uses to avoid paying benefits. This policy does not become a factor until the VA has decided that your disability is not 100 percent, given the various percentages of disability that the VA schedule normally would assign to your condition.

First Hurdle: What Is Unemployability?

In the past, the Board of Veterans' Appeals has often said "Being unemployed is not the same as being unemployable." Neither the BVA nor the regional office says much more. They may recite that they have "carefully" considered your education and training. They conclude, however, that you have not proven that you cannot work. VA decisions typically give no indication that an evaluation of your skills was conducted, of whether there are jobs for which you qualify, or of whether those jobs are available. Have an evaluation done for yourself. See the discussion of this in Chapter 5.

Officially, there is no single, comprehensive definition of "unemployability" or what the VA means when it says, "unable to secure and follow a substantially gainful occupation by reason of disabilities." You need to know some of the VA rules that apply to these cases so that you can recite the rules to the VA and then explain why the rules apply to you. For example, according to a VA manual, "unable to secure" suggests failed attempts to obtain work. "Unable to follow or maintain employment" suggests sporadic or temporary work. Another rule reminds VA officials, "a person may be too disabled to engage in employment although he or she is up and about and fairly comfortable at home or upon limited activity" (38 C.F.R. 4.10). Yet another rule says that age is a factor in evaluating pension claims (38 C.F.R. 4.19).

In reality, the VA does not consider unemployability as an issue unless it has decided that it cannot rate your disabilities at 100 percent but has decided that you have at least one disability rated at 60 percent. If you have more than one disability, the VA will consider unemployability if one disability is at least 40 percent and all others combined are at least 70 percent.

If you have only one disability, which is rated at 60 percent on the VA schedule, or you have two disabilities and their ratings total 70 percent, the VA should consider increasing your rating to 100 percent if you have said that you cannot work because of the disability (38 C.F.R. 4.17). This is the rule after Dec. 15, 1991.

★ NOTE ★

The VA does not add the different percentages it assigns to your disabilities, it "combines" them. You should confirm any "combined rating" by using the combined ratings table in 38 C.F.R. 4.25. (See discussion on page 102).

The rule before Dec. 15, 1991, was more lenient. If you were rejected for a pension before Dec. 15, 1991, and you were 55 to 59 years old, you had to have one disability rated at 60 percent or a combined rating of 60 (not 70) percent. The old rule also said that if you were 60 to 64, you had to have one disability rated at 50 or a combined rating of 50 (not 70) percent. If you met these percentages (and ages) in an earlier application but there is no indication on the VA rating decision that it considered VA regulation 38 C.F.R. 4.17, tell the regional office that it made a "clear and unmistakable error."

Second Hurdle: Forcing the VA to Read Its Own Rules

Anticipate that a regional office's rating specialist must first look at the ratings you currently have when he or she reviews a request for a total rating based on unemployability. The VA employee has memorized the percentages just described. He or she has been told that you must have these particular percentages before he or she will seriously consider your application. The percentages that the specialist has memorized come from the first part of a three-part VA rule (38 C.F.R. 4.16[a]). If you do not already have those ratings, you must make sure that the VA applies the next rule.

Under the next rule (38 C.F.R. 4.17[b]), even without the specific itemized percentages, "claims of all veterans who fail to meet the percentage standards but who . . . are unemployable" will be referred by the rating board to the Adjudication Officer under 38 C.F.R. 3.321(b)(2). In a letter to the VA regional office, you should state, "Please consider my claim for a total rating under 38 C.F.R. 3.321(b)(2)." The Adjudication Officer is the head of the adjudication division at the regional office and is the person authorized to approve a total rating even if the various percentages, noted previously, are not met.

Third Hurdle: Some Work Does Not Preclude a Total Rating

You can anticipate that the VA may deny your claim even if you have not had a steady job for the past several years but you have done some volunteer work or you have worked a few hours a week and earned some money. The VA will say that such work proves that you are employable. The VA is incorrect.

If in a year's time (or on the average during the past few years) you make less than the amount set as the poverty threshold, your employment is "marginal." Marginal employment cannot be used to deny a total disability rating. In 1993, the poverty threshold for an individual was $7,143.

```
━━━━━━━━━━━━━  ★ IMPORTANT ★  ━━━━━━━━━━━━━
 The money you make from marginal employment will reduce the
 amount of the VA pension (unless you have medical expenses that
 offset the earnings).
```

Fourth Hurdle: Getting the VA to Take into Account an SSA Disability Finding

Unlike what you must do in the VA disability system, which assigns ratings between 10 percent and 100 percent, to obtain disability benefits from the Social Security Administration you must prove that you are totally disabled (i.e., you cannot engage in substantial gainful activity). Otherwise you get nothing. If you have convinced the SSA that you are totally disabled, the VA should consider making the same determination. Until recently, however, the VA routinely and completely ignored SSA decisions.

Permanent Disability

Getting VA pension payments requires not only a total rating but also that the disability is reasonably certain to continue for the rest of your life. The VA used to presume that if you were 65 years old you were permanently and totally disabled. This is no longer the law. The VA may presume that a condition is permanent if it required hospitalization for at least 6 months or for an indefinite period.

If you are in an accident or suffer a heart attack or a stroke, the VA will guess whether you are likely to recover fully and regain the ability to work, but it must give "due consideration" to your age, educational level, occupational background, and prior physical condition. If there is a question about whether your condition is permanent after a heart attack, a stroke, or an accident, the VA should rule that your condition is permanent and schedule you for a future examination.

```
━━━━━━━━━━━━━  ★ IMPORTANT ★  ━━━━━━━━━━━━━
 The money you are paid in Social Security Disability Insurance
 Benefits will reduce the amount of the VA pension (unless you
 have medical expenses that offset the SSA money).
```

LIMITED INCOME

To get a VA Improved Pension, you must have limited income and re-sources. The VA Improved Pension program is intended to keep you slightly above the poverty level. It is an income-maintenance program. Some would say it is a welfare program. Regardless of what you call it, the VA adjusts the amount that it will pay if you are receiving money from other sources. The VA doesn't care about some money you get; it does care about other money and counts it against you. The money that the VA cares about is called "countable income."

You care about what the VA considers countable income because for every dollar of countable income, you get one dollar less of VA pension. Basically, Congress has decided what sum of money it thinks is appropriate for you to have, and the VA is supposed to make sure that you don't get more than that, at least not during the time the VA is paying you. For example, in 1994, if you were single, the maximum income that Congress believed appropriate was $7,818. If you won $1,000 playing the lottery, the VA would reduce its annual payment by $1,000 so that during the year you would still have only a maximum income of $7,818. The VA refers to the Congressional cap as the maximum annual pension rate (MAPR).

The maximum amount that the VA pays, or the MAPR, increases with the number of dependents you have. For example, in 1994, the amount paid if you had no dependents was $7,818 ($651 per month) but the amount paid if you had one dependent was $10,240 ($853 per month). For each additional dependent, the MAPR increased by $1,330.

The rest of this section will discuss (1) what the VA counts as income, (2) what the VA does not count as income, and (3) what the VA will let you deduct from what it counts. This section describes the initial considerations regarding income. After a pension is awarded, you have a continuing obligation to notify the VA about changes in your life (and your family's) that might affect your VA pension payments.

Technically, you must have limited resources in order to qualify for VA pension payments. Under VA rules, you must not have "too much" property, enough that someone at the VA will think "it is reasonable that some part of your estate be consumed for your maintenance" (38 C.F.R. 3.274). The house that you live in does not count as part of your estate. VA rules provide no hard-and-fast dollar value of what the VA views as too much property. In reality, this is seldom an issue. If the VA makes it an issue, you can appeal its decision. See Chapter 3.

What Counts as Income

The short answer is that everything counts unless the VA says it doesn't count. Under VA rules, "payments of any kind from any source shall be counted as income" unless specifically excluded by another rule (38 C.F.R. 3.271). Payments that are excluded (i.e., that do not count) are listed in another VA rule, 38 C.F.R. 3.272, and are discussed next. The following list of income that is included is taken from the VA rule and VA Manual M21-1, Part IV, para. 16.41.This VA manual provides detailed instructions on income calculations and can be reviewed at any VA regional office.

Put a check mark in each box that describes the money you are getting or expect to get during the next year.

- ☐ business, farm, or professional income
- ☐ compensation for injury or death
- ☐ your earnings
- ☐ income of a spouse
- ☐ earnings of children
- ☐ income of children
- ☐ retirement or survivors' program income
- ☐ interest
- ☐ dividends
- ☐ life insurance
- ☐ unemployment compensation
- ☐ benefits subject to garnishment
- ☐ social security lump sum death benefit
- ☐ IRA distributions
- ☐ withdrawal of contributions from a retirement fund
- ☐ Department of Labor employment programs such as the Green Thumb Program and the Older Americans Community Service Employment Program
- ☐ VA benefits such as burial, education, compensation, and Dependency and Indemnity Compensation and accrued benefits
- ☐ value of room and board
- ☐ gifts and inheritances
- ☐ waived income
- ☐ gains from gambling
- ☐ payment to World War II Japanese internees
- ☐ Vietnam War bonus payment
- ☐ U.S. Government Life Insurance (USGLI) or National Servicemen's Life Insurance (NSLI) insurance payments

How to Exclude a Child's Income

Your child might have two kinds of income: (1) a social security benefit or (2) earnings from employment. The VA presumes that any income of your child's, such as a social security check, is "reasonably available to or for" you (38 C.F.R. 3.23[d][4]). You can overcome that presumption by showing that your annual expenses for "reasonable family maintenance exceed the sum of countable annual plus VA pension entitlement." The expenses to include in this calculation include expenses for basic necessities such as food, clothing, shelter, and other expenses "which are necessary to support a reasonable quality of life." You can use VA Form 21-0571 to claim this hardship exclusion. It is available by calling the nearest VA regional office. More detailed information about this hardship exclusion is contained in VBA Circular 21-89-7, which is also available through the nearest VA regional office.

A certain amount of a child's earnings are automatically excluded (38 C.F.R. 3.272[j]). In 1990, the amount excluded was $5,300. If your child is earning more but also attending postsecondary education or vocational rehabilitation or training, the amount of those education expenses is excluded.

What Does Not Count as Income

Payments you might get that are excluded (i.e., that do not count against you for VA purposes) are listed in VA rule 38 C.F.R. 3.272 and are explained in VA Manual M21-1. The following list is compiled from VA Manual M21-1, Part IV, para. 16.41, and the VA rule. Put a check mark in the box next to any income that you or members of your family receive:

☐ welfare and supplemental security income
☐ maintenance
☐ proceeds of casualty insurance (if you lose property due to fire, flood, theft, etc., and you collect on an insurance policy, the amount received is not countable so long as it does not exceed the value of the lost property)
☐ profit from sale of property
☐ income from Domestic Volunteer Service Act programs
☐ Agent Orange settlement payments (see discussion of this case in Chapter 15)
☐ mineral royalties
☐ income tax refunds

☐ withheld social security
☐ distributions from VA Special Therapeutic and Rehabilitation Activities Fund
☐ Home Energy Assistance Act
☐ interest on IRAs
☐ chore services payments
☐ loans
☐ Crime Victims Compensation Act payments
☐ provisional income
☐ scholarships and grants for school
☐ survivor's benefit annuity
☐ California State renter's credit
☐ relocation expenses
☐ disaster relief payments
☐ FHA construction grants
☐ insurance dividends
☐ timber sale
☐ payments to foster parents
☐ joint accounts

Expenses That Can Reduce Your Income

If, after reviewing the previous lists, you think you have income that the VA would count against you, don't stop. Read this section to see if you had (or will have) expenses during the next year that you can use to reduce your countable income. This is one time when keeping track of your expenses may actually pay off. Put a check mark in the boxes that apply to you:

☐ medical expenses that will not be reimbursed
☐ education expenses for you or your spouse (including tuition, fees, books, materials)
☐ spouse's or child's final expenses (amounts paid for the last illness and burial)

Medical Expenses

It often seems that the less income you have, the more likely you and your family will have medical expenses, and the less likely you will have health insurance that will reimburse you for those expenses. Fortunately, the VA will let you use your medical expenses and those of your children and spouse to offset the amount of countable VA income (38 C.F.R. 3.272[g]). This helps only if you or your family have a source of income other than the VA pension. If you do, and you have medical expenses, you may be able to keep most of your other income.

The exclusion for medical expenses is available under the following circumstances:

★ the expenses will not be reimbursed by anyone; and
★ the expenses were paid or will be paid by you or your spouse for you, your spouse, your children, your parents, other relatives, or a constructive member of your household; and
★ the expenses will total more than 5 percent of your Maximum Annual Pension Rate (MAPR).

The VA has a list of medical expenses that you may be able to claim. This list does not cover everything: If you think you have an expense similar to any of those on the following list, tell the VA about it. The VA regional office personnel are under orders to "allow all expenses which are directly related to medical care."

LIST OF POSSIBLE MEDICAL EXPENSES

abdominal supports
acupuncture service
ambulance hire
anesthetist
arch supports
artificial limbs and teeth
back supports
braces
cardiographs
chiropodist
convalescent home
crutches
dental service
dentures
dermatologist
eyeglasses
food or beverages specially prescribed by a physician
gynecologist
hearing aids and batteries

home health services
hospital expenses
insulin treatment
medical insurance premiums
invalid chair
lab tests
lip reading lessons
neurologist
nursing services
occupational therapist
ophthalmologist
optician
optometrist
oral surgery
osteopath, licensed
pediatrician
physical examinations
physical therapy
physician
podiatrist
prescriptions and drugs
psychiatrist
psychoanalyst
psychologist
psychotherapy
radium therapy
sacroiliac belt
seeing-eye dog and maintenance
speech therapist
splints
supplementary medical insurance (Part B) under Medicare
surgeon
telephone/teletype special communications equipment for the deaf
transportation expenses for medical purposes (20 cents per mile plus
        parking and tolls or actual fares for taxi, buses, etc.)
vaccines
vitamins prescribed by a doctor
wheelchairs
whirlpool baths for medical purposes
X-rays

Additional possible deductible medical expenses include these:

★ nursing home fees if you are a patient, not a resident, at the home
★ all reasonable fees paid to an in-home attendant (does not have to be a licensed health professional) if the VA is paying the housebound or aid and attendance allowance (discussed later in this chapter); if the VA has not agreed to pay the housebound or aid and attendance allowance, the fees paid to an in-home attendant may be deducted only if the attendant is a licensed health professional
★ fees paid for custodial care as long as some medical treatment is provided or the person is participating in a program of therapy or rehabilitation supervised by a doctor
★ non-prescription drugs if a doctor directed that they be taken
★ mechanical and electronic devices that compensate for disabilities

All these possible expenses and further examples of such expenses are found in VA Manual M21-1, Part IV.

"Plug into" Formula

After you determine whether the money you receive annually is counted or excluded as income and you deduct any allowable expenses, you arrive at the "IVAP," the countable income for VA purposes. Plug this figure into the following formula to calculate how much you should get each month from the VA:

─────────── ★ IMPORTANT ★ ───────────

File a statement of medical expenses each month with the VA regional office. You do not need to send copies of receipts to the VA, but you should save all your receipts. Do not wait until you receive the annual questionnaire from the VA asking you about your expenses. The value in filing each month is that if you die, your spouse may be entitled to use those expenses as deductions. If the expenses have not been filed with the VA as of the date of your death, the VA will *not* allow your surviving spouse to claim them.

MAPR = _____
minus countable income for VA purposes = _____
divided by 12 months = _____ per month

If you cannot figure all this out, sit down with your service representative and with the VA manual and VA rules and work through the calculation. If all else fails and you can't figure this out but you think you are close, go ahead and complete VA Form 21-526. The VA will be happy to evaluate everything for you. You should understand, however, that if it decides against you, it may exclude you from reopening your claim for a full year. Just as you can appeal because of questions about your disability, you can also appeal a VA denial if the VA counts certain income and calculates that your income is too high. You have 1 year in which to file your Notice of Disagreement. See Chapter 3 for details about appealing.

Adjustments in Income

After you begin to receive a VA pension, you will have to be careful to keep it. Each year on the anniversary of the effective date of your pension award, the VA will send you an almost-impossible-to-understand form called the Eligibility Verification Report (EVR). You can't ignore it, and sometimes you can't wait for it to arrive. Each year, several thousand veterans are terminated from the pension program because they do not return the EVR.

There are two big ways (and several smaller ones) in which questions about income occur. First, the VA may be wrong about the kind of money you have, that is, whether money you have is countable or not. Second, the VA may be wrong about when to start counting that money as part of the IVAP. You can appeal either VA decision. See Chapter 3.

We hope that, from the lists given earlier in this chapter, you will be able to confirm whether the VA counted what's countable, didn't count what's not countable, and excluded what's excludable.

As if that is not complicated enough, what happens when you report to the VA on the Eligibility Verification Report (EVR) that your income has changed or you are divorced is even more complicated. If these changes coincide with the week that you get the EVR from the VA, you suffer minimal discomfort. On the other hand, if your change in income or number of dependents occurred in one of the other 51 weeks of the year, your level of discomfort may rise sharply and be directly proportional to the

---
★ WARNING ★

You are obligated to notify the VA about any change in material circumstances that may affect your VA payments. The VA compares your computer records with those of the SSA and other federal and state agencies to try to catch veterans who may not be properly reporting their income or marital status.

Don't wait for the comparison to happen. Call the VA regional office. Explain what has happened. Get the VA employee's name. Don't believe the person on the phone if he or she says you do not have to worry about your change in status. Write to the regional office and report the change. Keep a photocopy of the letter you send. If the change is that you have begun to receive social security disability insurance benefits or retirement benefits, send along a copy of your award letter and your first check. If the VA sends the same amount the next month, repeat the process. If the VA sends the same amount the next month, repeat the process.

You can keep the check, but don't think that you can spend all the money without having to repay some it. Consult your service representative and try to calculate how much is correct and safe to spend and how much you will have to repay. If you know that you are not entitled to any of the money, mark the check "void," make a photocopy for your records, and enclose it with a letter to the regional office.

---

length of time between the date of the change and the date when you return the EVR.

The VA must make adjustments in its payment when you are no longer entitled to the same amount of VA pension. Even if you call the VA the same day that something happens to affect your payment, the VA will not be able to make the necessary adjustments to its check-writing computers to avoid paying you the old amount. This means in many cases that the VA automatically generates overpayments, which at some time will have to be repaid.

To adjust your pension, the VA will take one of three actions. It will (1) terminate your payments, (2) reduce your payments, or (3) increase your payments. If the VA terminates or reduces your payments or declares that it overpaid you, review Chapters 2 and 3 to understand your rights.

VA adjustments are spread over the 12-month period from the effective date when the adjustment was required. The VA calls this "annualizing." For example, if the VA has been paying you $616 each month (for a total of $7,397 for the year), and you report that you won $7,397 in the lottery, the VA will terminate its payments to you. The VA will not send checks to you for the next 12 months. You are expected to live on the lottery winnings for the next 12 months by depositing all the lottery winnings and withdrawing from your savings account no more than $616 each month. Good luck.

Sometimes the VA mistakenly adjusts its payments based on when it thought you began to receive social security benefits. For example, the VA may have been told by the SSA that it awarded you benefits on June 1. Perhaps the SSA did, but you may not have received your first check until December 1. The proper time for the VA to make its adjustment is when you actually have the first SSA check in your hands, not the technical "effective date of the award."

Your circumstances will change somewhat year to year. Do your best to report the changes as they occur. If you anticipate a big change that could otherwise terminate your pension for 12 months, you may be able to limit the loss. There is a little-used process known as "renouncing" (or giving up) your pension. This is discussed in Chapter 2. Renouncing your pension is dangerous these days because you may find that you cannot requalify for the pension. Work very closely with a knowledgeable service representative if you even think about doing this.

If You Need Help to Get Through Your Day

You may be eligible for extra pension payments each month if you need someone to help take care of you or if you are housebound. Needing someone to help take care of you may mean that you qualify for the aid and attendance (A&A) allowance. These extra payments are referred to as a "special monthly pension." If you are single, the maximum annual pension rate increases about 22 percent if you qualify for the housebound (HB) allowance and 60 percent if you qualify for the A&A allowance.

You do not need to wait until the VA notifies you that you are entitled to a pension before asking for either the HB or A&A allowance. You can speed the process if you ask your doctor to prepare a statement describing your limitations. The *VA Physician's Guide to Disability Evaluation Examinations* contains a format for VA doctors to use in these cases. Private doctors can also follow it. The format based on the guide is provided on p. 130.

Housebound Allowance

In VA rules, to qualify for the housebound allowance means that you are first entitled to a pension because you have a single disability rated at 100 percent (not based on unemployability) and another disability rating of 60 percent for a different body system than the one in which you have the 100 percent rating. Another way you qualify for the housebound allowance is to be "substantially confined" to your house or, if you are institutionalized, to be substantially confined to the ward. You must also show that your disability "will continue throughout your lifetime" (38 C.F.R. 3.351[d]).

Effective Dec. 1, 1993, the housebound rates were as follows:

single veteran $9,556/year, or $796/month
with one dependent $11,997 per year / $998 per month
for each additional dependent add $1,330 per year / $110 per month

Aid and Attendance

To qualify for the A&A allowance, you must be helpless or "so nearly helpless as to require the regular aid and attendance of another person" (38 C.F.R. 3.351[b]). The VA will consider you eligible for the A&A allowance if you are blind or nearly blind, if you are a patient in a nursing home because of a mental or a physical incapacity, or if you meet certain other criteria.

The "other criteria" include such factors as the inability to dress or undress yourself, to be ordinarily clean and presentable, or to feed yourself; a need to adjust prostheses or orthopedic appliances frequently; an inability to feed yourself through loss of upper extremity coordination or through extreme weakness; incontinence; or a need due to a mental or a physical incapacity to be protected from the hazards or dangers of your daily environment. The VA rules are clear that you do not need to meet each of these factors to qualify for the A&A allowance. Also, you do not need to be so helpless that someone must attend you constantly (38 C.F.R. 3.352[a]).

Effective Dec. 1, 1993, the A&A rates were as follows:

single veteran $12,504 per year / $1,042 per month
with one dependent $14,927 per year / $1,243 per month
for each additional dependent add $1,330 per year / $110 per month

Effects on Your SSI Benefits When Your VA Pension Begins

Supplemental security income (SSI) does not count against you as far as the VA is concerned. SSI payments are excluded from countable income. The reverse is not true: the Social Security Administration will reduce, if not terminate, SSI payments when you begin to receive a VA Improved Pension. Loss of SSI eligibility can mean loss of Medicaid eligibility. As you will see in Chapter 9 on VA medical services, there is no guarantee that you will be able to walk into a VA hospital to get treatment. Certainly, there is no entitlement to care in a VA hospital for your family.

If you are now receiving SSI, confirm with the nearest legal aid or legal services office what may happen to your SSI and your Medicaid eligibility if you begin to draw a VA pension. Perhaps in your state the VA pension payment does not affect your Medicaid eligibility.

Format for Private Doctor's Report: A&A or HB Benefits

(Format based on the *VA Physician's Guide*)

Date of exam:_____

Place of exam:_____

Veteran's Name:_____

VA File Number:_____

Social Security Number:_____

A. Diagnoses:_____
_____

B. Capabilities:_____
_____

   1. Is this person able to dress or undress himself or herself? yes no

   2. Is this person able to keep himself or herself ordinarily clean and presentable?   yes no

   3. Is there a frequent need for adjusting special prosthetic or orthopedic appliances which by reason of the particular disability this person cannot do without aid?   yes no does not apply

   4. Is this person able to feed himself or herself?   yes no

   5. Has this person lost coordination of upper extremities or does he or she suffer from extreme weakness such that he or she is unable to feed himself or herself?   yes no

   6. Is this person unable to attend to urinary and bowel function?   yes no

   7. Does this person have difficulty performing urinary and bowel functions without assistance?   yes no

   8. Is there present incapacity, physical or mental, which requires care or assistance on a regular basis to protect this person from hazards or dangers incident to his or her daily environment?   yes no

   9. Does this person suffer from total blindness?   yes no

   10. Is the essential characteristic of this person's condition such that it requires him or her to remain in bed?   yes no

Examining Doctor's Signature:_____

Doctor's Name:_____

Address:_____

Telephone:_____

CHAPTER SIX

Educational Assistance and Vocational Rehabilitation

★ ★

This chapter tells you about educational assistance programs and vocational training programs that are available through the VA. The educational assistance currently available will not meet even half your educational expenses. In fact, it was not designed to do more than that. Seven years ago, when the most commonly used program began, its monthly payment was thought to cover just about half your expenses. After 7 years of inflation and increases in college tuition rates, the VA payments were increased from $300 to $350 in 1991. Even with that increase, however, the money is expected to meet less than 45 percent of your expenses. The current program, the Montgomery GI Bill, was named after the long-time chairman of the House of Representatives Committee on Veterans Affairs, Sonny Montgomery of Mississippi.

The major programs administered by the VA's Education Service include these:

★ Montgomery GI Bill—Selected Reserve Program
★ Montgomery GI Bill—Active Duty Program
★ Post–Vietnam Era Veterans' Educational Assistance Program

The VA also offers educational assistance to dependents and survivors of certain veterans. See Chapter 10.

In addition to educational assistance programs, the VA offers vocational rehabilitation to veterans with a service-connected disability rating of at least 20 percent.

These programs and their rules are very technical. At the same time, for almost any VA rule, there are exceptions and sometimes exceptions to exceptions. The laws change and the VA frequently changes the rules, too. Before you take "no" for an answer from the VA, make sure you are satisfied that the denial is based on the latest information. Sit down with a service representative at the nearest VA regional office and look at the latest rules. You can appeal a denial by the VA. See Chapter 3. Sometimes it may be necessary to start the appeal process just to get enough information from the VA to make sure it is right.

HOW TO BEGIN

You may already know exactly how much educational assistance you have available. If not, call the nearest VA regional office to confirm what is available to you. The regional office can also confirm whether the school you are considering and the courses you plan to take are approved. To apply to a particular school, deal directly with the school. Its financial affairs office will have the appropriate application form to use to tell the VA that you are admitted. Make sure that the school submits the application form to the VA.

MONTGOMERY GI BILL—SELECTED RESERVE PROGRAM

The Montgomery GI Bill—Selected Reserve Program covers members of the Army, the Navy, the Air Force, the Marine Corps and Coast Guard reserve elements, and the Army and Air National Guard. The law govern-

---

★ IMPORTANT ★

If you sign up for classes and then reduce your course load, withdraw from school, or are absent from several classes, call and write to the VA and tell it. If you have a good reason for reducing or withdrawing from courses or for being absent from classes, explain your reasons. See Chapter 2 for some of the official reasons that might excuse your withdrawal. Unless your excuse is good, the VA may come after you for the money it sent.

ing this program is not a VA law; it is a Defense Department law and is sometimes referred to as the Chapter 106 program (corresponding to Title 10, U.S. Code, Chapter 106). Because the VA administers the program, it has regulations regarding the program; you can find these regulations at any VA regional office. They begin at 38 C.F.R. 21.7500.

To be eligible for this program, you must be a reservist and must meet *all* the following requirements. You must

★ have a 6-year obligation that you signed after June 30, 1985, either to enlist, reenlist or extend an enlistment;

★ complete initial active duty for training;

★ meet the requirements for a high school diploma or an equivalency before completing initial active duty for training

★ participate satisfactorily in the Selected Reserve.

Amount of Money

Under the Montgomery GI Bill—Selected Reserve Program, you are entitled to 36 months of assistance. In 1992, the payments amounted to $190 per month. If you attend school on a less than full-time basis, the payments will be less but will last longer. If you attend school on a three-quarter-time basis, you received $143 per month; attending on a half-time basis entitled you to $95. More money may be available to you under the Montgomery GI Bill—Active Duty Program if you completed at least 2 years of active duty.

★ **DEADLINE** ★

You have 10 years from the date when you begin to be eligible for this program, or 10 years from the date when you separate from the Selected Reserve, to use all of your allotment. The VA can grant an extension of this 10-year period if you apply within 1 year of the ending date. An extension may also be granted if you apply within 1 year of the date when you recovered from health problems that prevented you from pursuing an education program. If those health problems were incurred or aggravated by your service in the Selected Reserve and were not the result of your willful misconduct, the VA may extend the deadline (38 C.F.R. 21.7551).

What You Can Do with Your Money

The VA offers counseling on courses to take, objectives to pursue, and suitable schools to attend. Take advantage of the offerings. Call the nearest VA regional office to schedule an appointment. The VA will not pay for everything you might want to do. For example, it will not pay for courses in bartending or personal development. Flight training is limited to schools that offer a standard college degree. The VA will not pay for courses that it considers "avocational and recreational" (for example, photography, dancing, music) (38 C.F.R. 21.7622). The VA may, however, pay for such courses if you can prove that they will be of use to you in pursuing your present or contemplated business or occupation. The VA will also not pay for postgraduate courses, audited courses, or correspondence courses.

MONTGOMERY GI BILL—ACTIVE DUTY PROGRAM

The Montgomery GI Bill—Active Duty Program covers you if you began active duty after June 30, 1985, and you paid into the program. The VA law governing this program is Chapter 30 of Title 38, U.S. Code, and it is often referred to as the Chapter 30 program.

To be entitled to payments from this program you

★ must have served for at least 3 continuous years; or

★ if you signed up for fewer than 3 years, you must have completed at least 2 years; or you

★ must have been discharged for a service-connected disability, for a preexisting medical condition, for certain other medical conditions, due to hardship; or you

★ must have been discharged for the convenience of the government and completed either 20 or 30 months of the initial period of active duty; or you

★ must have been discharged involuntarily as a result of a reduction in force.

One other requirement of this educational assistance program is unique: You must have a fully honorable discharge. A general discharge (or discharge under honorable conditions) is not good enough. If your discharge is not fully honorable, see Chapter 17 for suggestions on how to change it. If your discharge prevents you from using the money you contributed, ask for a refund. If you are denied a refund, appeal and consult an attorney.

You may also be eligible for this program if you were eligible for the earlier educational assistance program that expired on Dec. 31, 1989 (the Chapter 34 program). If this is your situation, you had to be on active duty on Oct. 19, 1984, and had to continue on active duty for 3 years after the beginning of the current program, which works out to June 30, 1988. If you were discharged just before that deadline due to health problems, hardship, or reduction in force, you may still be eligible. You did not have to pay into the program.

If you think you are eligible for this program, call the VA regional office. You can read the VA rules at the VA office or the office of your service representative (38 C.F.R. 21.7000).

Amount of Money

Under the Montgomery GI Bill—Active Duty Program, you are usually entitled to 36 months of assistance. As of this writing, the payments amount to $400 per month for full-time attendance. If you attend school on a less than full-time basis, the payments will be less but will last longer. Your months of entitlement may be less than 36 if you were discharged early. Generally, if you served 30 months of a 3-year tour, you have 30 months of benefits.

★ DEADLINE ★

You have 10 years from the date when you were last discharged from active duty to use your entitlement. Or, if you base your entitlement on service in the Selected Reserves, you have 10 years after you satisfied the 4 years of service in the Selected Reserves. If you initially were not eligible but had your military records corrected through a Board for Correction of Military Records or an upgrade of your discharge from a Discharge Review Board, you have 10 years from the date of the correction.

The VA can grant an extension of the 10-year period if you apply within 1 year of the ending date. An extension may also be granted if you apply within one year of the date when you recovered from health problems that prevented you from pursuing an education program. If those health problems were incurred or aggravated during or as a result of your service in the Selected Reserve and were not the result of your willful misconduct, the VA may extend the deadline (38 C.F.R. 21.7051).

What You Can Do with Your Money

You cannot get a refund of the money you contributed while on active duty. Use it or lose it.

As with the Montgomery GI Bill—Selected Reserve Program, the VA offers counseling on courses to take, objectives to pursue, and suitable schools to select. Take advantage of the offerings. Call the nearest VA regional office to schedule an appointment. The VA may reimburse your travel costs for the counseling.

The VA will not pay for unapproved courses or courses from an institution that engages in deceptive or misleading advertising. Confirm with the VA that the courses you intend to take are approved. The VA will also not pay for so-called avocational or recreational courses unless you can justify that you need them for your business (38 C.F.R. 21.7120).

Unlike the Montgomery GI Bill—Selected Reserve Program, the VA will pay for postgraduate courses under the Montgomery GI Bill—Active Duty Program.

POST–VIETNAM ERA VETERANS' EDUCATIONAL ASSISTANCE PROGRAM

The Post–Vietnam Era Veterans' Educational Assistance Program (known as VEAP) covers you if you began active duty between Jan. 1, 1977, and June 30, 1985, and you paid into the program. The VA law governing this program is Chapter 32 of Title 38, U.S. Code, and it is often referred to as the Chapter 32 program.

To be entitled to payments from this program

★ you had to participate by making payments during your active duty service;

★ you had to have served 181 or more continuous days; or

★ if you entered active duty after Sept. 7, 1980, you had to have completed at least 24 months or have been discharged for hardship, through an early-out program, or for a disability.

Participation in VEAP means that you allowed your active duty pay to be reduced by between $25 and $100 per month for as long as 12 months. You may have made a lump sum contribution. VEAP was voluntary, and you could withdraw from the program and receive a refund of the amount you contributed. If you do not use the program before your deadline expires, your contribution will be refunded, but you must request the refund within 1 year of the end of your delimiting date (38 C.F.R. 21.5060). Call the nearest VA regional office to request a refund if you think any funds remain. As of October 1993, the VA was looking for about 13,000 veterans due a refund. Call (800) 827-1000 for more information.

Amount of Money

For every dollar you contributed, the government added two dollars. The amount you will be paid monthly is determined by the amount of your contribution plus the government's divided by 36 months or the number of months during which you contributed to the program, whichever is less.

What You Can Do with Your Money

You can pursue an associate's degree, a bachelor's degree, or a graduate degree program. Courses at vocational, technical, or business schools that lead to a certificate or a diploma are also acceptable. On-the-job training, apprenticeships, cooperative courses, and certain correspondence courses may be pursued. Remedial or refresher training as well as tutorial assistance is also available.

VOCATIONAL REHABILITATION

Vocational rehabilitation is a VA program that pays you to overcome the effects of a service-connected disability. The program is intended to provide services and assistance necessary to enable you to achieve maximum

---

★ DEADLINE ★

You have 10 years from the date when you were last discharged from active duty. If you initially were not eligible but had your military records corrected through a Board for Correction of Military Records or received an upgrade of your discharge from a Discharge Review Board, you have 10 years from the date of the correction or upgrade. The VA can grant an extension of the 10-year period for health problems if you apply within 1 year of the date when you recovered from those health problems (38 C.F.R. 21.5042).

independence in daily living and to obtain suitable employment. The VA law governing this program is Chapter 31 of Title 38, U.S. Code, and it is often referred to as the Chapter 31 program. In 1992, 36,763 veterans were undergoing vocational training subsidized by the VA. Most of these veterans were attending colleges or universities.

Effective Oct. 1, 1993, eligibility for vocational rehabilitation is tied to the following three conditions. You must meet one of the first two conditions AND the third:

★ You suffer from a service-connected disability that entitles you to at least a 20 percent rating, or

★ You are receiving medical care while awaiting separation for disability, AND

★ The VA must determine that you need rehabilitation.

The first two conditions are pretty straightforward. In deciding whether you need rehabilitation, the VA requires you to participate in counseling that begins with an initial evaluation by a counseling psychologist at a VA regional office. The first evaluation is intended to determine as quickly as possible whether you have an employment handicap that is serious and whether achieving a vocational goal is reasonably feasible. If the VA says it will help you, it prepares an Individualized Written Rehabilitation Plan as a tool to help structure the services it will offer. You are entitled to a copy of this plan.

The VA actually makes two determinations about your disability: (1) Is it an employment handicap or (2) is it a *serious* employment handicap? You will qualify for additional services if your disability is considered to be serious. Ordinarily, if your disability rating is less than 30 percent, your disability will not be considered serious. The VA must also decide whether you have a "reasonable feasibility of achieving a vocational goal" (38 C.F.R. 21.53).

It is reasonably feasible that you will achieve a vocational goal if the following apply:

★ your goals have been identified, and

★ your physical and mental conditions permit training for the goals to begin within a reasonable period, and

★ you possess the necessary educational skills and background to pursue the goal, or

★ the VA will provide services to develop such educational skills.

If the VA says that it is not feasible for you to achieve a vocational goal, it must provide services to help you improve your potential to later achieve a vocational goal and services to enable you to achieve maximum independence in your daily life. You can appeal if the VA says no. You can pursue the normal appeals process described in Chapter 3 or you can request an administrative review by the VA Central Office in Washington, DC.

★ NOTE ★

The deadlines you must meet in the "normal" appeals process are not postponed while you pursue an administrative review.

Within each VA regional office, a Vocational Rehabilitation Panel consisting of the counseling psychologist, the vocational rehabilitation specialist, the medical consultant, the social services staff, and the various other specialists is responsible for reviewing cases brought to it by the counseling psychologist or vocational-rehab specialist. This is another informal route to obtain a review of your case.

The VA application form for this program, VA Form 28-1900, Disabled Veteran's Application for Vocational Rehabilitation, is usually sent with the VA letter that first awards you a service-connected disability rating of at least 20 percent.

Amount of Money

While you pursue a vocational rehabilitation program, you are paid a monthly subsistence allowance along with your service-connected compensation. Your tuition, fees, and books are paid, too. The subsistence allowance varies depending on whether you are pursuing the program as a full-time or a part-time trainee and also varies if you have dependents. The length of service is usually 48 months, but this period can be extended if your employment handicap is serious. For full-time training, the rate for a single veteran is $366 each month; for three-fourths-time training, $275; and for half-time training, $183.

The VA has some flexibility in making payments and can advance money against future benefit payments if you have a crisis during the program. The subsistence allowance also continues for 2 months after completion of training.

★ IMPORTANT ★

If the VA says training is not medically feasible and you cannot work because of your service-connected disability, give that notice to the regional office and ask it to increase your rating to 100 percent due to unemployability.

★ DEADLINE ★

You usually have 12 years from the date when you were discharged to use Chapter 31 benefits. However, this period can be extended if you have a serious employment handicap. Also, the deadline can be extended if for a period it was not feasible for you to pursue a program. If you were not determined to have a service-connected disability when you were discharged from the service, the 12-year period starts on the date when the VA notifies you that it agrees that you have a service-connected disability.

If the character of your discharge means that the VA does not consider you a veteran, changing the character of your discharge will mean that the 12-year period will begin on the date of the upgraded discharge. See Chapter 17 about changing your discharge.

What You Can Do with Your Money

Educational or vocational training can include the following:

★ enrolling in trade, business or technical schools or in college
★ training on the job or in an apprenticeship program
★ on-the-farm training
★ entering programs that combine school and on-the-job training
★ training in special rehabilitation facilities or at home when necessary

After the training is complete, the VA should assist you in finding a suitable job.

CHAPTER SEVEN

HOUSING

★★

This chapter tells you about the VA's home loan guaranty program. It's a big program: In 1992, the VA guaranteed 266,000 home loans. During the same period, another 153,389 veterans were late in their home loan payments.

The VA does not give you money to buy a house. Instead, the VA tells a private lender that if it will give you the money, the VA will guarantee to cover the lender's losses. In eight of ten cases, this means that the lender will not require a down payment; this is a big advantage to you. Also, the interest rate on VA-guaranteed mortgages is usually slightly lower than the rate for conventional loans.

VA HOME LOAN ELIGIBILITY

Whether you are eligible to use the VA home loan guaranty depends on when you served and how long you served, although as a practical matter almost anyone who served is eligible. If you are on active duty now, you also are eligible.

For each of the rules noted next, two additional criteria are required for eligibility to use the loan guaranty: (1) You must be officially a "veteran" and (2) if you did not serve the length of time noted next, you still qualify if you were discharged after a shorter period because of a service-connected disability. (To be sure you qualify as a veteran, refer to Chapter 1.)

Following are tours of duty and associated requirements for a VA home loan guaranty:

★ World War II: requires 90 days of total service
★ Post–World War II: requires 181 days of continuous active duty
★ Korean War: requires 90 days of total service
★ Post–Korean War: requires 181 days continuous active duty
★ Vietnam War: requires 90 days of active duty
★ Post–Vietnam War: requires 181 continuous days of active duty (Eligibility is also affected by whether you served the minimum length of duty required for persons who entered service on or after Sept. 7, 1980. See details on this in Chapter 4.)
★ Persian Gulf Conflict: requires 90 days of active duty (See the details in Chapter 1 about the minimum length of duty required for persons who entered service on or after Sept. 7, 1980. This now includes the National Guard and reserves who were called.)

★ NOTE ★

There is no deadline.

HOW TO BEGIN

First, call the nearest VA regional office. Ask for VA Form 26-1880, Request for Determination of Eligibility and Available Loan Guaranty Entitlement. If you are trying to put a loan application together quickly, visit the Loan Guaranty Service at the regional office and pick up the form.

Second, list your assets, debts, income, expenses, and other financial figures and determine what you can afford. You can ask a real estate agent to estimate what your monthly mortgage payments will be. Better yet, shop around for a reputable mortgage company and ask it for quotes on monthly mortgage payments. Also ask whether the VA interest rate is likely to go up or down soon.

If you get an estimate of what your monthly payments for a certain interest rate on a certain amount of mortgage would be, be sure to add

---

★ WARNING ★

As eager as you may be to buy a home, be extremely careful to report fully to a prospective lender your monthly income and expenses. Do not include wages you hope to get for overtime or otherwise stretch your income. You can quickly be in a lot of trouble if you move into the house and only then discover that you cannot afford to make the monthly payments.

---

enough to cover taxes and insurance to that estimate. This may mean another $100 to $200 per month beyond the quote for "principal and interest." Also, calculate the cash required to pay closing costs at settlement. These costs may include taxes to be escrowed, water bills, and assorted other fees. One potentially big cost is the funding fee that the VA requires.

The VA funding fee may be as much as 3 percent of the loan you are seeking (i.e., $3,000 for a $100,000 mortgage). This fee is not charged if you are receiving service-connected compensation or are entitled to receive compensation but instead are now getting retirement pay. The fee is also affected by the amount of the down payment you make or whether you are refinancing the loan (38 C.F.R. 36.4312). Your lender may let you include these costs in the loan, but be sure to find this out up front.

Third, find a house. Actually, you can use the VA loan guaranty to buy a so-called site-built home (new or previously owned), a condominium, or a manufactured home, or to make improvements or repairs on your current home. You can also use it to refinance an existing loan to take advantage of lower interest rates.

THE AMOUNT OF MONEY AVAILABLE

The private lender or mortgage company makes the final determination of how much money it will extend to you. The VA gives you nothing. The lender's determination is based on whether you are a good financial risk. The lender is supposed to follow VA underwriting rules to decide whether to extend you a loan. These guidelines are found in VA regulations (38 C.F.R. 36.4337 [for site-built homes] or 36.4206 [for manufactured homes]).

As a rule of thumb, you can usually get a loan for about four times what the VA says is your entitlement. Currently, the basic entitlement is $36,000, but the amount varies with the purpose of the loan and how much you want to borrow. As much as $46,000 may be available. You can use the current $36,000 basic entitlement even if your original entitlement after World War II was only $4,000.

If you used your loan guaranty once and then sold your home and repaid the lender, your loan entitlement should have been restored.

IF YOUR HOME IS IN DANGER OF REPOSSESSION

If you are late in making your mortgage payments, get help. Some veterans' service organizations offer cash assistance. Some social services agencies offer cash assistance. Even if they don't offer cash, they may be able to talk to your lender and the VA to arrange for help. Contact the nearest legal aid or legal services office for help. As depressed and hopeless as you may feel, try not to lose the house. The VA doesn't like it and has a long memory of such situations.

Help is supposed to be available from both the lender and the VA. As a practical matter, the VA does very little and instead relies on the lender to provide servicing. Even if the VA does little to help you, you must contact the Loan Guaranty Service at the VA regional office. Ask by phone and in writing for help. Having made such an effort may help you later, if the VA begins debt collection proceedings.

You are not alone in needing help. Each year, foreclosures occur on thousands of veterans' homes. The VA has sustained enormous losses recently from veterans who could not keep up their payments. The VA then pays off hundreds of millions of dollars to the lenders. The primary reasons for foreclosure are (1) extensive obligations, (2) curtailment of income, (3) marital difficulties, and (4) illness.

The "official" default and foreclosure process goes something like this (though the VA often is not as helpful as this outline may imply):

1. A default occurs.
2. If the default is not remedied, the lender reports to the VA within 105 days after the initial default.
3. The VA sends a supplemental servicing letter with advice on how to reinstate the loan.
4. The lender notifies the VA of its intent to foreclose after the loan has been in default for 90 days.
5. The VA has 15 days in which to respond to the lender's notice of foreclosure. If the VA does not respond within 30 days, the lender can terminate the loan.
6. The VA considers alternatives to foreclosure if the default cannot be remedied (for example, compromise agreement, voluntary conveyance, or refunding).
7. The lender initiates foreclosure either through a court proceeding or a nonjudicial proceeding, which may take from a few months to a year to complete.
8. The VA may pursue alternatives to foreclosure during this period, including paying the lender the guaranty amount and leaving the property with the lender or paying the lender the entire amount you owe.
9. At the foreclosure sale, the lender may bid the net value of the prop-

erty. Sometimes third-party bidding is permitted. If the lender acquires the property at the sale, it usually then conveys its purchase to the VA, which then attempts to resell it. In 1990, the VA had more than 16,000 properties to resell.

★ NOTE ★

If you are in the market for a home, you might consider purchasing one that the VA must resell. Ask a real estate agent about these or call the VA regional office loan guaranty service.

Help from the Lender

The lender should take a number of steps when you are behind in your payments. These steps, or servicing, are intended to make sure that the lender has no alternative but to foreclose. As soon as you are late in making a payment, the lender must notify the VA of your delinquency. The lender is also obligated to accept a partial payment from you in certain circumstances. For example, if you offer at least one-half of the amount due, the lender must accept it. However, there are a number of ways in which the lender can get around this requirement (for example, you might offer one-half but send a personal check instead of a certified check, or the lender may already have begun foreclosure proceedings). A lender is supposed to "extend all reasonable forbearance" to you (i.e., not foreclose if it is at all possible to work something out).

Working something out, of course, requires that you sit down with the lender and talk. It requires that you answer the phone and respond to the letters that are sent to you.

Help from the VA

By law, as soon as the VA learns from the lender that you are in default, the VA "shall provide" information on alternatives to foreclosure, including methods of remedying the default or of conveying a deed in lieu of foreclosure. The VA is also obligated to tell you that counseling is available. Generally, the VA relies on the lender to tell you all this.

You should push the VA to help you. One of the little-known and little-used options is for the VA to pay off the lender; then you begin making payments directly to the VA. This is called "refunding." The advantage to you is that the VA has the flexibility to extend the terms of the loan to lower monthly payments. Unfortunately, the VA takes a narrow view of this option and seldom extends it unless it is certain that you can continue to make the payments.

Another option is a compromise agreement in which you sell the property with VA financial assistance. The VA then holds you responsible for the amount that the VA paid. Another possibility is a voluntary conveyance. You voluntarily offer the property to the VA; then the VA holds you liable for its loss, which is likely to be less than after a lengthy foreclosure proceeding.

Again, you cannot explore these options if you don't pick up the phone or sit down with the VA Loan Guaranty Service staff.

Help from State Laws

In some states, there are laws regarding how far the lender and the VA may go to collect any losses that occurred as a result of the foreclosure (for example, if the home sold at a sheriff's sale for less than its original market value). Recently there have been lawsuits in several states where the VA has pursued veterans for deficiencies, despite a state's "antideficiency" law. In some of these cases, the VA won the right to insist that veterans repay the deficiency. In other states, the veterans won. Check with a consumer law specialist in your state to see if you might have such a law available. The lead attorney in the cases challenging the VA's practice of ignoring state antideficiency laws is David Leen (Leen & Moore; 520 E. Denny; Seattle, WA 98122).

Another state law that might help you is the right of redemption. Exactly how this right operates varies from state to state. You might have the right to remain on the property after the foreclosure for a short time or the right to repay the indebtedness and reclaim the property. Again, check with a consumer law specialist in your state to find out if such a law is available to you.

Bankruptcy

If push comes to shove and you simply have no other options, sit down with a competent bankruptcy attorney. If you declare bankruptcy, you will either eliminate the problem or make it worse. You must make sure that a bankruptcy petition names not only your lender but also the U.S. Department of Veterans Affairs. Failure to do so will mean that the VA is still free to pursue you on any deficiency. Filing bankruptcy is an extreme measure.

You must get good advice on how to do it and learn the consequences to your credit standing and other aspects of your life.

DANGERS OF LETTING SOMEONE ASSUME YOUR VA LOAN

One of the biggest headaches you may have, especially if you are on active duty, is trying to sell your house quickly when you are ordered to a new duty station. Thousands of servicemembers have been burned when they sold their houses by letting others assume their mortgages. If you were one of these people, it might have sounded like a good deal at the time because it allowed you to move on quickly and to no longer worry about the payments on the old house. No doubt the real estate agent you were working with thought it was a good deal, too.

However, unless you took the proper steps to make sure that the person assuming your mortgage was approved by the VA, you will be in trouble if the purchaser defaults. If the person who assumed your mortgage defaults on his or her payments, you may never hear about it at the time, but the VA will come after you for any deficiency that arises. You will be liable for a deficiency even if the person to whom you sold the home resold it to another person and then that person defaulted.

Before March 1988, you were obligated to go to the VA for prior approval of the transfer of your house. The VA probably sent you pamphlets that informed you of this obligation. However, the warning to get prior approval was buried among a lot of information. If you saw and understood the language and went to the VA first, the VA would have taken a few months to review the creditworthiness of the person who was to assume your mortgage and the assumption contract. If the VA was satisfied, it would have released you from liability at that time. If you were selling to another veteran who was entitled to a VA loan guaranty, the VA should have restored your entitlement to future use of the VA loan guaranty.

If you didn't do what you should have done, see Chapter 2 for the steps that the VA can take to pursue you for a debt. Also, apply to the VA regional office nearest the house you sold and ask for a "retroactive release of liability." Although the VA probably never told you this, you can apply years afterward for a release of liability. If you are successful, the debt is forgiven. You should immediately hire an attorney to help you with this problem. You do not have to wait to hire an attorney until after the Board of Veterans' Appeals denies your appeal.

For loans made on or after March 1, 1988, the VA required that the mortgage papers contain a large warning about the need to get prior approval. The language to be used must say: "THIS LOAN IS NOT ASSUMABLE WITHOUT THE APPROVAL OF THE DEPARTMENT OF VETERANS AFFAIRS OR ITS AUTHORIZED AGENT." Since March 1, 1988, you must go through the release of liability procedure before the sale, or else the lender can demand immediate and full payment from you when the lender discovers what you've done. If you didn't go through the process in advance and the lender learns about it, the lender is obligated to report your error to the VA or be liable for the damages that the VA may eventually sustain.

MOBILE HOMES

In the 1980s, the VA Inspector General uncovered a nationwide scheme by manufacturers of mobile homes to "pack" their invoices by itemizing certain add-ons that were not provided. This way, the VA would guarantee more of the price of the home than it should have. This also meant that if the mobile home was lost in foreclosure, the VA would pay off more than it should. The VA succeeded in getting settlements of several hundred thousand dollars from several manufacturers (including Fleetwood, Redman, and Guerdon). To find out whether the manufacturer of the mobile home you lost in foreclosure was one of those from which the VA collected money, write to the VA Inspector General (Assistant IG for Policy; Planning & Resources (53B); U.S. Department of Veterans Affairs; 810 Vermont Ave., N.W.; Washington, DC 20420). It is not clear, however, whether any of that money was credited to the debts that might have been established against the veteran. If the VA is pursuing you on a mobile home loan debt, ask the IG to determine whether the VA already collected from the manufacturer.

CHAPTER EIGHT

BURIAL AND
LIFE INSURANCE

★ ★

This chapter tells you about the two VA programs that are in a sense related: burial and insurance (in that order). The VA maintains 114 national cemeteries in 38 states and Puerto Rico. Of these cemeteries, 53 are full. In fiscal year 1992, 64,602 veterans and survivors of veterans were buried. Another 315,888 applications for headstones or markers were received from families of veterans who were buried in private cemeteries.

The VA's life insurance program is extensive: In 1992, the VA was covering 6.6 million veterans for more than $76 billion. The program is really a series of eight programs—some that the VA administers, others that it supervises. The programs supervised by the VA are actually handled by Prudential Insurance Company and the Bankers Life Insurance Company of Nebraska.

Note: This chapter does not cover the wide variety of insurance policies offered on late-night television. Even the programs that refer to themselves as "veterans life insurance" are not related to the VA. Ask your local insurance agent or your state's insurance commissioner about the value of such policies and about whether you can get a better deal by purchasing insurance from another company.

BURIAL BENEFITS

VA burial benefits include the opportunity to be buried in a VA national cemetery, to obtain a headstone or a marker, to be reimbursed for burial expenses, to receive a memorial certificate and a flag, and to get a cash payment. Many states also maintain veterans' cemeteries. For families of

---
★ IMPORTANT ★

If you are the surviving spouse of a recently deceased veteran, and you are considering applying for a VA death pension, do not do so until you have read Chapter 10. Acceptance of VA life insurance benefits may jeopardize your eligibility for obtaining the pension. On the other hand, paying the expenses for your spouse's last illness and death before you begin receiving a VA pension may reduce the pension payment you might otherwise receive. See Chapter 10 on that issue as well.

---

veterans who died on or after Nov. 1, 1990, the VA no longer offers an allowance in lieu of the government-provided headstone or marker. Nevertheless, this allowance may still be available even if you never applied before in the case of a death prior to that date.

As a practical matter, funeral directors will help you fill out applications for these benefits and may file the claims for you. Be sure to take a copy of the veteran's DD 214, Report of Separation, to the funeral home.

BURIAL IN A NATIONAL CEMETERY

Burial in a VA national cemetery includes the gravesite, opening and closing of the grave, and continuing maintenance. Some of the national cemeteries offer columbaria (a structure of vaults lined with recesses for urns) for inurnment of cremated remains or burial of remains. There is no expense to you for a headstone or a marker. Approximately 10 percent of families whose veteran member is eligible for burial in a national cemetery take advantage of the opportunity. The biggest drawback about this benefit has been that you cannot specify the cemetery in which you want to be buried, and many families do not want their loved ones buried hundreds of miles away. The VA is aware of this problem and is trying to expand the space available in certain urban centers. A list of all VA cemeteries is included in Appendix B.

Who Can Be Buried in a National Cemetery?

You are eligible for burial in a national cemetery if any one of the following applies:

★   You serve on active duty and are discharged under other than dishonorable conditions.

★ You die on active duty.
★ You are in the reserves, or the Army or Air National Guard, and you die while hospitalized or undergoing treatment at government expense, or you die as a result of an injury or a disease contracted while on active duty for training or inactive duty training.
★ You are a member of the Army, Navy or Air Force ROTC and you die while traveling to or attending an authorized training camp or practice cruise, or you die while hospitalized or under treatment at government expense for an injury or a disease incurred at the camp or traveling to the camp.
★ You serve during war with an allied force and you are a U.S. citizen when you die.
★ You are the surviving spouse of any of the above members and have not remarried.
★ You are a veteran's minor child.

The VA has the flexibility to designate other categories of persons to be eligible for burial. Call the director at the nearest national cemetery to find out if it has.

If you need to discuss burial arrangements during regular business hours, call the cemetery that you are interested in. During a weekend or on a holiday, arrangements for any national cemetery burial can be made through one of the following cemeteries that offers extended hours: Calverton in Calverton (Long Island), New York; Jefferson Barracks in St. Louis, Missouri; or Riverside in Riverside, California. Nevertheless, burials themselves are not offered on weekends unless you make an "extraordinary request." For example, if your religious beliefs dictate a burial within 24 hours, the burial can usually be arranged even during a weekend.

Although perhaps the best known, the Arlington National Cemetery is not a VA cemetery. It is operated by the Department of the Army, has its own rules on eligibility for burial, and is quite exclusive. Write the Superintendent, Arlington National Cemetery, Arlington, VA 22211, or call (703) 695-3250 if you want to pursue burial in that cemetery.

Headstones, Markers, Grave Liners

Monuments available for placement in national cemeteries include flat ones made from bronze, granite, or marble or upright ones made of marble. Niche markers are also available. Replacement monuments are also provided at government expense when the original becomes illegible or there is a mistake in the inscription. It takes about 2 weeks for the VA to process a request and for a monument to be received. An order for a monument should be made on the date of burial at a national cemetery or by submitting a VA Form 40-1330 to obtain a marker in a private cemetery.

A headstone or a marker will be placed in a national cemetery to memorialize a veteran whose remains are not available for burial either because the remains were not recovered or because they were buried at sea, cremated, or donated to science. To request a marker or headstone, call (800) 697-6947.

When a casket is used to bury remains, a grave liner is required.

Almost anyone eligible to be buried in a national cemetery but who was not, and almost anyone who was buried in a national cemetery or a post cemetery is eligible to have his or her grave marked. The VA does not provide headstones for family members or for U.S. citizens who fought with allied forces.

Cash Allowance Instead of Government Marker

For deaths before Nov. 1, 1990, if you chose not to get an official government headstone or marker, you could ask for cash instead. The cash equaled the government's cost to make a marker. In 1994, the amount was $98. Basically, you could use the allowance to defray the cost of the headstone that you bought for the veteran, which no doubt cost more than $98. For deaths after Nov. 1, 1990, however, this allowance is not available.

There used to be a two-year deadline to apply for the allowance. However, the VA's General Counsel ruled that the deadline was illegal, so currently there is no deadline to apply for the allowance.

If you never applied for this allowance or applied and were turned down as having applied too late, it may still be available to you. Apply by calling or writing the nearest VA regional office and asking for an application for the "monetary allowance in lieu of a Government-furnished headstone or marker." According to a confusing VA regulation, to be eligible for the allowance, the veteran must

★ have been eligible to be buried in a national cemetery but was not, or
★ died under circumstances precluding the recovery of the body (including burial at sea), and
★ have been buried on or after Oct. 18, 1978, and died before Nov. 1, 1990.

Also, the headstone that was purchased must either mark the grave or memorialize the veteran, or the veteran's identifying information must be added to an existing headstone or marker (38 C.F.R. 3.1612).

Reimbursement of Burial Expenses

Four different payments are available to defray the cost of burials: One payment is for deaths that are not service connected ($300), and one is for deaths that are service connected ($1,500). In addition, reimbursement for the cost of transporting the body to a national cemetery in the case of a service-connected death is available. Also, a plot allowance is available for certain deaths.

SERVICE-CONNECTED DEATH

The VA should agree that a service-connected disability led to death "when the evidence establishes that such disability was either the principal or a contributory cause of death" (38 C.F.R. 3.312). For example, even if the immediate cause of death was not heart disease but the veteran was service connected for a heart problem, it may be possible to convince the VA that the cause of death was service connected.

★ DEADLINE ★

There is no deadline. Until 1989, VA rules said that there was a 2-year deadline. According to the VA's General Counsel, those rules were unlawful. If you never applied for this benefit or were denied because your claim was too late, file now.

NONSERVICE-CONNECTED DEATH

The $300 nonservice-connected death burial allowance is available if, at the time of death, the veteran was receiving VA pension or compensation or had a claim pending. For compensation and pension claims pending at the date of death, the evidence on file has to be sufficient to make an initial award of benefits. If the pending claim is a reopened one, the VA can ask for additional information to support the claim. The $300 allowance is also available to pay for burials of veterans who have no next of kin (38 C.F.R. 3.1600).

The $300 payment is also available if the veteran with a nonservice-connected disability died in a VA hospital, a nursing home (either a VA home or one paid for by the VA), or a domiciliary.

PLOT ALLOWANCE

A plot allowance of $150 is available if a veteran was discharged from active duty because of a disability, died while receiving a pension or compensation, or died while in a VA facility. This allowance is available as long as the veteran is not buried in a national cemetery (either a VA or other U.S. government cemetery). This allowance is not available if the cause of death was service connected. If this is the case, refer to the previous discussion on service-connected death.

★ DEADLINE ★

A claim for reimbursement of the plot allowance or nonservice-connected burial allowance must be filed within 2 years from the date of burial.

TRANSPORTATION EXPENSES TO A NATIONAL CEMETERY

For certain veterans, the VA will pay for the cost of transportation to the nearest national cemetery that has space available. Given the limited number of open cemeteries and the distance to them, the cost of transporting remains can be prohibitive without this reimbursement. The items covered include shipping, permits, shipping case, cost of sealing the case, and two pickups by hearse (38 C.F.R. 3.1606).

★ DEADLINE ★

There is no deadline to apply for reimbursement of transportation expenses. Until 1989, VA rules said that there was a 2-year deadline. According to the VA's General Counsel, those rules were unlawful. If you never applied for this benefit or were denied because your claim was too late, file now.

Presidential Memorial Certificates and Flags

This certificate bears the signature of the President and an inscription expressing recognition for the veteran's service. It is issued to the next of kin, a relative, or a friend. There is no deadline to request the certificate from any VA regional office. Certificates are usually provided within one week.

An American flag used to drape the casket of a veteran can be obtained through any VA regional office, national cemetery, or most post offices. The VA also issues flags to the family of servicemembers missing in action and presumed dead.

LIFE INSURANCE

Life insurance for veterans had its origins in war risk insurance for ships that began just before World War I. After war was declared in 1917, commercial insurance companies began either to exclude payments for any death resulting from wartime military service or to charge prohibitively excessive rates. Ever since, various policies have been offered to cover veterans.

Given the complexity of the various policies, it is fortunate for you that the VA offers a convenient, single point of contact: (800) 669-8477. Use this number to report address changes, to confirm whether dividends are due to be paid to you, or to confirm when you are expected to pay premiums to the VA. Your survivor can also use the number to file a claim

---

★ WARNING ★

Traditionally there has been much litigation involving insurance matters. In the past, the $10 limit on attorney's fees did not apply to insurance cases. There was a 10 percent limit based on the amount of money recovered. You were free to contest the matter in the U.S. district court closest to you (38 U.S.C. 1984). With the creation of the U.S. Court of Veterans Appeals in 1988, this arrangement has become more complicated.

Now, if you appeal an insurance matter to the Board of Veterans' Appeals, the only court you appeal to after that is the U.S. Court of Veterans Appeals (*Young v. Derwinski*, No. 90-53 [Oct. 25, 1990]). You are still free to appeal to the nearest federal district court as long as you do so *before* appealing to the Board of Veterans' Appeals. Be careful about the deadline for appealing to the BVA. It is not likely that your district court case will end in time for you to file an appeal with the BVA. It is unclear whether the VA would grant an extension of the BVA filing deadline.

See Chapter 3 for details on calculating the deadline. You may discover that you are arguing with a former spouse whose name was mistakenly left on the insurance policy as the beneficiary. If you are the current spouse, insist on seeing the formal change of beneficiary notice that was filed with the VA.

Consult with an attorney to learn the advantages and disadvantages of federal district court versus Court of Veterans Appeals.

---

when you die. Do your spouse a favor now: Look up your insurance policy number and write it on the page provided at the back of this book. Then tell your spouse that if you die, she or he should refer to this book. Also tell your spouse where you keep all your old VA papers. In addition, if you remarried and did not change the name of the beneficiary on your policy, do so now. Otherwise, your current spouse will not receive benefits.

We will not give you all the details about insurance policies and whether you can convert your current term plan to one of eight different permanent plans or, if you can, which of the plans is best for you. Pamphlets addressing the various policies are available through any VA regional office. Sit down with a local life insurance agent to discuss your needs. We assume that you have a policy that began automatically while you were on active duty.

We will tell you briefly about the plans that are currently open for new enrollments and about five matters that should be of particular interest: (1) how to borrow against your policy or cash it in, (2) how to get paid cash each month if you become disabled, (3) who gets dividends, (4) how to avoid the infamous insurance dividend hoax, and (5) what your spouse needs to know about your policy.

Available Insurance

Life insurance programs available to veterans and servicemembers, the policy prefix letter, and beginning and ending dates follow:

Service-Disabled Veterans Insurance
This policy is available to you if you are suffering from a service-connected disability but are otherwise insurable. You may select any person, firm, or corporation as your beneficiary and arrange for settlement options of a lump sum, installments with interest, a monthly life income with 120 payments guaranteed, or a refund life income. Premiums are waived if you become totally disabled for 6 months or more before you reach age 65.

Servicemen's Group Life Insurance
This policy provides as much as $100,000 of life insurance coverage for servicemembers on active duty. Active-duty personnel are covered full-time; reserves are covered part-time. Coverage is automatic upon entry on active duty. If you don't want this coverage, you have to specifically elect not to be covered. Short of canceling coverage, you can reduce your

---

★ INSURANCE ★

U.S. Government Life Insurance (USGLI) K Jan. 1, 1919, to April 24, 1951

National Service Life Insurance (NSLI) V Oct. 8, 1940, to April 24, 1951

National Service Life Insurance (NSLI) H Aug. 1, 1946, to Dec. 31, 1949

Veterans Special Life Insurance (VSLI) RS and W April 25, 1951, to Dec. 31, 1956

Service-Disabled Veterans Insurance (S-DVI) RH April 25, 1951, to present

Veterans Reopened Insurance (VRI) J, JR, JS May 1, 1965, to May 2, 1966

Veterans Mortgage Life Insurance (VMLI) Aug. 11, 1971, to present

Servicemen's Group Life Insurance (SGLI) Sept. 29, 1965, to present

Veterans' Group Life Insurance (VGLI) Aug. 1, 1974, to present

---

★ DEADLINE ★

You must apply for Service-Disabled Veterans Insurance within 1 year of becoming service-connected disabled.

---

coverage. Proceeds of this policy can be paid either in a lump sum or over a 36-month period. You may select any beneficiary you want.

Veterans' Group Life Insurance

This program is actually a post-discharge insurance that converts the Servicemen's Group Life Insurance to a 5-year term policy. At the end of that term, you have the right to convert the policy to one of about 300 commercially available life insurance policies. You have the right to convert to a commercial policy at standard premium rates, regardless of your health status. To apply for coverage, you must submit an application and a premium payment within 120 days after discharge. The amount of the premium varies depending on the amount of the coverage and your age. Call the VA toll-free number above to obtain an application and to find out the amount of the premium. The annual premium varies from about $6 per year to about $40. Send the application to the following address: Office of Servicemen's Group Life Insurance; 213 Washington Street; Newark, NJ 07102.

Veterans Mortgage Life Insurance

This policy is restricted to disabled veterans who have received grants to purchase specially adapted housing and is intended to pay off your mortgage company at your death. The monthly premium can be deducted from your compensation payments.

How to Borrow Against Your Policy or Cash It In

As long as the VA's records show no evidence of incompetency and your policy has been in effect for at least 1 year, you can take out a loan for as much as 94 percent of the cash surrender value of any permanent plan. The loan value is determined based on the length of time the policy is in effect, which plan is involved, and your age at the time it was issued. NSLI policy loans are charged interest at an adjustable rate that changes each October. Interest rates on USGLI policy loans do not change.

To obtain a loan, call the toll free number, (800) 669-8477, and ask for an application, VA Form 29-1546, and the amount of coverage available to you. You can also submit an informal application to the nearest VA regional office. Simply state in a letter that "This is an application for a loan of $_____ on policy number _____. Please send the check to the following address: _____." Be sure to sign the letter. You can also surrender your policy and request its cash value. You can obtain a lump sum or installment payments. Before surrendering your policy, confirm that it has a cash value. Note that term policies do not. You can use VA Form 29-1546 (available by calling the nearest VA office) or file an informal application.

How to Get Paid Cash Each Month If You Become Disabled

If you now have an NSLI policy (not the RH, or JR, or JS policies), you may be able to add a Total Disability Income Provision (TDIP) to your policy. If you do, you will pay an additional premium. Since Jan. 1, 1965,

---

★ IMPORTANT ★

Policies surrendered for cash are not eligible for reinstatement.

a provision to permit payment of $10 per month per $1,000 of insurance has been available.

To add this provision to your policy, you must not yet be 55 years old and you must be in good health. The "$10 Age 65 Provision" begins to pay after 6 months of continuous disability. Total disability is defined under VA rules as "any impairment of mind or body which continuously renders it impossible for the insured to follow any substantially gainful occupation" (38 C.F.R. 8.43). This includes permanent loss of use of both feet, of both hands, of both eyes, of one foot and one hand, of one foot and one eye, the total loss of hearing in both ears, or the loss of speech.

Who Gets Dividends

Regular dividend payments began in 1952 on participating V policies. Now, dividends are paid to holders of V, K, RS, W, J, JR, and JS insurance. A dividend can be paid to you by check, can be credited to you to pay future premiums and gain interest, can remain on deposit and earn interest, can be used to pay premiums in advance, can be used to pay on a loan, or can be used to buy paid-up insurance. The VA pays more than $1 billion in dividends each year. Some 2.2 million World War II veterans with the NSLI V policy will receive an average payment of $389. Korean War veterans with the VSLI RS and W policies will receive an average of $394. Veterans Reopened Insurance policyholders will receive $290 (for the J), or $521 (for the JR), or $531 (for the JS).

Infamous Insurance Dividend Hoax

Periodically, dog-eared photocopies of what alleges to be documentation of a dream-come-true opportunity for a special dividend sweep the country and flood the VA Insurance Center in Philadelphia. This hoax apparently began after the 1948 Special Dividend that was announced in 1949. Annual reruns of the original publicity surrounding the special dividend started appearing in the mid-1960s. It is not true that there is a dividend payment still awaiting you from a policy in effect in 1948.

The only dividends that the VA is currently paying are the regular dividends paid on policies currently in effect. These dividends are paid automatically, with no application necessary. If you see what looks like a too-good-to-be-true opportunity to apply for a special dividend, pass it up. Don't waste your money photocopying the phony application for all your friends.

What to Tell Your Spouse About Your Insurance Policy

If you have a VA insurance policy, write the policy number on the page provided at the back of this book. Get a copy of your insurance file and make sure that the intended beneficiary is officially listed as the beneficiary at the correct VA office. If you failed to change the beneficiary or if the VA lost the change you sent it, the right person will not get the proceeds.

There are two VA offices that handle insurance matters. For states east of the Mississippi River, contact this office: Regional Office and Insurance Center; P.O. Box 8079; Philadelphia, PA 19101.

For Minnesota, Wisconsin, Illinois, Indiana, Mississippi, and states west of the Mississippi River, contact this office: Regional Office and Insurance Center; Bishop Henry Whipple Bldg.; Fort Snelling; St. Paul, MN 55111.

Tell your spouse to be prepared to send the appropriate office a marriage certificate and a death certificate as well as children's birth certificates. If the VA insurance file number is not known, your spouse should submit the VA claim number, your social security number, your military service number, dates of service, and the branch of service. Also tell your spouse to call the toll-free insurance number: (800) 669-8477.

CHAPTER NINE

MEDICAL SERVICES

★ ★

This chapter tells you, the veteran, about some of the health care services that *might* be available in your area. What you find when you go to your nearest VA facility may be much different than what we discuss here. To locate the nearest VA medical facility, see Appendix B at the end of this book. There are 171 VA medical centers, 128 VA nursing homes, 35 domiciliaries, 191 clinics, and 200 vet centers scattered across the country.

In 1992, the VA employed more than 204,000 people who treated more than one million patients in VA hospitals and 23.9 million outpatients, at a cost of almost $13.6 billion. Half of the health care treatment was provided to veterans aged 65 and older.

Many VA hospitals are affiliated with medical schools, thus many medical students are used in the VA system. These students are supposed to be supervised by fully licensed doctors.

Exactly who is eligible for VA health care has changed drastically during the last few years and is likely to change more. Also, regardless of whether you are eligible for care, there is no guarantee that you will get the treatment you need when you need it.

Just like national health care, VA medical care needs reform. It is inefficient and bureaucratic. Periodically, the quality of care that is provided is questioned by veterans and surviving family members, by the media, and by Congress. The VA system is under enormous pressure to handle an increasing number of older veterans. At the same time, VA facilities in rural areas are not operating anywhere near their capacity. In 1992, then–VA Secretary Derwinski proposed providing care to indigent nonveterans in some of these rural hospitals. His proposal contributed to his departure from the VA. Nevertheless, you can expect to hear about other proposals for changes, including making the VA competitive with private facilities.

This chapter describes the basic rules for getting health care and lists many of the kinds of care that are offered. These rules may change dramatically if a national health care plan is enacted.

ELIGIBILITY FOR VA HEALTH CARE

VA health care may be especially important for you if you have no health insurance. Although almost every veteran is potentially eligible to receive treatment in a VA hospital, an elaborate system of priorities determines who receives treatment first. There are basically two kinds of eligibility: (1) mandatory and (2) discretionary. Regardless of your eligibility for VA health care, the VA must first agree that you need the care. Also, just because you are eligible for hospital care does not mean that there is a bed available. Eligibility for hospital care does not mean that you are also eligible for nursing home care or outpatient treatment, or other services.

Mandatory Care

The law says that the VA "*shall* furnish hospital care, and *may* furnish nursing home care" (emphasis added) to certain veterans. Basically, if you already have a service-connected disability, you are to be treated for virtually any other disability you might have. If your disability is not service connected, but you have limited income, you *shall* be treated.

★ CAUTION ★

VA medical care is often inferior to private care. If you cannot afford private care and you qualify for VA care, you have little choice but to take your chances with the VA system. If, however, you can afford private care and you have a medical problem that requires the best possible care, you should either simply seek private care or carefully investigate whether the VA care available to you will be as good as, or even better than, private care. (For instance, the VA medical center in your area may be unusually good in general or may specialize in the kind of problem you have.)

```
┌──────────── ★ FURTHER CAUTION ★ ────────────┐
│ Whenever possible, call the hospital first for an appointment or to │
│ find out the procedures at the facility you will be visiting. You can │
│ expect to fill out forms asking for lots of financial information. │
│ You can also expect to wait, and wait, and wait. Check with a │
│ veterans' service organization volunteer at the facility for details │
│ on what to expect. Ask the volunteer if some days or times of day │
│ are less busy than others. │
└────────────────────────────────────────────┘
```

```
┌──────────────── ★ WARNING ★ ────────────────┐
│ If you are denied care because the VA does not consider your │
│ disability to be service-connected, review Chapter 3 to see if you │
│ can make a case that your condition is related to your service. │
└────────────────────────────────────────────┘
```

Officially, the VA *shall* treat you for any disability you have (regardless of whether it is service connected) if you are a veteran who

★ was discharged from service for a disability,
★ is receiving (or entitled to receive) disability compensation,
★ has a service-connected disability rated at 50 percent or more,
★ has a service-connected disability,
★ is a former POW,
★ served in the Mexican border period or World War I, or
★ is unable to defray the expenses of necessary care.

If you fit into the first category, you have the highest priority for admission and so forth down the list.

In addition, the VA *shall* treat a service-connected disability of any veteran. If you were exposed to Agent Orange in Vietnam or radiation at one of the nuclear test sites or in Japan, you *shall* be treated for any disability even though you cannot prove that the disability resulted from your exposure. On the other hand, if the VA can prove that your disability resulted from something besides your exposure to Agent Orange or radiation, it can deny you care. Even if the VA denies you care because it says there is another reason for your problem, it may treat you if you meet any of the other criteria.

Inability to Defray Expenses of Necessary Care

The law says that you are eligible for free VA care when you are unable to defray expenses of necessary care. You are unable to defray expenses if any of the following is true:

★ You are eligible for Medicaid.

★ You are receiving a nonservice-connected pension (see Chapter 5).

★ Your income is not greater than a certain amount (explained next), which varies each year, and your assets are below a certain level.

The income limit increases each year by the same percentage that the cost of living allowance increases (about 4 percent). Also, not all the money you might get each year counts as far as the VA is concerned in calculating your income. For example, supplemental security income (SSI) checks do not count. All the rules about counting money that are described in Chapter 5 for the VA pension are used to calculate eligibility for medical care.

As of 1993, a single veteran with countable income of less than $19,912 and a veteran with one spouse with income of less than $23,898 were considered eligible for free VA care. If you own two homes, the VA may say that you have too many assets, and it may refuse to provide free care. This is not usually the reason the VA denies medical services.

Discretionary Care

Anyone not covered under the mandatory care section is covered here. You may still be treated by the VA, but you have to pay for the services. For example, for up to 90 days of inpatient care, you have to pay either the cost of the care or an amount equal to the Medicare deductible. If you need a longer period of care, you have to pay one-half the Medicare deductible for each additional 90-day period of care. In 1993, the Medicare deductible was $696.

★ WARNING ★

If the VA turns you down because you have too much income or too many assets, get the refusal in writing. Don't take a verbal no from an admissions clerk. Whether you can get the denial in writing or not, you have a right to appeal. To start your appeal, file a notice of disagreement with the Medical Administrative Service at that VA facility and with the nearest VA regional office. Chapter 3 describes the appeal process.

KINDS OF MEDICAL SERVICES AVAILABLE

Hospitals

VA hospitals provide a variety of services, but they don't all offer the same services. Certain surgical procedures are not performed at every facility. Some facilities do no surgery and devote most of their beds to handling patients with psychiatric conditions. Some facilities (such as those in San Francisco, West Los Angeles, Miami and New York) offer special care for veterans with AIDS. Still, start with the nearest VA facility. If you need care that the local facility cannot provide, it should steer you to the nearest VA facility that can (or in some cases a Defense Department facility).

After you are in a VA hospital, the VA may decide that you have received the care needed and that no more treatment would be useful, and therefore decide to discharge you to a private nursing home. Before the VA can do so, the VA must give 1 week's notice to you or your family. If you or your family object, the VA is required to give you 2 weeks to submit medical information to contest the discharge plan.

Outpatient Clinics

Most outpatient clinics are located in a VA medical center, although some satellite clinics are separate from the main center. The VA *shall* treat you on an outpatient basis if you need treatment for any of the following:

★ your service-connected disability
★ any disability if you have a service-connected disability rated at least at 50 percent
★ a disability caused by the VA through its malpractice (malpractice in the legal sense, as determined by VA claim or under lawsuit under the Federal Tort Claims Act)

Medical services necessary either to prepare for a period of hospitalization or to avoid hospitalization *shall* be provided if either of the following is the case:

★ You have a service-connected disability rated at 30 or 40 percent.
★ You are eligible for mandatory care and do not have more income than the rate paid to a veteran on the VA Improved Pension who

is entitled to the aid and attendance allowance (A&A). As of December 1, 1993, this meant $12,504.

Medical services *may* be provided free of charge if you are a former POW, or a veteran of the Mexican border period or World War I, or if you are receiving an A&A allowance or the housebound allowance with either a VA pension or compensation. If you do not fit into one of these groups, you may still be treated in an outpatient clinic, but you will have to pay for a portion of the cost of the service.

Nursing Homes

Nursing home care is a service that the VA *may* provide. The law does not require the VA to provide nursing home care. The priority for admission to a nursing home is the same as the priority in the list found in the mandatory care section and usually follows a period of care in a VA hospital. Nursing home care may mean care in a VA facility or in a private community facility.

If the nursing home care is needed for a service-connected disability, the VA will pay for it indefinitely. If the care is needed for a nonservice-connected disability, the VA will pay for care in a community facility for 6 months following a period of VA hospitalization. The VA may pay for a 45-day extension if you need more time to arrange for Medicaid to pick up the cost. You may get a longer extension if you are terminally ill and not expected to live more than 6 months.

As soon as you learn that you may be transferred to a community nursing home, work with the VA's social workers and try to be admitted to the facility of your choice. Because the rate the VA pays for the 6-month period is higher than the Medicaid rate, most nursing homes should not be reluctant to accept you as a patient. You should, however, find out about the reputation of the nursing home. Call the nearest legal aid office or county elder affairs office and talk to its staff who work with nursing home issues and ask their opinion about the quality of care at the facility. You should also check with the state office that licenses the facility to make sure that it is not about to lose its license.

Alternatives to Nursing Home Care

The VA offers several alternatives to traditional nursing homes. For example, certain VA facilities offer adult day health care either in the VA medical center or through a contract with a community health care center. This is available if you are rated at least 50 percent for a service-connected disability.

Hospital-based home care is offered by almost half of all VA medical centers. This care involves visits from VA staff to homebound veterans (for example, those with Alzheimer's disease). In-home hospice care for veterans who are terminally ill is also offered by some VA centers. If your spouse is caring for you at home but needs a break, some VA facilities offer short stays for respite care. VA employees also visit community residential care homes to provide care. These homes must meet certain minimal standards.

VA domiciliaries are facilities that provide limited rehabilitation services and minimal health care services. You may be admitted to a domiciliary if you have an annual income that is less than the VA pension plus the A&A rate (or less than about $12,000 per year). You have to be able to feed yourself and to brush your teeth.

Alcohol and Drug Dependence Treatment

Most VA facilities offer specialized treatment for drug or alcohol abuse problems. The VA treats about four times as many veterans for alcohol problems as it does drug abuse problems. Treatment usually begins with an inpatient stay, followed by outpatient visits. The VA also offers treatment through community facilities and through halfway houses.

Readjustment Counseling

The VA offers a network of almost 200 community-based vet centers that provide individual and group counseling and limited family counseling to Vietnam, Panama, Grenada, and Persian Gulf veterans who cannot readjust to civilian life. The program began in response to the unmet needs of Vietnam veterans suffering from post-traumatic stress disorder (PTSD). Instead of requiring veterans to make their way through a maze of red tape to get help and losing most along the way, vet centers are designed to minimize the bureaucratic hassles and to offer their services at convenient locations. Most vet center staff are also veterans. For the nearest vet center, see the list in Appendix B at the end of this book. Vet center staff can also help arrange for inpatient treatment of PTSD at selected VA medical centers.

Dental Care

Outpatient dental treatment and appliances are available but only for a dental condition or disability that meets one of the following requirements:

★ is service connected and rated at least 10 percent
★ is service connected and due to combat wounds or in-service trauma
★ is aggravating some other service-connected disability for which you began to get treatment while in a VA hospital and which needs to be completed
★ is a condition or disability of a veteran who is rated totally disabled from a service-connected disability
★ requires treatment to prepare for hospital admission
★ is needed by a former POW

Dental treatment is also available if your dental condition is service connected but rated at 0 percent—if it existed when you were discharged and you apply within 90 days of your discharge. If your Report of Separation, DD 214, says that you received proper dental care within 90 days before discharge, the VA won't provide it.

Prosthetics

Wheelchairs, artificial limbs, trusses and similar appliances, and special clothing required because of prosthetic appliances are considered medical services and are offered to veterans receiving VA hospital care. These services are also offered to veterans eligible for outpatient care. If you need a prosthetic appliance, you must be fitted for it and trained to use the device. Guide dogs fall under this category of services, too. Replacement or repair of prosthetics is also available although there may be a considerable delay in scheduling the repairs. If the prosthetic appliance causes extra wear and tear on your clothes, you may be entitled to an annual clothing allowance. In 1993, that allowance was $452.

Medication

VA pharmacies used to fill prescriptions for whatever drug a VA doctor prescribed. This can mean drugs such as aspirin that are available over the counter, AZT, or narcotics and other controlled substances that require prescriptions. Recently, there have been reports of pharmacies dropping certain drugs due to budget cuts.

Almost all VA pharmacies offer to fill or refill prescriptions through the mail. During the next few years, the VA will consolidate its mail-order service so that your medical center may not be the location that fills your prescription. However, each center will retain a pharmacy that fills prescriptions in person, if you have the time to wait.

In late 1990, the VA began charging $2.00 per 30-day supply of drugs supplied. Some, but not all, VA pharmacies offer 90-day quantities. Unless the drugs you need are narcotics or other controlled substances, you should request a 90-day supply so that you won't have to have three prescriptions filled.

Special Physical Examinations: Agent Orange, Radiation, and Persian Gulf

For certain veterans, VA medical centers offer a general physical examination on request. If you served in Vietnam, were at an atomic bomb test site, or served in the Persian Gulf, the VA will conduct an Agent Orange, atomic radiation, or Persian Gulf exam. These examinations are not designed to measure residual levels of Agent Orange or other toxic substances or radiation-related damage. Having one of these exams is not the equivalent of applying for service-connected benefits. If you want to file a claim for compensation, see Chapter 4.

However, the examinations are thorough and are an opportunity to get a good checkup free of charge. Also, your name will be kept in either the Agent Orange, Radiation, or Persian Gulf Registry so that you can be contacted if the VA decides that additional services or information should be offered to you.

Women Veterans' Examinations

If you are a woman veteran, you do not have access to health care equal to that of men. Only 60 percent of VA facilities have women's clinics offering gynecologic care and preventive health and counseling services. Thorough physical examinations, including cancer screening, of women inpatients is sporadic. Only 19 VA medical centers have mammography programs and, as revealed in press accounts in 1992, the machines are not properly monitored.

Cancer screening is especially critical for women veterans, who have an unusually high incidence of cancer—almost twice the rate of nonveteran women. If you are in a VA facility undergoing an examination and you did not have a Pap smear, a breast or pelvic exam, or a mammogram in the past 6 months, insist that the tests be done.

YOUR RIGHTS AS A PATIENT

Whether you are a patient at a VA hospital, nursing home, or domiciliary, you have rights (38 C.F.R. 17.34 and 17.34[a]). And you must be given a copy of these rights when you are admitted. These rights do not cover every situation, and sometimes the VA may say that giving you a copy of your rights is medically contraindicated. Your rights include these:

★ the right to consent or withhold your consent to a procedure after being fully informed about it
★ the right to be treated with dignity and with respect for your privacy
★ the right to receive prompt treatment free from excessive medication or restraints
★ the right to have visitors and to use a telephone in private and to receive unopened mail
★ the right to wear your own clothes
★ the right to exercise and go outdoors
★ the right to confidentiality of your medical records

The primary method of enforcing these rights is for you to present a grievance. See the next section for some ideas of whom to talk with.

If you are committed to a VA hospital involuntarily, your exact rights are less clear. Some state laws permit someone to have you committed for a short period of observation. Other state laws provide strict protections to ensure review of such commitments. Nevertheless, the VA does not always agree that it is required to follow state laws when they conflict with what the VA wants to do. Each state has special advocates for persons who are mentally ill (or alleged to be ill), and these advocates should be consulted with questions about involuntary commitments. Call the nearest Legal Aid office for the name of the special advocate.

What If the Quality of Care Was Poor?

Health care in VA facilities (or private ones) is not guaranteed to be perfect. You won't always get better. In fact, you may get worse or die. However, if your condition worsens as a result of the care you received in the VA facility, you can try to get money for being made worse. There are two ways to get money: first, through the VA; second, through a medical malpractice claim. If you want to pursue both, pursue them at the same time. You should also consider complaining loudly in hopes that no other veterans will be treated as you were.

Informal VA Malpractice Claim

The VA does not post signs in its medical centers telling you about either option to obtain cash. Nor does the VA have an application form for you to use. Still, you can ask for monthly compensation benefits for any injury that you suffer as a result of VA hospital or nursing home care, as a result of a VA examination, or even during VA vocational rehabilitation. This benefit was formerly called the Section 351 benefit. Since the VA renumbered all its laws in 1991, it is now called the Section 1151 benefit. This corresponds to Section 1151 of Title 38, United States Code.

You or your surviving spouse can claim the Section 1151 benefit by writing a letter to the nearest VA regional office. Include in your letter how your condition is worse now than it was before and say that you want "service-connected compensation under 38 U.S.C. 1151."

★ **DEADLINE** ★

There is no deadline to make a Section 1151 claim. Because of a decision by the U.S. Court of Veterans Appeals in November 1991 (in *Gardner* v. *Derwinski*, No. 90-120), the VA has put these cases on hold. An appeal is pending at the U.S. Court of Appeals for the Federal Circuit. Depending on the results of this appeal, the VA may write new regulations for processing these claims.

Formal Malpractice Claim

Apart from the VA informal process, you should consider whether the injury you suffered at the hands of a VA physician might warrant a potentially larger payment from the government under the Federal Tort Claims Act. With this formal process, you must file a claim (use Standard Form 95, which you can obtain from any federal courthouse and which is reproduced in Appendix A) with the VA regional office within 2 years of the date of the injury. You or your surviving family must claim that you were hurt as a result of VA medical malpractice. Strict deadlines must be met under this process. Work with a lawyer who specializes in medical malpractice claims. If the VA does not agree to pay the amount you claimed on your form, you can appeal to the federal district court. (Of course, the case must be large enough to interest a lawyer. The VA limits contingency fees to 20 percent in cases settled before litigation and 25 percent in cases concluded after a lawsuit is filed.)

If the VA agrees to pay you the Section 1151 benefits each month and then you are awarded money under the Federal Tort Claims Act, the VA will suspend its payments for awhile. Don't worry about this now. Because you don't know whether either claim will pay off, file both claims as soon as possible.

Informal Claims

If you don't file a claim, but you are unhappy with how you were treated, complain. Unless someone hears from you about your experience with the VA health care system, the system will not improve. You can make an anonymous call to the VA Inspector General's hotline at (800) 488-8244.

The VA also has a Medical Inspector at the Washington, DC, Central Office who will soon have assistants working out of four regional offices (in Baltimore, MD; San Francisco, CA; Jackson, MS; and Ann Arbor, MI). You can write to the Director of the VA Medical Center and to both committees in Congress that keep track of the VA's activities: the Committee on Veterans Affairs of the U.S. Senate (Washington, DC 20510) or the Committee on Veterans Affairs of the U.S. House of Representatives (Washington, DC 20515). You can also write to your own senator or representative.

If you think that the doctor who treated you should not be practicing medicine, make a complaint to the state licensing board. Also ask a veterans' service organization what it can do to help you. Also consider calling a newspaper or a television news reporter. Many radio stations offer call-in shows that you can use to air your concerns.

MEDICAL PAYMENT ISSUES AND PROBLEMS

The VA used to pay you to travel to a VA facility to get treatment. These days, in the face of increasing demands for service and tighter budgets, the VA is less likely to reimburse you for your travel expenses and more likely to demand that you pay for care before it will provide any. The VA can pay for certain treatment that you might get in an emergency at a non-VA facility. Sometimes the VA will agree in advance to pay for civilian treatment that you cannot receive at the VA. If you are receiving monthly compensation benefits and enter a hospital, your benefits may increase. On the other hand, if you are getting the extra A&A allowance each month along with the 100 percent compensation rate, that allowance may decrease upon admission to a VA hospital or a VA nursing home. Pension payments are also affected after admission to a VA nursing home or domiciliary.

Reimbursement to You for Travel to the VA

The VA will reimburse you for part of the cost of travel to the VA facility if you have a service-connected disability rated at 30 percent or more. If you have a lower rating but are going to the VA for treatment of that particular disability, the VA will reimburse you. Also, if you are receiving a VA pension (or have no more money than the VA pays in pension), the VA will reimburse you. When you are ordered to have a compensation or pension examination, the VA will reimburse you for travel expenses. There is a $3 per trip deductible and an $18 per month cap on reimbursement. These amounts are subject to change. You should claim reimbursement before you leave the facility.

If you can't afford to travel to the VA facility in the first place, call the nearest veterans' service organization and ask about any transportation services they offer. Some VSOs have volunteer drivers who provide door-to-door service.

Reimbursement to You for Care or Services in a Private Facility

Sometimes you can make prior arrangements with the VA to pay for care in a private facility or through a private doctor (38 C.F.R. 17.50[d]). This may be possible if the nearest VA facility is not easily accessible or if it does not offer the care you need. You must need treatment for a service-connected condition or a nonservice-connected disability that is aggravating a service-connected disability. This program is referred to as the "fee-basis" program.

Prior authorization is essential. If, however, an emergency arises and you must go to a non-VA facility, make sure someone calls the nearest VA facility within 72 hours. The VA may accept the call as "prior" authorization. Otherwise, you may have to pay the full cost yourself. Be sure that the date and time of the call and the name of the VA employee who speaks with you or a family member is recorded. Also make sure someone writes down the details of the conversation and sends a letter to the VA confirming what was discussed.

If no prior arrangements are made and you cannot call within 72 hours but you need emergency care, the VA may still pay the private hospital bill (38 C.F.R. 17.80). The VA limits reimbursement to veterans who don't have prior approval who have a service-connected disability.

To receive VA payment for care that was not approved in advance, you would have to get treatment for the service-connected disability or a nonservice-connected disability that was aggravating the service-connected disability. If you are rated permanently and totally service-connected disabled, you can be treated for any disability (not just the service-connected one). In addition, the care you received at the non-VA facility must have been for a medical emergency and no VA facility could have been feasibly available.

Even if you fit all these requirements, the VA will not pay for the full cost of the non-VA care. It pays only through the date that the medical emergency ended and will pay only a Medicare rate. See Chapter 3 for guidance on how to appeal a VA denial.

★ DEADLINE ★

You have 2 years from the date treatment was provided in which to apply for reimbursement through the Chief, Outpatient Service, at the nearest VA medical center.

Reimbursement from You to the VA

If you receive care in a VA facility and the VA later decides that you were not eligible for free care, the VA will send you a bill. The VA may decide that you had more income than you reported and consequently decide that you are in the "discretionary," not "mandatory," eligibility category. You can appeal this decision. See Chapter 3 for details on how and where to file an appeal.

The VA may also refer the bill for debt collection actions. If so, you can dispute the accuracy of the bill and ask for a waiver to avoid repayment. See Chapter 2 for details on how to contest a VA debt and to request a waiver. The VA is not supposed to deny you care in the future if you have not been able to pay a bill.

Effect of VA Health Care on Compensation and Pension Payments

If you are receiving monthly benefits from the VA and you are hospitalized, you may receive more money, or less.

The VA has a rule referred to as "paragraph 29" (38 C.F.R. 4.29), which requires the VA to temporarily increase its compensation disability rating to 100 percent if you are hospitalized for treatment of a service-connected condition for more than 21 days. Also, after a period of hospitalization, the VA may keep the 100 percent rating in place for a month or two for convalescence (this is called a "paragraph 30" rating). Because the VA medical center may not tell the VA regional office that you were hospitalized, you should.

If the VA has been paying you the A&A allowance under 38 U.S.C. 1114(r) along with a 100 percent compensation rate, the VA should cut off the higher A&A allowance when you are admitted to a VA hospital or a VA nursing home. Still, VA medical centers frequently do not tell the regional office when you are admitted and even if told, the regional offices frequently do not make the necessary adjustment. You should make sure the VA does. If the VA medical center does not tell the regional office or if you do not tell the regional office, the regional office will blame you and charge you with an overpayment. See Chapter 2 for suggestions on how to contest repayment.

If you have no family and are admitted to a VA facility and you have more than $1,500, the VA will cut off payments of compensation or pension until your money (including *everything*, such as your home and car) is reduced to a worth of $500.

If you are receiving pension payments and you have a family, and you are admitted to a VA hospital, your pension should not be reduced. If you do not have a family and are admitted to a domiciliary or a nursing home at VA expense, your pension payment will be cut to $90 per month after the third full month of care.

★ VOLUNTEERS ARE WELCOME ★

Most veterans' service organizations use volunteers to provide many services to patients in VA hospitals and nursing homes. If you are interested contact the nearest VSO or the volunteer coordinator at the nearest VA medical facility to see how you can help.

CHAPTER TEN

DEPENDENTS AND SURVIVORS

This chapter is for the spouse, child, or dependent parent, or the surviving spouse, child, or parent, of a veteran. It tells you about several VA programs that may provide either monthly cash payments or services that can save you money. If your veteran-spouse is not living with you and is not adequately supporting you or your children, this chapter will also tell you how to ask the VA to send part of his or her benefits directly to you or your children.

There are more dependents and survivors than there are veterans. Veterans total about 26.9 million. Spouses total 20.7 million, children 18 years old or younger total 12.7 million; and parents dependent on veterans total 9.6 million. Add to that 1.6 million survivors. Your total strength: 44.6 million.

As a survivor, one of two basic requirements must be met in order for

---

★ IMPORTANT ★

Get help. No book can substitute for the experience of a veterans' service representative who has daily, hands-on experience with the VA process and the VA decision-makers. Unless your claim was denied by the Board of Veterans' Appeals (BVA) within the last 12 months, you cannot hire and pay a private attorney. Although you may not be able to hire an attorney and pay him or her directly, a third party could do that for you at any time. See Chapter 1 for details on locating a service organization representative or an attorney.

★ **EXTREMELY IMPORTANT** ★

It is essential that you make the strongest case the first time. You do not want to waste your time on a half-hearted effort. If you lose, you will have to overcome difficult legal requirements just to reopen your claim, let alone win it. Take the time to talk to a service representative. Ask the rep what kind of evidence is essential. Get that evidence. Get it right the first time.

---

you to obtain monthly cash benefits: (1) your deceased veteran-spouse must have died of a service-connected condition or (2) if not, he or she must have served during a period of wartime. If you can't prove one of these, you can't receive monthly cash payments, but you may qualify for lump sum cash payments.

This chapter is divided into three sections: (1) how to prove your relationship to the veteran, (2) how to obtain benefits while your veteran-spouse is alive, and (3) how to obtain benefits after your veteran-spouse dies. Some VA programs offer benefits whether the veteran is alive or dead. For example, if the veteran is totally and permanently disabled because of a service-connected disability, you can receive educational assistance. When the veteran dies, you can also obtain educational assistance. The same is true of health care. Other VA benefits are available to surviving family only after the veteran dies (for example, compensation, death pension, home loan guaranty [see Chapter 7], insurance proceeds [see Chapter 8], burial benefits [see Chapter 8]).

Eligibility for any of these benefits is described later in this chapter. Just as for veterans, however, in order to get a benefit, you must ask for it. Before the VA will tell you what benefits you can get, the VA will insist that you prove who you are.

Before proceeding further, send for your spouse's military service records. If your spouse already did this, locate the records. If your spouse did not get the records, you must do so. Follow the directions in Chapter 25 to make a formal request for official military personnel and medical records. If your spouse ever filed a claim for VA benefits or has VA life insurance, get those records, too. Locate in the VA insurance file the form listing exactly who is the beneficiary of the policy.

If you were not married to the veteran while he or she was in the service, or if you don't recall some key details of his or her experiences in the service, and he or she is still alive, ask about those experiences: what kind of training he or she had; what kind of work he or she did; exactly

---

★ NOTE ★

You, just like a veteran, have a right to appeal if the VA says that you are not the survivor of a veteran. You must meet certain deadlines when you appeal. Review Chapter 3 to understand the application and the appeal processes. If you are in a dispute with another former spouse over who was properly married to or divorced from the veteran, the VA refers to your case as a "contested" case and the deadlines for appealing are much shorter than usual. Get help with all this. Service representatives with veterans' service organizations are often available free of charge in VA regional offices or state or county veterans' offices.

If you are facing debt collection action by the VA or you have been denied by the Board of Veterans' Appeals, you may be able to hire an attorney to represent you. A list of attorneys in private practice who represent veterans and survivors is available from the National Organization of Veterans' Advocates (P.O. Box 42334, Washington, DC 20015). If you have limited income, free legal representation may be available through the nearest legal aid or legal services office.

---

where he or she was stationed; the names of those with whom he or she served, whether he or she was ever sick, even for a day. If your spouse is unable to write all this down, make a tape recording of your spouse addressing each of these issues. You don't know when this information may be useful.

PROVING YOUR RELATIONSHIP TO THE VETERAN

A veteran has to prove that he or she is a veteran by submitting a Form DD 214, Report of Separation. Likewise, you must prove your relationship to a veteran. You will be asked to submit a birth certificate, a marriage license, a death certificate, or all three. Getting some VA benefits requires only that you prove you are or were married to a veteran. For other VA benefits, you have to prove how long you were married or why you weren't living together when your spouse died.

As with all VA programs, there are detailed rules describing who is a dependent and how to prove it. We will describe those rules now, but remember that there are exceptions to these rules and exceptions to exceptions. We cannot describe every variation of behavior that the VA will recognize as constituting marriage or that will cause the VA to say there was, for instance, a lack of continuous cohabitation. Nor can we guarantee that the VA will pay you benefits. We will, however, give you an idea of how to satisfy the VA's curiosity.

Qualifying as a Spouse

Under VA rules, a spouse is a member of the opposite sex who is a husband or a wife. A wife (or husband) is someone who is married to the veteran. Marriage does not have to be a formal wedding with a license. If the state in which you began living together recognizes common-law marriages, so will the VA (38 C.F.R. 3.1[j]).

The VA will demand proof of marriage. Proof can be in the form of a certified copy of your marriage license, an affidavit from the magistrate who married you, or affidavits from eyewitnesses. Proof of common-law marriage can be in the form of an affidavit describing all the circumstances of the marriage (i.e., when you began living with your spouse and where

---

★ WARNING ★

If the VA asks that you supply a "certified" copy of a marriage, birth, or death certificate, try to supply it. But do not miss a deadline just because you cannot find the proper person to certify the document. If you wait too long, you may lose a lot of money. Send a photocopy immediately, then get a copy certified and send it to the VA. You rarely ever need to supply an original document. Certified copies of marriage, birth, and death certificates can be obtained from the state department of vital statistics (or similar state or county office). Call the operator in the state's capital or your county seat to get the phone number for this office.

VA rules allow several classifications of employees to certify a document (for example, the government official who has official custody of the document, a VA employee who is authorized to administer oaths, an accredited veterans' service representative, military or civilian personnel under orders of the commander of a military installation, or an official at a school). You may need to show the original to one of these persons and ask him or her to sign a statement that he or she has looked at the original document, is satisfied that the document is genuine, and certifies that the photocopy is a true and exact copy of the original.

---

you were living). The VA also demands affidavits from two people who personally knew that you and your spouse were accepted in your community as husband and wife (38 C.F.R. 3.205).

Sometimes the VA will want to know about prior marriages to make sure that your marriage to the veteran was valid.

Qualifying as a Surviving Spouse

In addition to requiring proof that you were married to the veteran, the VA will require proof that you lived continuously with the veteran from the date of marriage to the date when the veteran died. The VA will want to know if you were married for at least 1 year prior to the veteran's death. If you moved out during the last year, the VA will want to know who was at fault.

Living continuously with the veteran does not necessarily mean under the same roof. For example, if he or she was an alcoholic and you had to leave for your own protection, the VA can still say that you lived continuously with the veteran. If you separated by mutual consent because of health or business reasons, for convenience, or for other reasons, the VA won't have a problem with this. If you separated for a short while and it was your fault, you will probably still qualify as a spouse. As long as no one (including your former mother-in-law) calls the VA and suggests that you left the veteran just because you felt like doing so, separations such as these should not be an issue.

On the other hand, if you gave birth to another person's child when you were not living with the veteran, or you took up residence with someone else of the opposite sex, the VA will presume that you were not living with the veteran. Of course, if you obtained a divorce, you are not a surviving spouse.

Sometimes veterans were married to more than one person at the same time and hid this fact. It is to your advantage if you didn't know about the other marriage or marriages. Marrying someone who is still legally married means that your marriage is illegal. The VA can still consider your marriage valid if you did not know about the prior marriage and about the veteran's failure to get a divorce. You can have a problem with getting VA benefits if the earlier spouse (the one never officially divorced) appears and tries to claim VA benefits.

Before Nov. 1, 1990, if the veteran died, you remarried, and that marriage ended in death or divorce, the VA would permit you to again say that you were the surviving spouse of the veteran. In 1990 and 1991,

Congress changed the law. For claims beginning Nov. 1, 1990, the law said that if you remarried, you could not be considered the veteran's surviving spouse despite a later divorce. But if you filed for a divorce before Nov. 1, 1990, the change in law does not affect you. A subsequent divorce restores your eligibility as a surviving spouse. If you did not file for divorce before Nov. 1, 1990, and you remarried and got divorced, you are not considered a surviving spouse. An annulment or voiding of the remarriage does restore you to the status of a surviving spouse.

Qualifying as a Child

The VA will demand proof of the veteran's relationship to the children. This proof can include a certified copy of a birth certificate, an affidavit from the doctor who delivered the child, two affidavits from persons who have personal knowledge that the children are the veteran's, or school records.

Children are children until they reach age 18, unless they are in school, in which case they can be children until they turn age 23. They are not children if they get married before age 18 (or 23 and in school). Children can be children forever if at or before age 18 they are permanently incapable of self-support. An award of SSA benefits is relevant information if you must appeal a VA denial.

To decide questions of self-support, the same VA rating boards that evaluate veterans' disability claims conduct an evaluation. Nevertheless, the VA applies special rules to decide children's incapacity for self-support (38 C.F.R. 3.356). Under these rules, the VA looks for physical or mental defects that would prevent the child from working. If the child has no work history, the VA may still look at daily activities that might indicate a capacity to work. The VA looks at the child's condition as of his or her 18th birthday. If, however, the child was incapable of self-support sometime before age 18 but on his or her birthday was working, the VA should see if that employment continued or was only temporary or charity work. If so, the child still can be deemed incapable of self-support.

Children can be adopted, legitimate, illegitimate, or stepchildren. A child remains the child of a veteran even if he or she is adopted out of the veteran's family. Adoptions must take place before age 18 (38 C.F.R. 3.57). A special rule applies to adoptions of a foreign child. To be valid, the child must receive one-half or more of his support from the veteran and must not remain living with his natural parents.

Children not in the custody of the veteran or surviving spouse are still considered the veteran's or surviving spouse's children as long as they have not lost legal custody.

Qualifying as a Parent

In some cases, a parent of a veteran can qualify for VA benefits. It's easy to prove the identity of the veteran's mother from his or her birth certificate. Birth certificates in some states also list fathers. However, a more difficult question arises when the birth certificate does not list the father or the parents were not married at the time. In this case, the VA requires a statement from the father that he assumed the legal and moral obligation of a parent. Statements from others who knew about the relationship will also be requested.

Adoptive parents and foster parents can qualify. The VA requires that foster care arrangements began prior to the veteran's reaching age 21 and existed for a year before the veteran entered military service. Technically, a brother or a sister can be considered a foster parent if he or she assumed such duties.

On the other hand, a veteran rated at least 30 percent for a service-connected disability can receive a dependent's allowance for a parent if the vet can prove that the parent has limited income. The VA will accept a single parent's monthly income of $400 as establishing "conclusive dependency" (38 C.F.R. 3.250).

Documenting Death

The VA will ask for proof of death before processing a claim by a survivor. A death certificate is not the only document that may be acceptable to the VA. For example, a coroner's report of death, a VA hospital's clinical summary, or a report of death provided by the military can be sufficient. If another federal agency (like the Social Security Administration) decided that the veteran was dead, the VA will accept this decision. If this kind of evidence is not available, an affidavit from someone who saw the body is proof (38 C.F.R. 3.211).

If the veteran disappeared and has been gone for at least 7 years, the VA can say that he or she is dead. The VA requires a "diligent search" for the veteran (38 C.F.R. 3.212). The VA also insists that a full 7 years is required even if a state law might permit a shorter period.

OBTAINING BENEFITS WHILE THE VETERAN IS ALIVE

Getting What You Are Due

Benefits for you, the dependent (child or spouse) of a living veteran, come in three kinds: (1) extra monthly cash benefits sent to the veteran because he is disabled, (2) cash to attend school, and (3) reimbursement for health care. A parent who is dependent on the veteran may also generate extra monthly cash benefits for the veteran.

Getting a Portion of the Veteran's Benefits

Veterans who have a disability that the VA agrees is related to their military service get a disability rating expressed in a percentage between 0 and 100. This is the service-connected compensation benefit. (See Chapter 4.) In 1993, the VA paid an extra $105 to a veteran rated 100 percent disabled for a service-connected condition. A veteran rated 50 percent disabled received $52. A veteran rated 30 percent received $31. The VA does not pay this extra "dependent's allowance" if the veteran is not rated at least 30 percent disabled.

Veterans who are totally disabled for reasons not connected to their military service may get a monthly pension from the VA if they have little income. This is the nonservice-connected pension benefit. As of December 1, 1993 if the veteran has no other income, the VA pays $7,818 per year, or $651 per month. With one dependent, the VA pays $10,240 per year, or $853 per month.

Veterans pursuing a vocational rehabilitation program may also get an extra amount of money for each dependent.

The VA does not consider these extra amounts to be yours, the dependent's. The VA sends one check to the veteran. If you divorce the veteran, the VA wants to know so that it can stop sending the extra portion. The VA does not ask the veteran whether he is supporting his spouse or children. The VA does not ask whether you are getting the support you need from the veteran.

If you are not living with the veteran but you are not divorced (final decree) and if the veteran is not providing support to you, you can ask the VA to send money directly to you. Even if you are divorced and the veteran is not receiving any extra money for you, as a spouse, you may still be able to get the VA to send money directly to you for child support. This is called making a claim for an "apportionment." Special rules apply to these cases (38 C.F.R. 3.450).

Asking for an apportionment is also important if the veteran is convicted of a felony and sent to prison. After the first 60 days of the vet's being imprisoned, the VA cuts off (or drastically reduces) its payment of compensation or pension, unless you ask that all the payments denied the veteran be apportioned to you.

You may not know whether the veteran is receiving any VA benefits. You (or anyone else) can ask any VA regional office for this information. You must supply the full name (and, if possible, the VA claim number or social security number). By law, anyone can find out how much a veteran is being paid per month (38 C.F.R. 1.502). You will not be told the diagnosis for the disability that warrants the payment, but you will be told the name of the VA benefit program involved. Knowing the amount of money the VA is paying per month and the name of the program, you can calculate whether the veteran is continuing to draw extra money for dependents.

HOW TO APPLY FOR AN APPORTIONMENT

The VA does not stock application forms for this benefit in its waiting rooms. In fact, it does not have an application form for you to use. Instead, to claim the benefit, write a letter to the nearest VA regional office and state that you are the spouse or the custodial parent of the veteran's children. State that the veteran is not "reasonably discharging his responsibility for your support." State that you are claiming a "special apportionment." List the ages of the children, list your monthly income from all sources, and list your monthly expenses. If you know whether the veteran is employed or receiving social security benefits or other income, state this information also. Finally, make a reasonable estimate of the amount of money you need.

Do not limit the amount to just the extra that the veteran is sent as a dependent's allowance. This amount is not enough to support anyone. You can ask for any portion or even all of the veteran's benefits, although the VA will not usually send more than 50 percent.

After the VA receives your letter, it should stop paying the extra dependent's allowance to the veteran and redirect the money to you. The VA should then take steps to see how much more it should send. It will contact the veteran and tell him or her that you have made a claim; the VA will then ask the vet to list his or her sources of income and his expenses. With information from both parties, the VA decides what is a reasonable level of payment to apportion to you.

The VA refers to these cases as "contested cases." Either party can appeal the VA's decision.

In child support cases outside the VA, you might consider asking for enforcement through your state court or state child support enforcement agency. Nevertheless, you should understand that the VA will not honor a state court order to garnishee a veteran's benefits. The law prohibits direct garnishment (38 U.S.C. 5301). The law does not prohibit garnishment if part of what the veteran receives from the VA is a result of waiving receipt of military retirement pay. The law also does not prohibit a state court from ordering the veteran to turn over child support payments even if the veteran's only income is VA benefits. A 1987 U.S. Supreme Court case made this ruling.

★ DEADLINE ★

If the VA refuses to send you a portion of the veteran's benefits or if the VA says that it will send only a small amount, you can appeal. The process is the same as that outlined in Chapter 3, but instead of 1 year, you have only 60 days in which to file your Notice of Disagreement (NOD). After receiving the Statement of the Case, you have only 30 days to file your appeal to the Board of Veterans' Appeals (BVA).

Educational Assistance for Spouses and Dependents

The VA offers educational assistance to families of certain veterans who are living or to families of veterans who died under certain conditions. These benefits are often referred to as Chapter 35 benefits because that is the chapter of the VA law book containing the laws for the program. The rules for family of living veterans are discussed next; the rules for survivors are discussed later in this chapter.

For the spouse or children to be eligible, the veteran must be permanently and totally disabled from a service-connected condition. A total disability is one that is set at 100 percent and may be based on unemployability. Still, that is not enough. The 100 percent disability also must be considered "permanent," which means likely to continue for the rest of the veteran's life. The VA uses special rules to decide if a total rating is permanent (38 C.F.R. 3.340).

In addition to families of disabled veterans, families of servicemembers missing in action, captured, or detained by a foreign government may also qualify for VA educational assistance. A child's marriage does not affect the child's eligibility for this assistance (38 C.F.R. 3.807[d]).

AMOUNT OF MONEY AND USES FOR IT

The educational assistance offered by the VA amounts to $404 per month if you attend school on a full-time basis, $304 if you attend on a three-quarter-time basis, or $202 if you attend on a half-time basis. As many as 45 months of full-time payments can be made. If you do not have a high school diploma or need refresher, remedial, or deficiency training, the VA will pay for 5 months of this training before it begins to reduce your 45 months of assistance. Additional payments are available for special restorative training for a child to overcome the effects of a physical or mental disability (38 C.F.R. 21.3300).

Educational assistance is available only if you pursue approved courses at approved institutions. Assistance will be paid for correspondence work, on-the-job training, or apprenticeship programs, and enrollment in colleges or universities. Recreational or avocational courses or courses in bartending do not qualify.

Private sources for scholarships should be considered, too. Some veterans service organizations offer scholarships. See Appendix D for a list of VSOs. The American Legion publishes *Need a Lift*, a guidebook for college financial aid. Write The American Legion; Emblem Sales Division; 700 N. Pennsylvania St.; Indianapolis, IN 46206.

★ DEADLINE ★

You usually have 10 years from the date when the VA decides that the veteran is permanently and totally disabled from a service-connected disability. Children usually must begin a program before their 26th birthday and generally must complete the program by their 31st birthday. However, if a veteran becomes totally disabled after the child turns age 18 but before the child turns age 26, an 8-year period is available beginning on the date when the VA notifies the veteran of his or her permanent and total rating. Extensions of these deadlines are permitted if the pursuit of education is "medically infeasible" (38 C.F.R. 21.304). Medical infeasibility can be based not only on other conditions but also on alcoholism.

Reimbursement for Health Care, CHAMPVA Benefits

The family of a veteran who has a permanent, total, service-connected disability are eligible for benefits through the Civilian Health and Medical Program of the Department of Veterans Affairs (CHAMPVA) unless they are already eligible under Medicare. In 1990, the VA spent $90.5 million on this program.

The VA uses no special rules to decide exactly which medical services it will reimburse or refuse to pay. Instead, it uses the same rules as those that apply to the Defense Department's CHAMPUS program. See Chapter 21. The CHAMPVA Registration Center operates a toll-free telephone line from 7:00 A.M. to 5:00 P.M. (Mountain Time): (800) 733-8387. The mailing address of the center is CHAMPVA Registration Center; VA Medical Center; 4500 Cherry Creek Drive South; Denver, CO 80222.

The VA has the option of insisting that you be treated in a VA medical center if it is properly equipped. This seldom happens.

OBTAINING BENEFITS AFTER THE VETERAN DIES

Getting What You Are Due

There are five kinds of benefits for the surviving spouse, child, or dependent parent of a deceased veteran: (1) monthly cash benefits sent to you, (2) cash to attend school, (3) cash to cover burial expenses, (4) cash from an insurance policy, and (5) reimbursement for health care. There are three monthly cash programs: one tied to whether the veteran had a service-connected disability (Dependency and Indemnity Compensation, or DIC), another tied to whether the veteran had wartime service and you have limited income (Death Pension), and another that the VA handles for the Social Security Administration (the Restored Entitlement Program for Survivors, or REPS).

You may not be eligible for monthly payments. If your deceased spouse was in perfect health while he or she served in the military and had few health problems afterwards, there may be no reason to say that the death was related to military service. If you can't prove that the death was service connected, you can fall back on the VA pension program, unless your deceased spouse served only between Feb. 1, 1955, and Aug. 4, 1964, or between May 8, 1975, and Aug. 1, 1990—peacetime.

Even if you do not think that the veteran died because of something that happened while he or she was on active duty, read the next section anyway. The VA has a lot of flexibility in deciding whether a death might be considered service connected and whether you qualify for the VA's DIC benefits. There may be information in the veteran's military service records or VA claims file that could lead to a favorable determination. It may be best to apply for everything and let the VA sort it out. If the VA says no, you can appeal through the same process that a veteran would use. (See Chapter 3.) For instructions on claiming insurance policy proceeds, see Chapter 8.

Service-Connected Death: Dependency and Indemnity Compensation Benefits

The VA's Dependency and Indemnity Compensation (DIC) benefits are for survivors of veterans who died on or after Jan. 1, 1957. There is a VA program covering deaths before this date, but only a small number of survivors are covered by it. In 1992, the DIC program paid benefits to 347,000 survivors. Surviving spouses made up 80 percent of the total. Surviving children totaled about 36,000; dependent parents totaled about 34,000.

You can apply for this benefit by writing to the nearest VA regional office or by completing the appropriate form: either VA Form 21-534, Application for Dependency and Indemnity Compensation or Death Pension by Surviving Spouse or Child, or VA Form 21-535, Application for Dependency and Indemnity Compensation by Parent(s). Both forms are available at the nearest VA regional office.

The most direct way to qualify for this benefit is to prove that you were married when your spouse died on active duty. If this is not your situation, you will have to prove not only that the veteran's death was service connected and that you were married to the vet but also that

---

★ IMPORTANT ★

If your veteran-spouse had a claim pending at the time of death, you may be entitled to any benefits that were due your spouse. These benefits are called "accrued" benefits and the VA should automatically determine this for you. You should get a copy of the VA claims file and review it with a service organization representative to see if anything was pending. The VA will pay only 1 year's worth of accrued benefits, regardless of how long a claim may have been pending.

★   you were married within 15 years after the veteran was discharged from the period of service during which he or she was injured, or

★ you were married for at least 1 year, or
★ you had a child and were married.

★ **DEADLINE** ★

There are no deadlines for applying for monthly cash payments from the VA. For service-connected deaths, it is best to apply as soon as possible. For nonservice-connected deaths, however, it may be best, before applying, to wait at least 45 days after the veteran dies if you are to receive any insurance proceeds.

In certain situations when the veteran was totally disabled at the time of death, the VA will presume that the death was service connected. In these cases, you will have to show that you were married for a least 1 year prior to the death or that you had a child and were married.

PRESUMING THAT A DEATH WAS SERVICE CONNECTED

If the following scenario fits, you may not need to go through a detailed medical analysis of the cause of the veteran's death. In two situations, the VA will presume that the cause of death was service connected.

First, if the veteran was rated totally disabled for the 10 years preceding death, or, second, if the veteran was rated totally disabled for the first 5 years after discharge, the VA will presume that the death was service connected. The death must not have been due to willful misconduct, such as driving while drunk and dying in an automobile accident. Also, even if the veteran was not actually receiving VA compensation at the 100 percent rating, the fact that he or she was entitled to it will qualify you. Consider this carefully if the veteran retired from the service either after 20 years of service or because of a disability (in this situation the vet probably was entitled to compensation but was not receiving it because retirement pay was higher).

If you cannot meet these requirements and convince the VA that it should presume that the death was service connected, read on.

PROVING THAT A DEATH WAS SERVICE CONNECTED

Proving that a death was service connected can be a complicated chore. A problem that the veteran had on active duty could have developed into something else that may have contributed to his or her death. This may not be obvious to you or to the VA. You need to get all the in-service treatment records. (See Chapter 25 for suggestions on how to do so.) If the veteran was not already service connected for a condition, you will need to show that he or she should have been. (See Chapter 4 for how to do this.) Then you will have to show that the condition was either the principal cause of death or the contributory cause of death.

Sometimes no in-service medical records are available or relevant. Still, there have been cases in which the veteran committed suicide and the surviving spouse succeeded in showing that the veteran was suffering from post-traumatic stress disorder (PTSD), which arose from combat experiences. One surviving spouse had a PTSD expert conduct a psychiatric postmortem from a review of the veteran's letters home from Vietnam and from his behavior as she described it. The VA agreed that his death was service connected.

You need to work closely with the doctors who were most familiar with the veteran's condition and try to determine whether there was a connection. In order for you to win, these doctors must prepare carefully worded evaluations that (1) review the in-service medical problems (or perhaps a condition that the VA already agreed was service connected), (2) describe the postdischarge medical problems, and (3) conclude that there is a definite likelihood or a high degree of certainty that the in-service condition contributed to death in a substantial way. You should share with these doctors the exact language of the VA's rule on these cases (38 C.F.R. 3.312).

The VA will pay little attention to these claims unless it believes there is a "reasonable probability" that the death might be related to service. You must have the veteran's doctors document the connection. The VA will pay more attention to a case in which the veteran was rated with a service-connected disability during his or her life if that disability involved the cardiovascular or genitourinary system, a vital organ, or any of the chronic diseases listed in VA regulations. These chronic diseases are listed in Chapter 4.

Another category of service-connected death cases can be particularly complicated. These are cases in which the veteran died in a VA medical center. The VA is supposed to treat the death as service connected even if the vet was not hospitalized for a service-connected condition.

AMOUNT OF DIC MONEY

Before 1993, the law dictated that payment of DIC to a surviving spouse was tied to the military pay grade. That is to say, the surviving spouse of an enlisted servicemember will get less than the surviving spouse of an officer. Beginning in 1993, this changed.

★ WARNING ★

Deaths in a VA medical center or a nursing home may be a result of medical malpractice. Much more money may be available through a claim filed under the Federal Tort Claims Act (FTCA) than the VA will pay. There are very strict deadlines involved in such cases. In order to determine your best option, consult with an attorney who is experienced with medical malpractice cases. VA payments will be reduced if you receive an award under the FTCA.

★ SPECIAL OPPORTUNITY ★

Survivors of veterans who participated at the site of a nuclear weapons test and certain other locations and who died of one of 13 specific cancers might be able to obtain a $75,000 one-time payment from a program handled by the U.S. Department of Justice. According to the Justice Department, you do not need an attorney to apply. However, if you accept the payment from the Justice Department, you will be giving up forever your right to receive VA or social security benefits based on your spouse's death. Doing so may be justified if there is no reasonable chance of getting a VA check each month for the rest of your life. For details on this program, write: Assistant Director, Radiation Exposure Compensation Program; U.S. Department of Justice; P.O. Box 146; Washington, DC 20044-0146; or call (800) 729-7327. If you want to consult an attorney who is experienced with representing veterans, you can obtain a list of members of the National Organization of Veterans' Advocates by writing to P.O. Box 42334; Washington, DC 20015.

As of December 1, 1993, a surviving spouse is entitled to $769 per month as a DIC payment. An extra $169 will be paid if the veteran had been rated totally disabled for eight years at the time of his or her death and the spouse was married to the veteran for those eight years. If the veteran died before January 1, 1993, a survivor might have the option of taking a higher payment that is tied to the pay grade of the veteran when he was on active duty. For example, survivors of high-ranking enlisted personnel (an E-7 or higher) and survivors of warrant officers and commissioned officers, might receive more.

If you are a patient in a nursing home, or are helpless, blind, or need the regular aid and attendance of another, an additional sum (the aid and attendance [A&A] allowance) of $195 each month is paid. If you are permanently housebound but need less care than necessary to qualify for the A&A allowance, an extra $95 is paid. An additional monthly sum of $150 for each child is included (this payment will increase to $200 beginning in October 1994). If you have a child who is permanently incapable of self-support, an additional payment of $327 is available. Finally, if the child is attending school, a payment of $166 per month is available until the child reaches age 23.

When there is no surviving spouse, monthly payments are made directly to the children, but those payments are not tied to the pay grade. Instead, Congress dictates the amount each year. In 1992, about 36,000 children received monthly payments according to the following schedule:

DIC RATES FOR CHILDREN

number of children	monthly rate
1	$327
2	471
3	610
more than 3	120 per additional child

An additional sum of $195 is paid if the child is permanently incapable of self-support.

Surviving parents with limited income may also receive DIC payments. Parents' DIC payments are reduced by certain countable income (see the explanation of "countable income," later in this chapter) but not on a dollar-for-dollar basis. If a parent has no other income, the VA will pay $370 per month.

Wartime Service and Limited Income: VA Improved Death Pension

The VA Improved Death Pension provides a surviving spouse with almost two-thirds the amount paid to a single veteran. Nonetheless, as of September 1992, 459,285 survivors were drawing VA pensions. Of these survivors, 28 percent were survivors of World War I veterans and 57 percent were survivors of World War II veterans.

Although VA pension plans were available before the current Improved Death Pension began in 1979, we do not address those plans. We also do not repeat all the details provided in Chapter 5 that discussed the

VA Improved Pension program for veterans. Almost all the rules that apply to veterans apply to you as a surviving spouse.

One big difference is that you do not need to prove that you are disabled. You do need to show that you have limited income. First and foremost, you need to show that your veteran-spouse served during a period of wartime.

The form to use to apply for this benefit is VA Form 21-534, Application for Dependency and Indemnity Compensation or Death Pension by Surviving Spouse or Child, which is available by calling the nearest VA regional office.

WARTIME SERVICE

Locate your deceased spouse's DD 214, Report of Separation, and note the date when his or her service began and ended. If you do not have the DD 214, see Chapter 25 for details on how to get it. Or, write to the VA for a copy of the veteran's VA claims file (see Chapter 11). Most likely, a copy of the DD 214 is in the claims file, too. Compare the dates against the official periods of wartime listed in Chapter 1.

Entitlement to the VA pension program requires service during a period of wartime. It also requires a minimum period of service. The veteran did not have to see combat, he or she only had to serve during the period officially designated as wartime.

In addition to serving during a particular time period, the veteran also had to have served a particular length of time that began, ended, or occurred during wartime: The active military service was during wartime for 90 days or more, the vet was discharged for a service-connected disability, the service was for at least 90 days that either began or ended during a

---

★ CAUTION ★

If you expect to get the proceeds from a life insurance policy, do not apply for a VA pension until after you receive the proceeds and at least 45 days have passed since the veteran died. If you get insurance proceeds after you are eligible for a VA pension, the VA will terminate your pension for as long as a full year. Also, do not pay the expenses of your spouse's final illness; do not pay the funeral bill (if at all possible) until after you are receiving pension payments. You can use those expenses to offset other income you may have and maximize the VA payment, but only if you pay those bills after becoming eligible for pension.

period of wartime, *or* the service during two or more periods of wartime totaled 90 days. Note that your veteran-spouse must have met only one of these requirements.

LIMITED INCOME

To get VA Improved Death Pension, you must have limited income and resources. The VA Improved Pension program is intended to keep you slightly above the poverty level. It is an income maintenance program. Some would say that it is a welfare program. Regardless of what you call it, the VA adjusts the amount that it will pay if you are receiving money from other sources. The VA doesn't care about some of the money; it does care about other money and counts it against you. The money that the VA cares about is called "countable income."

You care about what the VA considers countable income because for every dollar of it you get one dollar less of VA pension. Basically, Congress has decided the sum of money that it thinks is appropriate for you to have, and the VA is supposed to make sure that you don't get more than that, at least not while the VA is paying you. For example, as of December 1, 1993, if you have no children younger than age 18, the maximum income that Congress believes is appropriate is $5,239, or $436 per month. If you win $1,000 playing the lottery, the VA will reduce its annual payment by $1,000 so that during the year you still have only a maximum income of $5,239. The VA refers to the Congressional cap as the maximum annual pension rate (MAPR).

The maximum amount that the VA pays, or the MAPR, increases with the number of dependents you have. For example, if you have one dependent, the amount you would be paid increases from $5,239 to $6,863 (or from $436 per month to $571 per month). For each additional dependent, the MAPR increases by $110 per month.

To calculate what you might get from the VA each month, fill in the following formula:

MAPR = _____
minus countable income for VA purposes = _____
divide by 12 months = _____ per month

You cannot fill in this formula until you calculate your "countable income for VA purposes." The VA abbreviates this as "IVAP." IVAP is calculated by knowing first what income the VA counts or doesn't count. If you have income that counts, you may be able to offset some or all of the income by whatever deductions you can take. For example, you may have $2,000 in outside income that the VA will count against you, but you may also have $2,000 in deductions for medical or burial expenses that offset your income. This would leave you with 0.00 IVAP and permit the VA to pay you the maximum amount (the MAPR).

Chapter 5 discusses (1) what the VA counts as countable income, (2) how long the VA will count the money against you, (3) what the VA does not count as income, and (4) what the VA will let you deduct from what it counts. The following section describes the initial considerations regarding income. After a pension is awarded, you have a continuing obligation to notify the VA about changes in your life (and your family's) that may affect your VA pension payments. Unless you report promptly any changes in the amount of money you may receive, the VA will put you through a complicated reduction and debt collection process.

Technically, having limited resources or a low net worth is also required for you to qualify for VA pension payments. Under VA rules, you cannot have "too much" property, enough that someone at the VA will think "it is reasonable that some part of your estate be consumed for your maintenance" (38 C.F.R. 3.274). The house you live in does not count as part of your estate. Unlike Medicaid's resource limits, VA rules provide no hard-and-fast dollar value of what the VA views as too much property. In reality, this is seldom an issue. If the VA makes it an issue, you can appeal its decision. See Chapter 3.

What Counts as Income

Under VA rules, "payments of any kind from any source shall be counted as income" unless specifically excluded by another rule (38 C.F.R. 3.271). Chapter 5 provides detailed lists of the kinds of payments that are excluded and included. Review those lists and place a check mark in the boxes that describe the money you are receiving or expect to receive during the next year. Try to estimate roughly what your next year's income will be.

Expenses That Can Offset Your Income

If, after reviewing the lists in Chapter 5, you think you have income that the VA could count against you, don't stop. Read this section to see if you had (or will have) expenses during the next year that you can use to reduce the amount of your countable income. This is one time when keeping track of your expenses may actually pay off. Put a check mark in the boxes that apply to you:

☐ Medical expenses that will not be reimbursed
☐ Education expenses for you
☐ Spouse's expenses of last illness
☐ Spouse's just debts

"Expenses of the last illness" means those expenses incurred at the onset of the acute attack that caused death. If the illness was prolonged, the VA considers the onset to be when it was necessary to have someone attend to the veteran on a daily basis. Usually the VA will not permit more than 1 year of expenses prior to the death to count as expenses of the last illness. Nevertheless, you should list expenses prior to the 1-year period as "just debts." "Just debts" include those debts incurred solely by the veteran or jointly with the spouse that do not involve the purchase of real or personal property.

Perhaps the most significant expenses you will incur are medical expenses. Fortunately, the VA will let you use your medical expenses and those of your children to offset the amount of income that the VA counts (38 C.F.R. 3.272[g]). This helps only if you have a source of countable income other than the VA pension. If you do, and you have medical expenses, you may be able to keep most of your other income.

The exclusion for medical expenses is available when *all* of the following circumstances apply:

★ The expenses will not be reimbursed by anyone.
★ The expenses were paid or will be paid by you for your medical expenses or those of your spouse, children, parents, other relatives, or
★ on behalf of a person who is a member or constructive member of your household.
★ The expenses will total more than 5 percent of your MAPR.

The VA has a lengthy list of medical expenses that you may be able to claim. This list does not cover everything, but if you think you have an expense similar to any of those on the list, tell the VA about it. The VA regional office personnel are under orders to "allow all expenses which are directly related to medical care" The list of possible medical expenses can be found in Chapter 5.

"Plug into" Formula
After you determine whether the money you receive annually is counted or excluded as income and you deduct any expenses, you arrive at the IVAP,

that is, the countable income for VA purposes. Plug this number into the following formula:

Maximum Annual Pension Rate = _____
minus countable income for VA purposes = _____
divided by 12 months = _____ per month

If you cannot figure all this out, sit down with your service representative and with the VA manual and VA rules, and work it out with the rep. If all else fails and you can't figure this out, but you think you are close, complete VA Form 21-534. The VA will be happy to evaluate everything for you. You should understand, however, that if the VA decides against you, it may exclude you from reopening your claim for a full year. If your claim is denied, you will be sent a form letter listing the income that the VA counted. If the reasoning in that letter is not clear to you, be sure to obtain a copy of the rating decision that details how the VA made its calculations. You can appeal a VA denial based on income questions. You have 1 year in which to file your Notice of Disagreement. See Chapter 3 for details on appealing.

After you begin to receive a VA pension, you will have to be careful to keep it. Each year on the anniversary of the effective date of your pension award, the VA will send you an almost-impossible-to-understand form called the Eligibility Verification Report (EVR). You can't ignore it and sometimes you can't wait for it to arrive. Each year, several thousand veterans are terminated from the pension program because they do not return the EVR. Others are terminated because they waited for the EVR to arrive before reporting income they had received earlier in the year, income they should have reported at the time rather than waiting for the EVR.

★ CAUTION ★

You are obligated to notify the VA about any change in circumstances that may affect your VA payments. The VA matches your computer records with those of the SSA and other federal and state agencies to try to catch surviving spouses who may not be properly reporting their income or marital status. Don't wait for this to happen: Call the VA regional office; explain what has happened; get the VA employee's name; don't believe the person on the phone if he or she says that you do not have to worry about the change; write to the regional office and report the change. Keep a photocopy of the letter you send.

If the change is that you have begun to receive Social Security Disability Insurance Benefits or retirement benefits, send along a copy of your award letter and a copy of the first check. If the VA sends the same amount the next month, repeat the process. If the VA sends the same amount the next month, repeat the process.

You can keep the check, but don't think you can spend the money. If you know that you are not entitled to any of the money, mark the check "void," make a photocopy of it for your records, and enclose it with a letter to the regional office. If, after you consult your service rep, you believe you are clearly entitled to a part of the check, cash it and use the part that is yours, but set aside the part that is not. The VA will eventually want a refund.

There are two big ways (and several smaller ones) in which questions about income occur. First, the VA may be wrong about the kind of money you have; that is, whether it is countable or not. Second, the VA may be wrong about when to start counting the income as your money. You can appeal either VA decision. See Chapter 3.

We hope that, from the previous discussions and the information in Chapter 1, you will be able to confirm whether the VA counted what's countable, didn't count what's not countable, and did exclude what is excludable.

As if this is not complicated enough, what happens when you report to the VA on the Eligibility Verification Report (EVR) that your income has changed is even more complicated. If this change coincides with the week that you get the EVR from the VA, you suffer minimal discomfort. On the other hand, if your change in income or number of dependents occurred in one of the other 51 weeks of the year, your level of discomfort may rise sharply and be directly proportional to the length of time from when the change in your life took effect to the date when you return the EVR.

The VA must make adjustments in its payment when you are no longer entitled to the same amount of VA pension. Even if you call the VA the day something happens to affect your payment, the VA cannot make the necessary adjustments to its check-writing computers to avoid paying you the old amount. This means that in many cases the VA automatically generates overpayments that eventually must be repaid.

The VA will adjust your VA pension payments in one of three ways: (1) terminate your payments, (2) reduce your payments, or (3) increase your payments. If the VA terminates or reduces your payments or declares that it overpaid you, review Chapter 2 to understand your rights to contest the VA determination and avoid repayment.

VA adjustments are spread over the 12-month period from the effective date when the adjustment was required. The VA calls this "annualizing." For example, if the VA has been paying you $413 each month (for a total of $4,957 for the year), and you report that you won $4,957 in the lottery, the VA will terminate its payments to you. The VA will not send checks to you for the next 12 months. You are expected to live on the lottery winnings for the next 12 months by withdrawing from your savings account no more than $413 each month. Good luck.

Sometimes the VA mistakenly adjusts its payments based on when it thought you began to receive social security benefits. For example, the VA may have been told by the SSA that it awarded you benefits on June 1. Perhaps this is true, but you may not have received your first check until December 1. The proper time for the VA to make its adjustment is when you actually get the SSA check in your hands, not the technical "effective date of the award."

Your circumstances will change somewhat from year to year. Do your best to report changes as they occur. If you anticipate a big change that could otherwise terminate your pension for 12 months, you may be able to limit the loss and shield your income. There is a little-used process known as "renouncing" (or giving up) your pension. This is discussed in Chapter 2. Work closely with a knowledgeable service rep if you even think about renouncing your pension. (Doing so can be dangerous. You may not requalify for a pension.)

Extra Pension Payments

You may be eligible for extra pension payments each month if you need someone to help take care of you or if you are basically housebound. Needing someone to help take care of you may mean that you qualify for the aid and attendance (A&A) allowance. These extra payments are referred to as a "special monthly pension." The maximum annual pension rate increases about 22 percent if you qualify for the housebound (HB) allowance and 60 percent if you qualify for the A&A allowance.

You need not wait until the VA notifies you that you are entitled to a pension before asking for either the HB or the A&A allowance. You can speed the process if you ask your doctor to prepare a statement describing your limitations. The *VA Physician's Guide to Disability Evaluation Examinations* contains a format for use by VA doctors in these cases. A format based on the guide is provided at the end of Chapter 5.

Effect of VA Pension on SSI Benefits

Supplemental security income (SSI) does not count against you as far as the VA is concerned. SSI payments are excluded from countable income.

The reverse is not true: The Social Security Administration will reduce, if not terminate, SSI payments when you begin to receive a VA Improved Pension. Loss of SSI eligibility can mean loss of Medicaid eligibility. If you are receiving SSI, confirm with the nearest legal aid or legal services office what may happen to it and your Medicaid eligibility if you begin to draw a VA pension. In your state the VA pension payment may not affect your Medicaid eligibility.

The Restored Entitlement Program for Survivors

In 1981, during the annual round of last-minute budget fights in Congress, several thousand survivors of veterans who died on active duty before Aug. 13, 1981, lost certain social security benefits. The Restored Entitlement Program for Survivors (REPS) is a hybrid VA-SSA program. The VA handles the application forms but uses SSA rules. The VA issued some rules itself (38 C.F.R. 3.812).

Basically, and briefly, if an active duty servicemember died before Aug. 13, 1981, his survivors may be paid REPS benefits. If the servicemember died after discharge but as a result of a disease contracted before Aug. 13, 1981, his survivors may still qualify for the REPS benefits. The program is needs based with a limit on the annual amount of earnings.

Benefits for the surviving spouse are payable if the spouse is a parent whose youngest child is age 16 or 17. Benefits for a child are payable from age 18 through 21 if the child is in school full time. The amount of the benefits is calculated using SSA insurance amounts.

The application form is VA Form 21-8924. It can be obtained from any VA regional office and turned in to that office. Given the complexity of the rules, however, only selected regional offices process these applications. The standard VA rules for appealing a denial can be followed. (See Chapter 3).

★ **NOTE** ★

In May 1992, the Court of Veterans Appeals threw out a portion of the VA's rules on the REPS program that said a claim must be filed within 11 months of a child's 16th birthday in order for the child to be eligible for benefits as of that date (*Cole v. Derwinski*, No. 89-30). If you were affected by this rule, reapply now and refer to the *Cole* case.

EDUCATIONAL ASSISTANCE FOR SURVIVORS

Under the VA's Chapter 35 program, surviving spouses and children are eligible for monthly educational assistance payments if the veteran

★ died as a result of a disability incurred in active service, or
★ died while rated permanently and totally disabled from a service-connected disability.

Veterans who had a permanent and total service-connected disability did not have to die of that particular service-connected disability for the survivors to qualify for assistance. See the previous description of monthly payments available to you. Some veterans' service organizations and many private organizations offer scholarships to surviving children of veterans so that they can attend college. Consult the financial aid office at the university you plan to attend. Also, consult your state department of veterans' affairs for special programs that may be available to you (see Appendix B).

REIMBURSEMENT FOR HEALTH CARE, CHAMPVA BENEFITS

Under the VA's CHAMPVA program, surviving spouses and children are eligible for reimbursement of health care provided at private facilities if the veteran

★ died on active duty, or
★ died as a result of a service-connected disability, or
★ died while rated permanently and totally disabled from a service-connected disability.

The CHAMPVA toll-free telephone number is (800) 733-8387. The mailing address is CHAMPVA Registration Center; VA Medical Center; 4500 Cherry Creek Drive South; Denver, CO 80222.

CHAPTER ELEVEN

VA RECORDS, RESEARCH, AND RESOURCES

★★★★★★★★★★★★★★★★★★★★★★★★★★★★★★★★★★★★★★

This chapter is intended to help you get your own records, get records about your military activities, research VA rules to see if the information in this book is still current, and find additional books or organizations that can help you.

GETTING YOUR OWN VA RECORDS

The basic record kept by the VA about you is a VA claims folder. The regional office keeps other files pertaining to you. For example, if you have a VA-guaranteed home loan, you have a loan guaranty file. If you were evaluated for vocational rehabilitation, you have a vocational-rehab file. If you have VA life insurance, you have an insurance file. If the VA says that you are incompetent to handle your funds, you have a guardianship file. And, of course, if you have been treated in a VA hospital or an outpatient clinic, you have a medical file. All these files may be in the same city and sometimes in the same building, but there is no cross-reference from one file to another.

You may not need all these files at once. Perhaps you trust the VA

★ IMPORTANT ★

If you have no time to do all the work outlined in this chapter, look for someone who stays current on VA matters. Shop around at the nearest VA regional office for a veterans' service organization representative who has some of the materials available.

never to lose your files. Perhaps you don't want to bother getting your own copy. Do yourself a favor. Get the files; a copy is free. Put the copy in a fireproof place (and tell your family where you put it).

If you are pursuing a claim for VA benefits, you especially want your claims folder. The claims folder contains the application that you filed for VA benefits, the service medical records that the VA obtained, the rating decisions, letters to you telling you about your claim, and letters from you telling the VA about your claim. One of the biggest reasons the VA denies claims is that it does not have the information it needs to allow the claim.

Unless you know what the VA has, you will not know what it relied on in making a decision. If you know what it relied on, you can tell either that it didn't get what it should have or that it mistakenly skipped an important portion of the records.

You can drive a few hundred miles to the regional office that has your file and ask to copy it (and hope that the VA can find it while you wait and hope that the photocopy machine works). Or, you can mail a letter called a "Privacy Act Request" to the office and ask it to make the copy and mail it to you. One copy of your file is free of charge. In your letter, be sure to say, "This is a Privacy Act Request for a complete and true copy of the entire claims file to include the reverse side of any page that contains text or is date stamped and to be in the exact order as the original." Include your VA claim number, and social security number, and current address. Keep a copy of your request.

If you are told to come to the VA office to inspect the file or that you have to pay for the copy, or you hear nothing for 30 days from the date when you sent your request to the VA, send a letter called a "Privacy Act Appeal" to the following person: General Counsel (024); U.S. Department of Veterans Affairs; 810 Vermont Ave., NW; Washington, DC 20420. In this letter, tell the General Counsel, "This is an appeal under the Privacy Act. Enclosed is a copy of the request I sent to get my records. As of today—more than 30 days after requesting them—I have not received my records."

After you get the file, keep the paperwork in the order in which you received it. Review it carefully to make sure that the VA prepared a rating decision every time you sent a claim. Also, make sure that every time you filed a Notice of Disagreement the VA acted on it and prepared a Statement of the Case. Use Post-It notes (or similar notes) to label these documents.

Tracking these documents may show that the VA failed to set the correct effective date for your claim. If the VA failed to do this, it may have committed an administrative error that is considered a "clear and unmistakable error" and is worth lots of money in back benefits. Also review the file to see what evidence the VA considered in evaluating your claim.

If you were seen by a counseling psychologist for a vocational-rehab evaluation, send a Privacy Act request to the psychologist for a copy of that file. If the evaluation you read in the file says that it is not medically feasible for you to undergo vocational-rehabilitation, this evaluation may be good evidence that you should have a 100 percent rating. If you are facing debt collection by the VA for $27,500 on a house you sold 10 years ago, get the VA loan guaranty file from the loan guaranty service office at the VA regional office closest to the property.

Every time you come home from a stay in a VA hospital or a visit to the outpatient clinic, ship a Privacy Act Request to the VA Medical Center, to the attention of the Medical Administration Service, and ask for a copy of any and all doctors' notes, nurses' notes, surgical procedure notes, laboratory reports, discharge summaries, consultants' reports, and so forth that may have been created. You should not, however, unload all 300 pages of this on the VA regional office to support a claim for increased benefits. Look for the records that contain a doctor's conclusion that your condition is "serious" or a summary of the period of hospitalization.

If your medical records involve psychiatric matters, the VA may write back and refuse to release them directly to you. The VA is concerned that if you read the psychiatrist's opinion about your condition, your condition may worsen. In this case, ask your service representative or another doctor to get the records.

VA medical centers do not keep your records in their buildings forever. They also do not transfer them to the next VA hospital that may treat you when you move, unless someone asks that the records be transferred. It's not like being in the military, where you had one set of medical records that followed you from duty station to duty station. Also, 3 years after the date of the last treatment, records are "retired" to a federal records storage center and only a key number (a number that identifies the location of the file in the storage facility) is kept on file at the medical center that treated you. VA medical records are destroyed 72 years after they are retired to the records center. Even if you do not need them now, get them and keep them safe in case your survivors need to prove that you were treated for a particular condition.

After you make the first request for your files, make other requests occasionally (for example, after you reopen your claim). Do not ask for the entire file again. If you do, the VA will charge you for it. Instead, ask for the records that were added to your file since the VA sent you the last copy.

★ **YOUR VA FILE IS PRIVATE AND CONFIDENTIAL** ★

Almost all the information in your VA file must be kept confidential. You can give up your right to privacy and give someone else permission to obtain your VA records. For example, you may give a VSO representative permission to examine your records. Or, you may give a member of Congress permission to see your records.

You may be asked to "waive your rights under the Privacy Act" when you apply for certain jobs. However, if you agree to give up one record and the VA turns over others, the VA may have violated your privacy and have to pay a penalty to you.

Certain records are considered extremely sensitive and require special release forms to be reviewed. For example, records of treatment and any reference to treatment for drug or alcohol abuse, AIDS, or sickle-cell anemia are specially protected. If these records are important to your claim for VA benefits, tell your representative that the records exist. Otherwise the rep may not discover them.

GETTING OFFICIAL RECORDS ABOUT YOUR MILITARY SERVICE

Sometimes you may need records about the nature of your military service. For example, if you are claiming you were in combat in Vietnam, you might want unit records documenting the operations in which your unit participated. This kind of information is not available in your military service personnel file, although evidence that you were attached to the particular unit should be. Each branch of the service maintains historical records. Some divisions have "division historians" who may be helpful. The primary addresses for historical records follow:

AIR FORCE:
Office of History
Reference Services
Forestall Bldg., 1000
   Independence Ave., SW
Washington, DC 20314

ARMY:
U.S. Army Military History
   Research Collection
Upton Hall
Carlisle Barracks
Carlisle, PA 17013

MARINE CORPS:
Marine Corps Historical Center
Research Section
Bldg. 58, Washington Navy
  Yard
Washington, DC 20374-0580

NAVY:
Navy Historical Center
Washington Navy Yard
Washington, DC 20374-0571

You can expect to be shuttled from office to office depending on exactly what records you need. Still, the addresses just listed are good starting points. Also don't forget your local library.

If you need records about your military experiences in Vietnam, a massive collection of such records is located at the Federal Records Center in the Washington, DC, area. In addition, an office at Ft. Belvoir, Virginia, conducts research with these records to support claims of exposure to Agent Orange in Vietnam or to document "stressful" combat experiences in Vietnam. Here is its address:

USA & JOINT SERVICES ENVIRONMENTAL SUPPORT GROUP
7798 Cissna Rd., Ste. 101
Springfield, VA 22150-3197

GETTING YOUR OWN PRIVATE MEDICAL RECORDS

Medical records of treatment you received in private hospitals or by private doctors or psychologists may be very helpful to your VA claim. Some states, including California, Colorado, Connecticut, Florida, Massachusetts, Minnesota, and New York, give you the right of access to and the right to copy your medical records. Other states leave this up to individual hospitals.

If you request these records, you can anticipate a high copying fee; find out what it is before you proceed. If you let the VA request the records, you will not have to pay. As a general rule, though, you should see the records before they go to the VA. Perhaps they are not relevant to your claim. Or, perhaps only a few pages need to go to the VA to support your claim.

If a hospital refuses to release your records and you really need them, ask the director of the VA regional office to issue a subpoena to get them. If the VA receives records that may not support your claim, be prepared to argue that the VA is misreading the records or is not reading other records that *do* support the claim.

GETTING SOMEONE ELSE'S VA RECORDS

Basically, you cannot obtain someone else's VA records. However, anyone is entitled to know the dollar amount that any veteran is receiving in VA benefits. If you are the spouse of a veteran who moved out, and you are considering asking the VA to send you a portion of the veteran's benefits, you should ask the VA regional office how much the vet is receiving. The regional office is required by VA regulation 38 C.F.R. 1.502 to release this information.

RESEARCHING VA LAW AND POLICY

When you call a VA regional office and ask why you received a particular letter, the official response often is "because that's what Title 38 says." If you pressure the person you are talking with for more detail, you probably won't get any. VA employees don't read Title 38 every day. Title 38 is a portion of the laws of the United States that covers VA benefits, health care, insurance, the appeals process, and the Court of Veterans Appeals. Most public libraries and all law libraries open to the public have a copy of Title 38.

If you are pursuing a claim, equally important to you than the law are the regulations contained in Title 38, Code of Federal Regulations (C.F.R.). We have included references throughout the preceding chapters to various sections of Title 38, C.F.R. Sometimes the regulations just repeat the text of the law, but usually there is more detail that explains how the VA applies the law. Title 38, C.F.R., is published once a year by the Government Printing Office (GPO) in Washington, DC, and sold at GPO bookstores and through the mail. You can reach the GPO at (202) 783-3238. The C.F.R. is also available at most public libraries. Part 3, Title 38, C.F.R., contains rules for processing claims at the VA regional offices; Part 4 contains the VA Schedule for Rating Disabilities; Part 17, the rules of eligibility for medical care; Parts 19 and 20, the rules for how the Board of Veterans' Appeals (BVA) operates. In advance of the annual publication of the C.F.R.s, proposed and final rules are published in the Federal Register, a daily compilation of rules from federal agencies that is also published by the Government Printing Office and available in most public libraries.

It is possible for a veteran to file a claim for VA benefits and win (or lose) without ever researching a single VA rule. Sometimes it seems that VA employees do the same thing. Maybe technically it is not necessary for a veteran to know what the rules say. The Court of Veterans Appeals has told the VA that veterans do not have to list the rules that they want the VA to apply; the VA is obligated to apply all the right rules. If you are in no hurry, don't bother looking up the rules. Leave it to the VA to do the right thing.

If you are not that trusting, go to the library. Take a copy of the Statement of the Case that you received from the VA regional office. It should list certain regulations and may even reproduce the text of the regulations. Look up the Code of Federal Regulations section numbers to which the statement of the case refers. Then read the sections just before the number the VA gave you and just after it. You may discover that the VA quoted only the first portion of the regulation and that the last portion is relevant to your case. If so, recite the last portion in a letter to the regional office or ask your service representative what it may mean to your case.

VA regulations are probably the most important to you. You should know, however, that VA employees rely on other VA publications that give them even more detailed instructions on how to process claims and instructions on what kinds of evidence are necessary to prove a claim. For example, the VA adjudication division relies on VA Manual M21-1, Adjudication Procedure. This manual is supplemented with periodic changes. The VA Central Office regularly communicates with regional offices through circulars and often announces many months in advance how it will process claims under new laws, even before regulations have been put into the C.F.R.

The BVA has its own manual, MBVA-1, which is supplemented with changes. The chairman of the BVA regularly issues memoranda that explain how the BVA will change its process in reaction to a decision by the Court of Veterans Appeals. The BVA keeps a subject matter index of its decisions and will give you free copies of selected decisions. You may want to use the index to see how the BVA handles claims such as yours. The BVA Index to Decisions is available in each regional office and at the BVA in Washington. The BVA plans to place copies of its decisions on CD-ROM to make them more available as a research tool.

The Veterans Health Administration has its own massive set of manuals that describe how each department within a medical center should operate. The Deputy Secretary issues circulars providing additional detail.

The VA Inspector General frequently publishes audits of various VA programs and the operations of individual regional offices and medical facilities. The audits often explain both how the rules should be applied and how they are actually applied or don't work.

You could spend a lot of time trying to understand all this. Instead, take a short cut, go to your service representative and ask the rep to list the materials that are important to your particular claim. If the rep does not have these research tools, ask the VA's Veterans Services Officer at the VA regional office to let you see the M21-1, for example, and the index to BVA decisions.

All VA publications are available for inspection in any VA regional office and may often be available through university libraries that are designated as federal depositories. All VA publications are available on request through the mail, through a Freedom of Information Act Request (FOIA). The FOIA is a federal law that requires the VA to turn over documents that are not normally for sale (in a bookstore or anywhere else). Nevertheless, the VA will usually charge a fee to copy the documents.

The M21-1 is several hundred pages in length. Use the manual at the VA office. If you look at it at the VA office and you think that you need a copy for your own use, ask the VA to copy selected pages or ask your local librarian to request a copy and then check out the document from the library.

One way to get documents free of charge is to work through a local veterans' organization or legal aid office. Ask the local service representative or legal aid attorney to make the FOIA request and ask for a waiver of fees.

The decisions of the Court of Veterans Appeals must be followed by the VA regional offices and the BVA. You can let the VA determine which decisions are relevant to your case, or you can do some research on your own. West Publishing Company (800) 328-9352 publishes an official set of the court's decisions in its *Veterans Appeals Reporter*. You may find this in some public libraries, or you may have to look in a law school library. You can find it at each VA regional office. The court also distributes its opinions through the GPO to major libraries designated as federal depositories. The court is also considering creating a public electronic bulletin board to make its decisions more quickly available. You do not have to be a lawyer to read court cases. You do have to be patient. It may help you to use a legal dictionary as well as other reference materials that a law librarian can recommend to you.

RESOURCES TO HELP YOU STAY UP-TO-DATE

The most convenient way to stay up to date with changes in VA benefits is to belong to a veterans' service organization. Each of the major VSOs offers a newspaper or magazine that regularly reports on new laws and new VA policies. You may not have the money to buy a life membership in a VSO, but it may be smart to be a member of three or four of them at least for the life of your claim. The addresses of VSOs are listed in Appendix D at the end of this book. There is also an electronic network of service reps, veterans, and attorneys around the country. Prodigy offers a Veterans Bulletin Board and CompuServe offers a Military Forum to share information relevant to VA claims.

The next most convenient way to keep track of changes is to work with your local librarian to review those publications that report on new laws and regulations. The district office of your U.S. representative or senator is also a good source of laws currently being considered or recently passed.

A service in Illinois has been publishing an annual compilation of VA benefits information for more than half a century. Although it does not offer advice on preparing claims, it collects much official information in one source and updates its figures every year. Contact the Veterans Information Service; P.O. Box 111; East Moline, IL 61244; ask about the book *What Every Veteran Should Know*.

The National Veterans Legal Services Project is a nonprofit organization in Washington, DC, that receives funding from the Legal Services Corporation and the Agent Orange Class Assistance Program. It offers a number of publications, some aimed at veterans, others aimed at service representatives including a newsletter (The Veterans Advocate) and a three-volume legal manual (Veterans Benefit Manual). For a list of these publications, write to the National Veterans Legal Services Project; 2001 S St., N.W., Dept. P (VB); Washington, DC 20009.

PART TWO

Special Programs, Opportunities, and Problems

CHAPTER TWELVE

BENEFITS AND BREAKS FROM NON-VA FEDERAL AGENCIES AND STATES

★ ★

This chapter tells you about a variety of services, benefits, or advantages you may get as a result of your status as a veteran from offices besides the U.S. Department of Veterans Affairs. The VA is not the only federal agency that offers programs and services for you. Also, many states offer cash bonuses, breaks on taxes and licensing fees, home loan guaranties, reduced college tuition, and nursing home care.

PROGRAMS AVAILABLE THROUGH FEDERAL AGENCIES BESIDES THE VA

Social Security Administration

Since January 1957, an amount for social security has been withheld from military service pay and has counted toward social security benefits. In fact, for every 3 months of active service you had, an extra credit was applied to your social security account. Obtaining social security benefits does not require that you wait until you are age 65, although at age 65 you may qualify for Medicare coverage.

Disabilities, even those resulting from your military service, may entitle you to social security disability insurance benefits. If you cannot convince the VA that you are entitled to service-connected compensation, you are always free to try to convince the SSA that you are disabled. Youhave to convince SSA that your disability is "total" because the SSA does not use a graduated system of measuring disability as the VA does.

The SSA has more than 1,000 offices around the country.

Department of Labor, Small Business Administration

See Chapter 13 for details about Department of Labor programs, the Small Business Administration (SBA), and veterans' preference in hiring and promotion.

Immigration and Naturalization Service

An honorable discharge can entitle aliens to full citizenship if they served during a period of war or served in the theater of operations of certain periods of hostilities (such as Grenada). For this to apply, you had to have been lawfully admitted to the United States for permanent residence. If not, you may still be able to take advantage of this if you were inducted or you enlisted while in the United States (including Puerto Rico, Guam, the U.S. Virgin Islands, the Panama Canal Zone, or American Samoa). Service during a period that was not wartime or a period of hostilities can still qualify you for naturalization if you had 3 years of service and you apply within 6 months of discharge. Although your status as a veteran may help some, it does not appear to speed the lengthy process.

Federal Housing Administration

Whether you used your VA home loan entitlement or not, the Federal Housing Administration (FHA) offers special terms for veterans to buy homes. This usually translates into a lower down payment. For more details, work with a local lender.

STATE PROGRAMS

Most states offer a broad range of benefits. Some of these state benefits are not particularly significant. However, cash bonuses, state nursing home care, reduced fees on licenses, and reduced college tuition can be substantial. For example, the state of Virginia waives all fees and charges for disabled veterans' children attending state-subsidized schools. The veteran parent must be permanently and totally disabled (or deceased) as a result of conditions that originated during a period of wartime. Scholarships that were tied to performing service for the state are considered satisfied by military service. Virginia also operates a state veterans' home and is in the process of developing a state veterans cemetery.

Massachusetts offers an annual pension to blind or paralyzed veterans, free tuition for Vietnam veterans attending a state college, cash educational assistance to surviving children of certain veterans, and a cash bonus of $300 for foreign service or $200 for stateside service during the Vietnam War.

California offers a farm and home purchase program that finances as much as $80,000 toward the purchase of a farm or $20,000 toward the purchase of a home. California also exempts a certain amount of military pay from income tax and exempts a portion of the value of a veteran's property from property tax.

Iowa offers a burial allowance through the county government. Ohio, through its county relief commissions, offers emergency cash relief to veterans in the event of accident, sickness, or "great destitution." Almost all states offer numerous advantages to veterans in obtaining employment in either state or local government.

The U.S. House of Representatives Committee on Veterans Affairs has published a compilation of state veterans' benefits. A copy of the publication (Committee Print No. 4, Jan. 28, 1992) may be available free (at the discretion of the committee) through the committee's publications office at (202) 225-3527. It is also offered for $11.00 from the GPO Congressional Sales at (202) 512-2470; ask for stock no. 552-070-11911-6. You can also get the latest information about state benefits through either your local county veterans' service agency or the State Department of Veterans Affairs office (located in your state capital).

If you apply for a benefit and are denied because you were not a resident of the state when you entered the service, the state's law may be unconstitutional. The U.S. Supreme Court struck down residency requirements in two states (one in New Mexico, another in New York). Ask a lawyer whether your state's decision is correct. Of course, if the benefits in question are small, a lawyer will not be interested in your case unless he or she believes it might form the basis for a class action: a case brought on behalf of all persons in the same situation.

CHAPTER THIRTEEN

EMPLOYMENT AND UNEMPLOYMENT

★★★★★★★★★★★★★★★★★★★★★★★★★★★★★★★★★★★★★★

The job market is tight. You need all the help you can get. This chapter tells you about help to get your old job back, to get a new job, or to get cash if you can't find a job after you're discharged from active duty. This chapter also explains some of the services offered by the Small Business Administration (SBA). Your status as a veteran may also increase the likelihood of getting a job with the federal, state, or local government. If you have a disability, a new law, the Americans with Disabilities Act, may prevent you from being discriminated against when you seek a job.

If you are still on active duty, look for and take advantage of the Transitional Assistance Program seminars. These seminars are not available at every base, but if you can find one, go. They offer practical advice on searching for jobs, writing a strong resumé, and developing interviewing skills—basic civilian survival skills.

YOUR RIGHT TO BE REHIRED FOR YOUR OLD JOB

If you left a job to go into the service, you probably have a right under federal law to get it back, but you have to ask for it quickly. Whether you left a job voluntarily to enlist or your reserve unit was activated, you have rights under the Veterans' Reemployment Rights Act.

You do not have to ask in writing to be rehired, but doing so is the safest thing to do in case there is a problem. Don't just talk to your former foreman or supervisor. Go to the personnel office or the person responsible for hiring. Be sure to say that you are a returning servicemember. If you are told that the company is not hiring anyone, explain again that you are a returning servicemember and mention the "federal Veterans' Reemployment Rights Act."

Generally, if you enlisted and served no more than 4 years and were discharged with an honorable or general discharge, you can expect to be rehired. Dishonorable discharges that are upgraded may qualify you to assert your rights under this law. "Entry-level separations" that are not characterized by the service are considered to be under honorable conditions.

If you enlisted and served more than 4 years and did so "at the request and for the convenience of the government," you may still be able to be rehired. Reservists called up for active duty for training may serve as long as they please without losing their right to reemployment.

What you can expect from your employer varies depending on whether you enlisted or were called up for active duty for training. If you were called up for active duty for training, you can expect to be returned immediately to your previous position with no loss in seniority, status, pay, or vacation. Otherwise, you can expect to be restored within a reasonable time to either the same position you had or a position of like seniority, status, and pay. You may also have as much as 1 year of job protection from firing (unless the employer has just cause).

If you have trouble with your former employer, the U.S. Department of Labor's Veterans' Employment and Training Service is responsible for enforcing the law through local U.S. attorneys. To locate the nearest Labor Department office, check your local telephone book under U.S. Government listings or call the Washington, DC, office at (202) 523-8611. The GPO sells a detailed handbook on these cases, the *Veterans' Reemployment Rights Handbook* (stock no. 029-007-00006-3). Call (202) 783-3238 to order a copy.

HELP IN GETTING A NEW JOB

Depending on the state in which you live, you may or may not have a strong state employment service program designed to help you. New York, for example, has a state jobs bill of rights for veterans and backs

---

★ NOTE ★

One of the little-known aspects of your right to reemployment is that your time in the service counts toward calculating your entitlement to the company's pension.

★ **DEADLINES** ★

You should ask to be reemployed as soon as possible. To get the protection of the federal law, you must request reemployment within either 31 days or 90 days. Reservists with less than 90 days' service usually have 31 days from their release to apply. Reservists released from active duty for training should ask before the end of the next regular work period and after their last travel day. Everyone else has 90 days. But don't wait.

---

it up with aggressive outreach and placement service. Each state operates a network of state employment security agency offices. In addition to maintaining lists of available jobs, these offices often offer counseling and testing services to help you determine what work you may be suited to perform.

Don't limit your search to the job lists in the state office or the lists in the local newspaper. Visit the nearest public library for books on finding jobs or on starting your own business. Also, locate the nearest vet center (see list in Appendix B), introduce yourself, and check the bulletin board. Use the introduction to explain what kind of work you want. Leave your resume with the vet center. Leave your name and telephone number on the bulletin board indicating that you are available. Join veterans' service organizations and find out where the local chapter or post meets; go introduce yourself.

Job hunting can be tedious and depressing, but persistence can pay off. Try not to get discouraged.

The U.S. Department of Labor, in addition to having reemployment rights responsibilities, also funds the Servicemembers Occupational Conversion and Training Program. This program can pay a participating employer up to $12,000 of your salary.

To be eligible for this program you must have been discharged after August 1, 1990. You must be unemployed at the time you apply for the program and have been unemployed for at least 8 of the previous 15 weeks before applying; or your military occupational specialty had to be one that is not readily transferable to civilian employment; or you must be rated at 30 percent disabled.

To find out if your occupational specialty qualifies you for this program and to apply for help, contact the nearest office of your state employment security agency.

Federal Veterans Preference

By law, the United States has an obligation to assist veterans of the armed forces in readjusting to civilian life because veterans, by virtue of their military service, have lost opportunities to pursue education and training oriented toward civilian careers. The official policy is to promote the maximum employment and job advancement opportunities for disabled and certain other veterans.

The Office of Personnel Management oversees federal agencies' hiring practices and is supposed to ensure that eligible veterans (and sometimes spouses, parents, or survivors) receive preference in federal employment. The reality varies widely from agency to agency. The preference includes adding either five or ten points to test scores, providing the first chance at some jobs, and furnishing limited protection from layoffs.

Veterans who are targeted for possible noncompetitive appointment to a federal job include Vietnam War veterans with service-connected disabilities and post–Vietnam War veterans. Listings of jobs available in the federal government are maintained at federal Job Information Centers; consult your telephone directory for the nearest center.

Federal funding is provided to state employment security agencies to provide a job counselor who provides special assistance to disabled veterans. Look for the Disabled Veterans Outreach Program (DVOP) specialist.

State Veterans Preference

Almost every state extends a preference in hiring to veterans. Some states require that you have been a resident of the state before you entered service. This and certain other residency requirements may be unlawful. See (Chapter 12.)

Private Employers with Federal Money

Affirmative action in hiring certain disabled veterans is also supposed to be the rule for any private contractor who has a contract for $10,000 or more with the federal government. Affirmative action applies to veterans with at least a 30 percent service-connected disability, those with a serious employment handicap, and those discharged from service because of a service-connected disability. If you believe affirmative action has not been applied to you either in hiring or promotion, complain to the nearest Department of Labor Office of Federal Contract Compliance Programs.

BAN ON DISCRIMINATION AGAINST DISABLED VETERANS

A new law, the Americans with Disabilities Act (P.L. no. 101-336), should make the job market a little more accessible for you if you have a disability. The act prohibits discrimination against you just because you are disabled, as long as you can perform the essential job functions. The ban on discrimination applies to the initial hiring stage (the employer cannot ask whether you have a disability), promotions, pay, health insurance, and other terms of employment. Not all employers are covered by this law. As of July 1992, employers with 25 or more employees must comply; after July 1994, employers with 15 or more must comply.

As long as you can perform the job, an employer must provide reasonable accommodations for you, such as modifying your work schedule or modifying equipment to make it easier to use. If you suspect that you did not get a job because of your disability, but you know you could do the job, there are two ways to make a complaint. The federal Equal Employment Opportunity Commission (EEOC) has enforcement authority. Call (800) 669-EEOC to locate the nearest EEOC office. As a practical matter, EEOC offices are overwhelmed with complaints and work very slowly. Fortunately, the new law does permit you to enforce the law privately through litigation.

Before filing a lawsuit, consult a veterans' service organization (VSO) such as the Paralyzed Veterans of America (PVA) or the Disabled American Veterans (DAV) for advice. The VSO may be able to help you resolve the problem or negotiate a resolution to the problem. The PVA has taken the lead in the fight to end discrimination against persons with disabilities, and it offers a series of pamphlets on the new law. Contact the PVA office at the nearest VA regional office.

UNEMPLOYMENT BENEFITS

If you have no job prospects after your release from service, consider applying for unemployment compensation. It's often a tedious process, but you are entitled to the money, and collecting unemployment is nothing to be ashamed of.

You may not want to apply at the nearest state unemployment office. The level of benefits paid varies from state to state, and you can apply in any state. If you live in Virginia, consider going to the office in Washington, DC. The Washington, DC, office will probably pay you more than the

Virginia office will. Call around to find out whether it's worth your time to travel to another state to apply. After you file an application, however, that state's laws apply to you. In any state unemployment office (in your state, it may be called an "employment security" office), pick up a pamphlet titled *Unemployment Insurance for Ex-Service Members*, prepared by the U.S. Department of Labor; it lists at least one unemployment office in each state.

The amount of the payment also varies depending on your pay grade at discharge. Whether you have to wait a week before you are eligible for benefits depends on the state. The payments can last as long as 26 weeks, and if the economy is weak, your claim can be extended, sometimes several times. To apply, visit your state unemployment office, taking copy number 4 of your DD 214, Certificate of Release, and your social security card. The first thing to do is register with the job placement office. If there is no job available, file for unemployment compensation.

If you served your entire tour of duty and received an honorable or a general discharge, you should not have a problem qualifying. You may have a problem if you left service before the end of your first full term unless you left for one of several specific reasons. You should still qualify if you served at least 1 year and your DD 214 shows that you left early for one of the following reasons:

★   for the convenience of the government under an early release program
★   because of medical problems (including pregnancy)
★   because of hardship
★   because of a personality disorder or an inaptitude

If you were on active duty in the reserves and served at least 90 days, you should qualify.

Each branch of the service has lists of the official narrative reasons for separation that, if found on your DD 214, will qualify you for these benefits. If you are considering an "early out" under one of the drawdown programs, make sure that your early departure will result in an official narrative reason for separation that will qualify you.

If you are denied benefits because of the character of your discharge, see Chapter 17 for information regarding how to apply for an upgrade. If you are denied because of the narrative reason for separation, consult your service's discharge regulations to determine whether the reason was accurate. The fastest approach may be to visit the nearest recruiting station and ask to review its copy of the discharge regulations. If you think the listed reason is incorrect, see Chapter 17 to learn how to apply for a correction to your military records.

Finally, if you applied for unemployment compensation before November 1991, you may have been limited to 13 weeks of benefits. If you are now unemployed again, you can reapply for benefits.

HELP IN STARTING YOUR OWN BUSINESS

The U.S. Small Business Administration (SBA) is supposed to give veterans special attention. The SBA can, but rarely does, make direct loans. Instead, the SBA will guarantee a loan extended by a private lender. This means that you need to convince a bank that you have a good idea for a small business and that you have adequate collateral for the bank to extend you a loan. Occasionally, if two private lenders refuse your request, the SBA may give you a direct loan if you are a Vietnam War veteran or are disabled. However, the SBA imposes its own credit standards that make it difficult to get a direct loan.

The SBA does sponsor a variety of seminars that offer training, counseling, and other help in preparing a detailed written business plan. To locate the nearest SBA field office, call (800) 368-5855.

CHAPTER FOURTEEN

HOMELESS AND INCARCERATED VETERANS

★ ★

Veterans who are homeless or incarcerated face extra hurdles in dealing with the VA. Congress saw the need to direct the VA not to deny VA benefits to a veteran just because he or she had no fixed address. Congress also saw fit to cut off VA benefits to most veterans shortly after incarceration.

HOMELESS VETERANS

Some surveys of homeless persons have found that as many as 50 percent of them are veterans. The VA offers no "homeless benefit" program. Being homeless does not automatically qualify you for a cash payment from the VA. You are eligible for the same benefits (for example, compensation or pension) as a veteran living in a house. Not only that: The fact that you are homeless should signal to the VA that you need extra attention and you need it quickly, but you need to tell this to the VA.

Each VA regional office has an employee who is the homeless coordinator. If you are near a VA regional office, go find that person and introduce yourself. This coordinator knows about services in the community to help you with food and temporary shelter. While you are at the regional office, visit each of the veterans' service organization representatives and find out how they can help you. For example, the Disabled American Veterans maintains an "indigents' fund" that might be a source of emergency cash. Other veterans service organizations offer short-term emergency assistance and sometimes longer-term assistance.

Getting Your Mail

Although Congress ordered the VA not to deny your claim for benefits because you have no fixed address, the problem of getting letters to you remains. The VA will need to ask you for more information; it will need to schedule you for an examination; it will need to tell you whether you were awarded or denied benefits. If all goes well, it will also need to know where to send your checks.

If you live near the VA regional office, ask the homeless coordinator to arrange for you to pick up your VA mail at the regional office. If that person refuses to do so, ask veterans' service organization representatives whether they will help you. If you are staying in a shelter that has an address and you trust the managers to relay your mail, use that address.

Of course, if you have money, you can rent a post office box. If you have no money, ask the postal service clerk for a Form 1527, Application for General Delivery. You will probably need to meet with the Postmaster to get his or her approval to use a general delivery address. Postmasters have the authority to offer you this service free of charge. Mail sent to a general delivery address will be held for only 30 days, so you must be able to check for any mail at least once each month. Be prepared to show a picture ID to pick up your mail. If you move out of the area and set up a new general delivery address, call the VA regional office (see Appendix B) and give it your new address. An address change made by the 10th of the month means that any check to be mailed the next month will go to your new address.

Replacing a Check

If you miss a VA check and you suspect that it was stolen or lost, you can get a replacement. The official advice that you are likely to get over the telephone from a regional office is that you have to write to the VA and request a replacement check. The official process will take several weeks. If you need the money and will not be able to afford to eat unless you receive the check sooner, go to the nearest VA regional office, explain your situation to the homeless coordinator, and ask for extra help. The regional office can arrange for a special check within a few days.

If you don't get a commitment from the VA homeless coordinator, ask each service representative to help you and, if necessary, ask for an appointment with the director of the regional office. Finally, if you get nowhere with the VA officials, call the local newspaper to see if it is interested in reporting your situation. The VA can move quickly in the face of potentially adverse publicity.

INCARCERATED VETERANS

Being incarcerated does not strip you of your status as a veteran. It does make your dealings with the VA more difficult. If you are getting a VA compensation or pension check, you can expect the VA to cut it off or sharply reduce it shortly after you are incarcerated, unless you have a family. If you have not previously applied for VA benefits, it is very difficult to do after you are imprisoned.

Reduction of VA Payments

The reduction or termination of payments caused by conviction of a felony should not happen if you have a family and they ask for the payments to be "apportioned" to them. See Chapter 10 for the apportionment process. Your spouse, dependent child, or dependent parent needs to apply and ask that your benefit be mailed directly to him or her.

If you have no family and you were drawing a 100 percent service-connected compensation, the VA will cut it to the 10 percent rate as of the 61st day after incarceration. If you were drawing a 10 percent rating, the VA should cut this payment in half. This is what is supposed to happen for veterans convicted of a felony that was committed after Oct. 7, 1980. If the VA notices a change of address to a post office box associated with a prison, it may ask you about your situation.

Although compensation payments are sharply reduced, pension payments are eliminated entirely unless you have a family. If you are convicted of either a felony or a misdemeanor and are incarcerated for more than 60 days, the VA should terminate the pension payments. Educational assistance is generally limited to reimbursement of expenses you incur. If tuition and books are provided free, the VA may pay you nothing. If you are in a halfway house the restriction does not apply.

You should tell the VA when you are incarcerated. The VA periodically compares lists of inmates with lists of its payees. If you fail to tell the VA that you are incarcerated and the VA continues to send the full payment automatically to your bank, then discovers you are incarcerated, not only will it make the reduction but it will also demand that you repay the overpayment. See Chapter 2 for information on how to apply for a waiver if this happens.

Payment of compensation or a pension to you should resume when you are released from prison. You must tell the VA that you are out of prison. Also, "release from prison" includes getting out on work release, being sent to a halfway house, or getting out on parole.

Applying for VA Benefits

Technically, you can apply just like any other veteran. The reality is that if you apply for disability benefits, the VA will want you to appear for an examination at a VA medical center. If your facility has made arrangements with the VA medical center to provide transportation and a guard, you may get past this hurdle. Some states provide transportation if you pay for it. If the facility has not made such an arrangement, ask for it. You might want to contact the team leader at the nearest VA vet center and ask him or her to help facilitate the arrangements. If no arrangement can be made, ask the VA to come to you. There is little chance that this will happen, but ask.

Finally, if you cannot get to a VA doctor and the VA will not come to you, ask the VA to give its guidelines for examinations to your facility's doctor. It may be necessary to make a formal request under the Freedom of Information Act to the regional office for a copy of the *VA Physician's Guide to Disability Evaluation Examinations*. See Chapter 11 for making a FOIA request. With the Physician's Guide, the prison doctor can perform an examination that should be acceptable to the VA. If the VA rejects your claim because it does not like the prison doctor's exam, appeal. See Chapter 3.

You may also consider arranging with an outside psychologist to give you a battery of written tests. For example, some tests are designed to identify the presence and severity of post-traumatic stress disorder (PTSD). The team leader at the nearest VA vet center may be able to facilitate this.

Getting Out of Prison

The fact that you are a veteran may have worked against you in sentencing. Having combat training may have made you appear more dangerous. Use your veteran's status to contact veterans' organizations to work with you. If you can show that you have support from your community, you strengthen your chance of getting parole. Especially, if you are up for parole review, ask someone to speak on your behalf. Ideally, that person will have worked with you while you were in prison and will have been able to arrange for a place for you to stay and work if you are released. All this should be included in a "Report to the Parole Board."

Use the national office addresses of vet organizations in Appendix B at the end of this book to ask for the local chapter or post. Some VSOs, for example, the VVA and AMVETS, have active programs for incarcerated veterans, including formation of chapters inside prisons.

Not Going into Prison

If you have not been convicted yet but are facing a trial and you believe that your combat experiences may have led to PTSD, which in turn contributed to your offense, say so. Ask your defense attorney to research PTSD. There is a good article in the March 1984 *Boston College Law Review* entitled "Paying the Price for Vietnam: Post-Traumatic Stress Disorder and Criminal Behavior" by C. Peter Erlinder; ask your lawyer to get it. If you had combat experience but have never been evaluated for PTSD, contact the nearest VA vet center team leader to arrange for an evaluation. The team leader may be able to work with your defense attorney to explain whether PTSD played a role in your offense.

Fort Leavenworth

If you are at Fort Leavenworth or another military prison as a result of a court martial, you or your family should contact this advocacy organization: M.O.M.S (Mothers Opposed to Maltreatment of Servicemembers); 8285 Black Hawk Court; Frederick, MD 21701; (301) 694-3668.

Pardons

After you have been out of prison for a few years, leading an exemplary life, consider applying for a pardon. Each state's rules are different on when you can apply and what you have to show to succeed. If your offense was a federal offense, contact the U.S. Department of Justice; ATTN: Pardon Attorney; Washington, DC 20530.

CHAPTER FIFTEEN

★

WAR VETS: WORLD WAR II, KOREA, VIETNAM

★★★★★★★★★★★★★★★★★★★★★★★★★★★★★★★★★★★★★★

If you are a veteran who experienced combat in World War I, World War II, Korea, or Vietnam (or perhaps in more than one period), you likely have memories that are more vivid (to put it mildly) than those held by veterans who were stateside their entire tour. You might even consider yourself a breed apart from noncombat veterans. When it comes to most benefits programs, however, it usually doesn't matter where or when you served.

There are exceptions to this, though, and this chapter focuses on the programs that are limited to certain groups of veterans of World War II, Korea, and Vietnam. These veterans also have common concerns that are related more to their age than to whether they served in combat, and these age-related issues are raised in this chapter, too.

World War II

Whether or not you saw combat during World War II, you served during a period of war. If you served at that time, you were part of the largest—and one of the oldest—groups of veterans. You also have the most colleagues dying each year. World War II veterans make up nearly one-third of the veteran population (about 8.5 million). At the same time, your ranks are shrinking at the rate of about 350,000 each year.

Your wartime service partially qualifies you for the VA nonservice-connected disability program. Until 1990, the VA considered you automatically disabled at age 65 for purposes of qualifying for the VA pension program. More than one-fourth of all veterans are 65 and older. Nevertheless, the age-65 presumption of disability was eliminated in 1990. Still, 75 percent of VA pension recipients (about 400,000) are World War II veterans. Details about the pension program are discussed in Chapter 5.

Because the VA pension payments are reduced by other income you receive, you should also consider whether your current health problems are related to your military service. Chapter 4 discusses service-connected compensation payments. These payments are not reduced by other income you may have. Although post-traumatic stress disorder (PTSD) is often associated with service in Vietnam, several thousand World War II veterans have also been awarded benefits for this condition. In particular, World War II veterans who were former POWs have a high incidence of PTSD. Approximately 116,129 servicemembers were captured and subsequently freed during World War II. An estimated 65,000 of these former POWs were alive as of 1992.

As you get older, you may become more concerned about nursing home care. Chapter 9 discusses the rules for being admitted to a VA nursing home. Keep in mind that new nursing homes are being built. Some states have veterans homes, too. Also, as more World War II veterans need care, you can expect changes in the VA rules regarding who is accepted into the homes. Unless many more beds become available, the rules are likely to further limit who is eligible. The role of the VA in the national debate on universal health care is unclear.

Also, as you get older, you may become more concerned about dying and making arrangements for your family. See Chapter 8 for a discussion of VA insurance programs. Make sure your spouse knows where to find your VA papers, your claim number, and the VA's toll-free insurance number. See Chapter 5 for a discussion of the VA pension program that is available to survivors regardless of their own disability. Also, see Chapter 10 for a discussion of benefits for survivors of veterans who had service-connected disabilities.

Korean War

The Korean War is sometimes referred to as the forgotten war and other times referred to as the first forgotten war (Vietnam was the second). If you are a veteran of the Korean War you are one of about 4.8 million, accounting for about one-fifth of all veterans. Only recently a national monument was begun in your honor.

For information on the Korean War Veterans Memorial, contact the Department of the Interior (18th & C Streets, N.W.; Washington, DC 20240). Although the larger veterans' service organizations include Korean

War veterans as members, there is a separate organization just for you. See Appendix D at the end of this book for the address of the Korean War Veterans Association.

Korean veterans, like those of Vietnam, continue to press for an accounting of the approximately 8,000 servicemembers still missing. Many of the missing were killed in combat in North Korea, which until 1992 was completely sealed off from visits by Westerners. In May 1992, North Korean officials returned the remains of several servicemembers. Whether more remains will be returned is unclear given the secretive nature of the North Korean government. Approximately 4,400 servicemembers were repatriated following internment as POWs. Of these, an estimated 3,155 were still living as of 1992.

Just as World War II veterans are pressuring the VA health care system to accommodate their needs for nursing home and expanded geriatric care, so too are Korean veterans trying to force some changes.

Vietnam War

During the Vietnam Era (1964 to 1975) about 9 million servicemembers were on duty. Of these, approximately 2.8 million spent time in Vietnam. A major study completed in 1981 found evidence that those veterans with exposure to combat later experienced dramatically more alcohol and drug use, arrests, medical problems, and stress-related symptoms than those not exposed to combat. The greater the degree of exposure to combat, the more serious the subsequent adjustment to civilian life. The study, *Legacies of Vietnam: Comparative Adjustment of Veterans and Their Peers*, was headed by Arthur Egendorf. The 900-page report was originally printed by the U.S. House of Representatives Veterans Affairs Committee; a copy may be available through your local library.

The unmet needs of Vietnam War combat veterans led to the creation of a network of vet centers across the country. For addresses, see Appendix B. These vet centers offer readjustment counseling that was not available through traditional VA facilities. An estimated 500,000 to 800,000 Vietnam War veterans are thought to have some symptoms of PTSD. Fewer than 10 percent are drawing service-connected compensation for this disability. See Chapter 4 for details on the compensation program.

Vietnam War veterans have continued to pressure the VA to recognize illnesses related to their exposure to herbicides in Vietnam. Although the VA officially recognizes that a handful of conditions are related to herbicide exposure (specifically to Agent Orange), the official list of such conditions does not begin to cover all those ailments complained of by veterans. Likewise, the VA has never agreed that children of Vietnam War veterans can be affected by their parents' exposure.

Through the efforts of many Vietnam War veterans who brought a lawsuit in 1979 against the chemical companies that manufactured Agent Orange, a settlement fund of $180 million was created in 1984. This fund was divided into two parts: one part to be used to make cash payments to veterans or survivors; the other part to pay organizations to provide services to veterans and their families. As of September 1991, approximately $86 million had been paid to 19,356 veterans and another $47 million had been awarded and remained to be paid to them. The average overall payment during the lifetime of the program will amount to about $5,800 per veteran. A total of 7,828 survivors of vets received $17.7 million or an average lump sum payment of about $2,500.

If you are a Vietnam War veteran and believe that you are totally disabled or if you are a surviving family member of a Vietnam War veteran, call the Agent Orange Payment Program at the following telephone number to receive an application: (800) 225-4712. You do not have to prove that your disability was directly caused by exposure to Agent Orange. This program is scheduled to expire in 1994.

Approximately 73 organizations have received settlement fund money amounting to about $13 million per year. This funding is expected to continue through 1994 and is managed by the Agent Orange Class Assistance Program at P.O. Box 27413; Washington, DC 20038; (202) 289-6173.

The small size of the payments to individual veterans was a bitter disappointment to many. Also, a comparison to what the VA should pay for the same condition is distressing: the total payment from the settlement fund during a 10-year period ($5,800) amounts to about one-fourth of what the VA pays in 1 year to a veteran rated as totally disabled (about $20,000). Nevertheless, very few veterans are being paid any VA benefits for Agent Orange-related conditions.

As of this writing, the issue of accounting for those missing in action in Vietnam continued to engage the attention of not only survivors but also numerous members of Congress and veterans' service organizations. The frequency of both official and unofficial trips to Vietnam to look for the remains of more than 2,000 soldiers has increased in the past few years. Whether they all can be accounted for is unknown. In late 1992, photographs of crash sites became available; these photos may lead to resolution of many cases.

In 1982, the Vietnam Veterans Memorial was built in Washington, DC. With its list (arranged in chronological order) of the more than 58,000 vets killed in Vietnam, it continues to draw the most visitors of any of the memorials in Washington, DC.

Finally, although the major veterans' service organizations include Vietnam War veterans as members, there is a separate organization just for you. See Appendix D for the address of Vietnam Veterans of America.

CHAPTER SIXTEEN

★

PERSIAN GULF VETERANS

★★

You are part of the latest group of former servicemembers to serve during wartime. The Persian Gulf War is defined as beginning on Aug. 2, 1990. As of the writing of this book, no ending date for this period was fixed. If you served in the Kuwaiti Theater of Operations, you were one of about 500,000 servicemembers. Despite the national media's interest in the advanced technology used against Iraq, your service was similar to that in other wars: long periods of waiting, sweating, eating strange food, and swatting flies— along with intense fear.

Casualties included 146 killed, at least 35 of these by friendly fire. Fortunately, your service was also characterized by a swift victory and overwhelming public support. When you returned, there were parades in your honor, something not experienced by either Korean War or Vietnam War veterans.

At the same time, you were exposed to diseases diagnosed only with difficulty and smoke from burning oil wells that may cause you problems later in life. There have also been reports of exposure to chemical and biological agents. This chapter is intended to alert you to some of these problems so that if your health is affected by your service you can get a head start in pursuing VA benefits.

POTENTIAL HEALTH PROBLEMS

The area of the world in which you served has many diseases not found in the United States. You may have been bitten by an infected sandfly, tick, or louse but not have any symptoms for months, even years. You may also have been given new drugs as a pretreatment for the expected nerve-gas attacks or a vaccine against biological warfare agents. These drugs may not be a problem, but you should make an extra effort to get a copy of your service medical records so that you know which drugs you were given.

Early reports suggest that fewer troops became ill than had been anticipated and that the most prevalent problem was diarrhea from eating locally grown lettuce. Congressional hearings in 1993, however, revealed new reports of increased sensitivity to multiple chemicals and noted the death from cancer of one 23-year-old veteran.

In addition to the delay in developing symptoms, the symptoms may not be correctly diagnosed because your condition is not something that most doctors would commonly encounter. For the rest of your life it will be very important to explain to any physician or other health care worker that your medical history includes service in the Middle East.

An article in the March 21, 1991, *New England Journal of Medicine* listed several diseases that may cause you to experience symptoms long after you became infected (for example, sandfly fever [postinfection fatigue], giardiasis, leishmaniasis, malaria, Q fever, brucellosis, schistosomiasis, and viral hepatitis). If you seek treatment in a VA medical center, health care workers there should be alert to your potential for developing these (and other) diseases. Still, even at a VA facility, you must be an advocate for yourself and make it clear that you served in the Middle East. Insist that your name be added to the Persian Gulf Registry so that you can be quickly contacted if additional tests become available to evaluate your health. In 1993, a label was created to describe a cluster of conditions (fatigue, imsomnia, sleep disorders, listlessness, weight loss, digestive disorders) that had commonly been reported: Persian Gulf Syndrome. In November 1993 the VA announced it would begin compensating Persian Gulf veterans suffering from chronic fatigue syndrome.

If you develop a problem that no one can diagnose, and the problem prevents you from working as efficiently as you used to, file a claim for disability compensation with the nearest VA regional office. At a minimum, you will want, as soon as possible, to start a record of your problems. Without a firm diagnosis, the VA is likely to deny your claim, but perhaps the VA will recognize the problem as one for which you should be paid compensation. This won't happen unless you apply. As of the end of 1993, the VA had granted only about five percent of Desert Storm claims based on exposure to toxic substances like smoke from oil wells. See Chapter 4 for more details regarding the VA compensation program.

In addition to the potential physical health problems, you may already have experienced (or you may later) disturbing recollections of combat. If you were in combat, treated wounded or burned soldiers, saw dead ones, or were in the barracks at Daharan that was hit by the Scud missile, stop by a vet center for some counseling.

Some noncombat vets or civilians may say that the combat didn't last long enough for it to affect your emotional health. When Vietnam War veterans first complained about their problems, they were given insensitive responses, too. Fortunately for you, vet center staff are often Vietnam War vets. They are sensitive to what you experienced and what you may be experiencing now. Take advantage of the services they provide.

A preliminary study of those vets particularly vulnerable to developing post-traumatic stress disorder (PTSD) include those who were either exposed to intensive combat or wounded in action, POWs, minorities, female troops, National Guard and reserve troops called to active duty with little advance warning, parents of small children, and troops who suffered economic hardship or family turmoil after their return home.

If the separation from your family left some scars or lingering resentment among your family members, also ask someone at a vet center for advice. A list of all vet centers around the country is included in Appendix B.

Most of the major service organizations are available for you to join. At this time, no organization of just Persian Gulf War vets exists and no memorial to your efforts has been built.

EMPLOYMENT AND TRAINING OPPORTUNITIES

One consequence of the Persian Gulf War was the passage of numerous changes to VA programs to help ease the difficulty for reservists who were called on short notice. For example, the Soldiers' and Sailors' Civil Relief Act, a law first enacted many years ago to protect families from evictions and soldiers from some debt collections was revised. The amount of life insurance coverage you could get was doubled. The Montgomery GI Bill monthly benefits were increased.

Given the large number of current civilian Defense Department employees who will also lose their jobs and look for work, it is important for you to take advantage of any education benefits you can get.

KEEPING UP ON NEW PROGRAMS

The changes in the GI Bill and the likely changes in postseparation benefits offered by each service may be important to you. Join a veterans' service organization to get a newsletter or magazine that reports these changes.

Also, consider extending or renewing your subscription to the *Army Times*, the *Navy Times*, or the *Air Force Times*. Each can be obtained by mail by addressing a letter to the name of the periodical, Springfield, VA, 22158-5898, or by calling (800) 368-5718. The *Times* routinely reports changes in benefit programs. You may discover that you are entitled to use the commissary after all.

CHAPTER SEVENTEEN

CORRECTING RECORDS AND CHANGING YOUR DISCHARGE STATUS

★★

This chapter tells you how to apply for a change in the kind of discharge that you had from the service. You may have received a regular discharge but think that you should have had a medical discharge, or you may have received a discharge that was under "other than honorable conditions" (that is, a discharge other than "honorable" or "general") and think that you deserved a general discharge. This chapter also describes how service-members can challenge a low evaluation rating or other adverse information in the file.

CORRECTING YOUR PERSONNEL FILE WHILE STILL ON ACTIVE DUTY

While you are on active duty, you receive periodic evaluations. A poor evaluation may prevent you from obtaining a promotion and may prevent

---

★ IMPORTANT ★

You are not prohibited from hiring an attorney to represent you on these claims. Service organizations often provide free representation in filling out the appropriate forms. These are difficult cases. Only a small percentage of these claims succeed. At the same time, if you do win, you may become eligible for several thousand dollars in VA benefits and sometimes in military retirement benefits. Calculate what you stand to gain; balance this against what you have to pay up front to hire a lawyer.

you from reenlisting or may force you out early. The regulations that the raters use require that any low evaluation be fully explained. If it is not, you may be able to have it removed or redone. If you appealed a low rating within your command and got no satisfaction, consider applying to the Board for Correction of Military Records.

You may also consider going this route if you received a nonjudicial punishment that you think was unfair. Get a DD Form 149, Application for Correction of Military Record, from your personnel office. Also consult with the base Judge Advocate General to make sure that there are no other options besides the Correction Board that you can pursue to have your record corrected. The address to use to file the DD 149 is on the back of the form. The members of the board who decide your case are civilian employees of the Defense.

If you discover that your personnel file contains a mistake, consider making a Privacy Act Request to your commander. The Privacy Act not only gives you the right to see your records; it also requires that only accurate, relevant, and timely information be kept in your files. The act gives you the right to correct mistakes or at least to include in the file your version of the mistaken information.

CHANGING YOUR DISCHARGE TO A MEDICAL DISCHARGE

Most servicemembers receive an administrative discharge. Chapter 22 describes those and the procedures involved. A small number of servicemembers receive a medical discharge following a physical evaluation board proceeding. See Chapter 24 for those procedures. Say you served for 5 years of a 6-year term and then you began to have problems and got into trouble that led to nonjudicial punishments.

Perhaps a mental status evaluation diagnosed you as having a schizoid personality disorder. Perhaps you completed a physical evaluation board but it decided that you were fit for duty. Perhaps, despite this diagnosis, your command discharged you because of disciplinary problems. Perhaps, within a few months your mother drove you to the nearest VA medical center and committed you for treatment. Perhaps you were diagnosed as suffering from schizophrenia and your VA psychiatrist offered an opinion that your schizoid personality disorder was really the early stage of schizophrenia.

This situation is only hypothetical. Still, if you were in a similar situation, you may want to consider asking the service to change your discharge. Before you do so, consider what the net gain may be. If the VA has already agreed to pay you service-connected compensation at the 100 percent rate (about $1,800 per month), you will not get additional money if your basic pay when you were discharged was less than the 100 percent rate. On the other hand, if your basic pay was higher or the VA did not agree to pay you compensation until 3 years after your discharge, it might be worth the initial investment to pay a lawyer to represent you.

A list of the names and addresses of attorneys who represent veterans at the Court of Veterans Appeals—and who may also be available to represent you in changing your discharge to a medical one—is available from the National Organization of Veterans Advocates; P.O. Box 42334; Washington, DC 20015.

If you intend to pursue a change, get a DD Form 149, Application for Correction of Military Record, by calling the nearest VA regional office. The address to use to file the form is on the back of the form. The application is processed by the Board for Correction of Military Records. There is one such board for each branch of the service. The members of the board who decide your case are civilian employees of the service.

CHANGING YOUR RE CODE OR OTHER INFORMATION ON DD 214

At discharge you are issued a Certificate of Release or Discharge from Active Duty, a DD 214. On this form, a narrative reason for your discharge is included as well as an RE code indicating whether you are considered immediately eligible for reenlistment. Another code, a three-letter separation program designator, or SPD (which used to be a three-digit SPN code), provides an abbreviation for the official narrative reason for your

---

★ **DEADLINE** ★

Technically, you have only 3 years from the date when you discovered the error in your discharge to apply to a Board for Correction of Military Records. Nevertheless, the board can excuse a late application if you give it a good reason. Examples may include that you did not discover the error until after you obtained a copy of your personnel file last month, or that you were out of the country, or that you were institutionalized for several years and could not pursue an application.

---

discharge. If you have a less than fully honorable discharge, your RE code will indicate that you are not eligible for immediate reenlistment.

If you want to reenlist or sign up for the reserves, talk to a recruiter. Some RE codes do not bar you from reenlisting and the recruiter can ask his or her command to waive the code. If you have your discharge upgraded, the RE code usually is automatically changed, but this does not guarantee that you will be able to reenlist. These days, the services have enough young recruits so that they seldom take the time to reconsider older vets' claims. You can confirm whether the SPD is correct by writing to the National Personnel Records Center (9700 Page Blvd.; St. Louis, MO 63132) and asking for an explanation of what the SPD means. If the SPD does not correspond to your official narrative reason for discharge, ask the Board for Correction of Military Records to correct it.

UPGRADING THE CHARACTER OF YOUR DISCHARGE

Most servicemembers receive an honorable discharge. As many as 10 percent of servicemembers may receive a less than fully honorable discharge (for example, a general discharge or, worse, a discharge under other than honorable conditions, which used to be called an "undesirable" discharge). Only a few receive (from a court-martial) either a bad conduct discharge or a dishonorable discharge from a court-martial.

Changing (upgrading) a discharge is difficult. Only about one of every ten applicants for an upgrade gets one. Discharges are not automatically changed.

A less than fully honorable discharge does not always prevent you from receiving VA benefits. If your main reason for wanting an upgrade is to qualify for VA benefits, apply for the benefits and, at the same time, apply for an upgrade. The VA will probably deny your claim because of your discharge, but you can appeal that within the VA. See Chapter 3 for a discussion of the VA appeals process.

The VA may say that your discharge does not prevent you from getting benefits. If you need medical treatment for a condition that occurred during a tour of duty that ended with an undesirable discharge, the VA should still treat you, even if it will not pay you compensation for the same condition (38 C.F.R. 3.360).

Whether you apply to the VA for benefits or not, a VA decision does not upgrade your discharge. Only a military Discharge Review Board (DRB) can upgrade a discharge. (There are separate DRBs for the Army,

Navy [including Marines], Air Force, and Coast Guard.) Use a DD Form 293, Application for the Review of Discharge. You can get this form by calling the nearest VA regional office. The deadline to apply for an upgrade is usually 15 years after discharge.

If you were discharged more than 15 years ago, instead of using a DD 293, use a DD 149 and apply for an upgrade through the Board for Correction of Military Records. If you were discharged by a general court-martial, go to the Correction Board. Also, if the Discharge Review Board rejects your request, go to the Correction Board. The Correction Board upgrades a higher percentage of cases than the Discharge Review Board does.

What to Tell a Discharge Review Board

Ask the Discharge Review Board to give you a hearing at which you can explain in person what happened. Most veterans don't bother with a hearing. Those who do stand a better chance of getting an upgrade. Ask for a hearing near where you live. With the downsizing of the military, you may have to travel to Washington, DC, for a hearing. If at all possible, try to do so. If you schedule an appointment, keep it. If you cannot keep it, call the board ahead of time and try to reschedule it. You may want to withdraw your application and resubmit it later when you will be able to keep an appointment.

The five high-ranking officers who consider your case usually stand by the records and do not take into consideration your behavior since your discharge. Take the time to explain the details of any punishment you received. The official record makes most offenses seem worse than they were. If you had a conflict with a particular supervisor or NCO, explain this and suggest that the conflict should not outweigh an otherwise good record.

If you were having personal, family, or medical problems that prevented you from performing your duties, explain this and try to have your spouse or doctor confirm your statements, too. They can testify by affidavit, but live appearances are generally more effective.

Special Resources on Discharge Upgrading

You should know about one publication that is designed for you and another that is designed for your lawyer. The 8-page *Self-Help Guide to Discharge Upgrading* is available from the National Veterans Legal Services Project in Washington, DC. Call (202) 265-8305 for the price and for information on ordering the guide. A technical manual (*Military Discharge Upgrading*) for lawyers is also sold by that project.

Living with a Bad Discharge

If all else fails and you cannot have your discharge changed, you must live with it. Some individuals lie about their discharges on employment applications. Others are never asked about their military service. Some are asked, explain the circumstances surrounding the discharge, and don't get hired; others do get hired. It's clear that if you lie, you can be fired for falsifying your application.

Whatever your situation was in the military, don't dwell on it. You are not a bad person just because you have a bad discharge. There is very little relationship between how you behaved in the military (perhaps as a teenager) and what you are capable of now. Unfortunately, many employers don't recognize this.

PART THREE

SERVICEMEMBERS AND THEIR FAMILIES

CHAPTER EIGHTEEN

★

BASIC SURVIVAL SKILLS

★ ★

If you are not on active duty, skip this chapter and this section. In fact, just read Part One of this book, the part on veterans. If you are on active duty, read on, and in anticipation of the day when you will become a veteran, read all of Part One as well.

The next seven chapters of this book are intended to flag some issues that you may face during your military career. Addressing these issues now will probably make your transition to becoming a civilian (and a veteran) much smoother than it otherwise would be. In particular, addressing these issues now will increase the likelihood that any contact you have in the future with the U.S. Department of Veterans Affairs will be successful.

Perhaps the best practical advice for making the most of your tour of duty is to read. Read the base newsletter, read the local civilian newspaper, read the newspapers that are aimed at you: for example, the *Army Times*, the *Navy Times*, and the *Air Force Times*. For subscription information, address a letter to the name of any of these three publications, Springfield, VA, 22158-5898 (no street address is necessary); you can also call (800) 368-5718. Ideas for maximizing your current pay, and your prospects for future employment and education are available. Particularly as the drawdown (personnel reduction) in defense increases, you need sources of good information.

OVERVIEW OF THE REMAINDER OF THE BOOK

The next chapter discusses financial matters: your pay, how to get more money, how to get out of financial trouble. Chapter 20 discusses the mil-

---
★ IMPORTANT ★

We will say again and again: Get help. The problems that we have flagged in the next few chapters are only a few that you may face. You may not know anyone who has had as many hassles as you are having, but be assured that of the millions of servicemembers who have preceded you, at least a few have had the same problems. The trick is to find someone who has already dealt with these problems and whom you can trust to give you good advice. You can always get advice, but you must get *good* advice.

You may also need to get confidential advice, and doing so may be difficult in the military. You must assume that what you say to a military psychiatrist, a chaplain, or a social actions officer will not be kept confidential.

Sometimes you may want to turn to support services available on the base, sometimes you may need to seek help off-base from civilian agencies or a private lawyer or doctor. We try to offer suggestions on where and when to look for help. Many civilians who were in the military in the past will lend you a hand, but you will have to ask for help.

---

itary disability retirement system; this system is important if you become unable to continue your military service as a result of an injury or illness. Chapter 21 covers medical care that is available (or should be available). Chapter 22 discusses some of the reasons you may be discharged early: Sometimes you can initiate a discharge; other times you don't have a choice. These days, with the new voluntary separation programs, there are many unknowns in your future.

Chapter 23 addresses some of the additional hassles that women and minority servicemembers sometimes face. Chapter 24 covers the benefits available to dependents, survivors and certain others. Chapter 25 addresses dependents' programs, while Chapter 26 describes how you can obtain a copy of important records about your military service.

CHAPTER NINETEEN

FINANCIAL ISSUES

★ ★

This chapter addresses some of the financial issues facing active duty personnel: how to confirm that you are getting the right pay, why you may be getting less than you thought, how to protect what you have, how to plan for survival after discharge. The information in this chapter may be changing as you read this. We will not give you 50 pages of charts itemizing the current dollar amounts of various kinds of pay. Such information would be too quickly out of date to be useful.

The most important advice we can offer is that you should question the amount of money you are receiving and should keep your eyes and ears open to changes. Get in the habit of reading the newspapers that are aimed at you: for example, the *Army Times*, the *Navy Times*, and the *Air Force Times*. For subscription information, address a letter to the name of any of these publications, Springfield, VA, 22158-5898, or call (800) 368-5718. These three papers routinely report on changes in pay, opportunities for bonuses, and options involving taxes. Particularly as the drawdown in the military increases, you need a weekly, if not daily, source of good information and advice.

See Chapter 10 for financial issues regarding dependents or survivors. See Chapter 13 for details regarding unemployment compensation for ex-servicemembers.

PAY

You can probably quickly recite how much pay you expect to receive in next week's check. But when was the last time you looked closely at your pay stub or compared it to the previous one? If you're in the army or the air force, your pay stub, or leave and earnings statement, may look different than it used to. These two services are using a new format for the statement.

The statement is divided into three columns: entitlements, deductions, and allotments. The statement also records the number of days of leave you used and the number remaining to be used. Save your statements. Review the new against the old. Review the new against the charts posted in the finance office for the correct amounts given your pay grade and years in service.

You already know that your pay rate changes with promotions and every year of service that you accumulate. But, do you know the date, day of the week and hour of the day that the next exam in your specialty is being offered? (And have you begun to study?) Some things you cannot control, other things you have some control over. Do what you can.

You are entitled to extra pay when your work involves certain hazardous duties. At the beginning of 1992, these duties warranted a $110 extra payment each month. Another increase in pay is available for those in "imminent danger." Those who participated in the Persian Gulf received $150 extra per month. Additional payments for those duties include flight pay, diving pay, submarine pay, and career sea pay. Special duty assignments and foreign duty also warrant additional pay. In addition, you can earn extra pay if you become proficient in a foreign language.

Hundreds of pages of details regarding how your pay is calculated and when you are entitled to more (or less) are contained in the *Department of Defense Pay and Allowances Manual*. This manual is available at any base, the post library, or the finance office.

EMERGENCY ASSISTANCE

You may find that your pay is inadequate and that you cannot put food on the table. If so, you should know about the food stamp program, operated by the U.S. Department of Agriculture. If your income is $16,510 or less and your family consists of you and at least three dependents, you qualify for food stamps. Your kids can get a free or reduced-price school lunch, too. It may seem demeaning to ask for this kind of help, but you have earned the benefit. Take advantage of it. Apply through the nearest county department of social services or a similar agency.

If you need emergency cash to pay for rent or other essentials, check with your base's family assistance office. If you're caught short while in transit, check with the nearest American Red Cross or USO office.

TAX ISSUES

You are not exempt from paying federal taxes just because you are in the military or stationed overseas. You do get some special breaks, though. For example, your basic allowance for quarters, family separation allowance, variable housing allowance, and certain other allowances are not counted as part of your gross income. Enlisted pay for service in the Persian Gulf on or after January 17, 1991, is not counted. If you did not earn enough to have to pay more taxes than the amount already withheld from your checks, you may not have to file a federal income tax return. Still, you should file, because you are probably entitled to a refund.

The state in which you are officially a resident can make a difference in your take-home pay. Some states charge no state income tax to anyone. Others exempt all active duty pay. Others exempt all retirement pay. Others exempt you from paying income tax while you are stationed overseas or if you are totally disabled and drawing disability retirement benefits. Some states will give you a break if you have to file late. Most states operate a toll-free tax information hotline.

Some tax issues are beyond the scope of this book. Among them are whether you owe taxes, how much you owe, whether you owe a penalty for not filing, and how to deal with federal and state tax agents. Get advice from your base's legal assistance office, call or write the IRS or your state tax office, or consult a reputable accountant or tax preparation company.

PROBLEMS WITH CREDITORS

When the VA Wants Money from You

The VA may come after you for money if you used your VA loan guaranty to buy a house. The VA has the authority to take as much as 15 percent of your base pay to repay a VA debt. You should be informed of the situation by the VA before your salary is reduced. You may learn of the problem first from your finance office. Or, you may get a call from a bill collector.

See Chapter 2 for a description of the VA debt collection program. Contact your base's legal assistance office for advice before calling or writing a VA office. Given the amount of money that the VA may want to recover, you should seriously consider hiring a lawyer to fight the VA.

─────────── ★ CAUTION ★ ───────────

Statements that you make to the VA can and will be used against you. Statements that the VA employees make to you may be accurate, but the statements may not take all factors into account. In addition, courts have ruled that you cannot rely on what a government employee tells you over the telephone. If the government employee's statements were incorrect but you relied on them, you cannot complain that you were misled.

In Debt

If you acknowledge that you're in debt, you've taken the first step to improving your financial situation. There are many different indicators of trouble: You can pay only the minimum due on credit cards, you borrow from friends in the last few days before you get paid, you have no savings, or you argue with your spouse about money.

If you acknowledge that you need to do something different than what you've been doing to get out of debt, you've taken another important step. Generally, you can do two things when you don't have enough money: Get more or make do with less. Both options may be painful. Making more can mean getting a part-time job. This may be unrealistic in the area in which you are stationed or given the hours when you must be on duty. Whether employment is possible for your spouse and whether your spouse can make enough to cover more than the extra expense for child care are also difficult questions. Making more money may mean preparing now for the next promotion exam.

If you can't get more money, try to cut expenses. Cutting expenses is also painful. If you're married, cutting expenses is more than twice as painful. Start by making a list of your credit card debts and required monthly payments and keeping a daily list of every expenditure. After keeping your list for 1 month, make a chart, showing the types of expenses you have (food, clothing, housing, child care, entertainment, credit cards, etc.) and how much you spend on each.

Review your list and try to identify essential and nonessential expenses. Maybe you can cut back on both.

Help in arranging a manageable repayment plan on credit cards may be available on the base or off the base. Family services offices on the base often offer counseling and may be willing to contact credit card companies to work out a repayment plan. Private consumer credit agencies also offer counseling. These agencies are often funded by credit card companies that are eager to help you avoid bankruptcy. You can locate the nearest agency by calling (800) 388-2227.

Debt collectors may begin to call you at home, but they cannot legally call you late at night. Also, if you send them letters telling them not to call you but to write you (or your attorney) instead, the calls should stop. You have other rights under the Fair Debt Collection Practices Act; ask your base's legal assistance office for more information about this law.

If you believe that declaring bankruptcy is the only way to resolve your problem, consult your base's legal assistance office or a private attorney who specializes in bankruptcy. You should expect to pay a few hundred dollars up front to an attorney and also expect to pay the court filing fee.

Declaring bankruptcy causes severe repercussions to your credit rating and will remain on your credit bureau report for 12 years. It may also (but should not) have a bad effect on your prospects for promotion. Not dealing responsibly with your finances is poor form; exercising your right to declare bankruptcy may be exactly the responsible thing to do.

Help from the Soldiers' and Sailors' Civil Relief Act

The Soldiers' and Sailors' Civil Relief Act is an old federal law that was amended during the buildup for the Persian Gulf War. It is intended to insulate you from some financial hassles that may be associated with entering active duty or being activated. For example, if you are being sued in a state court and your military service is halfway around the world, you should be able to postpone the case. Another key feature of this law is that it can reduce the interest rate on loans if your income is less on active duty than it was when you were a civilian. This law involves civil, not criminal, matters. According to an American Bar Association fact sheet:

★ You can request a delay in a court case if you have attempted to obtain leave and were unable to do so because of your military duty.

★ If a default judgment is entered against you while you are on active duty, your case can be reopened if you can show that your service prevented you from defending yourself, if you have a defense to at least part of the case, and if you apply to the court to reopen the case within 90 days following your service.

★ The interest rate on loans taken out before you entered active duty cannot exceed 6 percent per year while you are in the service unless the creditor can show that your ability to pay was not affected by your duty.

★ By giving notice to the landlord, you or your dependents may terminate a lease if it was entered into prior to entry into military service.

★ Repossession of property purchased on an installment contract that was entered into before you entered active duty is not permitted unless the creditor files a lawsuit; the lawsuit must be postponed if you request it and the court agrees that your duty has affected your ability to make payments on the contract.

★ Foreclosure on your house may be postponed or, if a foreclosure occurred, the foreclosure judgment may be reopened or the redemption period extended.

★ The deadline (under a statute of limitations) for you to file a lawsuit against someone may be postponed while you are on active duty.

Two other provisions of this law may also help you: (1) Your health insurance coverage must be reinstated automatically by your employer if you were called to active duty on or after Aug. 1, 1990, and (2) a private life insurance policy cannot be terminated for failure to pay the premiums while you are on active duty.

CHAPTER TWENTY

★

ON-THE-JOB INJURY (DISABILITY RETIREMENT)

★ ★

This chapter describes the process for obtaining what amounts in the civilian world to workers' compensation. In the military, it's called "disability retirement." Injuries that may lead to disability retirement are not limited to those incurred during combat. A disability due to an auto accident while you were home on leave or a disease you contracted while on active duty may also lead to disability retirement.

Our best advice is to get help. If you are facing a disability retirement, you are facing an extremely complicated, largely secret set of rules and procedures. Your decision may be affected by recent changes in separation policy that offer cash payments for certain servicemembers who leave early. Some official help is available through counselors who can help you understand the process or help you calculate the best options to pursue. Unfortunately, these counselors are often overworked.

If you are initially turned down or given a low disability rating, you have the right to representation by military counsel (a military lawyer) to pursue an appeal. You also have a right to hire a civilian lawyer. You should consider doing so. Contact lawyers you know or the nearest lawyer referral service (to find it, telephone your county bar association) to locate someone familiar with disability determinations. Certain veterans' service organizations also offer free counseling and representation. Getting good advice can mean the difference between a token, one-time payment or a substantial payment each month.

By law, the starting point toward disability retirement is a finding that you are "unfit to perform the duties of [your] office, grade, rank, or rating because of physical disability." Service regulations describe what consti-

```
─────────────── ★ IMPORTANT ★ ───────────────
```

Don't be in a hurry to complete this process. Do not believe anyone who tells you not to consider all options now and that if you don't get as much money from the service as you think you should, all you must do is ask the VA for more. Do not rely on the suggestion that the VA will pay you to undergo vocational rehabilitation to overcome your disability. There is nothing certain about benefits from the VA. Even if you have to remain on a medical hold beyond your expiration of term of service (ETS) to fight for the proper disability rating, at least you are drawing pay while you do so.

tutes a physical disability. If you have a medical condition listed in a regulation, you must be evaluated for possible disability retirement. These standards usually become important in one of three circumstances: while you are hospitalized for a serious injury or illness, after a period of light duty following a less serious injury or illness, or after a chronic illness has affected your ability to work.

For example, if your doctor believes that you are unfit for duty before you are released from the hospital, he or she may initiate a medical board proceeding at the hospital. If the board's medical findings agree with your doctor's, they are relayed to the physical evaluation board for processing to decide whether those findings mean you are unfit. If the medical board does not think that your case needs to be referred to the evaluation board, you can request an additional review. If your doctor is not sure whether you will recover completely, you may be given a light-duty profile for a few weeks. After this, your doctor may refer your records for review. Finally, you may be referred for evaluation even if you were not hospitalized recently but instead have had a chronic illness that has made it difficult to perform your duties.

You have a right to obtain copies of your medical records (see Chapter 25) and you should periodically review them. You will not usually see an explicit reference in your hospital records to the fact that you are "unfit." This is a determination made by the physical evaluation board.

The decision by the physical evaluation board about your fitness for duty begins with an assessment of your duties given your rank and an evaluation of whether you can reasonably perform these duties. The board also considers whether your health could worsen from continued duty or whether you pose a risk to the health of others.

Amount of Money at Stake

The money you get for a disability is intended to make up for what you will not be able to earn in the civilian world. How much money you get is determined partly by the percentage of disability found by a physical evaluation board, how long you have served, and your highest pay grade. If you came on active duty before September 8, 1980, your highest pay grade is used in this determination. If you started after that date, the average of your last three years' pay is used. Depending on the severity of your disability, you may be paid either a lump sum or a monthly payment. The monthly payment may be a temporary payment for as long as 5 years or a lifetime payment.

Disability Less Than 30 Percent

In general, if you have not served long enough to be retired based on years of service, and the percentage of disability is 0, 10, or 20 percent, you will be paid a one-time lump sum disability severance payment. The severance pay is calculated by multiplying the number of years of service (but not more than 12) by the amount of 2 months' worth of basic pay. Use the following formula to do your calculations:

Years of Service_____
    times
    Monthly Pay × 2_____
    equals_____

This sum is exempt from taxation if you entered service before Sept. 25, 1975. If you entered service after this date, you must pay taxes on this sum unless your disability is the direct result of combat-related injuries during armed conflict, extra-hazardous service, simulated war, or an instrumentality of war.

Disability Greater Than 30 Percent but Not Permanent

If your disability is found to be 30 to 50 percent disabling, but it is not clear if your condition is permanent, you may be put on a temporary disability retired list (TDRL). If you are on the TDRL, you will be paid monthly at least 50 percent of your basic pay for as long as 5 years. If your percentage of disability is higher than 50 percent, you get a higher percentage of your basic pay but not more than 75 percent of it.

Disability Greater Than 30 Percent and Permanent

If your disability is found to be permanent and there is no expectation that your condition will improve, you will be retired and paid one of two ways:

1. 2.5 percent of your creditable years of service multiplied by your base pay

Years of Service _____ × 0.025 = _____
    times
    Monthly Base Pay _____
    equals _____

or

2. the percentage of your disability multiplied by your base pay

Monthly Base Pay _____
    times
    Percent Disability _____
    equals _____

Either way you calculate the sum, the amount is capped at 75 percent of your base pay.

Line-of-Duty (On-the-Job) Injury

Unless the reason for being unfit is a result of an accident or illness that occurred in the line of duty, you will not be separated with a disability retirement. If you were injured in an accident on base, a preliminary investigation was probably already conducted. An accident report was probably also prepared that notes whether your injuries were the result of your "intentional misconduct or willful neglect" and whether your injuries were incurred during an unauthorized absence. One of the more common scenarios in which possible misconduct may be an issue is an automobile accident. If you were drunk at the time and arrested for drunk driving, the service may conclude that the injuries you sustained in the accident do not warrant disability retirement.

Another reason that you may be retired but not paid disability benefits is that the service may decide that your condition existed prior to enlistment. This is often the situation if you have a mental disability. The evaluation board may decide that certain behavioral problems that you had as an adolescent indicated that your condition existed prior to service. You may still succeed in obtaining disability benefits if you can show that your condition was worsened by military service, but this is difficult to do.

In deciding whether your condition existed prior to enlistment, you have in your favor a "presumption" that you were in sound physical and mental condition upon entering service unless the condition was noted and recorded at the time of your entrance physical examination. Nevertheless, this presumption can be overruled (and therefore you will lose) if your condition is congenital or hereditary and the natural progress of the condition has made you unfit for duty.

Certain other conditions that appear shortly after beginning active duty may also overrule the presumption of sound condition. Examples include fibrosis of the lungs and symptoms of chronic or communicable diseases.

The line-of-duty determination is not usually the problem for you. The problem is more often the particular percentage of disability that is assigned to your condition.

Percentage of Disability

The percentage of disability assigned to your condition is significant because it dictates whether you will receive a one-time lump sum payment or monthly payments. By law, the Department of Defense (DoD) uses the same charts that are used by the VA to establish a percentage of disability. These charts make up the 1945 VA Schedule for Rating Disabilities, 38 C.F.R. Part 4. ("38" means volume 38; C.F.R. means the Code of Federal Regulations, which can be found in law libraries and certain other libraries.) As its name implies, the schedule is almost 50 years out of date.

By law, the DoD must use the VA schedule in effect when the evaluation board makes its determination. Beginning in 1989, the VA proposed major changes in the schedule. Some of these changes went into effect in 1992. You must get a copy of the VA schedule currently in effect. If you are working with a counselor who has the current VA schedule, you're ready to proceed. If not, review it at the hospital or at a library on or off the base. Because the entire schedule will change soon, it is also important to get the latest changes. Your base's legal officer should be able to help you find the changes.

The VA schedule is basically a series of charts. There is one chart for each body system. For example, one chart deals with your nervous system, another with bones. Your disability is assigned a Diagnostic Code. For example, if you've lost a kidney, the Diagnostic Code is DC 7500. After you are assigned a Diagnostic Code, look it up on the chart to find the appropriate percentage of disability. The VA schedule in effect at the end of 1991 read as follows:

7500 Kidney, removal of one, with nephritis, infection, or pathology of the other

Severe	100
Mild to moderate	60
Absence of one, the other functioning normally	30

Therefore, as long as your remaining kidney is normal, losing one kidney is worth a 30 percent rating. Under rules likely to go into effect soon, the absence of one kidney will be worth 0 percent.

Documenting the Appropriate Percentage

In addition to obtaining a copy of the current VA schedule to confirm your disability rating, get a copy of your service's implementing regulations that explain in more detail what the VA schedule means, and get a copy of all your medical records. You are entitled to a copy free of charge. See Chapter 25. Take your medical records and a copy of the VA schedule and service department regulations to a nonmilitary doctor who specializes in your condition. Ask him or her to examine you, to review your records and the VA schedule, and to prepare a report that evaluates your condition.

As part of your exam, make sure that you explain the kind of work you did before your injury. Explain whether it is still possible to do this work or similar work. Ask the doctor to track the language of the VA schedule and to add his or her assessment of your ability to work. Although a civilian doctor's evaluation is not binding on the military (and will cost you money), if it is thorough and from a board-certified specialist, it may be persuasive.

If you were released from the hospital with a limited duty profile, another kind of documentation is critical. If you were not able to perform even the light duty to which you were assigned, much less the work that you previously did, or if you could perform the work but with obvious difficulty, ask your supervisor or co-workers to write a letter on your behalf. Ask your supervisor to describe your performance before your injury (and to include your evaluations and promotion potential up to that point) and after the injury.

For example, if you injured your right hand and you can no longer hold a wrench tightly enough to loosen a nut, ask your supervisor to include this fact in his or her report. If you were given extra time off, time to rest, or other special treatment, ask your supervisor to say so. Unless you have this kind of documentation, the evaluation board will have only a sterile, dry stack of papers with which to rate you. The members of the board will have no real idea what your situation entails. You want to show the evaluation board that before your injury you were a hard-working, self-motivated person. You do not want them to get the idea that you were only a marginal performer who performs only marginally worse after having been injured.

THE PROCESS, PART I

After the hospital refers your case to the physical evaluation board, the initial processing of your case is conducted in secret. You don't know when it's happening, and you don't have an opportunity to talk to the individuals making the decision.

Typically, three high-ranking officers—two line officers and one medical officer—informally review your medical records and prepare their findings. The medical officer may or may not be a specialist in the relevant field of medicine. The findings may be that you are fit for duty or that your condition existed prior to service. If the findings say you are unfit, they will also state a percentage of disability.

These findings are delivered to you and you have a choice: Accept the findings or appeal. The findings will also include a statement about your right to appeal and how long you have to make this decision. The army gives you 3 days to make the decision. If you go forward with an appeal, you may have a personal hearing before the evaluation board.

Deciding Whether to Appeal

Decide whether to appeal only after you consult someone you trust. If the only person available to you is so busy that he or she doesn't have time to counsel you, get an independent evaluation. Find a veterans' service organization representative or a private attorney and sit down and discuss your case. Make an appointment with a private doctor who specializes in your condition or who is a rehabilitation medicine specialist. Because getting such information can easily take more than 3 days, it is advisable to request a formal hearing. If after consulting with other persons you realize that what you were offered is all you can get, you can withdraw your request for a hearing.

You are entitled to a military lawyer to represent you in an appeal. If the military lawyer assigned to your case impresses you as being competent and interested in you as an individual and appears to have the time necessary to devote to your case, use him or her. On the other hand, given the amount of money potentially involved, you may be better off paying a private lawyer to represent your interests.

Deciding whether to appeal is more complicated now than in the past. The added complication is whether you can get more money under an early separation program than you are likely to get through the disability system. If the disability board has found you fit for duty, and you appeal, you may succeed in being found unfit. However, the percentage of disability is likely to be set low: 10 percent or 20 percent. This percentage will net you only severance pay that the VA will offset against its possible payments. With the early release programs now being used to reduce the armed forces, you may discover that you can get a larger payment through the early release program (with no offset of VA benefits) than from the disability retirement program.

Of course, the basic factor to consider when you are deciding whether to pursue your case further is whether the evidence in your records and a fair reading of the VA schedule would net you a higher percentage of disability. Review the current VA schedule with your counsel (lawyer). Also review the service's notes explaining the VA schedule (for example, Army Regulation 635-40). If your counsel cannot make a plausible argument for stretching your symptoms to match those necessary for a higher rating, take what's offered.

For example, if you developed epilepsy and your records document one major seizure in the past 6 months and an average of four minor seizures each week, you will not get a 40 percent rating. As of the end of 1993, a 40 percent rating required one major seizure and an average of five to eight minor seizures weekly.

It is possible, but only remotely so, that appealing may lead to a *reduction* in the percentage of disability initially offered. After the in-person hearing, there are usually further paper, not personal, reviews of your case. Whether you are separated or remain on active duty, after the final determination, you can seek further review through the Board for Correction of Military Records (BCMR). You should apply to the BCMR within three years of the final disability decision. (See Chapter 17.) It may also be possible to seek review in the U.S. Claims Court. You can also apply for veterans' benefits through the nearest VA regional office, even while you are on TDRL.

THE PROCESS, PART II

The appeals process includes an opportunity to appear in person before the physical evaluation board. The board members when you appear before will generally be the same ones who have already considered your case. Although this is convenient for the board members because they already know your case, it is unfair for you to have to present your case to members who have already made up their minds.

If you do not think that a member of the board can be impartial, you have the right to challenge his or her participation in the hearing. In the VA system, hearings must be held before employees who did not consider (and prejudge) the matter.

Take a tape recorder to the hearing to make sure that you will have a record of everything that occurs. At the formal evaluation board hearing, you have the right to testify under oath. If you do, you can be cross-examined. You may introduce witnesses, documents, or other evidence at the hearing. You may cross-examine witnesses whom the board examines. You also have the right to say nothing, which may be a valuable option if you are facing questions about symptoms that might have existed prior to enlisting.

Your counsel has certain duties to you: to prepare your case, to present it to the board, to examine and cross-examine witnesses, and to submit oral or written arguments. Your counsel is also obligated to discuss the board's findings with you and to assist in preparing a rebuttal if you are not satisfied with the outcome of the hearing.

Immediately after the hearing, the board will inform you of its findings and tell you that the findings are not final. You have the opportunity to submit a written statement at this time. In the Army, this opportunity must be exercised within 3 days. The evaluation board is required to consider what you have written and respond in writing to you.

The evaluation board's findings and recommendations are not the final word, although for all practical purposes the evaluation board's recommendation usually holds. After the evaluation board, there is another level of review by the disability review council.

The review council may disagree with the evaluation board and find that you are fit for duty or, for example, that your disability is only 20 percent, not 50 percent, disabling. If you did not appear in person before the evaluation board and instead simply accepted the initial, informal board's recommendations, you may now want to appear in person before the evaluation board. At a minimum, you should work with your counsel to prepare a rebuttal to the review council's findings.

Your rebuttal to the review council's findings is considered by the physical disability appeal board (or, in the Navy and the Marine Corps, the physical disability review board).

If you are already on disability retirement from the Army, a disability rating review board reviews the percentage ratings assigned by the evaluation board. The rating review board can modify or amend a retirement order if the original order was based on a mistake of law or fraud or if you were not granted a hearing even though you requested one. This board can also modify the order if new evidence is found that could not have been presented before and that warrants a higher rating. If you are a former Army servicemember, you have 5 years in which to apply for relief from this board.

THE PROCESS, PART III

After all the routine boards have considered your case, you can appeal to one other board, whether you are still on active duty or have been discharged. Each branch of the service has a Board for the Correction of Military Records. To apply to this board, use a DD Form 149, which can be obtained from any base or VA office. Civilian personnel sit on this board. The board has broad powers to correct any error or injustice in your records. See Chapter 17 for details on how to apply to the correction board.

Sometimes after the correction board denies you relief, you can further appeal your case to the U.S. Claims Court. Consult with an attorney for details about this procedure.

Part of the process you face if you are on temporary disability retire-

---

★ NOTE ★

Although the correction board has broad powers, it will seldom change a disability rating. Therefore, do not use its existence as an excuse not to exercise your right to demand a hearing in person before the physical evaluation board or your right to submit a rebuttal to the evaluation board's findings.

ment is reexamination every 18 months for as long as 5 years. At the end of 5 years, you may be found fit for duty and offered the opportunity to return to active duty. You may accept or decline this opportunity. You may also appeal a finding of fitness for duty before the physical evaluation board. Following each periodic examination, your percentage of disability may be adjusted; this could result in your receiving a lump sum in severance pay or being placed on the permanent retired list.

Relationship to SSA Benefits

During your military service (at least for service after January 1, 1957) you pay into social security. If you are disabled and cannot work as a result of your disability, you may be able to draw social security disability insurance benefits. Unlike VA benefits, which are offset by military disability pay, there is no offset of SSA (Social Security Administration) benefits if you receive severance pay.

As with the VA, however, a finding by the military that you are permanently disabled does not require the SSA to agree that you are entitled to its benefits. The SSA does not use the VA Schedule for Rating Disabilities. Instead, the SSA uses a listing of impairments. Contact the nearest SSA district office for an application. Also consult a lawyer who is experienced in SSA disability matters.

RELATIONSHIP TO VA BENEFITS

If you are permanently or temporarily retired or if you are awarded a lump sum disability severance, immediately apply to the nearest VA regional office for VA compensation benefits. You should understand that just because the service set your disability at 20 percent does not mean that the VA will award 20 percent; it may award a higher or lower rating. Also, if the VA says that you are 80 percent disabled and the military said you were only 20 percent disabled, do not think that the military was wrong.

If this does happen, however, ask the evaluation board to reconsider its decision or apply to the correction board for a change in your disability retirement. Keep in mind, though, that just as the percentage set by the military does not have to be followed by the VA, neither does the percentage set by the VA have to be followed by the military. See Chapter 4 for information on applying to the VA for disability compensation.

There is a complicated interplay between military disability payments and VA payments. The amount paid by the VA for a particular percentage of disability is not tied to your former base pay. The VA payment changes from year to year as set by Congress. See Chapter 4 for the 1994 rates. If you are awarded disability severance and the VA agrees that you are entitled to VA compensation for the same disability, you may not be paid VA benefits immediately. The VA offsets your severance pay against what it normally would pay you. You may have to wait years before you begin to receive VA benefits.

For example, if you are awarded a $10,000 severance payment and the VA agrees that you are 30 percent disabled, you will not begin to receive VA payments until 3 1/2 years have passed. This is how long it would take monthly VA payments at the 30 percent rate to total $10,000. Only after this time period will you begin to receive VA payments.

If you are drawing temporary or permanent disability retirement but the VA benefits are higher, you can waive receipt of the military retirement pay. You cannot draw the full amount of both the military retirement pay and the VA compensation. In calculating whether it is to your advantage to waive receipt of disability retirement in order to receive VA compensation, keep in mind that VA compensation is not taxable income.

★ IMPORTANT ★

The law might change to permit certain veterans to receive the full amount of both military disability pay and VA compensation. Call the nearest VA office to confirm that.

INCAPACITATION PAY FOR RESERVISTS

Incapacitation pay consists of pay in an amount not to exceed military pay and allowances for a reservist's pay grade and years in service. It is intended to compensate a reservist for a medical condition incurred in service. The pay can cover conditions which render the reservist unable to perform military duties or who, although he or she can perform military duties, cannot perform civilian employment. The pay is generally for a six-month period but can be extended. A determination of eligibility for incapacitation pay is initiated by the reservist by reporting to the commanding officer any condition which might affect his or her ability to perform military duties.

CHAPTER TWENTY-ONE

MILITARY MEDICINE

by
P. J. Budahn and
Soraya S. Nelson

This chapter tells you about some of the medical services available while you're still on active duty. Even in the best of times, military medicine has been confusing, with the services running their own hospitals and clinics, the federal government funding a health insurance system for family members and retirees, and, increasingly, various contractor-run clinics providing off-base care for military families.

The Defense Department's health care system is one of the largest in the world. With 164 hospitals worldwide and more than 500 freestanding clinics, it serves approximately 8.4 million people. This includes approximately 2 million uniformed members of the Army, Navy, Air Force, the Marines Corps, the Coast Guard, and Public Health Service; 2.6 million dependents of active-duty servicemembers; 1.7 million retirees; and 2.3 million dependents and survivors of retirees.

The system is in flux. At least 24 military hospitals are expected to close their doors by 1998 as bases shut down. The reduction in the active duty force will also trigger the realignment of services and the reduction and relocation of medical personnel to suit the number of patients.

To offset some of the reductions, more alternatives to the Pentagon's traditional health care system will become available to military servicemembers and their families. Some of the alternatives are contractual arrangements with civilian doctors and hospitals to treat military patients, and so-called "medical sharing agreements" with Department of Veterans Affairs hospitals that allow military servicemembers and possibly even dependents to go there for treatment. Adding to the confusion are various programs to increase efficiency and reduce costs in the medical system by decentralizing certain functions. This translates into varying rules and different out-of-pocket medical expenses depending on the branch in which you serve and the area of the country in which you are located.

Increasingly, you have to be a savvy consumer to get the most out of military medical care. The health care provided by the armed services is valuable to you: There are no premiums for basic medical coverage, on-base treatment is free, and most off-base care is a bargain. But being able to see a military doctor is not always easy, especially if you are a dependent or a retiree. Understanding the complexities of getting the government to pick up the tab for off-base care requires research.

THE MILITARY MEDICAL SYSTEM

Being treated at military hospitals can mean getting high quality care at not-so-high-quality facilities. Between 1987 and 1990, the Joint Commission on Accreditation of Healthcare Organizations, a private commission that inspects and accredits hospitals nationwide, found that the percentage of military hospitals meeting or exceeding the quality standards of medical treatment surpassed the percentage of civilian hospitals that did so.

Nevertheless, according to the commission, the hospital facilities, many of which are decades old and in need of renovation, do not always meet civilian standards. Still, no military hospitals lost their accreditation as a result of the 3-year study. Military hospitals were 100 percent in compliance with nationwide laboratory testing standards. Compared with civilian hospitals, they had half as many faults cited in emergency and special services, surgery, and medical record keeping.

Active-Duty Care

Everyone on active duty, including a reservist on active duty for training, is entitled to free medical care in a military-run hospital or clinic, from surgical procedures and outpatient treatment to dental care and pharmacy items. This right continues through a person's last day on active duty.

Here are some finer points in the rules:

★ Priority: Except in cases of genuine emergencies, active duty service-members are treated before other patients eligible for care in on-base facilities, such as dependents and retirees.

★ Sick call: Denials of medical care, including requests to go on sick call, are serious actions. Initially, complaints should be resolved through the chain of command. Servicemembers denied care also have the option of taking complaints to the Inspector General or to a military lawyer.

★ CHAMPUS: Active duty military personnel are ineligible to receive financial help under the government health insurance program known as CHAMPUS (the Civilian Health and Medical Program of the Uniformed Services), which helps pay the medical bills of military families dealing with civilian doctors and hospitals.

★ Emergencies: In rare cases, active duty personnel need to go to an emergency room and a civilian hospital is closer than a military hospital. In these instances, the government will reimburse the civilian facility for the costs of treating a military person.

Second Opinions

Active duty servicemembers are entitled to seek second opinions when they are treated at military hospitals. This is a matter of medical custom, not written military policy.

A military patient should check with his or her doctor, hospital commander, or local military hospital patient representative for information about how to get a second opinion. The patient representative can also help you if you have a complaint or a question concerning your medical care.

Medical Malpractice

If you are on active duty, you are barred by federal law and U.S. Supreme Court decisions from suing the military for medical malpractice or for negligence.

All other users of the military health care systems, such as dependents and retirees, can file medical malpractice claims through the services. When claims are rejected, they can take their cases to the federal court system.

Abortion

Since October 1988, abortion in military hospitals has been available only to women whose lives are endangered by the pregnancy. Military medical facilities are barred by Defense Department regulations from terminating a pregnancy, even when a fetus is suffering from fatal genetic defects. But with the advent of the Clinton presidency, unrestricted abortions are again becoming available at military hospitals. But the procedure comes at a cost. In overseas hospitals in 1993, women military health care users had to pay $477 to get an abortion.

Despite the partial lifting of the ban, it is difficult to find an overseas military hospital to perform the procedures. If local laws in the country a U.S. military hospital is located in forbid abortion, the military doctors cannot perform them. Some other military hospitals cannot offer them because they lack qualified doctors or needed equipment. Military doctors may also refuse on moral or religious grounds to perform the procedure.

Having an abortion does not affect your active duty career, although there have been isolated incidents where a security clearance has reportedly been denied on that basis. The most publicized incident was that of an air force recruit who in 1989 was denied a security clearance because service officials thought that her three past abortions indicated that she was irresponsible and untrustworthy.

ENROLLMENT IN THE DEFENSE ENROLLMENT ELIGIBILITY REPORTING SYSTEM AND OTHER PROGRAMS

To use on-base military health care, servicemembers, retirees, and dependents must be registered in the Defense Enrollment Eligibility Reporting System, or DEERS, which is a nationwide, computerized system to which military hospitals have access.

DEERS lists all active duty personnel and retired military people automatically. Servicemembers and retirees must register their dependents. Registration is done at the nearest military personnel office.

Changes in family status also affect eligibility for medical care and, thus, must be reported to DEERS. Among the events that must be reported are the following:

★ Births
★ Adoptions
★ Divorces
★ Deaths

Additional enrollments may be required at your local military hospital as the Defense Department converts to managed care or ''coordinated care'' medical systems.

CHAMPUS
Basic Rules and Expenses

Active duty dependents, retirees, and the dependents of retirees are eligible for treatment in military medical facilities. However, except in genuine medical emergencies, they always receive care after the active duty patients have been treated. Among other things, this can mean that a retiree will wait hours until all active duty patients have been treated.

To provide for timely treatment of non-active duty patients and to reduce the demands placed on military medical facilities, the Pentagon runs its own health insurance program. Called CHAMPUS, or more formally, the Civilian Health and Medical Program of the Uniformed Services, it allows non-active duty patients to use civilian doctors and private medical facilities, with CHAMPUS picking up most of the expense.

Here are some of the basic financial rules of CHAMPUS:

★ If you have some other form of health insurance, either privately purchased or employer provided, it must pay first for the expenses it covers before CHAMPUS can be used.

★ Patients must pay a certain amount of each year's medical expenses. This is called a "deductible." CHAMPUS deductibles range from $50 to $300 annually.

★ Patients also pay for a portion of approved medical expenses. This is called "cost sharing." Cost sharing for most medical procedures is 20 percent to 25 percent.

★ Patients admitted to a civilian hospital overnight must pay certain additional costs. In 1993, for example, active duty dependents paid $9.30 per day, but not more than $25 for the entire hospital stay. Other CHAMPUS-eligible patients paid $265 a day or 25 percent of the hospital bill, whichever was less.

★ Out-of-pocket expenses are capped at $1,000 a year for active duty dependents and at $7,500 a year for all other patients.

★ After reaching the yearly caps, CHAMPUS will pay 100 percent of all allowable charges. These are the rates that CHAMPUS officials set for treatments based on the average local cost.

Treatment Under CHAMPUS

Like any health insurance plan, CHAMPUS has a long list of treatments that it covers and a somewhat shorter list of typical procedures not covered.

─────── ★ NOTE ★ ───────

If a civilian doctor charges more than the allowable rate for a procedure, which is what CHAMPUS considers typical for your area, you may have to pay the difference between what the doctor charged and what CHAMPUS considers fair. To avoid this, it is best to ask civilian health care providers whether they participate in CHAMPUS. If they do, they agree to accept the rates set by CHAMPUS for each medical procedure. It also means they agree not to bill the CHAMPUS patient for any expenses.

Generally, CHAMPUS will help military families pay for routine costs of care by private physicians and treatment in civilian hospitals. It may be simpler to consider some of the routine treatments that CHAMPUS will *not* cover:

★ abortions, except in limited circumstances
★ birth control that doesn't require a prescription
★ chiropractors and naturopaths
★ cosmetic, plastic, or reconstructive surgery, except to restore function
    or to reconstruct a breast
★ dental care, except as part of medical care
★ experimental surgery
★ eyeglasses and contact lenses, except in limited circumstances
★ hearing aids, except as part of disability care
★ orthodontia
★ orthopedic shoes and arch supports
★ private hospital rooms, unless medically necessary
★ weight reduction services and supplies

Before Using CHAMPUS

Of the 8.7 million people eligible to use an on-base medical facility, almost three-quarters live within a 40-mile radius of a military installation. For medical matters, this is known as a "catchment area."

─────── ★ NOTE ★ ───────

The fact that CHAMPUS doesn't provide a given treatment doesn't mean that the treatment is unavailable to military families. Some procedures on CHAMPUS' not-covered list are available in military medical facilities. Others, principally dental care, are available through a government-backed dental insurance plan.

CHAMPUS-eligible patients within the 40-mile catchment area must go to their nearest military hospital for inpatient care and expensive out-patient treatment. One of two things will happen:

★ If on-base care is available, the patient must be treated on base. CHAMPUS won't pay any of the medical bills if the patient receives off-base care.

★ If care is not available at the military hospital, hospital officials should make a formal statement certifying this fact. This is called a "nonavailability statement." It is sent electronically to a computer that clears the way for CHAMPUS reimbursement.

Approximately 25 percent of potential military patients live outside the 40-mile catchment areas. They can seek civilian care without clearance by the military hospital commander.

CHAMPUS Resources

Nearly all on-base hospitals have a full-time counselor to help military families sift their way through their medical options. These counselors, called "health benefits advisors," are especially useful in understanding the finer points of CHAMPUS.

Among the printed material available from a health benefits advisor is *The CHAMPUS Handbook*, a free, 140-page, simple explanation of the program that is updated yearly.

CHAMPUS Cutoff

Career servicemembers planning to stay on active duty long enough to qualify for retirement often don't know about one important change in their health benefits: When retirees and their dependents reach age 65, they lose

---

★ IMPORTANT ★

Watch for changes affecting people outside the catchment areas. The 25 percent of all patients in those regions account for 75 percent of all CHAMPUS costs. In 1992, the Pentagon formed a special joint-service task force to devise new administrative procedures for those outlying regions. Since 1993, the Defense Department has begun offering government-contracted civilian care—often at reduced charges—to military health care users near closing military hospitals. Also, there are plans to offer a mail-order pharmacy. This concept will be tested in 1994.

CHAMPUS and are automatically enrolled in Medicare. With bases closing and limited military medical resources for retirees, medical experts advise retirees to sign up for the extra coverage known as "Medicare Part B." It costs about $40 a month.

THE TRANSITIONING SERVICEMEMBER

If you are leaving active duty, eligibility for military health care ends at midnight on the day when you are discharged or leave the service for reasons other than retirement or death. Usually any supplemental insurance your family bought to offset out-of-pocket CHAMPUS expenses also expires at this time.

Therefore, it is wise for you and your family to have physical exams and to address any ongoing medical problems before your discharge. Remember, preventive procedures such as well-baby visits, physicals, pap smears, and mammography may not be covered by civilian insurance plans. You can save money by taking care of those items while still in the military's health care system.

Desert Storm Veterans

Veterans of Operation Desert Storm must be especially careful to undergo a thorough separation physical, especially if they suffered any injuries in the Middle East or experienced any ailments since returning home.

★ WARNING ★

Servicemembers have a right to request physical examinations before they leave active duty. Because of the increasing numbers of military reduction discharges, some installations, instead of giving people physical exams, are asking them to fill out questionnaires about their health. Questionnaires won't identify many health problems. In addition, they may jeopardize future VA disability claims. If there is no record of a problem arising in the service, it's difficult to show that a later disability relating to that problem is service connected.

Get a physical exam and make sure that the medical records mention any ongoing health problems that may worsen in later years and make you eligible for a VA disability. (For more information on preparing for a disability claim, refer to Chapter 4.)

★ ADDITIONAL WARNING ★

Dental care is not offered under the military-sponsored transitional health care program. Families with the military's dependents' dental insurance plan should give themselves plenty of time for predischarge checkups, allowing time for additional visits if the dentist discovers problems.

Even if a problem is more of a nuisance than a physical disability, veterans should consider filing compensation claims with the Department of Veterans Affairs. They may not be entitled to VA benefits now, but their eligibility may change if the condition worsens.

A proper discharge physical and a prompt review now by a VA screening board will make it easier in later years to prove that an injury or ailment was service connected.

Dental Care After Discharge

Active duty servicemembers who were unable to get proper dental care before discharge are eligible for one-time treatment in a VA dental facility. The benefit comes with two deadlines:

★ You're not eligible if you went to a military dentist within 90 days of discharge and received proper treatment.

★ You must apply to the VA for care within 90 days of your discharge.

Continuing Military Medical Care

Until the recent cutdown in military personnel, after servicemembers accepted discharge papers, they were ineligible for treatment in military medical facilities. So were their families. CHAMPUS quit helping with the off-base medical bills.

★ NOTE ★

Some people can see a military dentist within 90 days of discharge and still qualify to see a VA dentist after their discharge if their military record shows that they didn't receive all the care recommended by the military dentist.

But Congress has directed the Pentagon to hold open the door that leads into the military medical system a little longer. Specific categories of people are eligible for continuing treatment, free of charge, in military hospitals, outpatient clinics, and rehabilitation clinics. They can also continue to participate in CHAMPUS.

The length of this continuing medical care is determined by the length of service on active duty:

★ 60 days if the servicemember spent less than 6 years on active duty
★ 120 days if the servicemember spent 6 years or more on active duty

However, not everyone who meets these length-of-service goals is eligible for postdischarge medical treatment on the base. To be eligible, the servicemember must also be included within certain other categories:

★ recipients of the Special Separation Benefit (SSB)
★ recipients of the Voluntary Separation Incentive (VSI)
★ recipients of separation pay, including recipients of half-separation pay

Among the groups specifically not eligible for continuing medical care are these:

★ enlisted servicemembers at the end of their enlistments
★ officers at the end of their obligated terms

Transitional Health Insurance

Even the new postdischarge medical benefits won't cover the care gap that many veterans will experience after leaving active duty. Because most Americans receive their health insurance through their workplace and many veterans will need months to find a civilian job, the government has sponsored a low-cost private health insurance plan that nearly all discharged veterans can purchase.

★ NOTE ★

Everyone who qualifies for continuing medical care, former servicemembers and their families, receives the same priority for treatment as the dependents of active duty servicemembers.

It's called the Uniformed Services Voluntary Insurance Program, or U.S. VIP. It is sold in 3-month periods by Mutual of Omaha and can be renewed for up to 18 months. In 1992, the cost of this plan started at $960 for a full year's coverage for an individual. Your local health benefits adviser should have information about U.S. VIP.

U.S. VIP will typically pay 80 percent of approved medical expenses. Policyholders usually pay the first $250 yearly for each covered person, a payment that's called a "deductible."

If out-of-pocket expenses reach $2,500 yearly per covered person, the company pays 100 percent of the eligible expenses, up to $1 million.

Like any other health insurance plan, U.S. VIP has a clearly defined list of services that are covered and another equally clear list of things that are not.

Spouses and children may sign up for the insurance even when former servicemembers don't purchase coverage for themselves.

Plans for National Health Care Reform

Contributing to the turmoil that touches all aspects of the military's health care system is how national health care reform will affect it. Officials privately estimate that it will take several years before the system adopts changes reflecting national health care reforms.

Among the features of the proposed new "managed-care" program are these:

★ Some patients will be asked to participate, or enroll, in programs in which local hospital commanders have contracted with civilian physicians, hospitals, or health care organizations to back up the military's medical system.

★ Whereas it will be easier and faster to get appointments, military families will have less choice regarding doctors and health care facilities.

★ Each patient will have a primary-care physician who will make all assignments to specialists.

★ For high-cost procedures such as organ transplants, the local hospital commander may send patients to specialized treatment facilities hundreds of miles away.

CHAPTER TWENTY-TWO

GETTING OUT

★ ★

This chapter describes the official process of discharge of enlisted personnel. It also explains the reasons for discharge. There are voluntary reasons—such as a hardship or an "early out," a discharge before the end of your period of enlistment, to attend school—and involuntary reasons, such as misconduct. Disability retirement is discussed in Chapter 20; retirement after 20 years of service is not addressed in this book. Because of the reduction in forces announced in 1991, there are increased opportunities for bonus payments to encourage an early out. Whether you are (or will be) eligible for an early out varies by branch of service and by what happens during the next few years.

Whether your discharge is voluntary or involuntary, you should care about the character of your discharge for three reasons:

★ It will affect your future job prospects.
★ It will affect your eligibility for unemployment benefits if you do not have a job after you're out.
★ It will affect whether you can use the money you set aside for education or are eligible for other VA benefits after you're out.

The Department of Defense uses five different characters of discharge: honorable, general, under other than honorable conditions, bad conduct, and dishonorable. Usually, if you are discharged at the expiration of your service obligation, because of a change in service obligation, or for the convenience of the government, you will receive a fully honorable discharge. However, if you are a marine or sailor, the character of your discharge relates to your evaluation marks.

Since 1982, the DoD has used a new "noncharacterized" kind of discharge called the "entry level separation" (ELS). Personnel discharged under the ELS do not receive an honorable, general, or any other character of discharge. An ELS discharge is an option for personnel identified as having problems adjusting to military service within the first 6 months of service.

Six months before the end of your tour, call the personnel office and get the details on any new early out programs or new job counseling opportunities (such as the Transitional Assistance Program). In particular, find out if your out-processing includes a physical examination and whether your personnel office plans to give you a copy of your personnel file. If the personnel office does not plan on delivering your personnel records to you at discharge, make arrangements to get a complete set of the entire record. Be sure to get a copy of all your medical records, too. You are entitled to a free copy of both your personnel and medical records. See Chapter 25.

In past years, discharge physical exams were often rushed. If you asked questions or had unusual problems, you could expect delays that could postpone the date of discharge. Because examinations were often conducted with 20 other members in the room at the same time, personal attention was limited.

If you have had no health problems during your tour of duty, such a cursory exam may be sufficient. If you have had any health problems while on active duty, whether these problems are currently bothering you or not, make sure that the problems are noted on your discharge exam medical history.

★ WARNING ★

It is extremely important to get an honorable discharge. Although you may think that your time in the military has little to do with the rest of your life, a less than fully honorable discharge is a lifelong stigma. Make every effort to get an honorable discharge. There is no automatic upgrade of a less than honorable discharge. You can apply to a discharge review board for an upgrade (see Chapter 17), but relatively few applicants win upgrades.

If you are a marine or a sailor and you calculate that, with 6 months left, your evaluation marks will not average out at the number you need for an honorable discharge, talk with your commander, work harder, change your attitude for 6 months.

This may mean a lengthy exam, but it may prevent a future problem with the VA. The VA often uses the absence of any problems noted at the separation exam as a reason to deny a claim for VA benefits. If you have indicated health problems on the medical history form, a doctor will review them with you. If the problems still bother you, make sure that the doctor indicates this fact on the form. If you think that you are not fit for duty, you may be eligible for a disability retirement, not an administrative discharge. Regarding disability retirement, see Chapter 20.

If a physical exam is not included as part of your out-processing and you have problems (even minor ones), have a checkup immediately. If the problem worsens after you are discharged, you will at least have a record of complaining about the problem while on active duty. This record will help you qualify for VA benefits for the problem.

DD 214, Certificate of Release or Discharge from Active Duty

The DD 214 is "a source of significant and authoritative information used by civilian and governmental agencies to validate veteran eligibility for benefits." Recorded on this form are the official reason for discharge, a so-called separation program designator (SPD), the character of discharge, reenlistment code, dates of service, job title, military training, awards and medals, and several other items of information. Employers will demand it. Some changes to the DD 214 are expected soon; these changes will describe military jobs in language that will make them sound more like civilian jobs.

DD 214 is a multipart form: The top copy (no. 1) is a short form that is sanitized; it does not include the character of or reason for discharge, the reenlistment code, or the SPD. Nevertheless, copies of the DD 214 with all this information *are* prepared: One copy (no. 4) should be offered to you (be sure to take it), one is sent to the VA, and three are retained by the service. At your request, a partially sanitized copy of the DD 214 is sent to the state department of veterans' affairs that you designate, and the other copy is sent to the U.S. Department of Labor's Unemployment Compensation Office.

Register a copy of your DD 214 by taking a copy to your county courthouse and asking a clerk to register it. Preserve your copies with other valuable papers in a safe (fireproof) place. If your service is characterized as honorable, you will also receive an Honorable Discharge Certificate, DD Form 256.

Processing Out

During the last few days of active duty, your personnel office will give you a checklist of other offices to visit: finance, base housing, security, the dispensary. Besides going through the official procedures, take the time to collect the names, home addresses, and service numbers of as many of the members of your unit as you can. They may be good contacts later both for business opportunities and to corroborate in-service health problems if you ever need to apply for VA disability benefits. Approach any supervisors who might give you letters of recommendation and either get these letters now or a commitment for them later if the need arises.

Don't ignore your personal finances. If you opened a local checking account and all your checks have cleared, close the account. If you live in off-base rental housing, meet all your obligations to the landlord. Bankers and landlords are increasingly feeding computer clearinghouses with the names of people who have failed to carry out their obligations. You may be unpleasantly surprised when you try to open a new bank account or rent another apartment only to discover that you are listed as a bad risk.

VOLUNTARY DISCHARGE

The Department of Defense (DoD) uses many official reasons for discharge as management tools to "promote the readiness of the Military Services." Although most servicemembers are discharged at the end of the enlistment period, you may ask to leave early. Official reasons for discharge include selected changes in service obligations as well as convenience of the government (for example, an early release to attend school, hardship, pregnancy, parenthood, conscientious objection, sole surviving family member).

Your command can force you out for several other official reasons (for example, having a personality disorder, being overweight, using drugs, or misbehaving). These reasons for discharge are discussed in the next section, which discusses involuntary discharge. Retirement because of a physical disability is discussed in Chapter 20.

Procedures for Discharge

Generally, if the official reason for discharge cannot result in a bad discharge, the discharge process is shorter; you have fewer procedural rights.

For example, you cannot get a hearing before a board of officers. On the other hand, if you are being discharged against your will, you have more rights. See the next section of this chapter, which discusses involuntary discharges. A brief description of the criteria for some of the voluntary reasons for discharge follow.

Selected Changes in Service Obligations

Each service secretary has a great deal of latitude in starting programs to reduce the numbers of servicemembers on active duty. Get the latest details from your personnel office. Some of the options may include cash payments and special benefits after discharge if you are willing to leave early. In addition to the inducement of the cash is the threat that if you don't take the money and go now, you risk being pushed out anyway without the cash.

In 1992, a Voluntary Separation Incentive or Special Separation Benefit was offered to certain members. Eligible members included those in pay grades or with occupational skills that were overstaffed. Check with your personnel office about this. The separation incentive is 2.5 percent of your annual base pay times the number of years of service and is to be paid out annually for twice the number of years you've served. The separation benefit is a one-time, lump sum payment of 15 percent of your annual base pay.

You may be eligible for these benefits if you have completed at least 6 years but fewer than 20 years of service or if you served at least 5 years of continuous active duty immediately before separation and agree to serve in the ready reserve. If you have a critical skill or are already pending an involuntary discharge, this program is not available to you. Details of the various options under the voluntary separation incentive programs and how you can evaluate their advantages and disadvantages are addressed in *Drawdown Survival Guide* by P. J. Budahn (published in 1993 by Naval Institute Press).

Early Out to Attend School

If you plan to attend school as soon as you are released, apply to the school a year in advance of the end of your tour. If the school term begins a few months prior to the end of your tour, give your commander an official letter of acceptance at the school and request an early release. Given the current need to reduce the size of the armed services, this kind of discharge may be readily approved.

Hardship or Dependency

Upon your request and if a genuine dependency or undue hardship exists, you may be able to get out early. As defined by DoD, a hardship that may qualify for discharge is not the usual inconvenience that comes from separating families. The hardship or dependency cannot be simply a temporary matter and conditions must have arisen or been aggravated after you entered the service. You have to show that you have tried every reasonable option to remedy the situation. You also have to show that your getting out will make a difference in relieving the hardship. If you are considering this kind of discharge, review your service's regulations at the base library to understand exactly what the process involves and what kinds of reasons can support a discharge. Ask the Red Cross to help you document the problems. Get letters from family and friends who know the details of the problem and how your presence may help solve it.

Pregnancy and Parenthood

Upon becoming pregnant, you should have the option of being discharged. Of women servicemembers separated each year, almost one-fifth were pregnant. If, as a result of becoming a parent, you are unable to satisfactorily perform your duties or are unavailable for worldwide assignment, you may be discharged. In this event, separation processing may not be initiated until you have had formal counseling and time to try to correct the unsatisfactory performance.

INVOLUNTARY DISCHARGE

This section describes the official reasons and procedures for discharge that are "involuntary"; that is, reasons for discharge that you may not be able to control.

Official Reasons for Involuntary Discharges

Following are some reasons to discharge you early:

★ convenience of the government (for example, certain physical or mental conditions such as personality disorder, chronic seasickness, enuresis, being overweight)

★ defective enlistment (for example, you enlisted when you were younger than age 17 or there were facts that would bar enlistment, defective enlistment agreement, fraudulent enlistment)

★ poor entry-level performance and conduct (for example, unsatisfactory performance during the first 6 months of service)
★ homosexuality (includes preservice or in-service conduct or statements)
★ failure of drug abuse rehabilitation
★ failure of alcohol abuse rehabilitation
★ misconduct (for example, minor disciplinary infractions, a pattern of discreditable involvement with civil or military authorities, commission of a serious offense, civilian conviction)
★ separation in lieu of trial by court-martial (where charges have been preferred for an offense that could result in a bad conduct or a dishonorable discharge)
★ security (when continued service is "clearly inconsistent with the interest of national security")
★ secretarial authority or other reasons
★ court-martial

Procedures for Discharge

Following is only a general description of the procedures for involuntary discharge; get the details from your personnel office or look up the rules at the base library.

Convenience of the Government

Although convenience of the government covers a wide range of reasons for discharge, some of which you may initiate, this chapter discusses the procedures that apply if the service is discharging you for reasons such as having a personality disorder or being overweight. Because this kind of a discharge is involuntary, you have more rights.

Personality Disorder

A personality disorder is more than simply a personality conflict with a superior. It is also something that does not suddenly appear after several years of service. Although it has not always done so, the DoD now requires that a psychiatrist or a psychologist officially diagnose the disorder before it can be used as a reason for discharge. You must receive written notification that the disorder is the reason that your commander proposes to discharge you. You must also be counseled about the problem. If you have more than 6 years in the service, you are entitled to appear with counsel before an administrative discharge board. As a practical matter, get a second opinion from a civilian psychiatrist or psychologist.

Overweight

How much over your ideal weight you can be and for how long varies. As a practical matter, given the current reduction of forces, after you receive a notice of proposed discharge due to being overweight, you have a problem. Counseling and dieting is no fun, but these days it is very serious business.

Homosexuality

In the past, you could be (and nearly always were) discharged for being a homosexual as soon as your commanding officer suspected your sexual preference. In a policy announced in 1993, unsupported suspicions of sexual preference are not sufficient reason to discharge you. If you declare openly that you are homosexual, or your command receives reliable information about your homosexuality, you still face discharge. Also, if you are caught (on base or off) engaging in homosexual conduct, you will be discharged. In 1993, a new administration policy and legislation by Congress and orders in court cases made these cases more complicated. A good resource for up-to-date information and possible assistances is the Military Law Task Force; 1168 Union St., Suite 201; San Diego, CA 92101; 619-233-1701.

Failure of Drug or Alcohol Abuse Rehabilitation

This reason for discharge applies only if you voluntarily entered a drug or alcohol rehabilitation program and were not rehabilitated. The service must find that you lack potential for continued military service and that long-term rehabilitation is necessary. If you seek rehabilitation after testing positive for drug use, the service is free to discharge you for misconduct.

Misconduct

Because of the likelihood of a bad discharge if you face separation due to misconduct, the discharge procedure for misconduct is the longest and gives you the most rights. Misconduct can be three or four minor nonjudicial punishments (NJPs), a conviction in a civilian court for a serious offense, or commission of a serious military offense. If the minor NJPs are considered to be a "pattern of misconduct," discharge proceedings may not be started until you have been formally counseled about the misconduct and offered an opportunity to change your behavior. After this opportunity has passed without a change in behavior, written notice of discharge proceedings must be provided, and you have the right to consult with a lawyer, to request an administrative discharge board hearing, and to be represented by either a military or a civilian lawyer (it's your option, but, remember, to hire a civilian lawyer, you must be able to pay legal fees).

Separation in Lieu of Court-Martial

If you are facing a court-martial for an offense that could lead to a BCD (bad conduct discharge) or a DD (dishonorable discharge), you can submit a written request for an administrative discharge instead. This will almost certainly lead to a UOTHC (under other than honorable conditions) discharge. You have the right to consult with counsel about this option. Before you ask for this kind of discharge, make certain that the reasons you are facing court-martial are actually punishable with a BCD or a DD.

Court-Martials

A court-martial can result in a punitive discharge (a bad conduct or dishonorable discharge), or it can result in a reduction in rank, a fine, a lengthy confinement, or a combination of these. Only rarely does a court-martial result in an acquittal (less than 10 percent of the time). A court-martial is an important event. This book is not intended to give you advice about defending yourself at a court-martial. The best advice we can give you is to be quiet and get a competent attorney as quickly as possible. Then let your attorney do the talking.

Ask your assigned military attorney which civilian attorney he has worked with and whom he or she respects, or call the local civilian bar association to get a referral to an attorney. Then quiz the attorney on his or her experience with court-martials and fees. If you feel comfortable with the civilian attorney and you have or can get the money to pay the fee, do so. Your assigned military counsel may be good. However, he or she probably has a heavy workload. Get all the help you can get.

The laws that govern your behavior are found in the Uniform Code of Military Justice (U.C.M.J.). You were told all this during boot camp but somehow these laws take on a new meaning when you are facing a court-martial. You can find a copy of the U.C.M.J. at your base's library. Look for Title 10, United States Code, Sections 801-940. The rules for conducting a court-martial are found in a separate book, *The Manual for Courts-Martials*.

Although the MP who arrested you may threaten to court-martial you, your commanding officer must first investigate the alleged offense and prepare a charge sheet (DD Form 458). The charge sheet includes the CO's recommendation for the type of court-martial: summary, special, or general court-martial. If a general court-martial is involved because a serious offense was allegedly committed, a separate Article 32 (of the U.C.M.J.) investigation must be conducted during which you may cross-examine witnesses. If the case goes to a general court-martial and you are convicted, the case may be reviewed by the Court of Military Review, the U.S. Court of Military Appeals, and potentially (but rarely), the U.S. Supreme Court.

Take advantage of any appeals process. If you are imprisoned—most likely at Ft. Leavenworth—be a model prisoner, try to line up a civilian job or civilian schooling, and apply for clemency or parole.

You and your family should get in touch with the following advocacy organization: M.O.M.S. (Mothers Opposed to Maltreatment of Servicemembers), 8285 Black Hawk Ct.; Frederick, MD 21701; (301) 662-7643; the director of the organization is the mother of a military prisoner. After you're released from prison, you can apply for an upgrade of your discharge, but upgrades are rarely given. See Chapter 17.

CHAPTER TWENTY-THREE

PROBLEMS SPECIFIC TO WOMEN AND MINORITY SERVICEMEMBERS

★★★★★★★★★★★★★★★★★★★★★★★★★★★★★★★★★★★

This chapter describes some of the issues facing women and minority servicemembers. Women comprise approximately 10 percent of the active duty armed services and 12 percent of the National Guard and reserves. Among the issues facing women in the military, two stand out: (1) limits on certain occupations and (2) sexual harassment. Minorities comprise approximately 21 percent of the armed forces contrasted with approximately 12 percent of the total U.S. population. Among the issues facing minorities in the military is continuing discrimination both on and off the base.

WOMEN

Job Limits

Women serve in all occupations except those prohibited by law or service policy. Traditionally, women served primarily in support and administrative occupations. Now, however, the total number of women serving in other occupations such as communications, electrical or mechanical repair, and medical fields is greater than the number of women serving in traditional occupations. In 1991, of 60,000 Navy women, 9,000 were serving at sea.

After the Persian Gulf War, Congress passed legislation to remove some of the remaining limits on occupations in which women can serve. In April 1993, the Clinton administration's new Secretary of Defense, Les Aspin, lifted the ban on women flying combat missions. Restrictions on infantry, armor, and cavalry and on service aboard navy warships remain but will be studied for possible changes.

In addition to certain official job limits, there are also unofficial limits. For example, tests used to screen whether an applicant is suited for an occupation continue to eliminate a disproportionate number of women. The tests measure an applicant's prior knowledge in traditionally male subject areas.

Servicemembers as Mothers

Difficulties that women servicemembers face include childbirth and child care. Women who become pregnant can usually leave the service upon request. (See Chapter 22.) Nevertheless, women who remain on active duty face the prospect of giving birth and then immediately being reassigned to a duty station that does not permit dependents. Such a policy obviously discourages retention of competent personnel. In recognition of this problem, Congress has ordered the Department of Defense to study the variations between the services' policies and to report to Congress with its findings.

Sexual Harassment

Sexual harassment encompasses a wide range of actions: from demeaning remarks to demands for sex. It is a frequent and common concern. Just as in the civilian world, sexual harassment hinders efficiency and lowers morale. Just as there is no place for it in the civilian world, there is no place for it in the military. Unfortunately, surveys suggest that there is a greater incidence of harassment in the military than in civilian life: Two-thirds of military women cited on-the-job harassment, contrasted with 30 percent to 40 percent of civilian women.

Fortunately, servicemembers can seek relief through unique avenues from those who are harassing them. Commanders have a strong duty to prevent harassment and to investigate complaints. In late 1991, an admiral was removed from a command position for failing to promptly investigate charges of blatant harassment of women at the Las Vegas Hilton earlier that year. In mid-1992, the Secretary of the Navy resigned as the investigation into the Tailhook scandal continued without resolution. In 1993, courts-martial began of Navy and Marine pilots who abused women at the Tailhook convention and numerous high-ranking officials were reprimanded by the new Secretary of the Navy.

It is up to you as the victim of harassment to choose how to handle the situation. You can immediately file a complaint, or you can tell the harasser to stop his or her behavior. You must decide what is the best step to take given your particular situation.

Filing a complaint can be difficult to do. If your complaint is anonymous, there probably will not be an investigation. In theory, filing a formal complaint is not supposed to subject you to further harassment or other retaliation; nevertheless, this may not always be the case.

If the harassment occurs in a location with no witnesses, make sure that your complaint is detailed; provide the time, the location, the reason you were there, the words used or the exact movements of the person and your reaction. If there are witnesses and they are willing to corroborate your complaint, include their names in your complaint.

Although it may be obvious to you that the behavior interferes with your ability to do your job, make this clear. You may get the attention of some persons in your chain of command more quickly if they think that their unit's performance may be adversely affected (which will reflect badly on them). Deliver the complaint to your superior officer. If your superior officer is the harasser, turn your complaint in to the next superior officer.

If you get no response within a few days, readdress your complaint to your commanding officer. If you get no response from your CO, the Uniform Code of Military Justice gives you a powerful tool to make sure that you do get a response. Under Article 138 of the U.C.M.J., if you file a grievance with your CO and the CO refuses to redress your grievance, you have a right to ask the CO's superior officer for help. The superior officer in turn is required by the U.C.M.J. to forward your complaint to the officer exercising general court-martial authority over your CO. This is likely to get a response.

There may be other avenues for getting help, too. The legal assistance office or social action office may be willing to arrange a training program about sexual harassment for your unit. A complaint to the Inspector General may be useful. Another alternative is to contact the local or national news media.

Rape

Rape is a crime that has very long-lasting consequences for the survivor. Report it. Get medical treatment immediately. If you do not get support from your hospital and command, go outside to civilian doctors. Contact the nearest rape crisis center.

Rape will likely affect job performance. But unless you have reported the rape, your evaluation marks may reflect an inexplicable drop in performance that will hurt your chances for either remaining in the service or getting an honorable discharge. If you do not get appropriate, professional help, you may become unfit for further duty. See Chapter 20 for an explanation of the disability discharge system.

Failing to press criminal charges may also result in your being denied medical care years later when you need it. Although more commonly associated with exposure to horror on the battlefield, post-traumatic stress disorder (PTSD) is a mental disability that can develop many years after a rape or an attempted rape. The VA officially recognizes the disorder but seldom pays disability compensation for it unless you can prove that the rape occurred. Unless you can convince the VA that your disorder is service connected, you are not likely to obtain medical treatment from the VA.

Resources

For several years, there has been a Defense Advisory Committee on Women in the Services. This committee periodically conducts hearings about sexual harassment and is always interested in hearing about instances of harassment or other issues of concern to women. Write the committee at DACOWITS (Defense Advisory Committee on Women in the Services) Staff Office; Room 3D769; Pentagon; Washington, DC 20301.

Both the U.S. House of Representatives and the U.S. Senate have committees that deal with the armed services. Write the House Subcommittee on Military Personnel and Compensation; Washington, DC 20515; or the Senate Committee on Armed Services; Washington, DC 20510. Also consult The National Organization for Women (1000 16th St., N.W.; Washington, DC 20036; [202] 331-0066) about services it offers. Complaints to the local or national news media may also pressure someone into addressing your problem.

MINORITIES

At the end of 1991, 21 percent of military personnel were African-American and 9 percent were Hispanic, Asian, Native American, or members of other minority groups. Thirty percent of Army personnel were African-American. Although it is clear that the services have come a long way since the 1940s and 1950s when segregated units were the rule, and that the services have done more than the civilian communities to combat racism, it is obvious that much more needs to be done to eliminate racism.

Obtaining an accurate statistical picture of the frequency of discriminatory actions is difficult. Still, statistics offered in the fall of 1991 documented that 45 percent of military prisoners were African-Americans. This means that African-Americans were more than twice as likely to be imprisoned as whites were.

According to an account published in November 1991 in the *Army Times*, complaints registered with the U.S. Civil Rights Commission from African-American servicemembers included concerns that the military justice system (pertaining to both courts-martials and nonjudicial punishments) and the evaluation system were prejudiced against minorities. The effect of lower evaluations of African-Americans desiring to stay in the service will likely be drastic.

Racial and Ethnic Harassment

Racial and ethnic harassment can include a broad range of actions or inactions: telling ethnic jokes; using derogatory slang terms, either publicly or privately; and assigning the most menial, most dangerous, or dirtiest chores to minority servicemembers more often than to others. Condoning such behavior by failing to condemn it or report it is almost the same as harassment. Failing to make an effort to understand and address the concerns of minority servicemembers perpetuates the harassment.

As with sexual harassment, a wide range of actions can be taken to address racial discrimination. Some would counsel taking strong, formal measures immediately, but, again, such may not be practical in your particular case. Casually stating that a colleague's behavior is demeaning may be enough to make some perpetrators stop. The next step may be to pointedly confront the person and demand that the action stop. If these informal efforts produce no results, put your complaint in writing.

Filing a complaint can be difficult to do. If your complaint is anonymous, there probably will not be an investigation. Filing a formal complaint is not supposed to subject you to further harassment or other retaliation, but what is supposed to happen and what does happen can differ. If the actions of a superior are discriminatory, document the actions in detail. If you are being given menial chores more often than whites, keep a daily log of your assignments and theirs.

Each facility has an equal opportunity officer. Approach this officer with your documentation. If you get no satisfaction, write your CO. If the

CO refuses to address your complaint, consider filing an Article 138 complaint with any officer superior in rank to your CO.

Although filing complaints may seem like a waste of time, it may be helpful to have documented the problem. For example, you may be discharged under honorable conditions, not with a fully honorable discharge, due to your evaluation marks. If you complained previously that your evaluation marks were lower than others' despite your good performance and that the lower marks were racially motivated, your complaint will give you a better chance at having your discharge upgraded. (See Chapter 17.)

Resources

The NAACP has longstanding concerns with the treatment of African-American servicemembers. The NAACP has numerous chapters throughout the United States and overseas near U.S. bases. Check the telephone book for the nearest chapter. The U.S. Commission on Civil Rights has demonstrated its interest in complaints of racially discriminatory actions in the military; contact the commission at 1121 Vermont Avenue, N.W.; Washington, DC 20425. Both the House of Representatives and the Senate have committees on the armed services. Write the House Committee on Armed Services; Washington, DC 20515; or the Senate Committee on Armed Services; Washington, DC 20510. Complaints to the local or national news media may also pressure someone into addressing the problem.

CHAPTER TWENTY-FOUR

DEPENDENTS, SURVIVORS, AND FORMER SPOUSES OF SERVICEMEMBERS ON ACTIVE DUTY

by P. J. Budahn and
Soraya S. Nelson

This chapter tells you about some of the programs, benefits, and services available to members of your family and to former spouses while you're on active duty. It also describes the benefits available to your survivors if you die while on active duty.

These benefits come with a variety of legal shadings: Some are absolute rights that belong to family members; some are merely extensions of a servicemember's rights; others are courtesies that can be taken away at the discretion of local commanders or limited when an installation's resources and personnel are scarce.

Approximately 2.8 million people are officially classified by the military as "dependents" and thus are eligible for a wide range of benefits. Many thousands more are the survivors or divorced spouses of servicemembers; these people qualify for a more limited variety of benefits.

Having the right to get something isn't the same as actually getting it. Throughout the 1990s, dependents, survivors, and former spouses are likely to encounter new obstacles to programs.

Personnel reductions, the shutdown of many bases, the reorganization of others, and the endless reconstruction of the military's medical system have made many services difficult to get. Prospects for the near future appear to be even worse. Look for a more limited access to benefits as tens of thousands of spouses and children of discharged servicemembers are, for the first time, given continued access to hospitals, clinics, commissaries, and exchanges.

In this kind of environment, servicemembers can't expect to be the guardians of their dependents' benefits. Spouses and older children need to know what they're entitled to, how to get it, and what to do if they're denied a benefit or program.

If you don't plan to give your family members a formal briefing on their dependents' benefits, perhaps you'll want to pass along this book after you've read it.

ELIGIBILITY FOR PROGRAMS

For spouses and children, the key to most military benefits is a card. It's formally known as DD Form 1173, also known as the Uniformed Services Identification and Privileges Card, but most people simply call it "the ID card." With a proper military ID card in hand, spouses, children, and other family members can have access to the programs and services they need, from medical care and shopping rights in the commissary to reduced-price tickets at the base's theater.

Not everyone who lives in a servicemember's household can get a dependent's ID card. Military rules restrict eligibility to specific groups of people:

★ the lawful spouse of a servicemember
★ the surviving spouse who hasn't remarried of a deceased servicemember
★ unmarried children, including adopted children and stepchildren, younger than age 21
★ unmarried children, including adopted children and stepchildren, older than age 21 who are incapable of self-support
★ unmarried children, including adopted children and stepchildren, younger than age 23 who are full-time students
★ parents or parents-in-law who receive more than one-half of their support from a servicemember
★ certain divorced spouses who haven't remarried

Getting an ID card for the first time for a family member often requires backup documentation, such as a marriage certificate; a birth certificate; medical records for older, disabled children; or proof of academic enrollment for students. Renewals, which are completed every 3 years, don't usually require the same documentation as the first application.

Military servicemembers don't have to get dependent ID cards from their parent service. That is, airmen don't have to travel to an air force base if an army or navy installation is more convenient. Each service fully honors the ID card of the others. If an army dependent is eligible to use a post's commissary, that family member can also shop at commissaries run by the navy and the air force.

For a dependent to get or renew an ID card, the signature of the active duty "sponsor" is usually necessary. But the military recognizes this isn't always possible. Servicemembers may be on assignment away from home when a spouse's ID card expires, or some argument between an active duty parent and an older child might strain relations, or communications between former spouses may break down entirely after a divorce.

The military has procedures that bypass the need for a servicemember's signature on a dependent's application for an ID card. The procedures vary by service and by category of dependent. People who think that they're being denied an ID card because a military sponsor refuses to sign the application should check with a military lawyer. The advice is free. Family service centers and the administrative offices that issue ID cards may also have helpful information.

DEPENDENTS

Resources Available to Dependents

A proper ID card will admit spouses, children and other family members of military servicemembers to a variety of free or low-cost facilities on the base.

Following are some places open to military dependents. An asterisk indicates that a facility may impose restrictions on access for dependents, mostly age limits that restrict children younger than age 12 who aren't accompanied by an adult.

★   chapels
★   clinics
★   clothing (uniform) stores*
★   clubs (Officer, NCO)

★ commissaries*
★ exchanges
★ family centers
★ hobby and auto shops
★ hospitals
★ laundries and dry cleaners
★ legal offices
★ libraries
★ package (liquor) stores*
★ recreation areas
★ theaters
★ swimming pools

SPOUSES' SURVIVAL CHECKLIST

Military families shouldn't wait for the next national emergency or sudden deployment to get their affairs in order. Spouses should take some necessary precautions now.

★ Have your active duty partner allot you a certain amount of money that's large enough to cover household expenses.
★ Get power of attorney, a legal document that allows you to take out loans, sell property and enter into contracts on behalf of your spouse.
★ Persuade your military spouse to make out a will.
★ Make sure that your spouse has taken advantage of the military's low-cost life insurance and named you as beneficiary.
★ Know your spouse's social security number.
★ Know the names and home telephone numbers of your spouse's commander and the senior NCO or petty officer.
★ Make an effort to meet two or three other spouses in your partner's unit and get their telephone numbers.
★ People living off base should keep a current base telephone book.
★ If your family's legal papers are in a bank's deposit box, make sure you're on the list of people who have access to it.

FINANCIAL SUPPORT OF DEPENDENTS

Desert Storm was only the latest, clearest reminder to military families of the financial hazards of the profession. Many servicemembers were only hours away from boarding planes for the Middle East when they had to fill out the paperwork necessary to send some of their paychecks directly to their families.

A military paycheck is made out to the person on active duty. Spouses can't cash it. And, as happened too many times during Desert Storm, the servicemember can't cash it, either (personnel often were called up and shipped out over a weekend, when most banks have limited hours or no hours at all). The military has provided a mechanism to avoid these anguishing family financial crises. The servicemember can designate a certain portion of a paycheck to be sent directly to a family member. A designated portion is called an ''allotment.''

Financial planners advise servicemembers not to wait for the next Desert Storm to authorize allotments for family expenses. Allotments to spouses should be large enough to pay a family's routine bills. The same result can be achieved by authorizing the pay center to deposit a paycheck electronically into a joint bank account.

The military servicemember who is contemplating or who thinks his or her spouse may be contemplating divorce, and who fears the spouse will abscond with the paycheck should realize that an allotment can always be canceled.

Some active duty servicemembers fail in their financial obligations to their families. This can result in an adverse comment in an efficiency rating, pressure from the chain of command to settle up, or even disciplinary action.

The military offers administrative remedies to the spouses and children of servicemembers who default on their financial obligations. Each service administers these remedies differently. Spouses who aren't being supported by their active duty partner should consult a military lawyer.

When family problems degenerate into divorce, a spouse can get a court order that tells the finance center to deduct money from a servicemember's paycheck and to send it directly to the spouse. Federal law sets maximum limits on withholdings for alimony or child support:

★　60 percent of earnings if the servicemember isn't supporting a second family

★　50 percent of earnings if the servicemember is supporting a second family

★　5 percent penalty if the servicemember is 12 weeks behind in alimony and child support payments

LAST RESORTS

The military prides itself on the network of programs and groups available to help families in crisis. Here are a few:

★ Family service centers: A one-stop site for a variety of problems, the family service center offers personalized counseling on making a family budget, classes to develop job skills, and specialized support groups such as Al-Anon for people grappling with particular problems.

★ Transition centers: At most locations, military spouses are eligible to use the job banks and attend the job searching seminars established for military servicemembers who are leaving active duty.

★ Relief societies: No-interest loans for military servicemembers in a budgetary squeeze are available from Army Emergency Relief, the Air Force Aid Society, the Navy-Marine Corps Relief Society, and Coast Guard Mutual Assistance. These are loans, not gifts, and repayment is expected through monthly payroll deductions.

★ Red Cross: The quickest way for families to get an urgent message to a military person deployed away from home is through the Red Cross. Red Cross channels are often faster than official channels.

★ Chaplains and military lawyers: Chaplains and military lawyers offer advice in strict confidence. Chaplains are experienced in dealing with the nonspiritual problems of daily living. Military lawyers, or legal assistance officers, can advise family members on tax questions, separation and divorce agreements, contracts, and claims against the government.

Chaplains, relief societies, and military lawyers can't solve every problem that can befall a military family. Families in crisis have other resources to draw on for various problems:

★ Food stamps: Military families are as eligible as anyone else to apply for food stamps, an invaluable aid to needy families trying to get the most from their limited income. Food stamps aren't a military program, and because of the strong gains in military pay during the 1980s, officials estimate only a few thousand military families are eligible. Social welfare agencies in the civilian community can help military families through the steps needed to qualify for food stamps. Military relief societies and family service centers can point the way, too.

★ Help for abuse cases: The abuse of spouses and children has been linked to families in crisis, households facing economic uncertainty, and breadwinners reeling from the blows to the ego that are a normal part of losing a job. These conditions are plentiful during a reduction in forces. Counselors warn families who are prone to the abuse of spouses and children that outside intervention is the only sure way to stop the abuse. When children are the victims, a host of people and agencies are prepared to step into the breach (from chaplains and military doctors to day care centers, school systems, and civilian child welfare agencies). The abuse of spouses often requires similar intervention by someone outside the home. Unfortunately, not only is the reduction in forces breeding some of the factors that contribute to spouse abuse, but also a spouse may fear that he or she will cause the servicemember to be discharged by raising issues that could damage the servicemember's military record. Indeed, this is a risk, but it must be balanced with the risk that the longer the abusive conduct continues, the more difficult it will be to stop and the more out of control it will become.

★ Aid for Alcoholism: The abuse of alcohol is another fairly predictable problem that will be growing in some households under the pressures of the reduction in forces. It's a problem that is difficult to solve but amazingly easy to begin to solve. The solution begins with a telephone call. Numbers for Al-Anon and Alcoholics Anonymous are listed for most communities. Al-Anon is for the families of problem drinkers. Alcoholics Anonymous is for the drinkers themselves. One telephone call will connect a person with strictly confidential support from people who have had similar experiences.

TRANSITION ELIGIBILITY

After people leave active duty, the main gate is usually barred to them and their families. This has changed with new rules designed to ease the transition of people leaving active duty during the reduction in forces. Many veterans, along with their spouses and children, will retain a form of their military ID cards and access to some facilities on the base.

At a minimum, the new cards will entitle the cardholders to shop in commissaries and exchanges. Other facilities may be opened at the discretion of base commanders. The cards will be stamped with the oversized letters "TA," for transition assistance. They will be issued on the day that the servicemember leaves active duty and they will expire in 2 years. They can't be renewed.

The new TA ID cards will be given to veterans and the families of veterans who fit into one of the following categories:

★ recipients of the Special Separation Benefit (SSB)
★ recipients of separation pay
★ people separated by formal reduction-in-force procedures

The new cards will not be given to veterans or their families when the veterans fit into one of the following groups:

★ recipients of the Voluntary Separation Incentive (VSI)
★ anyone retiring
★ enlisted members completing their enlistments
★ officers completing their obligation terms

SURVIVORS

Burial Assistance

A host of programs and benefits become available to the family of a servicemember who dies while on active duty. Some are offered by the military, others by the Department of Veterans Affairs, which is still most commonly known as the VA.

Among the things that survivors can expect are these:

★ Burial assistance: Both the military and the VA offer financial aid to meet funeral expenses. Amounts vary with the circumstances of

─────── ★ NOTE ★ ───────

Some of the people ineligible for the new TA ID cards will qualify for another reason for a different version of the military ID card. Retirees, for example, have a different type of ID card. VSI recipients must also serve in the reserves, for which they receive a limited-access reserve ID card.

the burial. In 1991, the basic benefit when servicemembers died on active duty was $1,750 from the military plus $2,000 for burial in a national cemetery or $3,100 for burial in a private cemetery.

★ National cemeteries: Servicemembers who die on active duty can be buried free of charge in any of the 113 national cemeteries or at Arlington National Cemetery.

★ Flags and headstones: The government provides free headstones and flags for the graveside rites. Funeral directors know the procedures for obtaining these items.

★ Honor guards: Personnel cutbacks have made it impossible for the military to supply honor guards for the burial of all veterans. Special efforts are made, however, to provide availability of an honor guard.

Survivor Programs

The survivors of servicemembers who die on active duty are eligible for annuities from the government, payment of life insurance claims (in most cases), and access to many on-base facilities.

Following are the major benefits:

★ Income programs: If a servicemember is eligible for retirement when he or she dies—even though he or she was still on active duty—the surviving spouse receives 55 percent of the servicemember's basic pay for life. The amount increases annually by the same percentage as military pay.

★ If a servicemember on active duty isn't eligible for a military retirement at the time of death, the survivors usually qualify for an annuity from the VA called "Dependency and Indemnity Compensation" (DIC). Rates vary by rank. For 1992, the DIC payments ranged from $616 monthly for the spouse of an E-1 to $1,005 for the spouse of an O-5.

★ Life insurance: Everyone on active duty automatically receives $100,000 of coverage under the government-backed Servicemen's Group Life Insurance program. Premiums are modest, and they're automatically withdrawn from monthly paychecks. This means that if an active duty servicemember does nothing, that person's spouse will receive $100,000 in SGLI insurance when the servicemember dies. However, military servicemembers can refuse the insurance or they can choose less coverage. Refusals or limited coverage require written applications by the service-member.

★   Health care: Spouses of servicemembers who die on active duty, plus their dependents, are eligible for treatment in a military hospital or an off-base military clinic, or under the military's CHAMPUS health insurance program.

★   Surviving spouses lose all entitlements to military health care if they remarry. When spouses turn 65 and qualify for Medicare, they lose their eligibility for CHAMPUS, although they retain the right to space-available care in a military hospital or clinic.

★   Regardless of age, the surviving spouses of servicemembers who die on active duty are entitled to other military benefits. They include a dependent's ID cards and access to commissaries, exchanges, and other on-base facilities.

Survivor Advocates

Even the smallest base has someone appointed part-time as the "casualty assistance officer" or "survivor assistance officer." Larger bases have people handling these duties full-time. They stay in touch with survivors, lead them through the paperwork needed to secure their benefits, and serve in later months as their advocates. Survivors shouldn't hesitate to call on these professionals when they're confused about benefits or believe that they are being unfairly denied benefits.

Survivor Benefit Plan and Retirees

One of the most important decisions that active duty servicemembers and their spouses make when the time approaches for a military retirement involves the Survivor Benefit Plan, or SBP. This program provides an income for a spouse after a retiree dies. Military retirement checks stop when a retiree dies, and without SBP many surviving spouses wouldn't have any income.

Following are some features of SBP:

★   Coverage and costs: The SBP gives a monthly check to the widows and widowers of military retirees. SBP coverage is purchased, like life insurance, by retirees during their lifetimes. Payments are made as automatic withholdings from the monthly retirement check. The maximum that survivors can receive is 55 percent of the monthly retired pay. The maximum that retirees pay for coverage is 6.5 percent of their total retirement check. Coverage and premiums for lesser amounts are determined by formulas.

★ Sign-up limit: Active duty servicemembers will be asked, as they approach retirement, to decide whether to participate in the SBP. If they decide to participate, they must also decide how much coverage they want. The spouse must sign a form agreeing to a decision not to take the SBP or to take anything less than the maximum coverage available. If the spouse won't sign, the government enrolls the veteran for the maximum SBP coverage.

★ After many of the basic SBP decisions are made near the retirement date, they can't be changed. Servicemembers who refuse to participate in the SBP can't change their minds later. Nor can they drop or reduce the SBP after coverage begins, although provisions are on the books for retirees to drop the coverage in cases of divorce or death of the spouse. Nor, generally, can the amounts of coverage be changed.

★ Supplemental coverage: When surviving spouses begin receiving social security at age 62, their SBP payments are reduced. For most, the SBP checks will then equal 35 percent of the original inflation-adjusted retirement check. Social security fills this gap, so most survivors won't see an overall decrease in monthly income.

★ Still, many retirees and their spouses don't want the SBP payments to be reduced. Since April 1992, the military has offered a new supplemental SBP plan. By withholding an additional amount monthly, military retirees can preserve the SBP at the original amount for their survivors.

★ Remarriage: Widows and widowers lose their SBP if they remarry before the age of 55. They regain the benefit if the new marriage ends for any reason. There is no loss of SBP coverage for survivors who remarry at age 55 or later.

FORMER SPOUSES

Garnishment of Active Duty Pay

Through court decisions and federal law, minimum protections have evolved that address some problems of both parties in a divorce involving a servicemember on active duty.

Former Spouses: The mobility of military life used to make it difficult, and sometimes impossible, for the former spouses of uncooperative military members to collect alimony, child support, or their legal share of joint property. Among the protections developed for these former spouses are the following:

★ Direct payments from a military finance center to a former spouse. These are basically deductions from a military member's paycheck.
★ Court-ordered direct payments, called "garnishments," if the active duty servicemember is uncooperative.

Military members: The reassignments and temporary deployments of military life sometimes acted against the interests of servicemembers on active duty. They've returned home to discover that they've suffered a major financial loss in a divorce proceeding of which they weren't aware. Among the protections on their behalf are these:

★ For the finance center to honor a garnishment, a marriage must have lasted at least 10 years while the military partner was on active duty.
★ The court that orders a garnishment can't have jurisdiction solely because an active duty person was transferred into the court's jurisdictional area. For the court to have jurisdiction, the military member must meet legal requirements for being a resident or for establishing a legal domicile or must accept the court's jurisdiction.

Garnishment of Retirement Pay

Few issues touching on military life have generated as much heat as the division of military retirement pay during divorce settlements. Congress has voted that retirement pay can be considered "community property"

★ NOTE ★

These protections, along with similar ones involving retirement pay, apply to contested divorces. The 10-year rule on garnishment, for example, is irrelevant when a military person voluntarily makes an allotment to a former spouse.

and that a former spouse can be entitled to a percentage of it. When retirement pay is awarded to a former spouse as community property, the payment continues even after the former spouse remarries.

Congress has also ordered military finance centers to make the necessary deductions from a servicemember's retirement pay and to send a monthly check directly to a former spouse when a proper court order has been filed with the finance center.

Following are a few of the legal fine points:

★ As with the garnishment of active duty pay, the finance center will honor the court order only if a marriage lasted at least 10 years while the military partner was on active duty.

★ Although a divorce court can award any proportion of retirement pay to a former spouse as community property, the finance centers will make direct payments only of less than 50 percent of retirement pay.

★ The 50 percent cap can be raised to 65 percent to honor debts for child support or spouse support.

★ The finance centers won't honor garnishments if a court has reopened a divorce settlement originally reached before June 26, 1981.

★ NOTE ★

Unless a veteran agrees, the finance centers won't send payments based on a disability retirement to any former spouse, even one with an explicit court order.

For example, if 40 percent of a veteran's retirement is based on a disability and a court awards a former spouse half of retirement pay, the former spouse will receive 30 percent of the total retirement pay: half of what the retiree gets after the disability pay is subtracted.

Benefits from the Military

A divorce court cannot award a former spouse any military benefits paid for by the government, although a few have tried. However, Congress has approved some on-base benefits for tightly defined groups of former spouses.

★ Military medical care for life, plus commissary and exchange privileges. These go to so-called "20/20/20" former spouses, who must meet *each* of the following conditions:

The marriage lasted at least 20 years.
The servicemember spent at least 20 years on active duty.
At least 20 years of the marriage occurred while the servicemember
  was on active duty.

These former spouses lose their government-paid benefits if they remarry. They can regain exchange and commissary privileges, but not free medical care, if the second marriage ends in divorce, death, or annulment.

★   Military medical care for life. This is a benefit of the so-called
    "20/20/15" former spouses, who must meet *each* of the following conditions:

    The marriage lasted at least 20 years.
    The servicemember spent at least 20 years on active duty.
    Between 15 and 20 years of the marriage occurred while the servicemember was on active duty.
    The final divorce decree was dated before April 1, 1985.
    These former spouses lose their military medical care if they remarry.

★   Military medical care for 1 year: This applies to some of the
    "20/20/15" former spouses, who must meet *each* of the following conditions:

    The marriage lasted at least 20 years.
    The servicemember spent at least 20 years on active duty.
    Between 15 and 20 years of the marriage occurred while the servicemember was on active duty.
    The final divorce decree was dated after April 1, 1985.

─────────── ★ NOTE ★ ───────────
Congress has given qualified former spouses a legal right to the medical care, commissary rights, and exchange privileges discussed previously. They don't need a court order, a divorce decree, or their former military partner's permission to claim these benefits.

Survivor Benefit Plan and Former Spouses

When a military retiree dies, the retirement checks stop. There is, however, a government program that provides a continuing income for survivors, including former spouses. This program was mentioned earlier in this chapter, in connection with spouses.

Called the Survivor Benefit Plan, or SBP, it allows retirees to purchase income protection for their survivors. Premiums are purchased through deductions from the monthly retirement check. Benefits paid to survivors are calculated as a percentage of the retirement pay; the most that a survivor can receive is 55 percent of the retirement pay.

Since 1982, military retirees have been able to designate former spouses as their SBP beneficiaries. Some fine points affect this decision:

★   After a retiree names a former spouse as a beneficiary, the decision can't be changed without the former spouse's permission.

★   If a retiree or an active duty servicemember has a former spouse and a current spouse, only one can be the SBP beneficiary.

★   Divorce courts can order retirees to name a former spouse as the SBP beneficiary. They can also order an active duty servicemember, when he or she retires, to give SBP coverage to a former spouse.

★   If a court orders a retiree to name a former spouse as beneficiary and the retiree later remarries, the retiree needs the court's permission to name the new spouse as the beneficiary.

★   Former spouses permanently lose their rights to SBP coverage if they remarry before age 55.

Support and Advocacy Groups

Support and advocacy groups have arisen along both sides of the marital divide. There is a group for former spouses called "EX-POSE," which offers practical advice and lobbies for expansion of former spouses' rights. An opposing group, the American Retirees Association, is actively trying to limit efforts by courts and Congress to award retiree benefits to former spouses.

To contact local representatives of either group, inquire at the family service center of the nearest military installation. Inquiries can also be directed to the national headquarters for the groups:

**EX-PARTNERS OF
SERVICEMEN/WOMEN FOR
EQUALITY (EX-POSE)**
P.O. Box 11191
Alexandria, VA 22312
(703) 941-5844

**AMERICAN RETIREES
ASSOCIATION**
2009 N. 14th St., Suite 300
Arlington, VA 22201
(703) 527-3065

CHAPTER TWENTY-FIVE

★

MILITARY RECORDS, RESEARCH, AND RESOURCES

★★

This chapter is intended to encourage you to get your own service records, to help you locate rules if you are facing particular problems, and to help you find additional sources of information. Also, if you never received the medals you were entitled to wear, this chapter will give you some addresses to contact.

GETTING YOUR OWN RECORDS

While on Active Duty

The basic record kept by the service about you is your Official Military Personnel File (OMPF). You are entitled to inspect it and to receive a free copy of it. The information is stored on microfiche. You need to regularly review the information in your personnel file. Although you should have received a copy of each evaluation, check your file to make sure you have them, especially if you are eligible for a promotion and have received any outstanding evaluations. You are also entitled to a copy of your medical records. Before you leave a duty station, give a letter to the hospital or clinic records clerk. State in your letter: "This is a request under the Privacy Act." Ask for a copy of any and all doctors' notes, nurses' notes, surgical procedure notes, laboratory reports, discharge summaries, consultant's reports, and so forth that may have been created.

If your medical records involve psychiatric matters, the service is likely to refuse to release them to you directly. The service is concerned that if you read about the psychiatrist's opinion about your condition, your condition may worsen. In this case, ask your parents' doctor to get the records. These records can be critical to you or your counsel if you are facing an early discharge and believe that a medical discharge is more appropriate.

After Discharge

Several months after you are discharged, your field OMPF and any information maintained at headquarters is combined and retired to the National Personnel Records Center (Military Personnel Records, 9700 Page Blvd.; St. Louis, MO 63132). After this happens, a copy can be obtained from the center. You can use either a Standard Form 180, Request Pertaining to Military Records, or you can write a letter to the center. The SF 180 can be requested from any VA regional office. A copy is included in Appendix A. It can take many weeks and sometimes months to get a response from the St. Louis records center. If you need help quickly, there is a private service that will search for you records (for a fee). Contact:

DATA FORCE ASSOCIATES
10412 Niblic
St. Louis, MO 63114
(314) 423-7084

Whether you write a letter to the center or send the SF 180, be sure to specify that you want a "complete copy of all my military and medical records." Also state on your request, "I want to confirm the accuracy and completeness of the files under the Privacy Act. Please waive any fees because I need the records to support a claim for VA benefits." Of course, also include the branch of service, dates of service, your service number, and your complete return mailing address, and be sure to sign and date the request. Your survivor can also request your records.

Records of medical treatment are not included in your OMPF. Only the initial and separation report of physical examination form and a report of medical history form are included. If you were hospitalized or you reported to sick call, these records are maintained in a separate building and are filed by the name of the facility at which you were treated. It may seem a waste of time to get years-old records of medical treatment, but you cannot rely on the government to preserve your records. A fire at the St. Louis Records Center in 1973 destroyed millions of records. In addition, the VA often denies claims because the records are not available. This punishes you for something you have no control over. Avoid the problem, get any and all medical records now and keep them in a safe, fireproof place. In your Privacy Act Request to the center, list the names of the hospitals in which you received treatment, the dates of treatment (as near as you can recall), and the kind of treatment you got (for example, for a broken back or hepatitis).

During the months between the time you are discharged and when the file arrives at the center, a request for your files goes to one address or another depending on your branch of service. These addresses are included on the reverse side of the SF 180. In 1993, the Army began to automatically ship a member's service medical records to the VA. These records do not include clinical records.

Other Records

There may be other records about you that are maintained by other offices. For example, if you were ever investigated by the service's investigators (the Army's Criminal Investigative Division, the Naval Intelligence Service, or the Air Force Office of Special Investigations), the office that investigated you has your name on file and maintains a file on you. If the investigation was closed, you should be able to get a copy. Although your personnel file may contain no reference to such a file, these files have a habit of surfacing at awkward times. You should learn what is in the file and, if necessary, complain about it before it is used to hurt your chance for promotion.

If you were involved in an auto accident on the base, the base security office has an accident report you may need.

Confidentiality of Records

Almost all the information in your military file must be kept confidential. Certain information, such as your rank and current duty station, can be released on request to anyone. You can give up your right to privacy and give someone else permission to read your records. For example, you may give a member of Congress or a newspaper reporter permission to look at your records.

When you apply for certain jobs, you may be asked to "waive your rights under the Privacy Act." If, however, you agree to give up your DD 214, Certificate of Release, and the service turns over more, such as medical records, it may have violated your privacy and have to pay a penalty to you for doing so.

Certain records are considered extra sensitive and require special release forms before they can be reviewed. For example, records of treatment or any reference to treatment for drug or alcohol abuse, AIDS, or sickle-cell anemia are specially protected.

Locating Someone You Served With

You cannot get the personnel files on someone you served with. If, however, that person is still on active duty, you can call the operator at the Pentagon at (703) 545-6700 and ask for the Locator Service. If the person is no longer on active duty, you can ask the director at the National Personnel Records Center to forward a letter to the home of record of the individual. Enclose with your request for this service a plain, unsealed envelope with the individual's name on it. Apply the proper postage but do not include your return address on the envelope. Put your letter inside. This way, the records center can verify that it is not sending debt collection demands or offensive materials.

You also might locate someone through an advertisement in a newspaper such as the *Army*, *Navy*, or *Air Force Times* or in the magazines published by the veterans' service organizations. See Appendix D for a list of VSOs.

GETTING YOUR MEDALS

If you were awarded medals but did not receive them (or lost them), you or your survivor can ask for them. The easiest way to ask is to use a Standard Form 180, Request Pertaining to Military Records, which you can request from any VA regional office. A copy is included in Appendix A. Send the completed SF 180 along with a copy of your DD 214, Report of Separation, to the following addresses:

★ for Navy, Marine Corps, and Coast Guard personnel: Navy Liaison Office, Room 3475, N-314, 9700 Page Blvd., St. Louis, MO 63132-5100

★ for Air Force personnel: National Personnel Records Center, Military Personnel Records, 9700 Page Blvd., St. Louis, MO 63132-5100

★ for Army personnel: Army Commander, U.S. Army Reserve Personnel Center, ATTN: DARP-PAS-EAW, 9700 Page Blvd., St. Louis, MO 63132-5100

RESEARCHING MILITARY LAW AND POLICY

As must be painfully clear, everything from the undershirt you can wear to the way you comb your hair, to the way you do your job, to the way you are discharged is covered by rules. You may never have seen the rules, only heard about them from a very authoritative voice. You may never want to see the rules. Nevertheless, if you question whether what you have been told is actually correct, you should be able to find the rule in black and white. If you are facing disciplinary action, ask your assigned counsel or the base defense counsel to show you the actual text of the law or rule that you supposedly violated. You can file an appeal of a nonjudicial punishment, but you have a deadline to do so. Ask the defense counsel to show you this rule, too.

If you are facing separation under a particular provision, ask to see the entire manual that contains that provision. These manuals and regulations can be found at the base's library or the Judge Advocate General's (JAG) office.

Although Title 32 of the Code of Federal Regulations (C.F.R.), which is sold through the Government Printing Office in Washington, DC, includes regulations issued by the military services, the services do not routinely publish in the C.F.R. their changes in regulations. So, don't buy the C.F.R. in order to stay up-to-date. As a practical matter, instead of using the C.F.R., get the latest AR, AFR, or SECNAVINST (i.e., Army Regulation, Air Force Regulation, Secretary of the Navy instruction) from your military library, JAG office, or personnel office.

You are entitled to use the Freedom of Information Act to request a copy of policies that you may have seen reported in the media but can't find at the library. Send FOIA requests to the secretary of the service. If you get no response within 10 days, send an appeal to the Office of the General Counsel for the service.

RESOURCES TO HELP YOU STAY UP-TO-DATE

The most convenient way to keep up-to-date with changes in service policies that may affect your future is to subscribe to a newspaper that covers these issues. For example, the Army Times Publishing Company, based in Springfield, Virginia, publishes a series of weekly newspapers that provide good coverage of personnel policy changes (not only the change but its potential effect on you) as well as practical advice on a wide range of issues. The *Army Times*, the *Navy Times*, and the *Air Force Times* include advice columns on financial matters, some veterans' benefits information, and in-depth features on life in the military. Contact the Army Times Publishing Company at (800) 368-5718. The Army Times Publishing Company announced in late 1993 that it was working with America Online, a computer information service, to offer "Military City Online," which will focus on offering current information useful to active duty members, retirees and their families. For more information about this service, call (800) 424-9335, ext. 8160.

The Uniformed Services Almanac in Falls Church, Virginia, annually publishes a series of almanacs: one on the uniformed services, one for the reserves, one for the National Guard, and one for retired military personnel. Each almanac has pay charts, various allowance amounts and descriptions, federal and state tax information, lists of installations, CHAMPUS telephone numbers, and much more. Contact the Almanac at P.O. Box 4144; Falls Church, VA 22044 or call (703) 532-1631.

APPENDIX A:

FORMS

****

LIST OF FORMS

★ VA Form 70-3288, Request for and Consent to Release of Information from Claimant's Records

★ VA Form 21-4142, Authorization for Release of Information

★ VA Form 572, Request for Change of Address/Cancellation of Direct Deposit

★ VA Form 21-8940, Veteran's Application for Increased Compensation Based on Unemployability

★ SF 95, Claim for Damage, Injury, or Death

★ SF 180, Request Pertaining to Military Records

★ U.S. Court of Veterans Appeals Form: Notice of Appeal

Form Approved
OMB No. 1900-0025

Veterans Administration

REQUEST FOR AND CONSENT TO RELEASE OF INFORMATION FROM CLAIMANT'S RECORDS

NOTE: The execution of this form does not authorize the release of information other than that specifically described below. The information requested on this form is solicited under Title 38, United States Code, and will authorize release of the information you specify. The information may also be disclosed outside the VA as permitted by law to include disclosures as stated in the "Notices of Systems of VA Records" published in the Federal Register in accordance with the Privacy Act of 1974. Disclosure is voluntary. However, if the information is not furnished, we may not be able to comply with your request.

	NAME OF VETERAN (Type or print)	
TO Veterans Administration	VA FILE NO. (Include prefix)	SOCIAL SECURITY NO.

NAME AND ADDRESS OF ORGANIZATION, AGENCY, OR INDIVIDUAL TO WHOM INFORMATION IS TO BE RELEASED

VETERAN'S REQUEST

I hereby request and authorize the Veterans Administration to release the following information, from the records identified above to the organization, agency, or individual named hereon:

INFORMATION REQUESTED (Number each item requested and give the dates or approximate dates—period from and to—covered by each.)

PURPOSES FOR WHICH THE INFORMATION IS TO BE USED

NOTE: *Additional items of information desired may be listed on the reverse hereof.*

DATE

SIGNATURE AND ADDRESS OF CLAIMANT, OR FIDUCIARY, IF CLAIMANT IS INCOMPETENT

VA FORM **70-3288**
JAN 1984

EXISTING STOCKS OF VA FORM 60-3288,
AND 00-3288, DEC 1976, WILL BE USED.

☆U.S. Government Printing Office: 1989-241-638/92599

VETERANS ADMINISTRATION

AUTHORIZATION FOR RELEASE OF INFORMATION

2. FILE NUMBER

C—

1. LAST NAME – FIRST NAME – MIDDLE NAME OF VETERAN (Type or print)

3. DATE OF BIRTH

4. SOCIAL SECURITY NO.

5. NAME AND ADDRESS OF HOSPITAL OR PHYSICIAN

6. DATES OF TREATMENT

I, the undersigned, hereby authorize the hospital or physician shown in item 5 above to disclose and release to the Veterans Administration any information that may have been obtained in connection with physical examination or treatment, with the understanding that the Veterans Administration will use this information in determining my eligibility to veterans benefits that I have claimed. The responses which are submitted may be disclosed as permitted by law outside the Veterans Administration.

7. DATE

8. SIGNATURE OF VETERAN

VA FORM 21-4142
MAY 1976

EXISTING STOCKS OF VA FORM 21-4142,
JAN 1971. WILL BE USED.

U.S.G.P.O 1983–421-488/0074

ⓋⒶ Veterans Administration

REQUEST FOR CHANGE OF ADDRESS/ CANCELLATION OF DIRECT DEPOSIT

NOTE: To notify the Veterans Administration of a change in address, cancellation of direct deposit, or both, complete this form and mail it to the VA office having your records. The information is requested under Title 38. United States Code, and will help insure that VA correspondence and any VA benefit checks to which you may be entitled are sent to your correct address. Disclosure is voluntary. However, if the information is not furnished, your mail may be lost or delayed and benefit payments, if any, may be suspended. Failure to furnish this information will have no other adverse effect on any benefit to which you may be entitled. The information may be disclosed outside the VA as permitted by law, or as stated in the "Notices of Systems of VA Records" which have been published in the Federal Register in accordance with the Privacy Act of 1974.

1. I REQUEST

☐ A CHANGE OF MY RESIDENCE ADDRESS ☐ BOTH

☐ A CANCELLATION OF MY DIRECT DEPOSIT ACCOUNT

3. VA FILE NO. (Include letter prefix, if any)

2. I RECEIVE BENEFITS AS THE

☐ VETERAN ☐ WIFE/HUSBAND ☐ WIDOW(ER)
☐ FATHER ☐ CHILD ☐ OTHER (Specify)
☐ MOTHER ☐ FIDUCIARY

4. VETERAN'S SOCIAL SECURITY NO. | **5. PAYEE NO. (if known)**

6. TYPE OF BENEFIT RECEIVED

☐ COMPENSATION OR PENSION ☐ OTHER (Specify)

EDUCATION

☐ CH. 31 (VOC. REHAB.) ☐ CH. 32 (VEAP)
☐ CH. 35 (DEA) ☐ CH. 30 (MONTGOMERY G.I. BILL-ACTIVE)
☐ CH. 34 (G.I. BILL) ☐ CH. 106 (MONTGOMERY G.I. BILL-RES.)

7. INSURANCE NO(S) (Only give these numbers if you are receiving payments on the insurance policy of a deceased veteran)

8. TYPE OF ADDRESS CHANGE (Complete if applicable)

☐ PERMANENT ☐ TEMPORARY

9. NAME OF PAYEE AS SHOWN ON CHECK (Type or print)

10. FIRST NAME - MIDDLE INITIAL - LAST NAME OF VETERAN

11. NEW ADDRESS (Complete only if applicable)

NUMBER AND STREET OR RURAL ROUTE (Include APT. NO., if appropriate)

CITY | STATE | ZIP CODE

12. TO BE COMPLETED BY DIRECT DEPOSIT PARTICIPANTS ONLY

IF YOUR BENEFIT PAYMENT IS CURRENTLY BEING SENT TO A FINANCIAL ORGANIZATION, BUT YOU WANT IT CANCELLED AND SENT TO YOUR HOME ADDRESS, CHECK THIS BOX ☐

Your payments will continue to be sent to the financial organization until the cancellation is processed. DO NOT close your bank account until your first payment is received at your home address.

13. SIGNATURE OF VETERAN OR PAYEE (DO NOT PRINT) | **14. DATE**

VA FORM 572
OCT 1987

EXISTING STOCKS OF VA FORM 572, APR 1984, WILL BE USED.

OMB Approved No. 2900-0404
Respondent Burden: 3/4 hour

Department of Veterans Affairs

VETERAN'S APPLICATION FOR INCREASED COMPENSATION BASED ON UNEMPLOYABILITY

NOTE — This is a claim for compensation benefits based on unemployability. When you complete this form you are claiming total disability because of a service-connected disability(ies) which have/has prevented you from securing or following any substantially gainful occupation. Answer all questions fully and accurately.

1. VA FILE NUMBER	2. VETERAN'S SOCIAL SECURITY NUMBER	3. DATE OF BIRTH

4. NAME OF VETERAN (First, Middle, Last) (Type or Print)	5. ADDRESS OF CLAIMANT (No., street or rural route, P.O., city or state and Zip Code)

6. TELEPHONE NUMBER OF CLAIMANT (Include Area Code)

SECTION I – DISABILITY AND MEDICAL TREATMENT

7. WHAT SERVICE CONNECTED DISABILITY PREVENTS YOU FROM SECURING OR FOLLOWING ANY SUBSTANTIALLY GAINFUL OCCUPATION?	8. HAVE YOU BEEN UNDER A DOCTOR'S CARE AND/OR HOSPITALIZED WITHIN THE PAST 12 MONTHS? ☐ YES ☐ NO	9. DATES OF TREATMENT BY DOCTOR(S)

10. NAME AND ADDRESS OF DOCTOR(S)	11. NAME AND ADDRESS OF HOSPITAL	12. DATES OF HOSPITALIZATION

SECTION II – EMPLOYMENT STATEMENT

13. DATE YOUR DISABILITY AFFECTED FULL TIME EMPLOYMENT	14. DATE YOU LAST WORKED FULL TIME	15. DATE YOU BECAME TOO DISABLED TO WORK

16A. WHAT IS THE MOST YOU EVER EARNED IN ONE YEAR?	16B. WHAT YEAR	16C. OCCUPATION DURING THAT YEAR

17. LIST ALL YOUR EMPLOYMENT INCLUDING SELF-EMPLOYMENT FOR THE LAST FIVE YEARS YOU WORKED

A. NAME AND ADDRESS OF EMPLOYER	B. TYPE OF WORK	C. HOURS PER WEEK	D. DATES OF EMPLOYMENT		E. TIME LOST FROM ILLNESS	F. HIGHEST GROSS EARNINGS PER MONTH
			FROM	TO		

18. DID YOU LEAVE YOUR LAST JOB/SELF-EMPLOYMENT BECAUSE OF YOUR DISABILITY?

☐ YES   ☐ NO *(If "YES" give the facts in item 25)*

19. DO YOU RECEIVE/EXPECT TO RECEIVE DISABILITY RETIREMENT BENEFITS?

☐ YES   ☐ NO

20. DO YOU RECEIVE/EXPECT TO RECEIVE WORKERS COMPENSATION BENEFITS?

☐ YES   ☐ NO

21. HAVE YOU TRIED TO OBTAIN EMPLOYMENT SINCE YOU BECAME TOO DISABLED TO WORK

☐ YES   ☐ NO *(If "YES" complete Items A, B and C)*

A. NAME AND ADDRESS OF EMPLOYER	B. TYPE OF WORK	C. DATE APPLIED

VA FORM
JAN 1990
21-8940

EXISTING STOCK OF VA FORM 21-8940, MAR 1984,
WILL BE USED.

SECTION III — SCHOOLING AND OTHER TRAINING

22. EDUCATION (Circle highest year completed)

GRADE SCHOOL 1 2 3 4 5 6 7 8   HIGH SCHOOL 1 2 3 4   COLLEGE 1 2 3 4

23A. DID YOU HAVE ANY OTHER EDUCATION AND TRAINING BEFORE YOU WERE TOO DISABLED TO WORK?

☐ YES   ☐ NO (If "YES" complete items 23B & 23C)

23B. TYPE OF EDUCATION OR TRAINING	23C. DATES OF TRAINING	
	BEGINNING	COMPLETION

24A. HAVE YOU HAD ANY EDUCATION AND TRAINING SINCE YOU BECAME TOO DISABLED TO WORK?

☐ YES   ☐ NO (If "YES" complete items 24B & 24C)

24B. TYPE OF EDUCATION OR TRAINING	24C. DATES OF TRAINING	
	BEGINNING	COMPLETION

25. REMARKS

SECTION IV – AUTHORIZATION, CERTIFICATION AND SIGNATURE

AUTHORIZATION FOR RELEASE OF INFORMATION – I consent that any physician, surgeon, dentist or hospital that has treated or examined me for any purpose or that I have consulted professionally may furnish to the VA any information about myself and I waive any privilege which makes this information confidential.

CERTIFICATION OF STATEMENTS – I CERTIFY that as a result of my service connected disabilities I am unable to secure or follow *any* substantially gainful occupation and that the statements in this application are true and complete to the best of my knowledge and belief and understand that these statements will be considered in determining my eligibility for VA benefits based on unemployability because of service-connected disability.

I UNDERSTAND THAT IF I AM GRANTED SERVICE-CONNECTED TOTAL DISABILITY BENEFITS BASED ON MY UNEMPLOYABILITY, THAT I MUST IMMEDIATELY INFORM THE VA IF I RETURN TO WORK. I ALSO UNDERSTAND THAT TOTAL DISABILITY BENEFITS PAID TO ME AFTER I BEGIN WORK MAY BE CONSIDERED AN OVERPAYMENT REQUIRING REPAYMENT TO THE VA.

26A. DATE SIGNED	26B. SIGNATURE OF CLAIMANT

WITNESS TO SIGNATURE OF CLAIMANT IF MADE BY "X" MARK. NOTE.–Signature made by mark must be witnessed by two persons to whom the person making the statement is personally known and the signature and address of such witnesses must be shown below.

27A. SIGNATURE OF WITNESS	27B. ADDRESS OF WITNESS
28A. SIGNATURE OF WITNESS	28B. ADDRESS OF WITNESS

PENALTY – The law provides severe penalties which include fine or imprisonment or both for the willful submission of any statement or evidence of a material fact, knowing it to be false or for the fraudulant acceptance of any payment to which you are not entitled.

PRIVACY ACT NOTICE: The responses you submit are considered confidential. (38 U.S.C. 3301). They may be disclosed outside the Department of Veterans Affairs only if the disclosure is authorized by the Privacy Act, including the routine uses identified in the system of records 58VA21/22, Compensation, Pension, Education and Rehabilitation Records – VA, published in the Federal Register. The requested information is considered relevant and necessary to determine maximum benefits provided under the law. Information submitted is subject to verification through computer matching programs with other agencies.

RESPONDENT BURDEN: Public reporting burden for this collection of information is estimated to average 3/4 hour per response, including the time for reviewing instructions, searching existing data sources, gathering and maintaining the data needed, and completing and reviewing the collection of information. Send comments regarding this burden estimate or any other aspect of this collection of information, including suggestions for reducing this burden, to VA Clearance Officer (70Y732), 810 Vermont Ave., NW, Washington, DC 20420; and to the Office of Management, and Budget, Paperwork Reduction Project (2900–0404), Washington, DC 20503. Do NOT send requests for benefits to these addresses.

☆U.S. Government Printing Office: 1990-262-755/06725

CLAIM FOR DAMAGE, INJURY, OR DEATH	INSTRUCTIONS: Please read carefully the instructions on the reverse side and supply information requested on both sides of this form. Use additional sheet(s) if necessary. See reverse side for additional instructions.	FORM APPROVED OMB NO. 1105-0008 EXPIRES 3-31-91

1. Submit To Appropriate Federal Agency:

2. Name, Address of claimant and claimant's personal representative, if any. (See instructions on reverse.) (Number, street, city, State and Zip Code)

3. TYPE OF EMPLOYMENT ☐ MILITARY ☐ CIVILIAN	4. DATE OF BIRTH	5. MARITAL STATUS	6. DATE AND DAY OF ACCIDENT	7. TIME (A.M. OR P.M.)

8. Basis of Claim (State in detail the known facts and circumstances attending the damage, injury, or death, identifying persons and property involved, the place of occurence and the cause thereof) (Use additional pages if necessary.)

PROPERTY DAMAGE

9.

NAME AND ADDRESS OF OWNER, IF OTHER THAN CLAIMANT (Number, street, city, State, and Zip Code)

BRIEFLY DESCRIBE THE PROPERTY, NATURE AND EXTENT OF DAMAGE AND THE LOCATION WHERE PROPERTY MAY BE INSPECTED. (See instructions on reverse side.)

PERSONAL INJURY/WRONGFUL DEATH

10.

STATE NATURE AND EXTENT OF EACH INJURY OR CAUSE OF DEATH, WHICH FORMS THE BASIS OF THE CLAIM. IF OTHER THAN CLAIMANT, STATE NAME OF INJURED PERSON OR DECEDENT.

WITNESSES

11.

NAME	ADDRESS (Number, street, city, State, and Zip Code)

AMOUNT OF CLAIM (in dollars)

12. (See instructions on reverse)

12a. PROPERTY DAMAGE	12b. PERSONAL INJURY	12c. WRONGFUL DEATH	12d. TOTAL (Failure to specify may cause forfeiture of your rights.)

I CERTIFY THAT THE AMOUNT OF CLAIM COVERS ONLY DAMAGES AND INJURIES CAUSED BY THE ACCIDENT ABOVE AND AGREE TO ACCEPT SAID AMOUNT IN FULL SATISFACTION AND FINAL SETTLEMENT OF THIS CLAIM

13a. SIGNATURE OF CLAIMANT (See instructions on reverse side.)	13b. Phone number of signatory	14. DATE OF CLAIM

CIVIL PENALTY FOR PRESENTING FRAUDULENT CLAIM	CRIMINAL PENALTY FOR PRESENTING FRAUDULENT CLAIM OR MAKING FALSE STATEMENTS
The claimant shall forfeit and pay to the United States the sum of $2,000, plus double the amount of damages sustained by the United States. (See 31 U.S.C. 3729.)	Fine of not more than $10,000 or imprisonment for not more than 5 years or both. (See 18 U.S.C. 287, 1001.)

95-108   NSN 7540-00-634-4046

Previous editions not usable.

STANDARD FORM 95 (Rev. 7-85)
PRESCRIBED BY DEPT. OF JUSTICE
28 CFR 14.2

PRIVACY ACT NOTICE

This Notice is provided in accordance with the Privacy Act, 5 U.S.C. 552a(e)(3), and concerns the information requested in the letter to which this Notice is attached.

A. *Authority*: The requested information is solicited pursuant to one or more of the following: 5 U.S.C. 301, 28 U.S.C. 501 et seq., 28 U.S.C. 2671 et seq., 28 C.F.R. Part 14.

B. *Principal Purpose*: The information requested is to be used in evaluating claims.

C. *Routine Use*: See the Notices of Systems of Records for the agency to whom you are submitting this form for this information.

D. *Effect of Failure to Respond*: Disclosure is voluntary. However, failure to supply the requested information or to execute the form may render your claim "invalid".

INSTRUCTIONS

Complete all items - Insert the word NONE where applicable

A CLAIM SHALL BE DEEMED TO HAVE BEEN PRESENTED WHEN A FEDERAL AGENCY RECEIVES FROM A CLAIMANT, HIS DULY AUTHORIZED AGENT, OR LEGAL REPRESENTATIVE AN EXECUTED STANDARD FORM 95 OR OTHER WRITTEN NOTIFICATION OF AN INCIDENT, ACCOMPANIED BY A CLAIM FOR MONEY DAMAGES IN A **SUM CERTAIN** FOR INJURY TO OR LOSS OF PROPERTY, PERSONAL INJURY, OR DEATH ALLEGED TO HAVE OCCURRED BY REASON OF THE INCIDENT. THE CLAIM MUST BE PRESENTED TO THE APPROPRIATE FEDERAL AGENCY WITHIN **TWO YEARS** AFTER THE CLAIM ACCRUES.

Any instructions or information necessary in the preparation of your claim will be furnished, upon request, by the office indicated in item #1 on the reverse side. Complete regulations pertaining to claims asserted under the Federal Tort Claims Act can be found in Title 28, Code of Federal Regulations, Part 14. Many agencies have published supplemental regulations also. If more than one agency is involved, please state each agency.

The claim may be filed by a duly authorized agent or other legal representative, provided evidence satisfactory to the Government is submitted with said claim establishing express authority to act for the claimant. A claim presented by an agent or legal representative must be presented in the name of the claimant. If the claim is signed by the agent or legal representative, it must show the title or legal capacity of the person signing and be accompanied by evidence of his/her authority to present a claim on behalf of the claimant as agent, executor, administrator, parent, guardian or other representative.

If claimant intends to file claim for both personal injury and property damage, claim for both must be shown in item 12 of this form.

The amount claimed should be substantiated by competent evidence as follows:

(a) In support of the claim for personal injury or death, the claimant should submit a written report by the attending physician, showing the nature and extent of injury, the nature and extent of treatment, the degree of permanent disability, if any, the prognosis, and the period of hospitalization, or incapacitation, attaching itemized bills for medical, hospital, or burial expenses actually incurred.

(b) In support of claims for damage to property which has been or can be economically repaired, the claimant should submit at least two itemized signed statements or estimates by reliable, disinterested concerns, or, if payment has been made, the itemized signed receipts evidencing payment.

(c) In support of claims for damage to property which is not economically repairable, or if the property is lost or destroyed, the claimant should submit statements as to the original cost of the property, the date of purchase, and the value of the property, both before and after the accident. Such statements should be by disinterested competent persons, preferably reputable dealers or officials familiar with the type of property damaged, or by two or more competitive bidders, and should be certified as being just and correct.

(d) Failure to completely execute this form or to supply the requested material within two years from the date the allegations accrued may render your claim "invalid". A claim is deemed presented when it is received by the appropriate agency, not when it is mailed.

Failure to specify a sum certain will result in invalid presentation of your claim and may result in forfeiture of your rights.

Public reporting burden for this collection of information is estimated to average 15 minutes per response, including the time for reviewing instructions, searching existing data sources, gathering and maintaining the data needed, and completing and reviewing the collection of information. Send comments regarding this burden estimate or

Civil Division
U.S. Department of Justice
Washington, DC 20530

Office of Management and Budget
Paperwork Reduction Project (1105-0008)
Washington, DC 20503

INSURANCE COVERAGE

In order that subrogation claims may be adjudicated, it is essential that the claimant provide the following information regarding the insurance coverage of his vehicle or property.

15. Do you carry accident insurance? ☐ Yes, If yes, give name and address of insurance company (Number, street, city, State, and Zip Code) and policy number. ☐ No

16. Have you filed claim on your insurance carrier in this instance, and if so, is it full coverage or deductible?

17. If deductible, state amount

18. If claim has been filed with your carrier, what action has your insurer taken or proposes to take with reference to your claim? (It is necessary that you ascertain these facts)

19. Do you carry public liability and property damage insurance? ☐ Yes, If yes, give name and address of insurance carrier (Number, street, city, State, and Zip Code) ☐ No

SF 95 (Rev. 7-85) BACK

☆ U.S. GOVERNMENT PRINTING OFFICE: 1989—241-175

REQUEST PERTAINING TO MILITARY RECORDS

Please read instructions on the reverse. If more space is needed, use plain paper.

PRIVACY ACT OF 1974 COMPLIANCE INFORMATION. The following information is provided in accordance with 5 U.S.C. 552a(e)(3) and applies to this form. Authority for collection of the information is 44 U.S.C. 2907, 3101, and E.O. 9397 of November 22, 1943. Disclosure of the information is voluntary. The principal purpose of the information is to assist the facility servicing the records in locating and verifying the correctness of the requested records or information to answer your inquiry. Routine uses of the information as established and published in accordance with 5 U.S.C.a(e)(4)(D)

include the transfer of relevant information to appropriate Federal, State, local, or foreign agencies for use in civil, criminal, or regulatory investigations or prosecution. In addition, this form will be filed with the appropriate military records and may be transferred along with the record to another agency in accordance with the routine uses established by the agency which maintains the record. If the requested information is not provided, it may not be possible to service your inquiry.

SECTION I—INFORMATION NEEDED TO LOCATE RECORDS (Furnish as much as possible)

1. NAME USED DURING SERVICE (Last, first, and middle)	2. SOCIAL SECURITY NO.	3. DATE OF BIRTH	4. PLACE OF BIRTH

5. ACTIVE SERVICE, PAST AND PRESENT   (For an effective records search, it is important that ALL service be shown below)

BRANCH OF SERVICE (Also, show last organization, if known)	DATES OF ACTIVE SERVICE		Check one		SERVICE NUMBER DURING THIS PERIOD
	DATE ENTERED	DATE RELEASED	OFFI-CER	EN-LISTED	

6. RESERVE SERVICE, PAST OR PRESENT   If "none," check here ▲ ☐

a. BRANCH OF SERVICE	b. DATES OF MEMBERSHIP		c. Check one		d. SERVICE NUMBER DURING THIS PERIOD
	FROM	TO	OFFI-CER ☐	EN-LISTED ☐	

7. NATIONAL GUARD MEMBERSHIP   (Check one): a. ARMY ☐ b. AIR FORCE ☐ c. NONE ☐

d. STATE	e. ORGANIZATION	f. DATES OF MEMBERSHIP		g. Check one		h. SERVICE NUMBER DURING THIS PERIOD
		FROM	TO	OFFI-CER ☐	EN-LISTED ☐	

8. IS SERVICE PERSON DECEASED
YES ☐   NO ☐   If "yes," enter date of death.

9. IS (WAS) INDIVIDUAL A MILITARY RETIREE OR FLEET RESERVIST
YES ☐   NO ☐

SECTION II—REQUEST

1. EXPLAIN WHAT INFORMATION OR DOCUMENTS YOU NEED: OR, CHECK ITEM 2: OR, COMPLETE ITEM 3

2. IF YOU ONLY NEED A STATEMENT OF SERVICE check here ☐

3. LOST SEPARATION DOCUMENT REPLACEMENT REQUEST
(Complete a or b, and c.)

		YEAR ISSUED	
a.	REPORT OF SEPARATION (DD Form 214 or equivalent) ☐		This contains information normally needed to determine eligibility for benefits. It may be furnished only to the veteran, the surviving next of kin, or to a representative with veteran's signed release (item 5 of this form).
b.	DISCHARGE CERTIFICATE ☐	YEAR ISSUED	This shows only the date and character at discharge. It is of little value in determining eligibility for benefits. It may be issued only to veterans discharged honorably or under honorable conditions; or, if deceased, to the surviving spouse.

c. EXPLAIN HOW SEPARATION DOCUMENT WAS LOST

4. EXPLAIN PURPOSE FOR WHICH INFORMATION OR DOCUMENTS ARE NEEDED

6. REQUESTER

a. IDENTIFICATION (check appropriate box)

☐ Same person identified in Section I   ☐ Surviving spouse

☐ Next of kin (relationship)

☐ Other (specify)

b. SIGNATURE (see instruction 3 on reverse side)   DATE OF REQUEST

5. RELEASE AUTHORIZATION, IF REQUIRED (Read instruction 3 on reverse side)

I hereby authorize release of the requested information/documents to the person indicated at right (item 7).

VETERAN SIGN HERE ▲

(If signed by other than veteran show relationship to veteran.)

7. Please type or print clearly –   COMPLETE RETURN ADDRESS

Name, number and street, city, State and ZIP code

TELEPHONE NO. (include area code) ▲

180-106

NSN 7540-00-142-9360

STANDARD FORM 180 (Rev. 7-88)
Prescribed by NARA (36 CFR 1228.162(e))

INSTRUCTIONS

1. **Information needed to locate records.** Certain identifying information is necessary to determine the location of an individual's record of military service. Please give careful consideration to and answer each item on this form. If you do not have and cannot obtain the information for an item, show "NA", meaning the information is "not available." Include as much of the requested information as you can. This will help us to give you the best possible service.

2. **Charges for service.** A nominal fee is charged for certain types of service. In most instances service fees cannot be determined in advance. If your request involves a service fee you will be notified as soon as that determination is made.

3. **Restrictions on release of information.** Information from records of military personnel is released subject to restrictions imposed by the military departments consistent with the provisions of the Freedom of Information Act of 1967 (as amended in 1974) and the Privacy Act of 1974. A service person has access to almost any information contained in his own record. The next of kin, if the veteran is deceased, and Federal officers for official purposes, are authorized to receive information from a military service or medical record only as specified in the above cited Acts. Other requesters must have the release authorization, in item 5 of the form, signed by the veteran or, if deceased, by the next of kin. Employers

and others needing proof of military service are expected to accept the information shown on documents issued by the Armed Forces at the time a service person is separated.

4. **Location of military personnel records.** The various categories of military personnel records are described in the chart below. For each category there is a code number which indicates the address at the bottom of the page to which this request should be sent. For each military service there is a note explaining approximately how long the records are held by the military service before they are transferred to the National Personnel Records Center, St. Louis. Please read these notes carefully and make sure you send your inquiry to the right address. Please note especially that the record is not sent to the National Personnel Records Center as long as the person retains any sort of reserve obligation, whether drilling or non-drilling.

(If the person has two or more periods of service within the same branch, send your request to the office having the record for the last period of service.)

5. **Definitions for abbreviations used below:**
NPRC—National Personnel Records Center PERS—Personnel Records
TDRL—Temporary Disability Retirement List MED—Medical Records

SERVICE	NOTE: (See paragraph 4 above.)	CATEGORY OF RECORDS	WHERE TO WRITE ADDRESS CODE ▶	
AIR FORCE (USAF)	*Except for TDRL and general officers retired with pay, Air Force records are transferred to NPRC from Code 1, 90 days after separation and from Code 2, 150 days after separation.*	Active members (includes National Guard on active duty in the Air Force), TDRL, and general officers retired with pay.	1	
		Reserve, retired reservist in nonpay status, current National Guard officers not on active duty in Air Force, and National Guard released from active duty in Air Force.	2	
		Current National Guard enlisted not on active duty in Air Force.	13	
		Discharged, deceased, and retired with pay.	14	
COAST GUARD (USCG)	*Coast Guard officer and enlisted records are transferred to NPRC 7 months after separation.*	Active, reserve, and TDRL members.	3	
		Discharged, deceased, and retired members (see next item).	14	
		Officers separated before 1/1/29 and enlisted personnel separated before 1/1/15.	6	
MARINE CORPS (USMC)	*Marine Corps records are transferred to NPRC between 6 and 9 months after separation.*	Active, TDRL, and Selected Marine Corps Reserve members.	4	
		Individual Ready Reserve and Fleet Marine Corps Reserve members.	5	
		Discharged, deceased, and retired members (see next item).	14	
		Members separated before 1/1/1905.	6	
		Reserve, living retired members, retired general officers, and active duty records of current National Guard members who performed	7	

ARMY (USA)	Reserve Control Groups: About 60 days after separation. U.S. Army Reserve Troop Unit personnel: About 120 to 180 days after separation.		
	Current National Guard officers not on active duty in the U.S. Army.		12
	Current National Guard enlisted not on active duty in the U.S. Army.		13
	Discharged and deceased members (see next item).		14
	Officers separated before 7/1/17 and enlisted separated before 11/1/12.		6
	Officers and warrant officers TDRL.		8
	Active members (including reservists on duty).—PERS and MED		10
NAVY (USN)	Navy records are transferred to NPRC 6 months after retirement or complete separation.		
	Discharged, deceased, retired (with and without pay) less than six months,	PERS ONLY	10
		MED ONLY	11
	Discharged, deceased, retired (with and without pay) more than six months (see next item)—PERS & MED		14
	Officers separated before 1/1/03 and enlisted separated before 1/1/1886—PERS and MED		6

*Code 12 applies to active duty records of current National Guard officers who performed service in the U.S. Army after 6/30/72.
*Code 13 applies to active duty records of current National Guard enlisted members who performed service in the U.S. Army after 6/30/72.

ADDRESS LIST OF CUSTODIANS (BY CODE NUMBERS SHOWN ABOVE)—Where to write / send this form for each category of records

1	Air Force Manpower and Personnel Center Military Personnel Records Division Randolph AFB, TX 78150-6001	5	Marine Corps Reserve Support Center 10950 El Monte Overland Park, KS 66211-1408	8	USA MILPERCEN ATTN: DAPC-MSR 200 Stoval Street Alexandria, VA 22332-0400	12	Army National Guard Personnel Center Columbia Pike Office Building 5600 Columbia Pike Falls Church, VA 22041
2	Air Reserve Personnel Center Denver, CO 80280-5000	6	Military Archives Division National Archives and Records Administration Washington, DC 20408	9	Commander U.S. Army Enlisted Records and Evaluation Center Ft. Benjamin Harrison, IN 46249-5301	13	The Adjutant General (of the appropriate State, DC, or Puerto Rico)
3	Commandant U.S. Coast Guard Washington, DC 20593-0001	7	Commander U.S. Army Reserve Personnel Center ATTN: DARP-PAS 9700 Page Boulevard St. Louis, MO 63132-5200	10	Commander Naval Military Personnel Command ATTN: NMPC-036 Washington, DC 20370-5036	14	National Personnel Records Center (Military Personnel Records) 9700 Page Boulevard St. Louis, MO 63132
4	Commandant of the Marine Corps (Code MMRB-10) Headquarters, U.S. Marine Corps Washington, DC 20380-0001			11	Naval Reserve Personnel Center New Orleans, LA 70146-5000		

STANDARD FORM 180 BACK (Rev. 7-86)

☆U.S. Government Printing Office: 1989-241-638/05970

UNITED STATES COURT OF VETERANS APPEALS

NOTICE OF APPEAL

_____,
)
               Appellant,)
)
     v.   ) VA FILE NO. _____
)
ANTHONY J. PRINCIPI,   )
Acting Secretary of Veterans Affairs,)
               Appellee.)

Notice is hereby given that _____, Appellant, appeals to the U.S. Court of Veterans Appeals from the decision of the Board of Veterans' Appeals (BVA).

Information pertaining to BVA decision being appealed:
a. Date of filing of Notice of Disagreement which led to BVA decision being appealed: _____
b. Location of VA Regional Office or other VA activity where Notice of Disagreement was filed: _____
c. Date BVA decision was mailed: _____
NOTICE OF APPEAL FILED BY: Appellant

                          _____
                          Signature of Appellant

---

name, address, phone number of appellant

CERTIFICATE OF SERVICE

A copy of this Notice of Appeal was mailed postage prepaid to
General Counsel (027)
Department of Veterans Affairs
810 Vermont Avenue NW
Washington DC 20420

I certify under penalty of perjury under the laws of the
United States of America that the foregoing is true and
correct.

---
date   Signature of appellant

FAX and mail the original to:
Clerk of the Court, U.S. Court of Veterans Appeals
625 Indiana Avenue NW #900, Washington DC 20004
202-501-5848 (FAX)

UNITED STATES COURT OF VETERANS APPEALS

MOTION AND AFFIDAVIT TO APPEAL WITHOUT PAYMENT OF COSTS

_____

     Appellant,

     v.   VA FILE NO. _____

ANTHONY J. PRINCIPI,
Acting Secretary of Veterans Affairs,
     Appellee.

I move for permission to appeal without payment of costs in this case and submit the following affidavit:

I, _____ am the appellant. I state that I am unable to pay the costs because of the hardship it will cause and that I believe I am entitled to redress. I state that I am
I swear that the answers to the questions below about my ability to pay the filing fee are true.

1. Are you now employed?

a. If the answer is yes, state the amount of your monthly salary or wages and the name and address of your employer.

b. If the answer is no, state the date of your last employment and the amount of your monthly salary and wages.

2. Within the past 12 months, have you received any income from a business, profession, other form of self-employment, rent payments, interest, dividends, retirement, annuity pay-

If the answer is yes, describe each source of income, and state the amount received from each during the past 12 months.

3. Do you have any cash or checking or savings accounts? _____ If the answer is yes, state the total amount of cash owned and the average monthly balance in any account.

4. Do you own any real estate, stocks, bonds, notes, automobiles, or other valuable property (excluding ordinary household furnishings and clothing)? _____ If the answer is yes, describe the property and state its approximate value.

5. List the persons whom you actually support and state your relationship to those persons.

6. Have you ever filed a motion in another case in this Court to appeal without payment of costs? _____ If the answer is yes, state the name and docket number _____ of the appeal.

7. State any other circumstances that you want the Court to consider about your ability to pay costs:

I state under penalty of perjury under the laws of the United States of America that the foregoing is true and correct.

_____
Date

_____
Signature of Appellant

_____
_____
_____
name, address, phone number of appellant

A FEW NOTES ABOUT THE FORMS INCLUDED IN THIS BOOK

You can usually get most government forms by calling any VA regional office [(800) 827-1000] or by visiting the office. If you cannot get a form that is listed in this guide, at least write to the VA and state that you want a particular benefit and ask that the office send you the proper form. Your letter should count as an informal claim as long as you follow up and file the correct form within one year.

Seven forms that you may need quickly or that may not be readily available are reproduced in this appendix. You can photocopy the form, fill it out, sign and date it and submit it to the correct office. If an official doesn't like your use of a photocopied form, he or she should provide an original one. What follows are a few notes about these forms and a cross reference to where you can find more information about the form in the book.

1. **VA Form 70-3288, Request for and Consent to Release of Information from Claimant's Records**

   Use a photocopy machine to copy this form before completing it. You can use this form to request one page of your VA claims folder or the entire folder. If you receive a VA letter denying your claim, you can be sure that a rating decision was made shortly before you were notified. Of course you will not know the exact date of the rating decision, but you can request it by stating in the box entitled "Veteran's Request," "I request a copy of the rating decision that led to your letter dated [*insert the date*]."

   If you want the entire VA claims folder, vocational rehabilitation folder, home loan folder, insurance file, or medical treatment file, state, "I request a complete and true copy of my entire claims folder or file. Please prepare an exact duplicate of my folder and keep the photocopy in the exact order as the original."

   In the block at the bottom of the page that asks for the purpose of your request, state, "This is a request under the Privacy Act and the Freedom of Information Act to confirm the accuracy and completeness of my VA file; please waive any fees for this service." Keep in mind that one copy of your entire file is free of charge (although some VA offices may try to discourage you from getting your file by charging you a fee). Mail or deliver this form to the VA office that has your records.

   For additional information about this form and problems you may have getting your VA records, see Chapter 11.

2. **VA Form 21-4142, Authorization for Release of Information**

This form is full size; just photocopy it and fill it out. If you want the VA to consider the medical records of your visit to a private doctor or a therapist or of your admission to a private hospital, you will need to give the VA permission to get these records. To save the VA (and yourself) several months' time, complete this form with the full name and mailing address (including ZIP code) of the doctor or hospital. Mail or deliver the completed forms to the nearest VA office along with a letter explaining why you want the VA to get the records (for example, the records show that you are seriously disabled and needed treatment for your condition).

If you are not sure what your doctor's records may say about your condition, don't use this form. Instead, request the records and review them yourself before giving them to the VA.

For additional information about this form and problems you may have getting your VA records, see Chapter 11.

3. **VA Form 572, Request for Change of Address/Cancellation of Direct Deposit**

This form is full size and self-explanatory. Use this form to make sure your benefit checks and VA letters come to the right address. Try to get this form to the nearest VA office before the tenth of the month if you want a check sent to a new address; after the tenth of the month, you may miss the mailing cycle for that month. Also, call the nearest VA office at (800) 827-1000 to report your new address.

4. **VA Form 21-8940, Veteran's Application for Increased Compensation Based on Unemployability**

Use a photocopy machine to copy this form before completing it. If you are already rated as service connected for a disability (no matter what percentage of disability has been assigned) and you believe that your disability prevents you from working, use this form. If you have not tried to get a job recently, try now before completing this form. If the employers say that they will not hire you because you are not able to do the job because of your disability, list their names and complete mailing addresses in block 21. If you have both a service-connected disability and a nonservice-connected disability, try to get a letter from the employer that says you cannot do the work specifically because of the service-connected disability. If you are receiving Social Security Administration disability benefits for the same condition for which you are service connected, list this fact in block 25.

For additional information about this form and problems you may have getting the VA to evaluate your ability to work, see Chapter 4.

5. **SF 95, Claim for Damage, Injury, or Death**

Use a photocopy machine to copy this form before completing it. This form is the first step in filing a medical malpractice case against the VA. You must submit this form to the nearest VA office within 2 years of the date when you were injured. Exactly when you were injured or knew you were injured might be a complicated question. Consult a lawyer experienced in the Federal Tort Claims Act. Most important, be sure to state the dollar amount you want in block 12d; ask for more, not less, because you can lower your demand but not increase it later.

For additional information about this form, see Chapter 9.

6. **SF 180, Request Pertaining to Military Records**

Use a photocopy machine to copy this form before completing it. Use this form to obtain a copy of your military personnel records or military medical records. If you want all your military records, state in Section II, block 1, ''Complete personnel and medical records.'' Make sure the Records Center doesn't send you only a few pages of your file. If you know the names of the military hospitals in which you were treated, list their names, dates of treatment, and the kind of treatment you received.

For additional information about this form and problems you may have getting military records, see Chapters 11 and 25.

7. **U.S. Court of Veterans Appeals Form: Notice of Appeal**

Use a photocopy machine to copy this form before completing it. If the Board of Veterans' Appeals has denied your claim, you must deliver this form to the Clerk of the court by the end of the 120th day after the date on the first page of the BVA's decision. Do not put this Notice of Appeal in the mailbox on the 120th day. You can send a copy by facsimile machine (found at the nearest photocopy shop) to (202) 501-5848. Also send the original to the Clerk, U.S. Court of Veterans Appeals, 625 Indiana Avenue, N.W., Ste. 900, Washington, DC 20004. For information from the clerk, call (800) 869-8654. If you do not know all the information requested on the form, don't worry about it, just submit the form on time.

For additional information about the Court of Veterans Appeals, see Chapter 3.

APPENDIX B:

VA FACILITIES

★ ★

WHERE TO GO FOR HELP

Veterans and dependents from throughout the country can obtain information on VA benefits from regional offices by calling a toll-free telephone
number, **(800) 827-1000**. Callers are automatically connected to the closest
VA regional office. Other telephone services nationwide include these:

Life Insurance   (800) 669-8477
Radiation Helpline   (800) 827-0365
Debt Management Center   (800) 827-0648
Education Loan   (800) 326-8276
Telecommunication Device for the Deaf (TDD)   (800) 829-4833
CHAMPVA   (800) 733-8387
Headstone and Gravemarker Helpline   (800) 697-6947

Many VA medical centers operate outpatient clinics. Some clinics
operate independently of medical centers. All clinics can make referrals for
care in VA medical centers.

──────────── ★ NOTE: ★ ────────────
The following information on VA facilities is taken from the 1993
edition of the pamphlet "Federal Benefits for Veterans and Dependents." This pamphlet is revised annually and sold through the
Government Printing Office (consult your telephone directory for
the nearest GPO or call the Washington, DC, office at 202-783-
3238 to order the latest edition.

The following designations for medical centers indicate additional programs available: * for nursing-home care units; # for domiciliaries.

Some national cemeteries can bury only cremated remains or casketed remains of eligible family members of those already buried. Contact the cemetery director for information on the availability of space.

Alabama

Medical Centers:

Birmingham 35233 (700 S. 19th St., 205-534-6581)
Montgomery 36109 (215 Perry Hill Rd., 205-228-4670)
*Tuscaloosa 35404 (3701 Loop Rd. East, 205-228-2760)
*Tuskegee 36083 (205-534-3550)

Clinics:

Mobile 36604 (1359 Springhill Ave., 205-690-2875)
Huntsville 35801 (201 Governor's Dr., SW, 205-533-1645)

Regional Office:

Montgomery 36104 (474 S. Court St., local, 262-7781; statewide, (800) 827-1000)
Mobile 36604 (1359 Springhill Ave., 205-690-2875)

Vet Centers:

Birmingham 35204 (1425 S. 21st St., Suite 108, 205-933-0500)
Mobile 36604 (951 Government St., Suite 122, 205-694-4194)

National Cemeteries:

Fort Mitchell Seale 36875 (553 Highway 165, 205-855-4731)
Mobile 36604 (1202 Virginia St.; for information, call Barrancas, FL, Nat. Cem., 904-452-3357)

Alaska

Clinics:

Anchorage Outpatient Clinic and Regional Office 99508-2989 (2925 De Barr Rd., 907-257-4700)
Fort Wainwright 99703 (Bassett Army Hospital, Rm. 262, 907-353-4208)

Regional Office:

Anchorage 99508-2989 (2925 De Barr Rd., local, 257-4700; statewide (800) 827-1000)

Benefits Office:

Juneau 99802 (P.O. Box 20069, Fed. Bldg., Rm. 103)

Vet Centers:

Anchorage 99508 (4201 Tudor Centre Dr., Suite 115, 907-563-6966)
Fairbanks 99701 (520 E. 5th Ave., Suite 200, 907-456-4238)
Kenai 99611 (P.O. Box 1883, 907-283-5205)
Wasilla 99687 (851 E. Westpoint Ave., Suite 109, 907-376-4318)

National Cemeteries:

Fort Richardson 99505 (P.O. Box 5-498, Bldg. 997, Davis Highway, 907-862-4217)
Sitka 99835 (P.O. Box 1065; Saw Mill Creek Rd.; for information, call Ft. Richardson, AK, Nat. Cem., 907-862-4217)

Arizona

Medical Centers:

*Phoenix 85012 (650 East Indian School Rd., 602-277-5551)
#Prescott 86313 (602-445-4860)
*Tucson 85723 (3601 S. 6th Ave., 602-792-1450)

Regional Office:

Phoenix 85012 (3225 N. Central Ave., local, 263-5411; statewide, (800) 827-1000)

Vet Centers:

Phoenix 85004 (141 E. Palm Ln., Suite 100, 602-379-4769)
Prescott 86301 (637 Hillside Ave., Suite A, 602-778-3469)
Tucson 85723 (3055 N. 1st Ave., 602-882-0333)

National Cemeteries:

National Memorial Cemetery of Arizona (Phoenix 85024, 23029 N. Cave Creek Rd., 602-379-4615/6/7)
Prescott 86313 (VA Medical Center, 500 Highway 89N., 602-776-6028)

Arkansas

Medical Centers:

Fayetteville 72703 (1100 N. College Ave., 501-742-5555)
#*Little Rock 72205 (4300 W. 7th St., 501-661-1202, 700-740-4601)

Regional Office:

North Little Rock 72115 (Bldg. 65, Ft. Roots, P.O. Box 1280, local, 370-3800; statewide, (800) 827-1000)

Vet Center:

North Little Rock 72114 (201 W. Broadway, Suite A, 501-324-6395)

National Cemeteries:

Fayetteville 72701 (700 Government Ave., 501-444-5051)
Fort Smith 72901 (522 Garland Ave., 501-783-5345)
Little Rock 72206 (2523 Confederate Blvd., 501-374-8011)

California

Medical Centers:

*Fresno 93703 (2615 E. Clinton Ave., 209-225-6100)
*Livermore 94550 (4951 Arroyo Rd., 415-447-2560)
*Loma Linda 92357 (11201 Benton St., 714-825-7084)
*Long Beach 90822 (5901 E. 7th St., 310-494-2611)
#*Palo Alto 94304 (3801 Miranda Ave., 415-493-5000)
*San Diego 92161 (3350 La Jolla Village Dr., 619-552-8585)
San Francisco 94121 (4150 Clement St., 415-221-4810)
*Sepulveda 91343 (1611 Plummer St., 818-891-7711)
#*West Los Angeles 90073 (Wilshire & Sawtelle Blvds., 310-478-3711)

Clinics:

Los Angeles 90013 (425 S. Hill St., 310-894-3902)
Benicia 94510 (N. Calif. System of Clinics, 5500 E. 2nd St., 510-372-2000)
Oakland 94612 (2221 Martin Luther King Jr. Way, 510-273-7096)
Redding 96001 (2787 Eureka Way, 916-246-5056)
Sacramento 95820 (4600 Broadway, 916-731 7300)
San Diego 92108 (2022 Camino Del Rio North, 619-557-6210)
Santa Barbara 93110 (4440 Calle Real, 805-683-1491)

Regional Offices:

Los Angeles 90024 (Fed. Bldg., 11000 Wilshire Blvd., serving counties of Inyo, Kern, Los Angeles, Orange, San Bernardino, San Luis Obispo, Santa Barbara, and Ventura, local, 479-4011; statewide, (800) 827-1000)
San Diego 92108 (2022 Camino Del Rio North, serving counties of Imperial, Riverside, and San Diego, local 297-8220; statewide, (800) 827-1000)
San Francisco 94105 (211 Main St., local, 495-8900; statewide, (800) 827-1000) serving the remaining counties in California except Alpine, Lassen, Modoc, and Mono. (Recorded benefits, 24-hour availability, 974-0138)
Counties of Alpine, Lassen, Modoc, and Mono served by Reno, Nev., RO.

Benefits Office:

East Los Angeles 90022 (5400 E. Olympic Blvd.)

Vet Centers:

Anaheim 92805 (859 S. Harbor Blvd., 714-776-0161)
Burlingame 94010 (1234 Howard Ave., 415-344-3126)
Commerce 90040 (VA East L.A. Clinic, 5400 E. Olympic Blvd., #140, 213-728-9966)
Concord 94520 (1899 Clayton Rd., Suite 140, 415-680-4526)
Eureka 95501 (305 V St., 707-444-8271)
Fresno 93721 (1340 Van Ness Ave., 209-467-5660)
Los Angeles 90003 (S. Central L.A., 251 W. 85th Pl., 310-215-2380)
Los Angeles 90025 (West L.A., 2000 Westwood Blvd., 310-475-9509)
Marina 93933 (455 Reservation Rd., Suite E, 408-384-1660)
Oakland 94612 (287 17th St., 510-763-3904)
Riverside 92504 (4954 Arlington Ave., Suite A, 714-359-8967)
Rohnert Park 94928 (6225 State Farm Dr., Suite 101, 707-586-3295)
Sacramento 95825 (1111 Howe Ave., Suite 390, 916-978-5477)
San Diego 92103 (2900 6th Ave., 619-294-2040)
San Francisco 94102 (1540 Market St., Suite 350, 415-522-6887)
San Jose 95126 (1022 West Hedding, 408-249-1643)
Santa Barbara 93101 (1300 Santa Barbara St., 805-564-2345)
Sepulveda 91343 (16126 Lassen St., 818-892-9227)
Upland 91786 (313 N. Mountain Ave., 714-982-0416)
Vista 92083 (1830 West Dr., Tri City Plaza, Suite 103, 619-747-7305)

National Cemeteries:

Fort Rosecrans (San Diego 92166, Point Loma, P.O. Box 6237, 619-553-2084)
Golden Gate (San Bruno 94066, 1300 Sneath Ln., 415-761-1646)
Los Angeles 90049 (950 S. Sepulveda Blvd., 310-824-4311)
Riverside 92508 (22495 Van Buren Blvd., 909-653-8417)
San Francisco 94129 (P.O. Box 29012, Presidio of San Francisco, 415-561-2008)

San Joaquin Valley (Gustine 95322, 32053 W. McCabe Rd., 209-854-2276)

Colorado

Medical Centers:

*Denver 80220 (1055 Clermont St., 303-399-8020)
*Fort Lyon 81038 (719-456-1260)
*Grand Junction 81501 (2121 North Ave., 303-242-0731)

Clinic:

Colorado Springs 80909 (1785 N. Academy Blvd., 719-380-0004)

Regional Office:

Denver 80225 (44 Union Blvd., P.O. Box 25126, local, 980-1300; statewide, (800) 827-1000)

Vet Centers:

Boulder 80302 (2128 Pearl St., 303-440-7306)
Colorado Springs 80903 (411 S. Tejon, Suite G, 719-471-9992)
Denver 80204 (1815 Federal Blvd., 303-433-7123)

National Cemeteries:

Fort Logan (Denver 80235, 3698 S. Sheridan Blvd., 303-761-0117)
Fort Lyon 81038 (VA Medical Center, 719-384-3152)

Connecticut

Medical Centers:

Newington 06111 (555 Willard Ave., 203-666-6951)
*West Haven 06516 (W. Spring St., 203-932-5711)

Regional Office:

Hartford 06103 (450 Main St., local, 278-3230; statewide, (800) 827-1000)

Vet Centers:

Hartford 06120 (370 Market St., 203-240-3543)
New Haven 06511 (562 Whalley Ave., 203-773-2232 or 773-2236)
Norwich 06360 (16 Franklin St., Rm. 109, 203-887-1755)

Delaware

Medical Centers:

*Wilmington 19805 (1601 Kirkwood Highway, 302-994-2511)

Regional Office:

Wilmington 19805 (1601 Kirkwood Highway, local, 998-0191; statewide, (800) 827-1000)

Vet Center:

Wilmington 19805 (VAMROC Bldg. 2, 1601 Kirkwood Highway, 302-994-1660)

District of Columbia

Medical Center:

*Washington, DC 20422 (50 Irving St., NW, 202-745-8000)

Regional Office:

Washington, DC 20421 (941 N. Capitol St., NE, local 872-1151)

Vet Center:

Washington, DC 20003 (801 Pennsylvania Ave., SE, 202-745-8400/ 02)

Florida

Medical Centers:

#*Bay Pines 33504 (1000 Bay Pines Blvd., N., 813-826-4011)
*Gainesville 32608 (1601 Southwest Archer Rd., 904-376-1611)
*Lake City 32055 (801 S. Marion St., 904-755-3016)
*Miami 33125 (1201 N.W. 16th St., 305-324-4455)
*Tampa 33612 (13000 Bruce B. Downs Blvd., 813-822-6011)

Clinics:

Daytona Beach 32117 (1900 Mason Ave., 904-274-4600)
Fort Myers 33901 (2070 Carrell Rd., 813-939-3939)
Jacksonville 32206 (1833 Boulevard, 904-791-2712)
Key West 33040 (1111 12th St., Suite 207, 305-536-6696)
Oakland Park 33334 (5599 N. Dixie Highway, 305-771-2101)
Orlando 32806 (83 W. Columbia St., 407-425-7521)
Pensacola 32503 (312 Kenmore Rd., 904-476-1100)
Port Richey 34668 (8911 Ponderosa, 813-869-3203)
Riviera Beach 33404 (Executive Plaza, 301 Broadway, 407-845-2800)

Regional Office:

St. Petersburg 33701 (144 1st Ave., S., local, 898-2121; statewide, (800) 827-1000)

Benefits Offices:

Fort Myers 33901 (2070 Carrell Rd.)
Jacksonville 32206 (1833 Boulevard, Rm. 3109)
Miami 33130 (Federal Bldg., Rm. 120, 51 S.W. 1st Ave.)
Oakland Park 33334 (5599 N. Dixie Highway)

Orlando 32806 (83 W. Columbia St.)
Pensacola 32503-7492 (312 Kenmore Rd., Rm. 1G250)
Riviera Beach 33404 (Executive Plaza, 310 Broadway)

Vet Centers:

Ft. Lauderdale 33301 (315 N.E. 3rd Ave., (800) 827-2204)
Jacksonville 32202 (255 Liberty St., 904-791-3621)
Lake Worth 33461 (2311 10th Ave., N. #13-Palm Beach, 407-585-
    0441)
Miami 33129 (2700 S.W. 3rd Ave., Suite 1A, 305-859-8387)
Orlando 32809 (5001 S. Orange Ave., Suite A, 407-648-6151)
Pensacola 32501 (15 W. Strong St., Suite 100 C, 904-479-6665)
Sarasota 34239 (1800 Siesta Dr., 813-952-9406)
St. Petersburg 33713 (2837 1st Ave., N., 813-893-3791)
Tallahassee 32303 (249 E. 6th Ave., 904-942-8810)
Tampa 33604 (1507 W. Sligh Ave., 813-228-2621)

National Cemeteries:

Barrancas (Pensacola 32508, Naval Air Station, 904-452-3357 or 452-
    4196)
Bay Pines 33504 (P.O. Box 477, 813-398-9426)
Florida (Bushnell 33513, P.O. Box 337, 904-793-7740)
St. Augustine 32084 (104 Marine St.; for information, call Florida
    Nat. Cem. 904-793-7740)

Georgia

Medical Centers:

*Augusta 30910 (1 Freedom Way, 706-251-7189--uptown; 706-251-
    3934--downtown)
*Decatur 30033 (1670 Clairmont Rd., 404-321-6111)
#*Dublin 31021 (1826 Veterans Blvd., 700-258-2717)

Clinic:

Savannah 31406 (325 W. Montgomery Crossroad, 912-920-0214)

Regional Office:

Atlanta 30365 (730 Peachtree St., NE, local, 881-1776; statewide, (800) 827-1000)

Vet Centers:

Atlanta 30309 (922 W. Peachtree St., 404-347-7264)
Savannah 31406 (8110 White Bluff Rd., 912-927-7360)
Marietta 30060 (500 Washington Ave., 404-428-5631)

Hawaii

Medical & Regional Office:

Honolulu 96850 (P.O. Box 50188, 300 Ala Moana Blvd., Rm. 1204, Medical office--808-541-1409; Regional Office: from Oahu, 541-1000; statewide, (800) 827-1000; toll-free service from Guam 475-8387)

Vet Centers:

Hilo 96720 (120 Kelwe St., Suite 201, 808-969-3833)
Honolulu 96814 ((1680 Kapiolani Blvd., Suite F, 808-541-1764)
Kailua-Kona 96740 (Pottery Terrace, Fern Bldg., 75-5995 Kuakini Hwy., #415, 808-329-0574)
Lihue 96766 (3367 Kuhio Hwy., Suite 101-Kauai, 808-246-1163)
Wailuku 96793 (Ting Bldg., 35 Lunalilo, Suite 101, 808-242-8557)

National Cemetery:

National Memorial Cemetery of the Pacific (Honolulu 96813, 2177 Puowaina Dr., 808-551-1431)

Idaho

Medical Center:

*Boise 83702 (500 West Fort St., 208-336-5100)

Clinic:

Pocatello 83201 (1651 Alvin Rickin Dr., 208-232-6214)

Regional Office:

Boise 83724 (Federal Bldg. & U.S. Courthouse, 550 W. Fort St., Box
044, local, 334-1010; statewide, (800) 827-1000)

Vet Centers:

Boise 83706 (1115 W. Boise Ave., 208-342-3612)
Pocatello 83201 (1975 S. 5th St., 208-232-0316)

Illinois

Medical Centers:

Chicago 60622 (Lakeside, 333 E. Huron St., 312-943-6600)
Chicago 60680 (Westside, 820 S. Damen Ave., P.O. Box 8195, 312-
666-6500)
*Danville 61832 (1900 E. Main St., 217-442-8000)
*Hines 60141 (Roosevelt Rd. & 5th Ave., 708-343-7200)
*Marion 62959 (2401 W. Main St., 618-997-5311)
#*North Chicago 60064 (3001 Green Bay Rd., 708-688-1900)

Clinic:

Peoria 61605 (411 Dr. Martin Luther King Dr., 309-671-7350)

Regional Office:

Chicago 60680 (536 S. Clark St., P.O. Box 8136, local, 663-5510;
statewide, (800) 827-1000)

Vet Centers:

Chicago 60637 (5505 S. Harper, 312-684-5500)
Chicago Heights 60411 (1600 Halsted St., 708-754-0340)
East St. Louis 62203 (1269 N. 89th St., Suite 1, 618-397-6602)

Moline 61265 (1529 46th Ave., Rm. #6, 309-762-6954)
Oak Park 60302 (155 S. Oak Park Ave., 708-383-3225)
Peoria 61603 (605 N.E. Monroe St., 309-671-7300)
Springfield 62702 (624 S. 4th St., 217-492-4955)
Evanston 60202 (656 Howard St., 708-332-1019)

National Cemeteries:

Alton 62003 (600 Pearl St.; for information, call Jefferson Barracks,
    MO, Nat. Cem., 314-263-8691/2)
Camp Butler (Springfield 62707, R.R. #1, 217-522-5764)
Danville 61832 (1900 E. Main St., 217-431-6550)
Mound City 62963 (P.O. Box 38, Hwy 37; for information, call Jef-
    ferson Barracks, MO, Nat. Cem., 314-263-8691/2)
Quincy 62301 (36th & Maine Sts.; for information, call Keokuk, IA,
    Nat. Cem., 319-524-1304)
Rock Island 61265 (P.O. Box 737, 309-782-2094)

Indiana

Medical Centers:

*Fort Wayne 46805 (2121 Lake Ave., 219-426-5431)
*Indianapolis 46202 (1481 W. 10th St., 317-635-7401)
*Marion 46952 (E. 38th St., 317-674-3321)

Clinics:

Crown Point 46307 (9330 Broadway, 219-662-0001)
Evansville 47713 (500 E. Walnut, 812-465-6202)

Regional Office:

Indianapolis 46204 (575 N. Pennsylvania St., local, 226-5566; state-
    wide, (800) 827-1000)

Vet Centers:

Evansville 47711 (311 N. Weinbach Ave., 812-473-5993 or 473-
    6084)
Fort Wayne 46802 (528 West Berry St., 219-460-1456)

Gary 46408 (2236 West Ridge Rd., 219-887-0048)
Indianapolis 46208 (3833 Meridian, 317-927-6440)

National Cemeteries:

Crown Hill (Indianapolis 46208, 700 W. 38th St.; for information, call
    Marion, IN, Nat. Cem., 317-674-0284)
Marion 46952 (1700 E. 38th St., 317-674-0284)
New Albany 47150 (1943 Ekin Ave.; for information, call Zachary
    Taylor, KY, Nat. Cem., 502-893-3852)

Iowa

Medical Centers:

#Des Moines 50310 (30th & Euclid Ave., 515-255-2173)
Iowa City 52246 (Hwy. 6 West, 319-338-0581)
#*Knoxville 50138 (1515 W. Pleasant St., 515-842-3101)

Clinic:

Bettendorf 52722 (2979 Victoria Dr., 319-332-9274)

Regional Office:

Des Moines 50309 (210 Walnut St., local, 284-0219; statewide, (800)
    827-1000)

Vet Centers:

Des Moines 50310 (2600 Harding Rd., 515-284-4929)
Sioux City 51101 (706 Jackson, 712-255-3808)

National Cemetery:

Keokuk 52632 (1701 J St., 319-524-1304)

Kansas

Medical Centers:

#*Leavenworth 66048 (4101 S. 4th St., Trafficway (913-682-2000)
*Topeka 66622 (2200 Gage Blvd., 913-272-3111)
*Wichita 67218 (5500 E. Kellogg, 316-685-2221)

Regional Office:

Wichita 67218 (5500 E. Kellogg, local 682-2301; statewide, (800)
    827-1000)

Vet Centers:

Wichita 67211 (413 S. Pattie, 316-265-3260)

National Cemeteries:

Fort Leavenworth 66027 (P.O. Box 1694; for information, call Leav-
    enworth, KS, Nat. Cem., 913-682-1748/9)
Fort Scott 66701 (P.O. Box 917, 316-223-2840)
Leavenworth 66048 (P.O. Box 1694; 913-682-1748/9)

Kentucky

Medical Centers:

*Lexington 40511 (Leestown Rd., 606-233-4511)
Louisville 40206 (800 Zorn Ave., 502-895-3401)

Clinic:

Colorado Springs 80909 (1785 N. Academy Blvd., 719-380-0004)

Regional Office:

Louisville 40202 (545 S. Third St., local, 584-2231; statewide, (800)
    827-1000)

Vet Centers:

Lexington 40503 (1117 Limestone Rd., 606-276-5269)
Louisville 40208 (1355 S. 3rd St., 502-636-4002)

National Cemeteries:

Camp Nelson (Nicholasville 40356, 6980 Danville Rd., 606-885-5727)

Cave Hill (Louisville 40204, 701 Baxter Ave.; for information, call Zachary Taylor, KY, Nat. Cem., 502-893-3852)

Danville 40442 (377 N. First St.; for information, call Camp Nelson, KY, Nat. Cem., 606-885-5727)

Lebanon 40033 (20 Highway 208, 502-893-3852)

Lexington 40508 (833 W. Main St.; for information, call Camp Nelson, KY, Nat. Cem., 606-885-5727)

Mill Springs (Nancy 42544; for information call Camp Nelson, KY, Nat. Cem., 606-885-5727)

Zachary Taylor (Louisville 40207, 4701 Brownsboro Rd., 502-893-3852)

Louisiana

Medical Centers:

*Alexandria 71301 (Shreveport Hwy., 318-497-0243)
New Orleans 70146 (1601 Perdido St., 504-682-5811)
Shreveport 71130 (510 E. Stoner Ave., 318-493-6411)

Clinic:

Baton Rouge 70806 (216 S. Foster Dr., 318-389-0628)

Regional Office:

New Orleans 70113 (701 Loyola Ave., local, 589-7191; statewide, (800) 827-1000)

Vet Centers:

Bossier City 71112 (2103 Old Minden Rd., 318-742-2733)
New Orleans 70116 (1529 N. Claiborne Ave., 504-943-8386)
Shreveport 71104 (Bldg. 3, Suite 260, 2620 Centenary Blvd., 318-
425-8387)

National Cemeteries:

Alexandria (Pineville 71360, 209 E. Shamrock St., 318-473-7588)
Baton Rouge 70806 (220 N. 19th St.; for information, call Port Hud-
son, LA, Nat. Cem., 504-389-0788)
Port Hudson (Zachary 70791, 20978 Port Hickey Rd., 504-389-0788)

Maine

Medical Center:

*Togus 04330 (Route 17 E., 207-623-8411)

Regional Office:

Togus 04330 (Route 17 E., local, 623-8000; statewide, (800) 827-
1000)

Benefits Office:

Portland 04101 (475 Stevens Ave., 207-780-3569)

Vet Centers:

Bangor 04401 (352 Harlow St., 207-947-3391)
Portland 04101 (63 Preble St., 207-780-3584)

National Cemeteries:

Togus 04330 (VA Medical & Regional Office Center; for information, call Massachusetts, Nat. Cem., 508-563-7113)

Maryland

Medical Centers:

Baltimore 21201 (10 N. Greene St., 410-605-7000)
Baltimore 21201 (Prosthetic Assessment Information Center, 103 S. Gay St., 410-962-3934)
*Fort Howard 21052 (N. Point Rd., 410-477-1800)
*Perry Point 21902 (410-642-2411)

Regional Office:

Baltimore 21201 (31 Hopkins Plaza, Fed. Bldg., local, 685-5454; counties of Montgomery & Prince Georges served by Washington, DC, RO, 202-872-1151; other areas, (800) 827-1000)

Vet Centers:

Baltimore 21230 (777 Washington Blvd., 410-539-5511)
Elkton 21921 (7 Elkton Commercial Plaza, South Bridge St., 410-398-0171)
Silver Spring 20910 (1015 Spring St., Suite 101, 301-589-1073 or 301-589-1236)

National Cemeteries:

Annapolis 21401 (800 West St.; for information, call Baltimore, MD, Nat. Cem., 410-962-4730)
Baltimore 21228 (5501 Frederick Ave., 410-962-4730)
Loudon Park (Baltimore 21229, 3445 Frederick Ave.; for information, call Baltimore, MD, Nat. Cem., 410-962-4730)

Massachusetts

Medical Centers:

#*Bedford 01730 (200 Spring Rd., 617-275-7500)
Boston 02130 (150 S. Huntington Ave., 617-232-9500)
*Brockton 02401 (940 Belmont St., 508-583-4500)

*Northampton 01060 (421 N. Main St., 413-584-4040)
West Roxbury 02132 (1400 VFW Pkwy., 617-323-7700)

Clinics:

Boston 02114 (251 Causeway St., 617-248-1000)
Lowell 01852 (Old Post Office Bldg., 50 Kearney Sq., 508-453-1746)
Springfield 01103 (1550 Main St., 413-785-0301)
New Bedford 02740 (53 N. Sixth St., 508-999-5504)
Worcester 01608 (595 Main St., 508-793-0200)

Regional Office:

Boston 02203 (JFK Federal Bldg., Government Center, local, 227-
    4600; statewide, (800) 827-1000)
Towns of Fall River & New Bedford, counties of Barnstable, Dukes,
    Nantucket, Bristol, part of Plymouth served by Providence, RI,
    RO.

Vet Centers:

Brockton 02401 (1041 Pearl St., 508-580-2730/31)
Boston 02215 (665 Beacon St., 617-424-0065 or 565-6195)
Lowell 01852 (73 East Merrimack St., 617-453-1151)
New Bedford 02740 (468 North St., 508-999-6920)
Springfield 01103 (1985 Main St., 413-737-5167)
Worcester 01605 (108 Grove St., 508-752-3526)

National Cemetery:

Massachusetts (Bourne 02532, 508-563-7113/4)

Michigan

Medical Centers:

*Allen Park 48101 (Southfield & Outer Drive, 313-562-6000)
*Ann Arbor 48105 (2215 Fuller Rd., 313-769-7100)
*Battle Creek 49016 (5500 Armstrong Rd., 626-966-5600)

*Iron Mountain 49801 (H St., 906-774-3300)
*Saginaw 48602 (1500 Weiss St., 517-793-2340)

Clinics:

Gaylord 49735 (850 N. Otsego, 517-732-7525)
Grand Rapids 49505 (3019 Coit, NE, 616-365-9575)

Regional Office:

Detroit 48226 (Patrick V. McNamara Federal Bldg., 477 Michigan
     Ave., local, 964-5110; statewide, (800) 827-1000)

Vet Centers:

Grand Rapids 49507 (1940 Eastern Ave., SE, 616-243-0385)
Lincoln Park 48146 (1766 Fort St., 313-381-1370)
Oak Park 48237 (20820 Greenfield Rd., 313-967-0040)

National Cemetery:

Fort Custer (Augusta 49012, 15501 Dickman Rd., 616-731-4164)

Minnesota

Medical Centers:

*Minneapolis 55417 (One Veterans Dr., 612-725-2000)
#*St. Cloud 56303 (4801 8th St. N., 612-252-1670)

Clinic:

St. Paul 55111 (Fort Snelling, 612-725-6767)

Regional Office:

St. Paul 55111 (Federal Bldg., Fort Snelling, local, 726-1454; state-
     wide, (800) 827-1000) counties of Becker, Beltrami, Clay, Clear-
     water, Kittson, Lake of the Woods, Mahnomen, Marshall,
     Norman, Otter Tail, Pennington, Polk, Red Lake, Roseau, Wilkin
     served by Fargo, ND, RO.

Vet Centers:

Duluth 55802 (405 E. Superior St., 218-722-8654)
St. Paul 55114 (2480 University Ave., 612-644-4022)

National Cemetery:

Fort Snelling (Minneapolis 55450, 7601 34th Ave. S., 612-726-1127/8)

Mississippi

Medical Centers:

#*Biloxi 39531 (400 Veterans Ave., 601-388-5541)
*Jackson 39216 (1500 E. Woodrow Wilson Dr., 601-362-4471)

Regional Office:

Jackson 39269 (100 W. Capitol St., local, 965-4873; statewide, (800) 827-1000)

Vet Centers:

Biloxi 39530 (767 W. Jackson St., 601-435-5414)
Jackson 39206 (4436 N. State St., Suite A3, 601-965-5727)

National Cemeteries:

Biloxi 39535 (P.O. Box 4968, 601-388-6668)
Corinth 38834 (1551 Horton St.; for information, call Memphis, TN, Nat. Cem., 901-386-8311)
Natchez 39120 (41 Cemetery Rd., 601-445-4981)

Missouri

Medical Centers:

*Columbia 65201 (800 Hospital Dr., 314-443-2511)
Kansas City 64128 (4801 Linwood Blvd., 816-861-4700)
*Poplar Bluff 63901 (1500 N. Westwood Blvd., 314-686-4151)

St. Louis 63106 (John Cochran Div., 915 N. Grand Blvd., 314-652-
   4100)
*St. Louis 63125 (Jefferson Barracks Div., 314-487-0400)

Clinic:

Mt. Vernon 65712 (600 N. Main St., 417-466-4000)

Regional Office:

St. Louis 63103 (Federal Bldg., 1520 Market St., local, 342-1171;
   statewide, (800) 827-1000)

Benefits Office:

Kansas City 64106 (Federal Office Bldg., 601 E. 12th St.)

Vet Centers:

Kansas City 64111 (3931 Main St., 816-753-1866 or 753-1974)
St. Louis 63103 (2345 Pine St., 314-231-1260)

National Cemeteries:

Jefferson Barracks (St. Louis 63125, 101 Memorial Dr., 314-263-
   8691/2)
Jefferson City 65101 (1024 E. McCarty St.; for information, call
   Jefferson Barracks, MO, Nat. Cem., 314-263-8691/2)
Springfield 65804 (1702 E. Seminole St., 417-881-9499)

Montana

VA Medical & Regional Office Center

Fort Harrison 59636 (William St. off Hwy. 12 W., 406-442-6410)

Medical Center:

*Miles City 59301 (210 S. Winchester, 406-232-3060)

Clinic:

Billings 59102 (1127 Alderson Ave., 406-657-6786)

Regional Office:

Fort Harrison 59636 (local, 447-7975; statewide, (800) 827-1000)

Vet Centers:

Billings 59102 (1948 Grand Ave., 406-657-6071)
Missoula 59802 (500 N. Higgins Ave., 406-721-4918)

Nebraska

Medical Centers:

*Grand Island 68801 (2201 N. Broadwell, 308-382-3660)
Lincoln 68510 (600 S. 70th St., 402-489-3802)
Omaha 68105 (4101 Woolworth Ave., 402-346-8800)

Regional Office:

Lincoln 68516 (5631 S. 48th St., local, 437-5001; statewide, (800)
    827-1000)

Vet Centers:

Lincoln 68508 (920 L St., 402-476-9736)
Omaha 68106 (5123 Leavenworth St., 402-553-2068)

National Cemetery:

Fort McPherson (Maxwell 69151, HCO 1, Box 67, 308-582-4433)

Nevada

Medical Center:

*Reno 89520 (1000 Locust St., 702-786-7200)

Clinic:

Las Vegas 89102 (1703 W. Charleston, 702-385-3700)

Regional Office:

Reno 89520 (1201 Terminal Way, local, 329-9244; statewide, (800) 827-1000) Also serving the following counties in California: Alpine, Lassen, Modoc, and Mono.

Vet Centers:

Las Vegas 89101 (704 S. 6th St., 702-388-6368)
Reno 89503 (1155 W. 4th St., Suite 101, 702-323-1294)

New Hampshire

Medical Center:

*Manchester 03104 (718 Smyth Rd., 603-624-4366)

Regional Office:

Manchester 03101 (Norris Cotton Federal Bldg., 275 Chestnut St., local, 666-7785; statewide, (800) 827-1000)

Vet Center:

Manchester 03104 (103 Liberty St., 603-668-7060)

New Jersey

Medical Centers:

*East Orange 07019 (Tremont Ave. & S. Center, 201-676-1000)
#*Lyons 07939 (Valley & Knollcrott Rd., 201-647-0180)

Clinic:

Brick 08724 (970 Rt. 70, 908-206-8900)

Regional Office:

Newark 07102 (20 Washington Pl., local, 645-2150; statewide, (800) 827-1000)

Vet Centers:

Jersey City 07302 (115 Christopher Columbus Dr., 201-656-6886 or 656-7484)
Linwood 08221 (222 New Road, Bldg. 2, Suite 4, 609-927-8387)
Newark 07102 (75 Halsey St., 201-622-6940)
Trenton 08608 (318 E. State St., 609-989-2260)

National Cemeteries:

Beverly 08010 (R.D. #1, Bridgeboro Rd., 609-989-2137)
Finn's Point (Salem 08079, R.F.D. #3, Fort Mott Rd., Box 542; for information, call Beverly, NJ, Nat. Cem., 609-989-2137)

New Mexico

Medical Center:

*Albuquerque 87108 (2100 Ridgecrest Dr., SE, 505-265-1711)

Regional Office:

Albuquerque 87102 (Dennis Chavez Federal Bldg., 500 Gold Ave., SW, local, 766-3361; statewide, (800) 827-1000)

Vet Centers:

Albuquerque 87107 (4603 4th St., NW, 505-345-8366 or 345-8876)
Farmington 87402 (4251 E. Main, Suite B, 505-327-9684)

Santa Fe 87505 (1996 Warner St., Warner Plaza, Suite 5, 505-988-6562)

National Cemeteries:

Fort Bayard 88036 (P.O. Box 189; for information, call Fort Bliss, TX, Nat. Cem., 915-540-6182)
Santa Fe 87504 (501 N. Guadalupe St., P.O. Box 88, 505-988-6400)

New York

Medical Centers:

*Albany 12208 (113 Holland Ave., 518-462-3311)
*Batavia 14020 (Redfield Pkwy., 716-343-7500)
#*Bath 14810 (Argonne Ave., 607-776-2111)
*Bronx 10468 (130 W. Kingsbridge Rd., 212-584-9000)
#*Brooklyn 11209 (800 Poly Place, 718-630-3500)
*Buffalo 14215 (3495 Bailey Ave., 716-834-9200)
#*Canandaigua 14424 (Ft. Hill Ave., 716-394-2000)
*Castle Point 12511 (914-831-2000)
#*Montrose 10548 (Old Albany Post Rd., 914-737-4400)
New York City 10010 (1st Ave. & E. 24th St., 212-686-7500)
*Northport 11768 (Middleville Rd., Long Island, 516-261-4400)
*Syracuse 13210 (Irving Ave. & University Pl., 315-476-7461)

Clinics:

Brooklyn 11205 (35 Ryerson St., 718-330-7785)
New York City 10001 (252 7th Ave. & 24th St., 212-620-6636)
Rochester 14614 (Federal Office Bldg. & Courthouse, 100 State St., 716-263-5734)

Regional Offices:

Buffalo 14202 (Federal Bldg., 111 W. Huron St., local 846-5191; statewide, (800) 827-1000) serving the remaining counties of New York

New York City 10001 (252 Seventh Ave. at 24th St., local, 620-6901;
   statewide, (800) 827-1000) serving counties of Albany, Bronx,
   Clinton, Columbia, Delaware, Dutchess, Essex, Franklin, Fulton,
   Greene, Hamilton, Kings, Montgomery, Nassau, New York, Orange, Otsego, Putnam, Queens, Rensselaer, Richmond, Rock-
   land, Saratoga, Schenectady, Schoharie, Suffolk, Sullivan, Ulster,
   Warren, Washington, and Westchester

Benefits Offices:

Albany 12207 (Leo W. O'Brian Federal Bldg., Clinton Ave. & N.
   Pearl St.)
Rochester 14614 (Federal Office Bldg. & Courthouse, 100 State St.)
Syracuse 13202 (344 W. Genessee St.)

Vet Centers:

Albany 12206 (875 Central Ave., 518-438-2505)
Babylon 11702 (116 W. Main St., 516-661-3930)
Bronx 10458 (226 E. Fordham Rd., Rms. 216-217, 718-367-3500)
Brooklyn 11201 (165 Cadman Plaza, E., 718-330-2825)
Buffalo 14209 (351 Linwood Ave., 716-882-0505 or 882-0508)
New York 10036 (120 West 44th St., 212-944-2931 or 944-2932)
Rochester 14608 (134 S. Fitzhugh St., 716-263-5710)
Staten Island 10301 (150 Richmond Terrace, 718-816-6899 or 816-
   4499)
Syracuse 13203 (210 North Townsend St., 315-423-5690)
White Plains 10601 (200 Hamilton Ave., 914-682-6850)
Woodhaven 11421 (75-10B 91st Ave., 718-296-2871)

National Cemeteries:

Bath 14810 (VA Medical Center, 607-776-2111, ext. 1293)
Calverton 11933 (210 Princeton Blvd., 516-727-5410 or 727-5770)
Cypress Hills (Brooklyn 11208, 625 Jamaica Ave.; for information,
   call Long Island, NY, Nat. Cem., 516-454-4949)
Long Island (Farmingdale 11735, 516-454-4949)
Woodlawn (Elmira 14901, 1825 Davis St.; for information, call Bath,
   NY, Nat. Cem., 607-776-2111, ext. 1293)

North Carolina

Medical Centers:

*Asheville 28805 (1100 Tunnel Rd., 704-672-5011)
*Durham 27705 (508 Fulton St., 919-671-6011)
*Fayetteville 28301 (2300 Ramsey St., 919-699-7000)
*Salisbury 28144 (1601 Brenner Ave., 704-699-2000)

Clinic:

Winston-Salem 27155 (Federal Bldg., 251 N. Main St., 919-631-5562)

Regional Office:

Winston-Salem 27155 (Federal Bldg., 251 N. Main St., local, 748-1800; statewide, (800) 827-1000)

Vet Centers:

Charlotte 28202 (223 S. Brevard St., Suite 103, 704-333-6107)
Fayetteville 28301 (4 Market Square, 919-323-4908)
Greensboro 27406 (2009 Elm-Eugene St., 919-333-5366)
Greenville 27834 (150 Arlington Blvd., Suite B, 919-355-7920)

National Cemeteries:

New Bern 28560 (1711 National Ave., 919-637-2912)
Raleigh 27610 (501 Rock Quarry Rd., 919-832-0144)
Salisbury 28144 (202 Government Rd., 704-636-2661)
Wilmington 28403 (2011 Market St., 919-632-2912)

North Dakota

Medical Center:

*Fargo 58102 (2101 Elm St., 701-232-3241)

Regional Office:

Fargo 58102 (655 First Ave. N., local, 293-3656; statewide, (800) 827-1000; mail only: 2101 N. Elm St.)

Vet Centers:

Fargo 58103 (1322 Gateway Dr., 701-237-0942)
Minot 58701 (108 E. Burdick Expressway, 701-852-0177)

Ohio

Medical Centers:

#*Brecksville 44141 (10000 Brecksville Rd., 216-526-3030)
*Chillicothe 45601 (17273 State Route 104, 614-773-1141)
#*Cincinnati 45220 (3200 Vine St., 513-861-3100)
Cleveland 44106 (10701 East Blvd., 216-791-3800)
#*Dayton 45428 (4100 W. 3rd St., 513-268-6511)

Clinics:

Canton 44702 (221 Third St., SE, 216-489-4660)
Columbus 43221 (2090 Kenny Rd., 614-469-5164)
Toledo 43614 (3333 Glendale Ave., 419-259-2000)
Youngstown 44505 (2031 Belmont, 216-740-9200)

Regional Office:

Cleveland 44199 (Anthony J. Celebrezze Federal Bldg., 1240 E. 9th St., local 621-5050; statewide, (800) 827-1000)

Benefits Offices:

Cincinnati 45202 (The Society Bank Center, Suite 210, 36 E. 7th St.)
Columbus 43215 (Federal Bldg., Rm. 309, 200 N. High St.)

Vet Centers:

Cincinnati 45219 (30 E. Hollister St., 513-569-7140)
Cleveland 44111 (11511 Lorain Ave., 216-671-8530)
Cleveland Heights 44118 (2134 Lee Rd., 216-932-8471)
Columbus 43205 (1054 E. Broad St., 614-253-3500)
Dayton 45402 (6 S. Patterson Blvd., 513-461-9150)

National Cemetery:

Dayton 45428 (VA Medical Center, 4100 W. Third St., 513-262-
    2115)

Oklahoma

Medical Centers:

Muskogee 74401 (Honor Heights Dr., 918-745-3011)
Oklahoma City 73104 (921 N.E. 13th St., 405-743-3011)

Clinics:

Lawton 73502 (Comanche Co. Hospital, P.O. Box 49, 405-357-6611)
Tulsa 74121 (635 W. 11th St., 918-581-7161)

Regional Office:

Muskogee 74401 (Federal Bldg., 125 S. Main St., local, 687-2500;
    statewide, (800) 827-1000)

Benefits Office:

Oklahoma City 73102 (200 N.W. 5th St.)

Vet Centers:

Oklahoma City 73105 (3033 N. Walnut, Suite 101W, 405-270-5184)
Tulsa 74101 (1855 E. 15th St., 918-581-7105)

National Cemetery:

Fort Gibson 74434 (1423 Cemetery Rd., 918-478-2334)

Oregon

Medical Centers:

#*Portland 97207 (3710 S.W. U.S. Veterans Hospital Rd., 503-220-8262)
*Roseburg 97470 (913 New Garden Valley Blvd., 503-440-1000)

Clinics:

Bandon 97411 (1010 1st St., S.E., Suite 100, 503-347-4736)
Eugene 97401 (138 W. 8th St., 503-465-6481)
Portland 97207 (8909 S.W. Barbur Blvd., 503-465-6481)

Domiciliary:

White City 97503 (Hwy. 62, 503-826-2111)

Regional Office:

Portland 97204 (Federal Bldg., 1220 S.W. 3rd Ave., local, 221-2431; statewide, (800) 827-1000)

Vet Centers:

Eugene 97403 (1966 Garden Ave., 503-465-6918)
Grants Pass 97526 (615 N.W. 5th St., 503-479-6912)
Portland 97220 (8383 N.E. Sandy Blvd., Suite 110, 503-273-5370)
Salem 97301 (318 Church St., NE, 503-362-9911)

National Cemeteries:

Eagle Point 97524 (2763 Riley Rd., 503-826-2511)
Roseburg 97470 (VA Medical Center, 503-440-1000)

Willamette (Portland 97266, 11800 S.E. Mt. Scott Blvd., 503-273-5250)

Pennsylvania

Medical Centers:

*Altoona 16603 (2907 Pleasant Valley Blvd., 814-943-8164)
#*Butler 16001 (New Castle Rd., 412-287-4781)
#*Coatesville 19320 (Black Horses Rd., 215-384-7711)
*Erie 16501 (135 E. 38th St., 814-868-8661)
*Lebanon 17042 (South Lincoln Ave., 717-272-6621)
*Philadelphia 19104 (University & Woodland Aves., 215-382-2400)
*Pittsburgh 15240 (University Drive C, 412-683-3000)
Pittsburgh 15206 (Highland Dr., 412-363-4900)
*Wilkes-Barre 18711 (1111 E. End Blvd., 717-824-3521)

Clinics:

Allentown 18103 (2937 Hamilton Blvd., 215-776-4304)
Harrisburg 17108 (Federal Bldg., 228 Walnut St., 717-782-4590)
Philadelphia 19102 (1421 Cherry St., 215-597-7244)
Sayre 18840 (Guthrie Square, 717-888-8062)

Regional Offices:

Philadelphia 19101 (RO & Insurance Center, P.O. Box 8079, 5000
    Wissahickon Ave., local, 438-5225; statewide, (800) 827-1000;
    recorded benefits information, 215-951-5368, 24-hour availabil-
    ity) Serves counties of Adams, Berks, Bradford, Bucks, Cam-
    eron, Carbon, Centre, Chester, Clinton, Columbia, Cumberland,
    Dauphin, Delaware, Franklin, Juniata, Lackawanna, Lancaster,
    Lebanon, Lehigh, Luzerne, Lycoming, Mifflin, Monroe, Mont-
    gomery, Montour, Northampton, Northumberland, Perry, Phila-
    delphia, Pike, Potter, Schuylkill, Snyder, Sullivan, Susquehanna,
    Tioga, Union, Wayne, Wyoming, and York
Pittsburgh 15222 (1000 Liberty Ave., local, 281-4233; statewide,
    (800) 827-1000) serving the remaining counties of Pennsylvania.

Benefits Office:

Wilkes-Barre 18701 (19-27 N. Main St.)

Vet Centers:

Erie 16501 (G. Daniel Baldwin Bldg., 1000 State St., Suites 1 & 2, 814-453-7955)
Harrisburg 17110 (1007 N. Front St., 717-782-3954)
McKeesport 15132 (500 Walnut St., 412-678-7704)
Philadelphia 19107 (1026 Arch St., 215-627-0238)
Philadelphia 19120 (101 E. Olney Ave., Box C-7, 215-924-4670)
Pittsburgh 15222 (954 Penn Ave., 412-765-1193)
Scranton 18509 (959 Wyoming Ave., 717-344-2676)

National Cemeteries:

Indiantown Gap (Annville 17003, R.R. 2, P.O. Box 484, 717-865-5254/5)
Philadelphia 19138 (Haines St. & Limekiln Pike; for information, call Beverly, NJ, Nat. Cem., 609-989-2137)

Philippines

Regional Office:

Manila 96440 (1131 Roxas Blvd., APO AP 96440, local, 810-521-7521; from U.S., 011632-521-7116, ext. 2577 or 2220)

Puerto Rico

Medical Center:

*San Juan 00927 (1 Veterans Plaza, Rio Piedras GPO Box 5800, 809-758-7575)

Clinics:

Mayaguez 00708 (Carr. Estatal #2, Frente A Res. Sultana, 809-831-3400)

Ponce 00731 (Reparada Industrial-Lot #1, Calle Principal, 809-841-3115)

Regional Office:

San Juan 00936 (U.S. Courthouse & Federal Bldg., Carlos E. Chardon St., Hato Rey, GPO Box 4867, local, 766-5141; all other San Juan areas and the Virgin Islands, (800) 827-1000) To call San Juan from U.S. Virgin Islands, (800) 827-1000

Vet Centers:

Arecibo 00612 (52 Gonzalo Marin St., 809-879-4510 or 879-4581)
Ponce 00731 (35 Mayor St., 809-841-3260)
Rio Piedras 00921 (Condomino Medical Center Plaza, Suite LC8A & LC9, La Riviera, 809-783-8794)

National Cemetery:

Puerto Rico (Bayamon 00960, P.O. Box 1298, 809-798-8400)

Rhode Island

Medical Center:

Providence 02908 (Davis Park, 401-273-7100)

Clinic:

Mt. Vernon 65712 (600 N. Main St., 417-466-4000)

Regional Office:

Providence 02903 (380 Westminster Mall, local, 273-4910; statewide, (800) 827-1000)

Vet Centers:

Cranston 02920 (789 Park Ave., 401-467-2046 or 467-2056)

South Carolina

Medical Centers:

Charleston 29401 (109 Bee St., 803-577-5011)
*Columbia 29209 (Garners Ferry Rd., 803-774-4000)

Clinic:

Greenville 29601 (120 Mallard St., 803-232-7303)

Regional Office:

Columbia 29201 (1801 Assembly St., local, 765-5861; statewide, (800) 827-1000)

Vet Centers:

Columbia 29201 (1313 Elmwood Ave., 803-765-9944)
Greenville 29601 (904 Pendelton St., 803-271-2711)
North Charleston 29418 (5603A Rivers Ave., 803-747-8387)

National Cemeteries:

Beaufort 29902 (1601 Boundary St., 803-524-3925)
Florence 29501 (803 E. National Cemetery Rd., 803-669-8783)

South Dakota

Medical Centers:

*Fort Meade 57741 (I 90/Hwy. 34, 605-347-2511)
#Hot Springs 57747 (Off 5th St., 605-745-4101)
*Sioux Falls 57117 (2501 W. 22nd St., 605-336-3230)

Regional Office:

Sioux Falls 57117 (P.O. Box 5046, 2501 W. 22nd St., local, 336-3496; statewide, (800) 827-1000)

Vet Centers:

Rapid City 57701 (610 Kansas City St., 605-348-0077 or 348-1752)
Sioux Falls 57102 (115 North Dakota St., 605-332-0856)

National Cemeteries:

Black Hills (Sturgis 57785, P.O. Box 640, 605-347-3830)
Fort Meade 57785 (VA Medical Center; for information, call Black
    Hills, SD, Nat. Cem., 605-347-3830)
Hot Springs 57747 (VA Medical Center, 605-745-4101)

Tennessee

Medical Centers:

*Memphis 38104 (1030 Jefferson Ave., 901-523-8990)
#*Mountain Home 37684 (Sidney & Lamont St., 615-926-1171)
*Murfreesboro 27129 (3400 Lebanon Rd., 615-893-1360)
Nashville 37212 (1310 24th Ave., S., 615-327-4751)

Clinics:

Chattanooga 37411 (Bldg. 6200 East Gate Center, 615-855-6550)
Knoxville 37923 (9047 Executive Park Dr., Suite 100, 615-549-9319)

Regional Office:

Nashville 37203 (110 9th Ave. S., local, 736-5251; statewide, (800)
    827-1000)

Vet Centers:

Chattanooga 37404 (425 Cumberland St., Suite 140, 615-752-5234)
Johnson City 37601 (703 S. Roan St., 615-928-8387)
Knoxville 37914 (2817 E. Magnolia Ave., 615-971-5866)
Memphis 38104 (1835 Union, Suite 100, 901-722-2510)

National Cemeteries:

Chattanooga 37404 (1200 Bailey Ave., 615-855-6590/91)
Knoxville (Mountain Home 37684, P.O. Box 8; call Mountain Home
    Nat. Cem. for information, 615-929-7891)
Memphis 38122 (3568 Townes Ave., 901-386-8311)
Mountain Home 37684 (P.O. Box 8, 615-929-7891)
Nashville (Madison 37115, 1420 Gallatin Rd. So., 615-327-5360)

Texas

Medical Centers:

*Amarillo 79106 (6010 Amarillo Blvd., W., 806-355-9703)
*Big Spring 79720 (2400 S. Gregg St., 915-263-7361)
#*Bonham 75418 (1201 E. Ninth, 903-583-2111)
#*Dallas 75216 (4500 S. Lancaster Rd., 214-376-5451)
*Houston 77030 (2002 Holcombe Blvd., 713-791-1414)
*Kerrville 78028 (3600 Memorial Blvd., 210-896-2020)
Marlin 76661 (1016 Ward St., 817-883-3511)
*San Antonio 78284 (7400 Merton Minter Blvd., 210-617-5300)
#*Temple 76504 (1901 S. First, 817-778-4811)
#*Waco 76711 (4800 Memorial Dr., 817-752-6581)

Clinics:

Austin 78741 (2901 Montopolis Dr., 512-389-1010)
Beaumont 77701 (3385 Fannin St., 409-830-2480)
Corpus Christi 78405 (5283 Old Brownsville Rd., 512-888-3251)
El Paso 79925 (5919 Brook Hollow Dr., 915-540-7811)
Laredo 78043 (2359 E. Saunders Ave., 512-725-7060)
Lubbock 79410 (4902 34th St., #10, 806-796-7900)
Lufkin 75901 (1301 Frank Ave., 409-637-1342)
McAllen 78501 (2101 S. Rowe Blvd., 512-618-7100)
San Antonio 78229 (9502 Computer Dr., 512-617-2672)
Victoria 77901 (2710 E. Airline Dr., 512-572-0006)

Regional Offices:

Houston 77054 (2515 Murworth Dr., local, 664-4664; statewide,
    (800) 827-1000, serves counties of Angelina, Aransas, Atacosa,
    Austin, Bandera, Bee, Bexar, Blanco, Brazoria, Brewster,

Brooks, Caldwell, Calhoun, Cameron, Chambers, Colorado, Co-
mal, Crockett, DeWitt, Dimitt, Dubal, Edwards, Fort Bend, Frio,
Galveston, Gillespie, Goliad, Gonzales, Grimes, Guadalupe, Har-
din, Harris, Hays, Hidalgo, Houston, Jackson, Jasper, Jefferson,
Jim Hogg, Jim Wells, Karnes, Kendall, Kenedy, Kerr, Kimble,
Kinney, Kleberg, LaSalle, Lavaca, Liberty, Live Oak, McCul-
loch, McMullen, Mason, Matagorda, Maverick, Medina, Me-
nard, Montgomery, Nacogdoches, Newton, Nueces, Orange,
Pecos, Polk, Real, Refugio, Sabine, San Augustine, San Jacinto,
San Patrico, Schleicher, Shelby, Starr, Sutton, Terrell, Trinity,
Tyler, Uvalde, Val Verde, Victoria, Walker, Waller, Washington,
Webb, Wharton, Willacy, Wilson, Zapata, Zavala)
Waco 76799 (1400 N. Valley Mills Dr., local, 817-772-3060; state-
wide, (800) 827-1000, serves counties not listed above)
Bowie County served by Little Rock, AR, RO, (800) 827-1000

Benefits Offices:

Dallas 75242 (U.S. Courthouse & Federal Office Bldg., 1100 Com-
merce St.)
Fort Worth 76102 (300 W. Rosedale St.)
Lubbock 79401 (Federal Bldg., 1205 Texas Ave.)
San Antonio 78229-2041 (3601 Bluemel Rd.)

Vet Centers:

Amarillo 79109 (3414 E. Olsen Blvd., Suite E, 806-376-2127)
Austin 78745 (1110 W. William Cannon Dr., Suite 301, 512-416-
1314)
Corpus Christi 78404 (3166 Reid Dr., Suite 1, 512-888-3101)
Dallas 75244 (5232 Forest Lane, Suite 111, 214-361-5896)
El Paso 79903 (2121 Wyoming St., 915-542-2851)
Fort Worth 76104 (1305 W. Magnolia, Suite B, 817-921-3733)
Houston 77004 (4905A San Jacinto, 713-522-5354 or 522-5376)
Houston 77007 (8100 Washington Ave., Suite 120, 713-880-8387)
Laredo 78041 (6020 McPherson Rd. #1, 512-723-4680)
Lubbock 79410 (3208 34th St., 806-743-7551)
McAllen 78501 (1317 E. Hackberry St., 512-631-2147)
Midland 79703 (3404 W. Illinois, Suite 1, 915-697-8222)
San Antonio 78212 (231 W. Cypress St., 512-229-4025)

National Cemeteries:

Fort Bliss 79906 (5200 Fred Wilson Rd., P.O. Box 6342, 915-540-6182)

Fort Sam Houston (San Antonio 78209, 1520 Harry Wurzbach Rd., 512-820-3891)

Houston 77038 (10410 Veterans Memorial Dr., 713-447-8686)

Kerrville 78028 (VA Medical Center, 3600 Memorial Blvd.; for information call Fort Sam Houston, TX, Nat. Cem., 512-820-3891)

San Antonio 78202 (517 Paso Hondo St;, for information, call Fort Sam Houston, TX, Nat. Cem., 512-820-3891)

Utah

Medical Center:

*Salt Lake City 84148 (500 Foothill Dr., 801-582-1565)

Regional Office:

Salt Lake City 84147 (P.O. Box 11500, Federal Bldg., 125 S. State St., local, 524-5960; statewide, (800) 827-1000)

Vet Centers:

Provo 84601 (750 North 200 West, Suite 105, 801-377-1117)

Salt Lake City 84106 (1354 East 3300 S., 801-584-1294)

Vermont

Medical Center:

*White River Junction 05001 (N. Hartland Rd., 802-295-9363)

Regional Office:

White River Junction 05001 (N. Hartland Rd., statewide, (800) 827-1000)

Vet Centers:

South Burlington 05401 (359 Dorset St., 802-862-1806)
White River Junction 05001 (Gilman Office Center, Bldg. #2, Holiday
Inn Dr., 802-295-2908)

Virginia

Medical Centers:

#*Hampton 23667 (Emancipation Dr., 804-722-9961)
*Richmond 23249 (1201 Broad Rock Rd., 804-230-0001)
*Salem 24153 (1970 Roanoke Blvd., 703-982-2463)

Regional Offices:

Roanoke 24011 (210 Franklin Rd., SW, local, 982-6440; statewide,
(800) 827-1000)
Northern Virginia counties of Arlington & Fairfax, cities of Alexandria, Fairfax, and Falls Church served by Washington, DC, RO,
202-872-1151

Vet Centers:

Norfolk 23518 (2200 Colonial Ave., Suite 3, 804-623-7584)
Richmond 23220 (3022 W. Clay St., 804-353-8958)
Roanoke 24016 (320 Mountain Ave., SW, 703-342-9726)
Springfield 22150 (7024 Spring Garden Dr., Brookfield Plaza, 703-
866-0924)

National Cemeteries:

Alexandria 22314 (1450 Wilkes St.; for information, call Quantico,
VA, Nat. Cem., 703-690-2217)
Balls Bluff (Leesburg 22075; for information, call Culpeper, VA, Nat.
Cem., 703-825-0027)

City Point (Hopewell 23860, 10th Ave. & Davis St.; for information, call Richmond, VA, Nat. Cem., 804-222-1490)

Cold Harbor (Mechanicsville 23111, Rt. 156 North; for information, call Richmond, VA, Nat. Cem., 804-222-1490)

Culpeper 22701 (305 U.S. Ave., 703-825-0027)

Danville 24541 (721 Lee St.; for information, call Salisbury, NC, Nat. Cem., 704-636-2661)

Fort Harrison (Richmond 23231, 8620 Varina Rd.; for information, call Richmond, VA, Nat. Cem., 804-222-1490)

Glendale (Richmond 23231, 8301 Willis Church Rd.; for information, call Richmond, VA, Nat. Cem., 804-222-1490)

Hampton 23669 (Cemetery Rd. at Marshall Ave., 804-723-7104)

Hampton 23669 (VA Medical Center, 804-723-7104)

Quantico (Triangle 22172, P.O. Box 10, 18424 Joplin Rd., 703-690-2217)

Richmond 23231 (1701 Williamsburg Rd., 804-222-1490)

Seven Pines (Sandston 23150, 400 E. Williamsburg Rd.; for information, call Richmond, VA, Nat. Cem., 804-222-1490)

Staunton 24401 (901 Richmond Ave.; for information, call Culpeper, VA, Nat. Cem., 703-825-0027)

Winchester 22601 (401A National Ave.; for information, call Culpeper, VA, Nat. Cem., 703-825-0027)

Virgin Islands

Vet Centers:

St. Croix 00820 (United Shopping Plaza, Suite 4--Christiansted, 809-778-5553 or 778-5755)

St. Thomas 00801 (Havensight Mall, 809-774-6674; for information on VA benefits, call (800) 827-1000)

Washington

Medical Centers:

*Seattle 98108 (1660 S. Columbian Way, 206-762-1010)

*Spokane 99205 (N. 4815 Assembly St., 509-328-4521)

#*Tacoma 98493 (American Lake, 206-582-8440)
*Walla Walla 99362 (77 Wainwright Dr., 509-525-5200)

Regional Office:

Seattle 98174 (Federal Bldg., 915 2nd Ave., local, 624-7200; statewide, (800) 827-1000)

Vet Centers:

Seattle 98122 (1322 E. Pike St., 206-553-2706)
Spokane 99201 (W. 1708 Mission St., 509-327-0274)
Tacoma 98408 (4801 Pacific Ave., 206-473-0731)

West Virginia

Medical Centers:

*Beckley 25801 (200 Veterans Ave., 304-255-2121)
Clarksburg 26301 (Milford/Chestnut Sts., 304-623-3461)
Huntington 25704 (1540 Spring Valley Dr., 304-429-6741)
#*Martinsburg 25410 (Route 9, 304-263-8011)

Regional Office:

Huntington 25701 (640 Fourth Ave., local, 529-5720; statewide, (800)
827-1000; counties of Brooke, Hancock, Marshall, and Ohio
served by Pittsburgh, PA, RO)

Vet Centers:

Beckley 25801 (101 Ellison Ave., 304-252-8220 or 252-8229)
Charleston 25311 (1591 Washington St., E., 304-343-3825)
Huntington 25701 (1014 5th Ave., 304-523-8387)
Martinsburg 25401 (138 W. King St., 304-263-6776/7)
Morgantown 26505 (1191 Pineview Dr., 304-291-4001)
Princeton 24740 (905 Mercer St., 304-425-5653 or 425-5661)
Wheeling 26003 (1070 Market St., 304-232-0587, ext. 271)

National Cemeteries:

Grafton 26354 (431 Walnut St.; for information, call West Virginia, Nat. Cem., 304-265-2044)
West Virginia (Grafton 26354, Rt. 2, Box 127, 304-265-2044)

Wisconsin

Medical Centers:

Madison 53705 (2500 Overlook Terrace, 608-256-1901)
#*Milwaukee 53295 (5000 W. National Ave., 414-384-2000)
*Tomah 54660 (500 E. Veterans St., 608-372-3971)

Clinic:

Superior 54880 (3520 Tower Ave., 715-392-9711)

Regional Office:

Milwaukee 53295 (5000 W. National Ave., Bldg. 6, local, 383-8680; statewide, (800) 827-1000)

Vet Centers:

Madison 53703 (147 S. Butler St., 608-264-5343)
Milwaukee 53208 (3400 Wisconsin, 414-344-5504)

National Cemetery:

Wood (Milwaukee 53295, 5000 W. National Ave., Bldg. 122, 414-382-5300)

Wyoming

Medical Centers:

*Cheyenne 82001 (2360 E. Pershing Blvd., 307-778-7550)
Sheridan 82801 (1898 Fort Rd., 307-672-3473)

Regional Office:

Cheyenne 82001 (2360 E. Pershing Blvd., local, 778-7396; statewide, (800) 827-1000)

Vet Centers:

Casper 82601 (111 S. Jefferson, 307-235-8010)
Cheyenne 82001 (3130 Henderson Dr., 307-778-7370)

APPENDIX C:

STATE DEPARTMENTS OF VETERANS AFFAIRS

In this appendix, we provide names, addresses, and telephone numbers for government offices of the states, American Samoa, the District of Columbia, Guam, the North Mariana Islands, Puerto Rico, and the Virgin Islands that provide services to veterans. This information is an adaptation of that published by the Department of Veterans Affairs (the VA). Among other things, these offices can provide veterans with information about benefits that may be available to them from their state government.

ALABAMA
DEPT. OF VETERANS AFFAIRS
P.O. Box 1509
Montgomery, AL 36102-1509
(205) 242-5077

ALASKA
DEPT. OF MILITARY AND VETERANS AFFAIRS
P.O. Box 5800
Ft. Richardson, AK 99505-5800
(907) 428-6014

AMERICAN SAMOA
OFFICE OF VETERANS AFFAIRS
American Samoa Government
P.O. Box 2586
Pago Pago, American Samoa 96799

ARIZONA
ARIZONA VETERANS SERVICE COMMISSION
3225 N. Central Ave., Suite 910
Phoenix, AZ 85012
(602) 255-4713

ARKANSAS
DEPT. OF VETERANS AFFAIRS
c/o VA Regional Office, Room 119
North Little Rock, AR 72115
(501) 370-3820

CALIFORNIA
DEPT. OF VETERANS AFFAIRS
1227 O St., Room 200A
Sacramento, CA 95814
(916) 653-2158

COLORADO
DIVISION OF VETERANS AFFAIRS
Dept. of Social Services
1575 Sherman St.
Denver, CO 80203-1714
(303) 866-2494

CONNECTICUT
CONNECTICUT DEPT. OF VETERANS AFFAIRS
287 West St.
Rocky Hill, CT 06067
(203) 721-5891

DELAWARE
DELAWARE VETERANS AFFAIRS COMMISSION
P.O. Box 1401
Old State House—The Green
Dover, DE 19903
(302) 739-2792

DISTRICT OF COLUMBIA
OFFICE OF VETERANS AFFAIRS
941 N. Capitol St., N.E., Room 1211-F
Washington, DC 20421
(202) 737-5050

FLORIDA
FLORIDA DEPT. OF VETERANS AFFAIRS
P.O. Box 31003
St. Petersburg, FL 33731
(813) 893-2440

GEORGIA
DEPT. OF VETERANS SERVICE
Floyd Veterans Memorial Bldg.
Suite E-970
Atlanta, GA 30334

GUAM
VETERANS SERVICE OFFICE
Office of the Governor
Government of Guam
P.O. Box 3279
Agana, Guam 96910
(671) 472-6002

HAWAII
OFFICE OF VETERANS SERVICES
733 Bishop St., Suite 1270
Honolulu, HI 96813
(808) 587-3000

IDAHO
DIVISION OF VETERANS SERVICES
P.O. Box 7765
Boise, ID 83707
(208) 334-5000

ILLINOIS
DEPT. OF VETERANS AFFAIRS
833 S. Spring St.
Springfield, IL 62794-9432
(217) 782-7937

INDIANA
DEPT. OF VETERANS AFFAIRS
302 W. Washington St., Room E-120
Indianapolis, IN 46204
(317) 232-3910

IOWA
VETERANS AFFAIRS DIVISION
7700 N.W. Beaver Dr.
Camp Dodge
Johnston, IA 50131-1902
(515) 242-5333

KANSAS
KANSAS VETERANS COMMISSION
Jayhawk Tower, Suite 701
700 S.W. Jackson St.
Topeka, KS 66603-3150
(913) 296-3976

KENTUCKY
DIVISION OF VETERANS AFFAIRS
Boone National Guard Center
Frankfort, KY 40601-6168
(502) 564-8514

LOUISIANA
DEPT. OF VETERANS AFFAIRS
P.O. Box 94095, Capitol Station
Baton Rouge, LA 70804-9095
(504) 342-5866, 342-5863

MAINE
BUREAU OF VETERANS SERVICES
State Office Bldg., Station #117
Augusta, ME 04333
(207) 289-4060

MARYLAND
MARYLAND VETERANS COMMISSION
Federal Bldg., Room 110
31 Hopkins Plaza
Baltimore, MD 21201
(301) 962-4700

MASSACHUSETTS
DEPT. OF VETERANS SERVICE
100 Cambridge St., Room 1002
Boston, MA 02202
(617) 727-3570

MICHIGAN
MICHIGAN VETERANS TRUST FUND
611 West Ottawa, P.O. Box 30026
Lansing, MI 48909
(517) 373-3130

MINNESOTA
DEPT. OF VETERANS AFFAIRS
Veterans Service Bldg., 2nd Floor
St. Paul, MN 55155-2079

MISSISSIPPI
STATE VETERANS AFFAIRS BOARD
4607 Lindbergh Dr.
State Veterans Home
Jackson, MS 39209
(601) 354-7205

MISSOURI
MISSOURI VETERANS COMMISSION
P.O. Drawer 147
Jefferson City, MO 65102
(314) 751-3779

MONTANA
VETERANS AFFAIRS DIVISION
P.O. Box 5715
Helena, MT 59604
(406) 444-6926

NEBRASKA
DEPT. OF VETERANS AFFAIRS
P.O. Box 95083
Lincoln, NE 68509
(402) 471-2458

NEVADA
COMMISSION FOR VETERANS AFFAIRS
1201 Terminal Way, Room 108
Reno, NV 89520
(702) 688-1155

NEW HAMPSHIRE
STATE VETERANS COUNCIL
359 Lincoln St.
Manchester, NH 03103-4901
(603) 624-9230

NEW JERSEY
DEPT. OF MILITARY AND VETERANS AFFAIRS
Eggert Crossing Rd. CN30
Trenton, NJ 08625-0340
(609) 530-7045

NEW MEXICO
VETERANS SERVICE COMMISSION
P.O. Box 2324
Santa Fe, NM 87503
(505) 827-6300

NEW YORK
DIVISION OF VETERANS AFFAIRS
194 Washington Ave.
Albany, NY 12210
(518) 474-3752

NORTH CAROLINA
DIVISION OF VETERANS AFFAIRS
Albemarle Bldg., Suite 10655
325 N. Salisbury St.
Raleigh, NC 27603

NORTH DAKOTA
DEPT. OF VETERANS AFFAIRS
15 N. Broadway, Suite 613
Fargo, ND 58102
(701) 239-7165

NORTH MARIANA ISLANDS
COMMONWEALTH OF THE NORTH MARIANA ISLANDS
2121 R St., N.W.
Washington, DC 20008
(202) 673-5869

OHIO
DIVISION OF VETERANS' AFFAIRS
30 E. Broad St., Room 1825
Columbus, OH 43266-0422
(614) 466-5453

OKLAHOMA
DEPT. OF VETERANS AFFAIRS
P.O. Box 53067
Oklahoma City, OK 73152
(405) 521-3684

OREGON
DEPARTMENT OF VETERANS AFFAIRS
Oregon Veterans' Bldg.
700 Summer St., N.E.
Salem, OR 97310-1270

PENNSYLVANIA
BUREAU FOR VETERANS AFFAIRS
Ft. Indiantown Gap,
Bldg. S-O-47
Annville, PA 17003-5002
(717) 865-8901

PUERTO RICO
PUBLIC ADVOCATE FOR VETERANS AFFAIRS
Cobian's Plaza Bldg., Stop 23
1603 Ponce de Leon Ave.
Santurce, PR 00909
(809) 725-4400

RHODE ISLAND
DEPT. OF HUMAN SERVICES
Division of Veterans Affairs
Metacom Ave.
Bristol, RI 02809
(401) 253-8000

SOUTH CAROLINA
DEPT. OF VETERANS AFFAIRS
226 Brown State Office Bldg.
1205 Pendleton St.
Columbia, SC 29201
(803) 734-0200

TENNESSEE
DEPT. OF VETERANS AFFAIRS
215 Eighth Ave., N.
Nashville, TN 37203
(615) 741-2930

TEXAS
TEXAS VETERANS COMMISSION
P.O. Box 12277
Austin, TX 78711
(512) 463-5538

UTAH
OFFICE OF THE GOVERNOR
210 State Capitol St.
Salt Lake City, UT 84114
(801) 538-1000

VERMONT
DEPT. OF STATE VETERANS AFFAIRS
120 State St.
Montpelier, VT 05620-4401
(802) 828-3379

VIRGINIA
DEPT. OF VETERANS' AFFAIRS
210 Franklin Rd., S.W., Room 1012
P.O. Box 809
Roanoke, VA 24004
(703) 857-7104

VIRGIN ISLANDS
OFFICE OF VETERANS AFFAIRS
#13-A Estate Richardmond
Christian St. Croix, VI 00820
(809) 773-6663

WASHINGTON
DEPT. OF VETERANS AFFAIRS
P.O. Box 9778, Mail Stop PM-41
Olympia, WA 98504-9778
(206) 753-5586

WEST VIRGINIA
WEST VIRGINIA DIVISION OF VETERANS AFFAIRS
1321 Plaza East, Suite 101
Charleston, WV 25301-1400
(308) 348-3661

WISCONSIN
DEPT. OF VETERANS AFFAIRS
P.O. Box 7843
30 W. Mifflin St.
Madison, WI 53707
(608) 266-1311

WYOMING
WYOMING VETERANS AFFAIRS COMMISSION
13 Dinwoody Circle
Riverton, WY 82501
(307) 777-6069

APPENDIX D:

VETERANS ORGANIZATIONS

★★★★★★★★★★★★★★★★★★★★★★★★★★★★★★★★★

In this appendix, we provide names, addresses, and, where available, telephone numbers, for selected veterans' organizations. Most of these organizations are national. This information is an adaptation of that published by the Department of Veterans Affairs (the VA). Many of these organizations employ service representatives who can provide advice to veterans regarding VA benefits issues and other matters.

Part One: Organizations Chartered by Congress

AMERICAN DEFENDERS OF BATAAN AND CORREGIDOR
P.O. BOX 12052
New Bern, NC 28561-2052
(919) 637-4033

AMERICAN EX-PRISONERS OF WAR
ROOM 9109 VARO
941 N. Capitol St., NE
Washington, DC 20421
(202) 208-1800

AMERICAN G.I. FORUM OF THE U.S.
1017 N. MAIN, SUITE 200
San Antonio, TX 78212
(512) 223-4088

AMERICAN GOLD STAR MOTHERS, INC.
2128 LEROY PL., N.W.
Washington, DC 20008
(202) 265-0991

THE AMERICAN LEGION
P.O. BOX 1055
Indianapolis, IN 46206
(313) 635-8411

THE AMERICAN RED CROSS
17TH AND D STS., N.W.
Washington, DC 20006
(202) 639-3586

AMERICAN VETERANS COMMITTEE
6309 BANNOCKBURN DR.
Bethesda, MD 20817
(301) 320-6490

AMERICAN VETERANS OF WWII, KOREA AND VIETNAM (AMVETS)
4647 FORBES BLVD.
Lanham, MD 20706
(301) 459-9600

AMERICAN WAR MOTHERS
2615 WOODLEY PL., N.W.
Washington, DC 20008
(202) 462-2791

ARMY AND AIR FORCE MUTUAL AID ASSOCIATION
FT. MYER
Arlington, VA 22211
(703) 522-3060

ARMY AND NAVY UNION, INC.
1391 MAIN ST.
Lakemore, OH 44250

BLINDED VETERANS ASSOCIATION
477 H ST., N.W.
Washington, DC 20001-2694

BLUE STAR MOTHERS OF AMERICA, INC.
4616 MAYBANK AVE.
Lakewood, CA 90712
(213) 428-2221

CATHOLIC WAR VETERANS, USA, INC.
419 N. LEE ST.
Alexandria, VA 22314
(703) 549-3622

CONGRESSIONAL MEDAL OF HONOR SOCIETY OF THE UNITED STATES OF AMERICA
U.S.S. INTREPID MUSEUM
W. 46th St. and 12th Ave.
New York, NY 10036
(212) 582-5355

DISABLED AMERICAN VETERANS
3725 ALEXANDRIA PIKE
Cold Springs, KY 41076
(606) 441-7300

FLEET RESERVE ASSOCIATION
125 N. WEST ST.
Alexandria, VA 22314
(703) 683-1400

GOLD STAR WIVES OF AMERICA, INC.
540 N. LOMBARDY ST.
Arlington, VA 22203-1060
(703) 527-7706

ITALIAN AMERICAN WAR VETERANS OF THE USA
122 MATHER ST.
Syracuse, NY 13203
(315) 479-8315

JEWISH WAR VETERANS OF THE USA
1811 R ST., N.W.
Washington, DC 20009
(202) 265-6280

LEGION OF VALOR OF THE U.S.A., INC.
92 OAK LEAF LANE
Chapel Hill, NC 27516
(919) 933-0989

MARINE CORPS LEAGUE
8626 LEE HIGHWAY, SUITE 201
Fairfax, VA 22031

MILITARY ORDER OF THE PURPLE HEART OF THE U.S.A., INC.
5413-B BACKLICK RD.
Springfield, VA 22151
(703) 642-5360

NATIONAL AMPUTATION FOUNDATION, INC.
12-45 150TH ST
Whitestone, NY 11357
(718) 767-0596

NAVY MUTUAL AID ASSOCIATION
ARLINGTON ANNEX, ROOM G-070
Washington, DC 20370-0001
(703) 614-1638

NON COMMISSIONED OFFICERS ASSOCIATION (NCOA)
10635 IH 35 NORTH
San Antonio, TX 78233
(512) 653-6161

PARALYZED VETERANS OF AMERICA
801 18TH ST., N.W.
Washington, DC 20006
(202) 872-1300

PEARL HARBOR SURVIVORS ASSOCIATION, INC.
DRAWER 2598
Lancaster, CA 93539
(805) 948-1851

POLISH LEAGUE OF AMERICAN VETERANS, USA
5413-C BACKLICK RD.
Springfield, VA 22151
(703) 354-2771

REGULAR VETERANS ASSOCIATION
2470 CARDINAL LOOP
B/217
Del Valle, TX 78617

SWORDS TO PLOWSHARES: VETERANS RIGHTS ORGANIZATION
400 VALENCIA ST.
San Francisco, CA 94103
(415) 552-8804

THE RETIRED ENLISTED ASSOCIATION
1111 S. ABILENE CT.
Aurora, CO 80012
(303) 752-0660

U.S. SUBMARINE VETERANS OF WORLD WAR II
862 CHATHAM AVE.
Elmhurst, IL 60126-4531
(708) 834-2718

VETERANS OF FOREIGN WARS OF THE UNITED STATES
406 W. 34TH ST.
(Broadway at 34th St.)
Kansas City, MO 64111
(816) 756-3390

VETERANS OF WORLD WAR I OF THE U.S.A., INC.
941 N. CAPITOL ST., N.E.
Room 1201-C
Washington, DC 20002-4234
(202) 208-1388

VIETNAM ERA VETERANS ASSOCIATION
250 PRAIRIE AVE.
Providence, RI 02905
(401) 521-6710

VIETNAM VETERANS OF AMERICA, INC.
1224 M ST., N.W.
Washington, DC 20005
(202) 628-2700

**WOMEN'S ARMY
CORPS VETERANS
ASSOCIATION**
P.O. BOX 5577
Ft. McClellan, AL 36205
(205) 820-4019

Part Two: Organizations Not Chartered by Congress

**AIR FORCE
ASSOCIATION**
1501 LEE HIGHWAY
Arlington, VA 22209-1198
(703) 247-5810

**AIR FORCE
SERGEANTS
ASSOCIATION**
P.O. BOX 50
Temple Hills, MD 20748
(301) 899-3500

**ALLIANCE OF WOMEN
VETERANS**
3200 E. SOUTH ST., APT.
710
Long Beach, CA 90805
(213) 630-2331

**AMERICAN MILITARY
RETIREES
ASSOCIATION**
68 CLINTON ST.
Plattsburgh, NY 12901
(518) 563-9479

**ASSOCIATION OF
EX-P.O.W. OF THE
KOREAN WAR, INC.**
1610 12TH AVE.
Manson, IA 50563
(503) 684-3270

**ASSOCIATION OF THE
U.S. ARMY**
2425 WILSON BLVD.
Arlington, VA 22201
(703) 841-4300

**BLINDED AMERICAN
VETERANS
FOUNDATION**
P.O. BOX 65900
Washington, DC 20035-5900
(202) 462-4430

**BROTHERHOOD
RALLY OF ALL
VETERANS
ORGANIZATIONS
(BRAVO)**
23917 CRAFTSMAN RD.
Calabasas, CA 91302
(818) 999-4174

CHINA-BURMA-INDIA VETERANS ASSOCIATION, INC.
560 AMRAP DR.
Parma Heights, OH 44130
(216) 884-9242

COMBINED NATIONAL VETERANS ASSOCIATION OF AMERICA
5413-C BACKLICK RD.
Springfield, VA 22151
(703) 354-2771

DESTROYER-ESCORT SAILORS ASSOCIATION
926 NATIONAL PRESS BLVD.
Washington, DC 20045
(202) 628-3400

KOREAN WAR VETERANS MEMORIAL ADVISORY BOARD
DEPARTMENT OF THE INTERIOR
18th & C Sts., N.W., Room 5024
Washington, DC 20240

KOREAN WAR VETERANS ASSOCIATION
2341 DALE DR.
Falls Church, VA 22043
(703) 560-4716

MILITARY JUSTICE CLINIC, INC.
960 MARTIN LUTHER KING JR. DR., S.W.
Atlanta, GA 30314
(404) 525-0240

MILITARY ORDER OF THE WORLD WARS
435 N. LEE ST.
Alexandria, VA 22314
(703) 683-4911

NAM-POWS, INC.
2757 ELM AVE.
Bexley, OH 43202
(614) 237-9908

NATIONAL ASSOCIATION FOR BLACK VETERANS, INC.
3929 N. HUMBOLDT BLVD.
P.O. Box 11432
Milwaukee, WI 53211-0432
(414) 265-8940

NATIONAL ASSOCIATION FOR UNIFORMED SERVICES
5535 HEMPSTEAD WAY
Springfield, VA 22151-4094
(703) 750-1342

NATIONAL ASSOCIATION OF ATOMIC VETERANS
P.O. BOX 44244
Salem, MA 01970
(508) 744-9396

NATIONAL ASSOCIATION OF CONCERNED VETERANS
501 CRESCENT ST.
New Haven, CT 06515

NATIONAL ASSOCIATION OF MILITARY WIDOWS
4023 25TH RD. N.
Arlington, VA 22207
(703) 527-4565

NATIONAL ASSOCIATION OF RADIATION SURVIVORS
P.O. BOX 20749
Oakland, CA 94620
(800) 798-5102

NATIONAL ASSOCIATION OF STATE DIRECTORS OF VETERANS AFFAIRS
C/O D.C. OFFICE OF VETERANS AFFAIRS
941 N. Capitol St., N.E., Room 1211-F
Washington, DC 20421

NATIONAL ASSOCIATION OF STATE VETERANS HOMES
P.O. BOX 409
Norfolk, NE 68702-0409
(402) 370-3177

NATIONAL ASSOCIATION OF VETERANS PROGRAM ADMINISTRATORS
C/O METROPOLITAN STATE COLLEGE
1006-11th St., Box 16
Denver, CO 80204
(303) 556-2993

NATIONAL CONGRESS OF PUERTO RICO VETERANS, INC.
304 PARK AVE., S.
New York, NY 10010
(212) 260-3000, Ext. 353

NATIONAL INCARCERATED VETERANS NETWORK
C/O MR. CRAIG T. MCLAREN, #115624
President
P.O. Box 37
Atmore, AL 36503-0037
(205) 543-8255

NATIONAL LEAGUE OF FAMILIES OF AMERICAN PRISONERS AND MISSING IN SOUTHEAST ASIA
1001 CONNECTICUT AVE., N.W., SUITE 219
Washington, DC 20036-5504

NAVAL RESERVE ASSOCIATION
1619 KING ST.
Alexandria, VA 22314-2793
(703) 548-5800

NAVY LEAGUE OF THE UNITED STATES
2300 WILSON BLVD.
Arlington, VA 22201
(703) 528-1775

RED RIVER VALLEY FIGHTER PILOTS ASSOCIATION
6237 S. GREENWICH RD.
Derby, KS 67307
(316) 788-7525

RESERVE OFFICERS ASSOCIATION OF THE UNITED STATES
1 CONSTITUTION AVE., N.E.
Washington, DC 20002
(202) 646-7715

SOCIETY OF MILITARY WIDOWS
5535 HEMPSTEAD WAY
Springfield, VA 22151-4094
(703) 750-1342

THE RETIRED OFFICERS ASSOCIATION
201 N. WASHINGTON ST.
Alexandria, VA 22314
(703) 549-2311

THE FORTY & EIGHT
777 N. MERIDIAN ST.
Indianapolis, IN 46204
(317) 634-1804

UNITED STATES ARMY WARRANT OFFICERS ASSOCIATION
462 HERNDON PARKWAY, SUITE 207
Herndon, VA 22070
(703) 742-7727

U.S. MERCHANT MARINE VETERANS OF WORLD WAR II
P.O. BOX 629
San Pedro, CA 90731
(213) 519-9545

WAVES NATIONAL
8 KENNEDY ST.
Alexandria, VA 22305
(703) 548-5272

WISCONSIN VIETNAM VETS, INC.
6523 W. MORGAN AVE.
Milwaukee, WI 53220
(414) 543-5706

WOMEN MARINES ASSOCIATION
1415 SPRINGVALE AVE.
McLean, VA 22101
(703) 356-1527

WOMEN AIR FORCE SERVICE PILOTS, WWII
9220 PRESIDENTIAL DR.
Alexandria, VA 22309
(703) 780-6346

INDEX

★ ABOUT THE AUTHORS ★

Keith D. Snyder is an attorney in private practice who focuses his legal work on the needs of veterans and their families. He is the founding president of the National Organization of Veterans' Advocates, whose membership is open to persons admitted to practice before the U.S. Court of Veterans Appeals. Before entering private practice, Snyder edited the *Veterans' Law Reporter*, a series of self-help guides, and a guide to veterans benefits, and conducted numerous training seminars. His military service consisted of four years as a Navy hospital corpsman during the Vietnam Era. He resides with his family in a Maryland suburb of Washington, D.C.

Richard E. O'Dell is Director of the Department of Veterans' Affairs of the Commonwealth of Virginia and is a combat veteran of the Vietnam War. He has testified before the U.S. Congress on a number of issues, most notably and successfully the creation of the U.S. Court of Veterans Appeals. Mr. O'Dell has conducted many training seminars for veterans advocates and has authored or coauthored various articles on the rights of veterans. He is a former national officer of a leading veterans organization. Mr. O'Dell resides with his wife in the beautiful Shenandoah Valley of Virginia.

Craig Kubey is a writer and is a member of the bars of California and the District of Columbia. He worked with Ralph Nader to establish the Equal Justice Foundation, a national public interest organization dedicated to promoting access for all citizens to courts and regulatory agencies. Three of Mr. Kubey's books have been national bestsellers. Mr. Kubey lives in northern California with his wife and children.

★ Key Information ★

Name: _____

SSN: _____

VA Claim #: _____

VA Insurance #: _____

VA Insurance Beneficiary: _____

VA Home Loan #: _____

Military Service #: _____

Branch of service: _____

Dates of service: _____

Telephone and address of nearest VA office:

_____

_____

_____

Name & phone of representative:

_____

_____